MOST WONDERFUL MACHINE

JUDITH A. McGAW

MOST WONDERFUL MACHINE

MECHANIZATION

AND SOCIAL CHANGE

IN BERKSHIRE

PAPER MAKING,

1801–1885

PRINCETON UNIVERSITY PRESS

Copyright © 1987 by Princeton University Press
Published by Princeton University Press, 41 William Street,
Princeton, New Jersey 08540
In the United Kingdom: Princeton University Press,
Oxford

ISBN 0-691-04740-5
ISBN 0-691-00625-3 (pbk.)

First Princeton Paperback printing, 1992

3 5 7 8 6 4 2

Publication of this book has been aided by a grant from
The Andrew W. Mellon Foundation

This book has been composed in Linotron Baskerville 95

Princeton University Press books are printed on acid-free
paper, and meet the guidelines for permanence and
durability of the Committee on Production Guidelines for
Book Longevity of the Council on Library Resources

Printed in the United States of America

FOR

BROOKE HINDLE

CONTENTS

ILLUSTRATIONS

TABLES

ACKNOWLEDGMENTS

It is a pleasure to acknowledge a few of the many debts I have accumulated over the course of this study. My dedication to Brooke Hindle expresses in a small way my enormous gratitude and esteem. After kindling my interest in the history of technology during my graduate studies at New York University, he kindly consented to supervise my dissertation from his new post at the Smithsonian Museum of History and Technology. His support and encouragement have continued to be an invaluable aid. Most of all, I thank him for setting an example of what is best in our profession, for providing a model worthy of emulation.

Vincent Carosso, Irwin Unger, and Carl Prince enriched my graduate education and lent their help over the following years. My friendships with Mary Kelley and Elizabeth Hitz also date from graduate school and have offered continuing intellectual and emotional sustenance. Somewhat older is my debt to John L. Thomas and Carl Bridenbaugh of Brown University, who presented history in a form that captured my undergraduate imagination.

My parents, Allan and Grace McGaw, have long provided the unconditional love that laid the foundation for this and all my work. Both taught me by example most of the important things I know. My thanks as well to Patricia McGaw Chichon and to Joseph, Michael, and Katie Chichon for welcoming me into their family whenever I have needed a haven and to Keith and Catherine McGaw Stouch for sharing their warmth and understanding.

I would not have come to know Berkshire County without the help of her people. In a sense this book began in 1971 during my first visit to the county, when I interviewed for a job with the Pittsfield Public Schools. Returning to my hotel, I stopped in the bar, where, as fortune would have it, I struck up a conversation with Bobby Higgins, whose family had long worked in Berkshire paper mills. I thank him for sparking my curiosity about the industry and for introducing me to his town and family. Thereafter, many Berkshire men and women afforded me access to company and town records and helped make my research time pleasant and productive. At Crane & Co., Winthrop M. Crane III, Mrs. Irving Witham, Mrs. Gertrude Kirby, Robert Taylor, and the late William G. O'Connell and Harry Stedman made me especially welcome during the months I worked among them. My thanks as well to Oscar Choquette of the Adams Historical Society, Margaret Angelini of the

Mead Corporation, Kathleen King of the Kimberly-Clark Corporation, and Thomas J. Fahey of the Byron Weston Company. Librarians in each of Berkshire's present and former paper mill towns made my task easier. I am particularly grateful to Betty Dennis, Denis Lesieur, and Polly Pierce. Florence Consolati and Frank Kelly of Lee shared an equally valuable resource: their enthusiasm for local history. My colleagues at Taconic High School initially made me welcome in the Berkshires and, later, Linda and Francis Curley and Paul and Peggy Nelson opened their homes to me during my research trips.

I have continued to be fortunate in my colleagues. At the University of Oklahoma, Robert and Mary Jo Nye, Ronald Snell, and Paul Glad gave me thoughtful readings and gentle criticism in the early stages of my writing. At the University of Virginia, Joseph Miller, Joseph Kett, and Fred Carstensen proved particularly helpful. Most recently I have been privileged to work among an outstanding group of scholars in the Department of History and Sociology of Science at the University of Pennsylvania. I am grateful to each of my colleagues and to the many fine graduate students who have forced me to think more clearly about the history of technology. I am most indebted to Charles Rosenberg and to Walter Licht of the history department for reading substantial portions of my manuscript and indicating how to improve it.

In ways that are impossible to measure, this is a much better book because of the years of supportive fellowship I have enjoyed in the Society for the History of Technology. Conversations with many members enabled me to refine my ideas, but I have made greatest demands on Carroll Pursell, Bruce Sinclair, and John Staudenmaier. I also thank Eugene Ferguson and Merritt Roe Smith for identifying errors and suggesting improvements in earlier versions of this work.

Several institutions supported this work financially. The University of Oklahoma Faculty Research Council funded the purchase of research materials and defrayed the cost of keypunching, and the College of Arts and Sciences granted me a summer research fellowship. I also received summer research support from the National Endowment for the Humanities and the University of Pennsylvania. Additional research was made possible through a grant from the Penrose Fund of the American Philosophical Society.

Librarians at each of the various institutions where I have worked have earned more than my thanks. I am especially grateful to Robert W. Lovett, formerly of the Baker Library, Harvard Business

School. Alice Foister proved an invaluable aid at the University of Oklahoma computing center, Carl Beetz has been a most helpful and able illustrator, and Pat Johnson has graciously typed countless pages and revisions. Gail Ullman and members of the staff of Princeton University Press also command my respect and gratitude.

Finally, without the patience and encouragement of a very special group of friends here in Philadelphia, this book would never have been completed. It is impossible to acknowledge them all, but let me at least mention Prue Martin and Tom Waldman. They have given me priceless gifts and maintain no record of my debt.

February 1986
Philadelphia

ABBREVIATIONS

Archival Collections

APS   American Philosophical Society, Philadelphia, Pennsylvania

BA   Berkshire Atheneum, Pittsfield, Massachusetts, Historical Room

BL   Baker Library, Harvard Business School, Cambridge, Massachusetts

BWP   Byron Weston Papers, Byron Weston Company office, Dalton, Massachusetts

CA   Crane Archive, Crane & Co. office, Dalton, Massachusetts

CMF   Crane Museum Files, Crane Museum of Paper Making, Dalton, Massachusetts

HP   Hurlbut Papers, Hurlbut Mill office, Mead Corporation, South Lee, Massachusetts

LLBP   L. L. Brown Papers, Adams Historical Society, Adams Public Library, Adams, Massachusetts

LLHR   Lee Library Historical Room, Lee Library, Lee, Massachusetts

MA   Massachusetts Archives, Boston, Massachusetts

NA   National Archives, Washington, D.C.

SL   Stockbridge Library Historical Room, Stockbridge Library, Stockbridge, Massachusetts

SP   Smith Papers, Peter J. Schweitzer Division office, Columbia Paper Mill, Kimberly-Clark Corporation, Lee, Massachusetts

Periodicals

AER   *American Economic Review*

AHR   *American Historical Review*

AQ   *American Quarterly*

BHR   *Business History Review*

EHR   *Economic History Review*

JEH   *Journal of Economic History*

JUH   *Journal of Urban History*

LH   *Labor History*

PM   *Paper Maker*

RHR   *Radical History Review*

SA   *Scientific American*

SF   *Superior Facts*

Signs   *Signs: Journal of Women in Culture and Society*

T&C   *Technology and Culture*

VG   *Valley Gleaner*

MOST WONDERFUL MACHINE

INTRODUCTION

Machinery fascinated nineteenth-century Americans. As the century dawned, political figures as disparate as Thomas Jefferson and Alexander Hamilton found machines intriguing. As the century drew to a close, literary men as diverse as Mark Twain and Henry Adams confronted the machine's cultural significance. Over the intervening hundred years, while entrepreneurs and mechanics discovered the machine's possible uses, artists and scientists explored the new technology's symbolic and theoretical potential. Simultaneously, American popular culture expressed widespread preoccupation with machines. Across the nation, local newspapers ran frequent accounts of new mechanisms, lyceum lecturers explained inventions to eager audiences, and mills opened their doors to travelers curious to examine the marvelous machines they housed. Lithographs and letterheads depicted mechanical contrivances; expositions and agricultural fairs featured displays and trials of new technology.[1]

Evidently, like the narrator of "The Tartarus of Maids," Herman Melville's tale of a man visiting a Berkshire paper mill, nineteenth-century Americans considered machinery worth going out of their way to see. And judging from the prevailing rhetoric and from the rapid adoption of mechanical technology, many Americans, at least in the industrializing Northeast, viewed machines with enthusiasm. Like Melville's fictional visitor they might have exclaimed, "Yours is a most wonderful factory. Your great machine is a miracle of inscrutable intricacy." Indeed, because they considered the machine such a wonder, they repeatedly endowed it with a significance transcending its capacity to produce or transport goods rapidly and cheaply. Newspapers and lecturers routinely credited mechanical technology with "the progress of the age," and planners of the great American Centennial Exposition organized exhibits so as to articulate the

---

[1] John Kasson, *Civilizing the Machine: Technology and Republican Values in America, 1776–1900* (New York, 1976); Brooke Hindle, *Emulation and Invention* (New York, 1981); Leo Marx, *The Machine in the Garden: Technology and the Pastoral Ideal in America* (New York, 1964); Carl Siracusa, *A Mechanical People: Perceptions of the Industrial Order in Massachusetts, 1815–1880* (Middletown, Conn., 1979); Bruce A. Sinclair, *Philadelphia's Philosopher Mechanics: A History of the Franklin Institute, 1824–1865* (Baltimore, 1977); Clarence H. Danhof, *Change in Agriculture: The Northern United States, 1820–1870* (Cambridge, Mass., 1969).

same reassuring message: mechanical innovation exemplified and guaranteed American progress.[2]

At least some Americans viewed the new technology with less enthusiasm. Yet even the minority of vocal critics conveyed fascination with the machine as they employed new technology to symbolize developments that evoked their fear and hostility. Melville's fictional visitor captured this dreadful fascination when, after describing the inscrutable paper-making machine, he mused:

> Something of awe now stole over me, as I gazed upon this inflexible iron animal. Always, more or less, machinery of this ponderous, elaborate sort strikes, in some moods, strange dread into the human heart, as some living, panting Behemoth might. But what made the thing I saw so specially terrible to me was the metallic necessity, the unbudging fatality which governed it.

Similarly, the horrifying denouement of Twain's *A Connecticut Yankee in King Arthur's Court* and Adams's sense of powerlessness before the dynamo in *The Education of Henry Adams* express profound technological fatalism.[3]

Few citizens of industrializing America could maintain Melville's ironic sense of the machine as symbol and tool of its creators, owners, and operators. In consequence, nineteenth-century America produced, along with its machines, a belief in technological determinism, a conviction that machines shape human destiny. Contemporary rhetoric expressed that conviction in various ways. In its strongest articulation, technological determinism meant that there was a logic inherent in technology, that new mechanical knowledge led inevitably to the production of new machines or that a new machine naturally suggested other new machines. Thereafter, people had no choice but to accept "progress" and cope with the inevitable consequences. In its more muted forms the rhetoric of technological determinism had less to say about the machines' origins, but attributed most social change to new inventions rather than to the

[2] See works cited above. Herman Melville, "The Paradise of Bachelors and the Tartarus of Maids," in Richard Chase, ed., *Herman Melville: Selected Tales and Poems* (New York, 1966), p. 228. The phrase "the progress of the age" becomes recurrent by about mid-century in the nineteenth-century journalistic accounts of technology that I have surveyed.

[3] Melville, "Tartarus," p. 227; Kasson, *Civilizing the Machine*; Marx, *The Machine in the Garden*.

ways in which people chose to use machines. In sum, whether they saw machines as dreadful or wonderful, many Americans were so fascinated they found it hard to look beyond them.

Until recently, historians have been less fascinated, less awed, less interested in looking at the machines that achieved so prominent a place in nineteenth-century American life and thought. Nor have they found Americans' ready adoption of machines remarkable, although, inspired by Arnold Toynbee's *The Industrial Revolution*, they have generally given industrialization a central role in nineteenth-century American history. Like Toynbee, American historians often mention textile machinery and steam engines in their accounts, but they have rarely gone out of their way to examine the new machines. As a result, they have tended implicitly to accept nineteenth-century technological determinism.[4]

Treating machines as "black boxes" and indulging in technological determinism remained acceptable historical scholarship as long as technology seemed benign. Since World War II, however, Americans have grown increasingly skeptical of "technological progress." But years of accepting technology as autonomous and its consequences as inevitable have made it easy for popular discourse simply to blame technology for disconcerting social ills. Technological determinism has itself become a critical social problem.

By the late 1950s growing public perception of technology as problematic encouraged some scholars to adopt a newly critical approach to technology's history. Their analyses of technology as a cultural product have helped to undermine the myth of technological determinism. These social historians of technology have now told us a great deal about the social origins of American invention, the cultural contexts shaping the transfer of British technology to America, the motivation for Americans' initial adoption of machines, and the circumstances that made some firms and locales reluctant innovators. They have made increasingly clear that the invention, innovation, development, and transfer of technology result from human choice, rather than from the inherent logic of technics.[5]

[4] Arnold Toynbee, *The Industrial Revolution* (Boston, 1956), originally published in 1884. For an excellent discussion of the strengths and weaknesses of economic historians' treatment of technology, see Nathan Rosenberg, "The Historiography of Technical Progress," in idem, *Inside the Black Box: Technology and Economics* (Cambridge, 1982), pp. 3–33.

[5] John M. Staudenmaier, S.J., *Technology's Storytellers: Reweaving the Human Fabric*

On the other hand, historians of technology have devoted comparatively little attention to the widespread diffusion of machines that distinguished nineteenth-century America. They have been concerned almost exclusively with the initial use of new machines by pioneering firms or "leading" industries, especially cotton textile mills and machine shops. They have also had much more to say about technology's social origins than about its apparent social consequences. Yet, nineteenth-century Americans developed the rhetoric of technological determinism to express their consciousness of machines' increasingly common use and pervasive social influence. Questioning the myth of technological determinism requires that we examine the general diffusion, use, and consequences of employing new technologies. Otherwise, we inadvertently convey the impression that, historically, social choice ceased at some point in the process of technological change—at the point when technology became part of most people's lives.

I consider technological determinism a crippling social malaise and I believe that a social history of technology can offer an effective antidote. Because the American rhetoric of technological determinism achieved clear articulation in the nineteenth century, I have chosen to examine the American experience with the machines of the Industrial Revolution. Because the rhetoric expressed awareness that the common use of complex mechanisms was novel and remarkable, I have focused on the phenomenon of mechanization: the general diffusion and widespread use of mechanical technology.

(Cambridge, Mass., 1985), offers an overview of scholarship and issues in the history of technology, and discusses the establishment of the leading scholarly organization and scholarly journal in the field. See also Staudenmaier's remarks on the occasion of the Society for the History of Technology's twenty-fifth anniversary and responses by John B. Rae and Melvin Kranzberg in *T&C* 25 (October 1984):707–49. Two other important assessments of the field are Thomas P. Hughes, "Emerging Themes in the History of Technology," *T&C* 20 (October 1979):697–711; and George Daniels, "The Big Questions in the History of American Technology," *T&C* 11 (January 1970):11–16.

In addition to several of the works cited earlier, outstanding examples of works treating the social shaping of technology in nineteenth-century America include Merritt Roe Smith, *Harpers Ferry Armory and the New Technology: The Challenge of Change* (Ithaca, 1977); David Jeremy, *Transatlantic Industrial Revolution: The Diffusion of Textile Technologies between Britain and America, 1790–1830* (Cambridge, Mass., 1981); David A. Hounshell, *From the American System to Mass Production: The Development of Manufacturing Technology in the United States* (Baltimore, 1984); Reese V. Jenkins, *Images and Enterprise: Technology and the American Photographic Industry, 1829–1925* (Baltimore, 1975).

In the following pages I have sought some preliminary answers to two questions about which the history of technology currently tells us little: What accounts for the widespread adoption of machines in nineteenth-century America? And what role did mechanization play in the social and cultural transformation of America? These are not simple questions and I have tried to avoid simple answers. I have indicated the challenge mechanization posed by examining the era's complex mechanisms and by sketching the intricate interaction of people and machines within an evolving social and economic context. Like nineteenth-century Americans, I have found the widespread use of machines a wonder and have placed it at the center of my tale. Unlike them, I have found human social and economic decisions accountable for the diffusion of machines and for most of the consequences of machine production. My title, *Most Wonderful Machine*, like Melville's phrase "most wonderful factory," expresses my simultaneous sense of amazement at mechanization and doubt that machines make history.

The mechanization of nineteenth-century America is a tale of epic proportions. In order to look closely at both technology and culture, I have reduced my task to the manageable dimensions of a case study. I have examined the dissemination and use of machines in the Berkshire County, Massachusetts, paper industry. Thus, one important contribution of this study is its treatment of one of many industries about which we know little. Like Thomas Cochran, I find it lamentable that students of America's Industrial Revolution have remained preoccupied with the industries and technologies that Toynbee identified as central to British industrialization, as though "the story of the New England cotton industry is the story of the industrialization of America." Among other things, this emphasis has helped obscure the common American experience of mechanization.[6]

Although there is certainly no such thing as a "typical" nine-

[6] Eugene S. Ferguson, ed., *The Early Engineering Reminiscences (1815–40) of George Escol Sellers* (Washington, D.C., 1965) called the need and opportunity for study of the history of paper-making technology to our attention several decades ago, but both the industry and its technology remain largely unexamined. Overviews include: Dard Hunter, *Papermaking: The History and Technique of an Ancient Craft* (New York, 1943); Lyman Horace Weeks, *History of Paper Manufacturing in the United States, 1690–1916* (New York, 1916); David C. Smith, *History of Papermaking in the United States (1691–1969)* (New York, 1970); the first is the work of a collector and the others are compendia published by a leading trade journal. Two scholarly works treat the industry after mechanization: Constance McLaughlin Green, *Holyoke, Mass.: A Case History of the Industrial Revolution in America* (New Haven, 1939); and Charles N. Glaab

teenth-century industry, the Berkshire paper industry provides a more representative example of most American manufacturing than do the "leading" industries, corporate enterprises, urban establishments, and government installations that have attracted most scholarly attention. Like Berkshire paper mills, most American factories during the Industrial Revolution were relatively small concerns, owned by proprietorships and partnerships, located in small towns or rural areas, and operated by relatively modest work forces and locally resident entrepreneurs. As in the Berkshire paper industry, the tale of American mechanization is essentially a story of many small men and women making small decisions; accumulating capital, acquiring machines, and reordering work incrementally.[7]

As well as being exemplary, the paper industry deserves attention in its own right. It was economically significant throughout the nineteenth century and its dramatic productivity increases, made possible by a series of technological changes, proved central to America's economic development and social transformation. As early as 1810 American paper mills produced by hand methods about 2.6 million dollars worth of paper, accounting for 2.5 percent of the value of the nation's manufactures. By 1899 the industry manufactured well over two million tons of paper, about sixty pounds for every man, woman, and child in the nation's greatly enlarged population and nearly nine hundred times its output in 1810. Nonetheless, reducing the industry's growing productivity to quantitative measures un-

---

and Lawrence H. Larsen, *Factories in the Valley: Neenah-Menasha 1870–1915* (Milwaukee, 1969).

Cochran's observations are stated most explicitly in "New Views on Industrialization" (paper presented in the Humanities Seminar Series, West Virginia University, 3/29/84). Many neglected issues and industries are surveyed in Brooke Hindle, *Technology in Early America: Needs and Opportunities for Study* (Chapel Hill, 1966); and Thomas C. Cochran, *Frontiers of Change: Early Industrialism in America* (New York, 1981). The quotation is from Caroline Ware, *The Early New England Cotton Manufacturers: A Study of Industrial Beginnings* (Boston, 1931), p. 3. Philip Scranton, *Proprietary Capitalism: The Textile Manufacture at Philadelphia, 1800–1885* (Cambridge, 1983), offers a critique of the "textile paradigm" and the assumptions that historians can safely confine their attention to large-scale operations, early mechanizers, and corporations.

[7] See n. 6. Important correctives to the limited focus of most scholarship on early nineteenth-century technological change include: Louis C. Hunter, *Waterpower: A History of Industrial Power in the Untied States, 1780-1930* (Charlottesville, 1979); Paul F. Paskoff, *Industrial Evolution: Organization, Structure, and Growth of the Pennsylvania Iron Industry, 1750–1860* (Baltimore, 1983); Lucius F. Ellsworth, *Craft to National Industry in the Nineteenth Century: A Case Study of the Transformation of the New York State Tanning Industry* (New York, 1975).

derstates its significance. The proliferation of cheap paper made possible a rapid rise in literacy, dramatic increases in long-distance communication, and the initiation and multiplication of specialized business, technical, and reform journalism, which facilitated economic, technological, and social change throughout the nation.[8]

Paper making offers outstanding advantages as a case study in the social history of mechanization. Its principal new machine, the Fourdrinier, was, as Melville described, "a miracle of inscrutable intricacy," one of the most complex mechanisms to be widely adopted in nineteenth-century America. At the same time, a number of paper-making tasks remaincd hand operations, sometimes despite the invention of machines that could perform these processes. Thus, the industry provides a laboratory for studying diverse patterns of technological diffusion. In contrast to the relatively labor-intensive machine shops and textile mills that have figured most prominently in previous scholarship, paper mills required comparatively few workers after mechanization, making them good places to examine the apparent "laborsaving" thrust of American technology.

Paper mills provide equally fine sites for studying the relationship of mechanization to subsequent social change. They offer a chance to observe the advent of machines without the distraction of many simultaneous changes usually lumped together under the phrase "Industrial Revolution." For example, paper making in Europe and America had always taken place in mills, so we cannot confuse the effects of mechanization in paper making with the effects of shifting work from home to factory. Likewise, preindustrial paper mills already had a marked division of labor by function and gender, so we can separate the impact of mechanization from the impact of the division of labor. In addition, mechanized paper mills continued to employ small work forces, so they did not spawn cities and they continued to require pure water, discouraging their relocation to cities. In consequence, they allow us to view the effects of mechanization apart from the effects of urbanization.

If paper making is admirably suited to the study of mechanization, Berkshire County, Massachusetts, is the obvious place to conduct such a study. During the 1820s and 1830s, when cylinder paper-making machines superseded hand manufacture, and the 1840s and 1850s, when Fourdrinier paper-making machines became a viable option and hand paper making virtually disappeared from the American scene, Berkshire County assumed national lead-

[8] Smith, *History of Papermaking*, pp. 18, 662.

ership in the industry, a position it continued to hold through the
Civil War years. By 1840 one Berkshire town, Lee, produced more
paper than any other town in the United States. By 1857 forty-three
mills operated in the county, and throughout the nineteenth century the county contained enough mills to permit examination of
the machine's diffusion to numerous and disparate establishments.[9]

Although large enough to afford a look at mechanization, the
Berkshire paper industry nonetheless provides a manageable context for closely scrutinizing the social shaping of machine purchases
and the social changes that accompanied and followed mechanization. Mill towns within the county shared similar populations, social
institutions, patterns of social interaction, and economic linkages to
urban markets, permitting a measure of generalization not possible
within a larger geographic unit. For a study of the social sources of
mechanization, the county possesses two added assets. As one of
western New England's Calvinist strongholds, it affords the opportunity to explore the interconnections between Calvinism, capitalism, and mechanization. In addition, the county's early and persistent orientation toward the New York market permits study of
technological change in the New York regional economy, whereas
most previous scholarship has treated developments in the Boston
or Philadelphia region.[10]

Within the context of the Berkshire paper industry, the dates
1801 through 1885 provide meaningful chronological boundaries.
In 1801 the county's first paper mill commenced operation. By 1885
competition from mills harnessing the substantial waterpower at
Holyoke and from mills processing the more abundant timber to
the north and west had already forced some Berkshire mills to close
and had deprived the county of paper industry leadership. The following year a flood in East Lee destroyed many of the county's remaining small mills, substantially altering the character of local paper making. Also, the study of paper industry mechanization
properly concludes with the 1880s, after the standardization of the
Fourdrinier paper-making machine, but before the widespread
shift to chemical wood pulp.

---

[9] Federal Writers' Project of the Works Progress Administration for Massachusetts, *The Berkshire Hills* (New York, 1939), p. 146; Weeks, *History of Paper Manufacturing*. See Appendix A for a chronology of mills.

[10] Cochran, *Frontiers of Change*, and Scranton, *Proprietary Capitalism*, discuss the
problems inherent in a scholarship that has focused disproportionately on firms
within the Boston region. They also exemplify and cite scholarship on the Philadelphia region.

I have underscored my concern with the origins, process, and aftermath of mechanization by dividing this book into three parts: "Before the Machine," "The Machine," and "After the Machine." Part I treats the years from 1799, when the local industry's founder first surveyed potential mill sites, to 1827, when one local mill installed the county's original paper-making machine. I describe the geographic and social assets that initially attracted paper makers to Berkshire County, establishing the natural resources and cultural climate that encouraged the local paper industry's growth both before and during the years of mechanization and that continued to shape the industry during the subsequent era of consolidation. I also depict the tools and skills of hand paper making and the social system of organizing paper manufacture that early paper craftsmen took for granted, factors ultimately influencing both mechanical technology and its uses. Finally, I trace the growth and increasing productivity of the hand paper industry over the decade of the 1820s as it responded to new economic opportunities offered by the New York market. I find that a period of productivity-enhancing innovation antedated and facilitated the introduction of machines; altered patterns of work and investment, patterns often attributed to the use of machines, actually originated prior to mechanization.

Part II introduces the new machines and the men who adopted them. I first depict the paper-making machinery developed in Europe and America, largely the creation of inventors and developers outside Berkshire County. Given Berkshire mill owners' prior concern with expanding output at particular stages of production, however, I find the arrival and diffusion of machines in Berkshire County a tale of local decision making and local innovation, not simply one of machines appearing and transforming the industry. More remarkable than the machine was local mill owners' ability to select machines and to finance industrial growth during the years between 1827 and 1857, when both technology and economic conditions changed continuously and unpredictably. Mill owners' knowledge of paper making and their ability to construct social networks that kept them abreast of mechanical and commercial developments account in large measure for the rapid, but selective, mechanization of the Berkshire paper industry.

Part III considers the consequences of adopting the new machine technology. The most direct consequences—chronic and periodic shortages of raw materials and natural resources once deemed abundant—led to additional technological innovations, encouraging the concentration of production in fewer mills and fewer towns.

In the years between 1857 and 1885 these developments combined
with incremental increases in the machines' productive capacities
and significant business innovation to transform the rapidly growing, rapidly changing paper industry that existed between 1827 and
1857 into an increasingly mature, predictable, capital-intensive enterprise. The more stable post–Civil War paper industry assured
success to established mill owners, enhanced their local influence,
and curtailed the movement of workmen into mill ownership. At
the same time, however, mechanization did not alter the skill, control over work, or personalized interaction of worker and owner
that had characterized masculine labor in preindustrial paper mills;
neither degradation nor organized protest accompanied the emergence of an identifiable working class. By contrast, women's tasks,
which remained largely unmechanized, appeared increasingly insignificant when compared to the more and more productive mechanized work of men. Although mechanization did not create the
sexual division of labor, it reinforced that division, underscored the
low assessment of women's marketable skills, and helped obscure
women's contribution to industrialization.

All told, I find mechanization a wondrous human accomplishment, fully warranting the fascination machinery elicited among
nineteenth-century Americans. The adoption of new technology
was accompanied by unanticipated consequences for mill owners,
mill employees, and citizens of the mill towns. But the use of machines did not create the new social order; I find that mechanization
and its consequences bore the imprint of assumptions and behavior
originating in hand paper mills and in preindustrial Berkshire
County and of social innovations made throughout subsequent decades. To begin this tale of mechanization, then, we need to look not
at the paper-making machine, but at a young, journeyman paper
maker entering a peaceful rural landscape.

PART I

BEFORE THE MACHINE

CHAPTER 1

A FINE PLACE FOR
PAPER MAKING:
BERKSHIRE COUNTY,
1799–1801

The young man who lay down to sleep one evening in 1799 at the small inn set between Pittsfield and Dalton in Berkshire County, Massachusetts, had never been so far from a paper mill. Twenty-two years earlier Zenas Crane had been born near the Bay State's first paper mill at Milton. Like any curious lad growing up in a mill village, he had undoubtedly glimpsed the local craftsmen at their work. Later, he had apprenticed at his brother Stephen's mill in Newton Lower Falls and studied the paper makers' craft more closely. Several subsequent years as a journeyman at Caleb Burbank's Worcester mill had perfected his paper-making skills. Having spent his entire life within walking distance of a paper mill, Crane had traveled on horseback to this remote spot in western Massachusetts to find a site for a new paper mill, a mill of his own.[1]

Increased real estate prices and diminished opportunity in the long-settled towns of eastern Massachusetts probably encouraged young Crane to travel west in 1799. Berkshire County land remained relatively cheap, allowing Crane in 1801 to purchase more than fourteen conveniently located acres, together with springs and waterpower rights, for only $194. The county also afforded considerable opportunity to the prospective paper mill owner. The Pittsfield town meeting's 1779 instructions to its representatives to use their "best endeavors, that any petition which may be preferred from this town, or from any individual of it respecting the erecting a Paper-mill in this town, be attended to and espoused by you in the General Court" expressed local citizens' keen awareness of the cost

---

[1] J.E.A. Smith, *Pioneer Paper-Maker in Berkshire: Life, Life-Work and Influences of Zenas Crane* (Holyoke, Mass., [1885]), pp. 10–13, 15. Crane's father had been one of the owners of the Milton mill before his death in 1778, and Crane's brother Stephen had trained there. Wadsworth R. Pierce, *The First 175 Years of Crane Papermaking* (North Adams, Mass., 1977), p. 11.

Fig. 1.1 Zenas Crane, the first Berkshire paper maker,
in 1801. Courtesy of the Crane Museum.

and difficulty of obtaining paper from distant mills. Twenty years
later Berkshire County and a wide bordering region still lacked paper mills. The nearest paper-making establishments operated in
Springfield, Massachusetts, to the east; Falls Village, Connecticut, to
the south; Bennington, Vermont, to the north; and Troy, New
York, to the west, and all of them had been founded within the previous fifteen years. Thirty-five miles away at Albany, New York, the
closest substantial population center, paper had remained so scarce
only ten years earlier that the publisher of the *Albany Register*
mended torn sheets with paste for use in printing.[2]

² Robert Brooke Zevin, *The Growth of Manufacturing in Early Nineteenth Century New
England* (New York, 1975), pp. 4–5; Smith, *Zenas Crane*, pp. 15, 23–24; Weeks, *History
of Paper Manufacturing*, pp. 125, 127; Chard Powers Smith, *The Housatonic: Puritan*

Young Crane had spent enough time around paper mills to know that successful paper making required more than demand for paper and land for a mill. After crossing the mountains into Berkshire County, he sought the other essentials of the paper maker's craft: falling water for power and pure water for processing, transportation routes by which he could secure imported ingredients and tools from the seacoast, and local supplies of his basic raw materials. In 1799, with national leaders engaged in a far-reaching debate over the role of manufactures, Crane may well have felt the need to test the social and cultural climate as well as to survey the natural environment. In any case, because he intended to live in the community where he built his mill, he probably assessed the local response to manufactures indirectly when he tried to gauge the welcome he and his family would receive. We do not know how much young Zenas learned on his first day in the Berkshires, but it would not be surprising if he entertained rosy dreams of the future that night in his room at the little inn. After completing his search for a mill seat among the mountains, he almost certainly returned east well pleased with what he had found. By any contemporary standard Berkshire County was a fine place for paper making.

Although we do not know Zenas Crane's itinerary or activities during his initial visit to the Berkshires, if he took the trouble to travel so far he probably surveyed the county extensively and inquired widely about its resources. Among those who might have supplied useful information were several contemporary residents who subsequently invested in early local paper mills. Viewing Berkshire County through the eyes of these men and of Zenas Crane will familiarize the reader with the geographic features and towns that recur throughout this book, establish the environmental and social context that shaped later development of the industry Crane founded, and provide a historical basis for assessing the environmental and social changes accompanying local industrialization. Equally important, Crane and his generation of investors had a distinctive vision of the Berkshire landscape. They saw neither the "hideous howling wilderness" noted by the Reverend Benjamin Wadsworth in his 1694 travels nor the "vast and charming park" celebrated in Franklin Chamberlin's 1876 oration. Rather, they viewed the land as fully exploited by contemporary farming methods,

River (New York, 1946), p. 251; Joel Munsell, *A Chronology of Paper and Paper Making* (Albany, 1864), pp. 35, 37–38.

awaiting employment of its latent manufacturing potential. Because their interpretation of the landscape as natural resources helped shape its future, we need to survey the county as they might have done.[3]

TRANSPORTATION

The preceding days' journey had been arduous for both Zenas Crane and his horse. Between the Connecticut River valley and the eastern boundary of Berkshire County, he traversed a rough plateau 1,000 to 1,500 feet high. Beyond lay the steep wall of the Hoosac Mountains, a natural boundary for the county. Ascending by one of the more gradual routes, from Westfield to the Berkshire town of Washington, required a climb of 1,211 feet in twenty-five miles, the most taxing part coming in the last half of the trip. There followed a steep descent into a long valley extending the length of the county. To the north and south more formidable mountains discouraged travel, including the 2,600-foot Hoosac Mountain, whose western slope dropped precipitously 2,000 feet to the valley floor in the town of Adams.[4]

In succeeding days Crane probably explored much of this valley. He must have learned that another, western wall of mountains, the

[3] Richard D. Birdsall, *Berkshire County: A Cultural History* (New Haven, 1959), pp. 17, 27–28; C. M. Hyde and Alexander Hyde, *Lee: The Centennial Celebration and Centennial History of the Town of Lee, Mass.* (Springfield, 1878), p. 51. Most local residents invested only briefly in paper mills, primarily during the War of 1812, when alternative investments grew scarcer. As discussed in Chapter 5, during the industry's early years most long-term paper mill proprietors were skilled craftsmen such as Crane. For a detailed chronology of mill ownerships, see Appendix A.

[4] J.E.A. Smith, ed., *History of Berkshire County, Massachusetts, with Biographical Sketches of Its Prominent Men*, 2 vols. (New York, 1885), 1:10. The Hoosac range of mountains and the similarly named mountain, town, river, and tunnel appear under various spellings, including Hoosic, Hoosick, Hoosuck, and Hoosuc, during the nineteenth century. Here, as elsewhere in this study, where no single name predominated in nineteenth-century usage, the modern name will be used. Where a single name predominated in nineteenth-century usage or where a particular name was used for most of the period 1801-85, that name will be employed. For example, the Hoosac Mountains were also referred to as the Green Mountains, Beartown Mountains, and Housatonic Mountains, but such usages were less frequent or were confined to particular localities within the county.

In New England the "town" is a geographic area rather than a center of population. Concentrations of population, of which there were often several within a single town, will be referred to as villages to distinguish them from the town in which they were located, especially where town and village bore the same name. No center of population in Berkshire County attained the legal status of a city during these years.

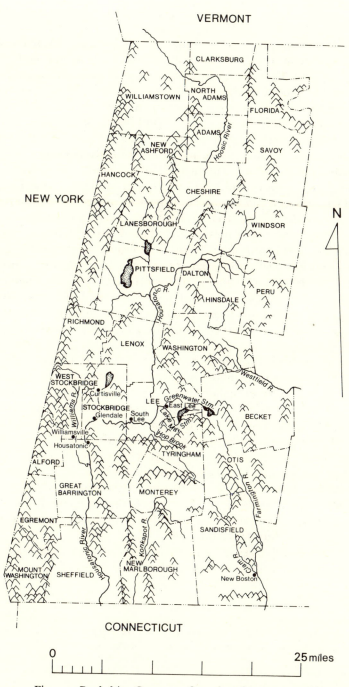

Fig. 1.2 Berkshire County, a fine place for paper making.

Taconics, enclosed the county along the New York border, making Berkshire a geographic, as well as a political, unit. By talking with county residents he might easily have discovered that, although the Taconics averaged five miles in width and rose as high as 2,100 feet above the valley floor, two low passes made travel to New York far easier than to eastern Massachusetts. On horseback he could complete the journey in an hour in good weather. To the north and south, extensions of the Hoosic and Housatonic River valleys facilitated travel to and from Vermont and Connecticut.[5]

His arduous journey from the eastern part of the state may have caused Crane some initial concern. If he built a paper mill in Berkshire County, he would need access to a seaport from which he could obtain those paper makers' supplies imported from Europe or manufactured in only a few American localities. If successful, he might also want to ship some paper to markets outside the county. Listening to the talk of farmers, small merchants, and craftsmen in various county towns, Crane would have abandoned earlier misgivings about transportation to and from the county. Access to mercantile centers, he learned, was adequate for a small paper mill in most Berkshire towns.

Even to and from Boston, a manufacturer could afford to ship commodities that weighed little relative to their cost, such as paper, paper molds, and paper makers' felts and chemicals. Estimating the selling price of a ream of writing or printing paper low at $3.50 and the weight of a ream high at 20 pounds, Crane could have calculated overland cartage 150 miles to Boston paying 30 cents per ton mile to be 45 cents a ream, or less than one-seventh of its retail price. By contemporary standards this was far from exorbitant.[6]

But transportation costs were only one consideration. When supplies spent long in transit, a mill owner needed to maintain an increased stock of tools and chemicals. Paper and raw materials in transit also constituted inventory and tied up additional capital. If Zenas Crane traveled as far south as Lee, he would have obtained a good sense of the problems and possibilities of local transportation

    [5] Ibid., pp. 11–12.

    [6] Weeks, *History of Paper Manufacturing*, pp. 119–20. Paper prices and weights are those of 1821, near the end of a period of sharp price deflation. George Rogers Taylor, *The Transportation Revolution, 1815–1860* (New York, 1951), pp. 133–34 passim. Cost per ton mile is that of the period from 1800 to 1819 or 1820. Douglass C. North, *Growth and Welfare in the American Past* (Englewood Cliffs, N.J., 1966), p. 111; James T. Lemon, *The Best Poor Man's Country: A Geographical Study of Early Southeastern Pennsylvania* (New York, 1976), p. 193.

by stopping at Nathan Dillingham's Red Lion Tavern, the hub of village activity, where citizens gathered regularly to hear the news or regale each other with well-worn tales. Built in 1778, the tavern was the town's first two-story structure and its buttery had served as the first local store. Dillingham might have recounted how the first load of salt delivered to the store had taken forty days to fetch from Boston. Of course, a local farmer would have added, our ox teams can generally haul twenty miles a day, reaching Boston in a little over a week, but winter snows and ice and spring mud slow overland commerce seasonally and unpredictably. Stephen Thatcher, a young man who worked nearby on his father's farm, could have il lustrated the point by recalling that his family's move from Wareham to Lee the previous winter had taken two and a half weeks. For a manufacturer of modest means, this was discouraging news. He could afford neither the production delays nor the larger working capital such unpredictable transportation schedules entailed.[7]

Young Thatcher might have advised Crane not to worry. Although a newcomer to Lee, the enterprising youth had already begun acquiring information about transportation west. Thatcher found farm work tedious and saw little opportunity for alternative employment in contemporary Berkshire. He had heard intriguing tales of whaling vessels fitting out across the New York state line before sailing down the Hudson to faraway places. The young man had learned that roads from southern, central, and northern Berkshire, respectively, led over the mountains thirty to fifty miles to Hudson City, Albany, and Troy. These river ports offered cheap, speedy transportation to New York City. Even under adverse weather conditions vessels from New York arrived at Hudson City in a week to ten days. In good weather sloops sailed upstream to Albany in only three days. Storekeeper Dillingham would have seconded Thatcher's advice. He had quickly ceased depending on unreliable Boston orders and brought most of his supplies on horseback from Hudson City.[8]

By the winter of 1801 Thatcher could have offered more detailed

<hr>

[7] Hyde, *History of Lee*, pp. 58, 68, 282; Taylor, *Transportation Revolution*, p. 138; Dwight E. Jones, *The Jones Story* (Pittsfield, Mass., 1966), p. 1; Penrose Scull, *Papermaking in the Berkshires: The Story of the Hurlbut Paper Company* (South Lee, Mass., 1956), p. 18.

[8] Hyde, *History of Lee*, pp. 187, 282; Judith A. McGaw, "The Sources and Impact of Mechanization: The Berkshire County, Massachusetts, Paper Industry, 1801–1885 as a Case Study" (Ph.D. diss., New York University, 1977), pp. 14–15; Robert Greenhalgh Albion, *The Rise of New York Port [1815–1860]* (New York, 1939), p. 144.

information to frequenters of the Red Lion. He had abandoned his dreams of whaling adventures, but he had escaped from the farm by finding seasonal work as a common laborer building the turnpike connecting Albany with Schenectady, employment that eventually led to an overseer's position. In the process, Thatcher acquired a good sense of transportation costs, knowledge that abetted his later careers as a Lee manufacturer of wire, chair-stuff, and, ultimately, paper. He might have estimated in 1801 that goods could be shipped upstream at only one-third the cost of wagon cartage. Downstream goods traveled at only one-twentieth of overland freight costs. In sum, a prospective Berkshire manufacturer would look to New York as a source of supplies and a market for surplus output. Assured of adequate transportation to New York from most Berkshire towns, Zenas Crane could concentrate on local natural resources in selecting his mill site.[9]

WATER

Given the limitations of transportation in 1799, Zenas Crane planned to rely on it only to a limited extent. He expected to depend primarily on the surrounding region to supply his mill's needs. Like most contemporary American manufacturing technologies, paper making made heavy use of local natural resources. Crane therefore surveyed the landscape with a far more sensitive eye than later manufacturers needed. Water, for power and for processing, especially interested him.

The importance of falling water to early American manufacturers can hardly be overstated. In 1799 it furnished virtually all of the motive power for mills such as the one Crane proposed to build. It would continue to drive nearly half of American industry and more than two-thirds of the mills in New England as late as 1870, twenty-five years after Zenas Crane's death in 1845. Because waterpower determined where subsequent generations of Berkshire paper makers built and operated the county's fifty-two paper mills, it is worth surveying the prospective mill sites Crane might have viewed.[10]

[9] Hyde, *History of Lee*, pp. 282–83; Albion, *New York Port*, p. 144.

[10] Hunter, *Waterpower*, pp. 1–203 passim; Nathan Rosenberg, "Selection and Adaptation in the Transfer of Technology: Steam and Iron in America, 1800–1870," in idem, *Perspectives on Technology* (Cambridge, 1976), pp. 175–77; Carroll W. Pursell, Jr., *Early Stationary Steam Engines in America: A Study in the Migration of a Technology* (Washington, D.C., 1969), pp. 85–86. See Appendix A.

Even to one accustomed to the plentiful rapids and falls of eastern Massachusetts, in 1799 Berkshire waterpower probably appeared inexhaustible. Major rivers and streams abounded. Many smaller streams, which deforestation later reduced to dwindling rivulets, remained, in the early part of the nineteenth century, rapid and reliable water courses. Rainfall was frequent and relatively regular. The large number of potential mill seats also reflected the small size of contemporary manufacturing establishments. Given their limited power requirements, mill owners often preferred a site on a small river or stream where they could construct a modest dam and canal cheaply and easily.[11]

Among contemporary Berkshire residents, David Campbell of Pittsfield was especially well prepared to extoll the county's waterpower prospects. Campbell had arrived from the Connecticut River valley only a decade earlier, but as an extensive dealer in local real estate and a promoter of various industrial ventures, he knew well the advantages offered by local rivers. In summarizing available waterpower, he might have begun by noting the division of the county into two principal watersheds, the Hoosic and the Housatonic. Both arose in the Greylock chain of mountains, which, extending south and west from Adams through Lanesborough to Pittsfield, separated the county into two river valleys. Springs only a few feet apart in a Lanesborough meadow began the flow either north to the Hoosic or south to the Housatonic.[12]

The smaller, swifter Hoosic presented few power sites until, descending from Cheshire, it entered Adams. Though little more than a rod across and a foot deep, it flowed rapidly through the town, its force augmented by ten tributary streams. Four of these tributaries each supplied enough power to drive small mills. Farther downstream, in North Adams, Campbell had heard of excellent water privileges along the Hoosic.[13]

[11] David D. Field, *A History of the County of Berkshire, Massachusetts, In Two Parts. The First Being a General View of the County; The Second, an Account of the Several Towns* (Pittsfield, Mass., 1829), p. 32; William Harvey Pierson, Jr., "Industrial Architecture in the Berkshires," 2 vols. (Ph.D. diss., Yale University, 1949), 1:8.

[12] Smith, *History of Berkshire*, 1:12, 15; 2:335, 338, 428.

[13] In 1878 what had been the town of Adams was divided into the towns of North Adams and Adams. Because of the greater geographical precision gained, the post-1878 designations will be used throughout. Likewise, maps and discussions of individual towns will reflect their boundaries at the terminal date of this study, 1885, rather than their varying dimensions and names during the period 1801–85.

In contemporary usage a water privilege was either a place where water provided sufficient power to drive machinery or the right to use the power at that place. For a

As a Pittsfield resident, Campbell had a more intimate acquaintance with the Housatonic, a longer, larger river. Although not one of the major rivers of the Northeast, the power of the Housatonic compared favorably with that of secondary rivers such as the Naugatuck and Mohawk. The Housatonic delivered its power intermittently, however, and Campbell, who later invested briefly in a Dalton paper mill and in Pittsfield woolen and cotton mills, knew where to find the best mill seats in central Berkshire. In its first eighteen miles the Housatonic descended six hundred feet, but meandered lazily in its early passage through Washington. Entering Hinsdale as a rushing mountain stream, by the time it arrived in the main village of Dalton two tributaries had fed it and transformed it into a considerable river. Falls and rapids whitened its surface through Dalton and just beyond the Dalton-Pittsfield border, where Zenas Crane watched it rush by from a window of his inn.[14]

From Pittsfield, where two powerful branches swelled it, the river dropped only four hundred feet in its circuitous path to the Connecticut border. During most of its travel south and west, it proceeded placidly, delivering its power in a few large bursts. Campbell's interests made him especially anxious to promote the several falls that occurred just south of Pittsfield's main village.

For testimonials to the Housatonic's power south of Pittsfield, James Whiton served as a better contemporary source than David Campbell. Whiton, who operated a furnace and a general store in East Lee, eventually joined with his sons to invest the family assets in an East Lee paper mill. Like Campbell, Whiton's financial interest in paper making was short-lived, but his enthusiasm for local manufactures was longstanding and fervent, manifested in prophesies that Lee would become an American Manchester. The town's waterpower resources provided the mundane basis for his extravagant vision of its future. Whiton might have begun by pointing out the substantial Housatonic falls that occurred in southeastern Lenox, near the Lee border. Crossing the town line, the river fell again in northern Lee, then flowed at a leisurely pace through the center of the town until it arrived at a steep declivity in South Lee village, not far from the Stockbridge border. As an East Lee resident, Whiton would also have called the visitor's attention to the numerous local mill sites along the Housatonic's tributaries. Most promising was the Lake May Stream, which ran past Whiton's premises. In only a few

more extended discussion of the waterpower resources of Berkshire County in 1799 see McGaw, "Sources and Impact," pp. 17–21.

[14] Smith, *History of Berkshire*, 2:335, 338.

miles it dropped over five hundred feet before joining the small but swift Greenwater Stream in East Lee center and, shortly thereafter, merging with the Housatonic south of Lee's center village.[15]

As a promoter of Lee's industrial possibilities, Whiton probably dismissed Housatonic mill privileges farther south and west. He was correct in minimizing their number. The Housatonic wandered quietly through much of Stockbridge, made a substantial drop in the village of Glendale, and fell again in the village of Housatonic, shortly after crossing the Great Barrington town line. Farther downstream in the center of Great Barrington, the river supplied several excellent water privileges, but all power in the town's center had been granted as a monopoly in 1762. Thus, Whiton could urge potential manufacturers to ignore Great Barrington in favor of Lee, where only an occasional small grist, saw, or fulling mill occupied the riverbanks and many mill seats remained unoccupied. Whiton and Campbell would have advised prospective mill owners to avoid the lower Housatonic, for by the time the river reached Sheffield it had delivered up its Berkshire waterpower and flowed peacefully through a broad agricultural plain.

Even in Sheffield, however, a man such as Crane might have found sufficient power for a small mill on one of the Housatonic's numerous tributaries. The Konkapot River, which joined the Housatonic in Sheffield, offered modest mill power near its source in Monterey and more numerous and substantial falls as it passed through the town of New Marlborough. In West Stockbridge the Williams River provided moderate power, and in Tyringham Hop Brook might drive several mills as it flowed through fields of wild hops before joining the Housatonic in South Lee.

Apart from the major watersheds of the Hoosic and Housatonic, Zenas Crane may have noticed on his journey west that the ridge of the Hoosac Range marked off additional watersheds. Along the eastern boundary of Becket, the west branch of the Westfield River ran rapidly toward its destination in the Connecticut. To the south and west, the Farmington River descended swiftly through Becket, Otis, and Sandisfield. Numerous brooks dashed down from the highland in East Otis to join the Farmington, offering mill seats along the way, as did the Clam River in New Boston village, Sandisfield.

To a man in search of waterpower, then, the Berkshires offered a bewildering array of choices. Moreover, none of these Berkshire

[15] Hyde, *History of Lee*, pp. 279, 312.

rivers was wide or rapid enough to require, as did the Connecticut or the Merrimac, a large outlay of capital merely to harness it. Like many other contemporary manufacturers, however, paper makers used water to process goods as well as for power. And paper makers such as Crane had to take special care in selecting process water. When they reduced rags to paper fiber and ground the fiber to produce pulp, paper mills employed extremely large quantities of water. Because hundreds of gallons of water came in contact with each pound of paper fiber, even small traces of impurities mounted up to much vitiating matter adhering to the rag stock. In particular, Crane needed to avoid iron-impregnated waters because they quickly added undesired color to paper.[16]

All this meant that Zenas Crane had to exercise far more care in selecting his process water than in choosing a power site. He rejected river water, which would have been full of silt during spring freshets and contaminated by the waste of tanneries, fulling mills, and other industries upstream. Instead, he looked for pure spring water. Springs also maintained a cool, even temperature throughout the year, an important asset in producing fine, long-lasting paper. Like other contemporary paper makers, Zenas Crane had to locate pure water without the help of chemical tests to identify it. Probably he depended on his sense of taste, using as his standard of comparison the waters near the mills where he had trained.[17]

By any standard Berkshire County was generously endowed with pure water. In Housatonic, Tyringham, Adams, and East Lee, soft-water springs bubbled to the surface near numerous mill privileges. At South Lee the springs on Beartown Mountain later revealed only .01 part per million of iron, no other coloring matter, not a trace of sulfur, and only slightly more calcium carbonate.[18]

For maximum access to local raw materials and markets, Crane may have preferred a more central location. As Campbell would have been quick to note, Pittsfield met this criterion best and had adequate transportation and abundant waterpower. But Pittsfield suffered early from a lack of good water. The rocky ledges beneath its

[16] Smith, *Zenas Crane*, p. 13; Ralph Snell, *Hurlbut's Papermaker Gentleman* 2 (January 1934):12; J. J. Clark and T. L. Crossley, *The Manufacture of Pulp and Paper: A Textbook of Modern Pulp and Paper Mill Practice*, vol. 3, *Elements of Chemistry* (New York, 1923), pp. 26–27.

[17] Clark and Crossley, *Elements of Chemistry*, p. 25; Snell, *Hurlbut's Papermaker Gentleman* 2 (January 1934):12.

[18] "Paper Making in Gt. Barrington and Stockbridge," *SF* 3 (February 1930):1; John A. Scott, *Tyringham Old and New* (Old Home Week Souvenir, August 7–13, 1905), p. 31; Snell, *Hurlbut's Papermaker Gentleman* 2 (January 1934):13.

soil meant that the first wells yielded only surface water, forcing its citizens to construct aqueducts by 1795. Later, after residents successfully drilled wells, they found the water heavy in iron. This fact alone led paper makers, beginning with young Crane, to avoid Pittsfield.[19]

Instead, Zenas Crane chose a site in Dalton, not many miles from where he had spent his first night in Berkshire County. Almost as central as Pittsfield, it also offered many mill sites. Equally important, a hill composed of very pure quartz flanked the Housatonic in Dalton. From its side issued springs so pure they approximated distilled water. One was so fine it would later be said, "The spring water was so good that the mill always made good paper regardless of the management."[20]

Zenas Crane had done more than discover a site suitable for his mill. He had identified a county able to support numerous papermaking establishments. But, accustomed to contending with the localism of the eighteenth-century economy, Crane probably asked a few more questions before committing himself. He sought assurance that he could obtain his principal raw materials nearby.

RAW MATERIALS

Cotton and linen rags were the paper maker's most important raw material and his single greatest expense. When he opened his mill, Crane intended to procure his rags in the surrounding countryside. Before beginning operation in 1801 he inserted a notice in the *Pittsfield Sun* announcing:

Americans!
Encourage your own Manufactories, and they will Improve. Ladies, save your RAGS.

As the Subscribers have it in contemplation to erect a PA-PER-MILL in Dalton, the ensuing spring; and the business being very beneficial to the community at large, they flatter themselves that they shall meet with due encouragement. And that every woman, who has the good of her country, and the interest of her own family at heart, will patronize them, by sav-

[19] Smith, *Zenas Crane*, pp. 17–19; Hamilton Child, comp., *Gazeteer and Business Directory of Berkshire County, Mass. 1725–1885* (Syracuse, N.Y., 1885), part 1, p. 283.

[20] Smith, *Zenas Crane*, p. 17; R. E. Toucey, "Subject: History of Artesian Wells Supplying Crane Mills, Dalton, Mass.," April 28, 1930, CMF; Byron Weston, "History of Paper Making in Berkshire County, Massachusetts, U.S.A.," *Collections of the Berkshire Historical and Scientific Society* (Pittsfield, Mass., 1895), p. 18.

ing her rags, and sending them to their Manufactory, or to the nearest Storekeeper—for which the Subscribers will give a generous price.[21]

Although local housewives needed to be taught their value, in 1801 a mill could expect better supplies of rags in Berkshire County than in the more populous towns to the east. Long-settled areas nearer the coast had experienced rag shortages by the late eighteenth century. In contrast to the situation of eastern mill owners, the absence of other paper mills in the Berkshires and the surrounding region meant that Crane would compete only with the housewife's rag carpet manufacture for discarded clothing and bedding. After several decades of rapid growth, the county's 1800 population of 33,885 certainly wore out more than enough garments to keep a small mill's rag room well stocked.[22]

Martin Chamberlin, the prosperous Dalton farmer who sold Crane the land for his mill, could have assured the young paper maker that Berkshire rags were high in quality as well as plentiful. Chamberlin's father had helped settle the town in the 1750s and had served as moderator of the first town meeting in 1784, giving Martin a good sense of the local agricultural heritage. Martin knew firsthand that many county farmers specialized in raising flax and had been told that domestic weavers had produced enough coarse linen tow cloth to export a surplus before the Revolution. At the time of Crane's visit, Berkshire rag bags held a much larger percentage of linen than those of port cities, whose inhabitants increasingly wore imported cotton. Crane welcomed the news; paper makers especially prized linen rags because their strong fibers made such durable paper.[23]

While listening to the young paper maker's plans and inquiries, Chamberlin no doubt had a number of personal concerns. As a successful farmer in a county where most good farmland had been brought under cultivation, he probably wondered what would become of the younger Chamberlins, including young Joseph, who

[21] Pierce, *Crane Papermaking*, p. 14.

[22] Sidney M. Edelstein, "Papermaker Joshua Gilpin Introduces the Chemical Approach to Papermaking in the United States," *PM* 30 (1961):3; Child, *Gazeteer*, part 1, p. 420.

[23] Smith, *History of Berkshire*, 1:640; 2:636; Bernard A. Drew, ed., *A Bicentennial History of Dalton, Massachusetts 1784–1984* (North Adams, Mass., 1984), pp. 10, 17, 24; Robert J. Taylor, *Western Massachusetts in the Revolution* (Providence, 1954), pp. 5–6; Aaron W. Field, "Sandisfield: Its Past and Present," *Collections of the Berkshire Historical and Scientific Society* (Pittsfield, Mass., 1894), p. 73.

later became the first local resident to build a Berkshire paper mill. Several years later Martin himself invested money in paper manufacturing, so he may have been looking for new uses for his growing wealth when Zenas Crane visited him. In 1799, however, he remained most interested in agriculture and was curious about any potential markets for his farm products. Like many local farmers who concentrated on raising beef cattle, Chamberlin learned that a paper mill would purchase waste products such as horns, hoofs, and scraps of hide, ingredients cooked in mill kettles to make size for coating writing paper. Chamberlin could also sell Crane the tallow and lard rendered from slaughtered animals to meet his mill's lighting and lubricating requirements. If Crane inquired about leather for belts to transmit power within his mill, Chamberlin knew many local tanners ready to supply it to him.[24]

As a second-generation farmer, Chamberlin probably engaged in lumbering in the off-season. He and his neighbors, including Daniel Boardman, another farmer who later invested briefly in a Dalton paper mill, assured Crane cheap building material for the modest frame structure he proposed to erect. Like the Chamberlins, the Boardmans had helped to settle Dalton, and Daniel had personally watched the county's development. He could report to Crane that several county turning establishments had recently sprung up to take advantage of Berkshire hardwoods. They could fabricate much paper mill equipment locally. Firewood for warming workrooms, cooking size, heating paper stock, and drying the finished product also remained plentiful in this recently settled region. Indeed, Crane may have noticed the leach tubs and kettles behind the Red Lion Tavern, allowing him to conclude that Nathan Dillingham engaged in potash production, a sure sign that wood was very cheap.[25]

Crane's industry shared its close ties to local agriculture with much early American manufacturing. Likewise, Crane and other contemporary mill owners looked to local mineral deposits for cheap and constant supplies of their remaining raw materials. Crane needed lime for breaking down his rags, and James Whiton might have told him that he could find all he needed at the lime kilns clustered around Lee, which burned the limestone and marble so abundant in the area. Later the lime would be converted into

---

[24] Taylor, *Western Massachusetts*, p. 8; "The History and Development of Paper Sizing," *SF* 1 (July 1927):2.

[25] Drew, *History of Dalton*, p. 10; Taylor, *Western Massachusetts*, pp. 5, 9; Hyde, *History of Lee*, pp. 279, 282.

bleaching powder for paper mills. For use as a filler to give weight, opacity, and smoothness to paper, Crane would have rejected the coarse clay used at the Lee pottery, but southern Berkshire yielded clay in sufficient quantity and fine enough quality. Alternatively, a paper mill owner could mix calcium carbonate from local limestone with rag fiber. Finally, as Whiton knew from his own enterprise, Berkshire's generous deposits of high-quality iron ore could meet the paper industry's modest metal tool requirements. Local furnaces refined the ore and blacksmiths like Cornelius Barlow of Lee stood ready to fabricate most metal implements and components, principally the numerous edge tools paper mills employed.[26]

After several days talk and travel, Zenas Crane concluded that western Massachusetts possessed nearly all of the raw materials of paper making. Only dyes, pigments, mordants, and a few specially crafted implements need come from any distance, and they were valuable enough to bear local freight rates. Berkshire County had the physical prerequisites, but what of the county's less tangible resources?

The Human Environment

It would be surprising if Zenas Crane found the potential importance of local skills and attitudes as easy to assess. Historians and economists blessed with both hindsight and statistics have struggled to measure the economic contribution of human skills and values in even a rough way. But Crane, like later scholars, must surely have sensed the importance of the human environment. If he could not calculate the value of local beliefs or project precisely how the character of the region's inhabitants would influence his endeavor, he could at least judge how comfortable an ambitious journeyman paper maker felt among Berkshire's overwhelmingly agricultural

[26] Hyde, *History of Lee*, pp. 277, 279–80, 301; Clark and Crossley, *Elements of Chemistry*, pp. 72, 83–84, 120–21; Smith, *History of Berkshire*, 1:5; Taylor, *Western Massachusetts*, pp. 9–10; Felicia Johnson Deyrup, *Arms Makers of the Connecticut Valley: A Regional Study of the Economic Development of the Small Arms Industry, 1798–1870* (Northampton, 1948), p. 35.

Barlow is the first identifiable individual to specialize in producing paper-making equipment in Berkshire County. He began making rag knives shortly after 1806, when Lee's first paper mill was established. Later, when his blacksmith shop burned down, he took advantage of the catastrophe to move from Lee to East Lee, where he established a waterpowered forge better suited to his new specialty. For further discussion of East Lee's community of machinery builders see Chapter 6.

population. By the time he built his mill in 1801, he must have noticed several cultural traditions that made him feel at home.[27]

Like most of his future neighbors, Zenas Crane customarily attended a Congregational church. If he worshipped in Dalton during his visit, Crane probably heard the youthful Ebenezer Jennings preach. As did many early members of the congregation, including the Chamberlin, Marsh, and Cole families, Jennings came from the Connecticut River valley. After experiencing a call to the ministry, he had traveled to the Berkshires to attend Williams College. During his student days Jennings had occasionally served Dalton as interim pastor, while simultaneously courting the Widow Cady's daughter Lovina. By 1800 the young couple had announced their intentions of marriage and Jennings had begun serving the still shepherdless flock of Dalton Congregationalists on a prolonged trial basis. He divided his time between Dalton and West Springfield, where the Reverend Dr. Joseph Lathrop directed his further ministerial studies along staunch Calvinist lines derived from Lathrop's mentor and former associate, Jonathan Edwards.[28]

As a result, Crane found that the sermons delivered in the Dalton meetinghouse differed noticeably from many of those preached to eastern Massachusetts congregations. If he visited Lee on a Sunday, he heard a similar Edwardsian message from the Reverend Alvan Hyde, who, like Jennings, filled a pulpit that had remained empty for some years because local parishioners preferred no minister to one they deemed unorthodox. Lee and Dalton typified the situation in a county whose settlers included many New Light veterans of neighboring Hampshire County's mid-eighteenth-century religious conflicts. Indeed, if the Calvinist tradition nurtured developing enterprise, few locales in America offered a more hospitable religious climate for a new industry than did Berkshire County. Beginning in 1743 three leading New Light theologians—Jonathan Edwards, Samuel Hopkins, and Stephen West—renewed the orthodox tradition while preaching and writing in the Berkshires. In 1801 Hopkinsians still held Arminianism at bay, and through the powerful

[27] Nathan Rosenberg, "Neglected Dimensions in the Analysis of Economic Change," in idem, *Perspectives on Technology*, p. 102; Paul John Uselding, *Studies in the Technological Development of the American Economy During the First Half of the Nineteenth Century* (New York, 1975), pp. 60–108; Robert E. Gallman, "Human Capital: How Much Did America Owe the Rest of the World?" *AER* 67 (February 1977):27–33.

[28] George B. Higgins, *A Pastoral Profile or Parsons in the Glen* ([Dalton, Mass.], 1978), pp. 25–26.

Berkshire Association of Congregational Ministers, founded by West and Hopkins in 1763, West and his colleagues maintained the rigor of local Calvinism and the authority of the pulpit well into the nineteenth century. They also published enough sermons and tracts to stimulate the paper business directly.[29]

Although Berkshire believers took their Calvinism seriously, it would be a mistake to picture them as dour, sober Puritans. On July 4, 1800, for example, James Whiton and Rowland Thatcher, young Stephen's father, gathered with about a hundred other men to raise a new meetinghouse in the center of Lee, an event accompanied by the firing of cannons and the sounds of fife and drum. Female parishioners had arrived somewhat earlier to prepare a hearty breakfast for the crowd. The Reverend Dr. Hyde offered up a prayer, but the highlight of the day was a spontaneous competition to climb and stand atop a ten-foot timber that rose above the rest of the frame. Rowland Thatcher finally succeeded and celebrated by tossing a bottle as far as he could. A mad dash to recover the bottle ensued. Dillingham, one of the committee that had made sure each parishioner contributed work and donated building materials, knew that much of the day's hilarity derived from the forty dollars worth of rum the committee had supplied. He also had reason to suspect that liquor helped maintain the unanimity of the ministerial association. Whenever Alvan Hyde entertained his mentor, West, and their colleagues, one of Hyde's sons was kept busy running to the store for libations. Indeed, some Lee Congregationalists attributed Hyde's "sonorous and musical" pulpit voice to the "Jamaica" he took before preaching.[30]

As a child of eighteenth-century America, Crane found this mixture of rum and religion quite familiar. But how much this tippling orthodoxy favored Berkshire economic development would have been, and remains, a nice question. If Crane or Whiton devoted any thought to the matter, they probably concluded, like good Calvinists, that the relationship of faith to works defied straightforward analysis.

[29] Hyde, *History of Lee*, pp. 64–66; Birdsall, *Berkshire Cultural History*, pp. 33–74 passim. The power of the Berkshire Congregational clergy through their association stands in marked contrast to the failure of most contemporary clergy to organize as effectively as did other interest groups. James A. Henretta, *The Evolution of American Society, 1700–1815: An Interdisciplinary Analysis* (Lexington, Mass., 1973), p. 211. Gregory H. Nobles, *Divisions Throughout the Whole: Politics and Society in Hampshire County, Massachusetts, 1740–1775* (Cambridge, 1983), offers an outstanding treatment of the conflicts that motivated a number of early Berkshire settlers to depart neighboring Hampshire County.

Both men found the implications of local political convictions easier to assess. Federalists championed American manufactures, and Federalists such as Crane and Whiton were numerous and powerful in Berkshire County. Later, during the bitter political disputes surrounding the War of 1812, Whiton thrice earned overwhelming local support to espouse Federalist policies as Lee's representative in the state legislature. Likewise, Crane served several terms as representative beginning in 1811. The influential orthodox clergy reinforced local Federalist strength. Most shared the sentiments expressed from his pulpit in 1815 by the Reverend Ebenezer Jennings: "If all democrats were not horsethieves, then all horsethieves were democrats."[31]

Yet Crane had little to fear from the county's growing Democratic-Republican minority. Small mills dependent on the surrounding agricultural community posed no threat to the Jeffersonian vision of America. Crane found friends in both political camps. Phineas Allen, publisher of the ardently Democratic-Republican *Pittsfield Sun*, guaranteed in advance to sell all the paper he made. Indeed, like religious controversy, political debate served primarily to stimulate the local paper market.[32]

The young paper maker also found Berkshire's social character congenial. The rugged mountain barrier had preserved virgin land here long after the settlement of southern and eastern New England. Only twenty-six years had separated the Pilgrim landing and the founding of Springfield, but eighty additional years intervened before the first pioneers ventured over the Hoosacs. As a result, nearly all of Berkshire's settlers were native New Englanders, coming from the south and east, where the land was either exhausted, too sandy, or too expensive. Adjacent Massachusetts hill towns, the Connecticut River valley, and the states of Rhode Island and Connecticut sent most of them, although Zenas Crane met men and women from eastern Massachusetts in Dalton and might have found larger numbers from Cape Cod in Lee, where they congregated along Cape Street.[33]

[30] Hyde, *History of Lee*, pp. 68, 199, 230–31.

[31] Hyde, *History of Lee*, p. 340; Smith, *Zenas Crane*, pp. 49–50; Birdsall, *Berkshire Cultural History*, pp. 85, 89–90 passim. Crane also served on the Executive Council, although not until the Jacksonian era, when he was a Whig party member.

[32] Smith, *Zenas Crane*, p. 29; Birdsall, *Berkshire Cultural History*, pp. 180–97.

[33] Smith, *Housatonic*, p. 11; Smith, *History of Berkshire*, 1:12, 26, 46, 50, 597, 635–36; 2:76, 126, 183, 233, 258, 285–86, 504, 607; Pierson, "Industrial Architecture," 1:81; Charles J. Taylor, *History of Great Barrington (Berkshire) Massachusetts, 1676–1882* (Great Barrington, Mass., 1929), pp. 287, 290; WPA Guide, p. 135.

The self-selection of Berkshire's early inhabitants acted as a sifting process, not unlike that which had occurred among America's
European settlers. Like the earlier colonists, Berkshire men and
women tended to be of the "middling" sort, for the wealthy had no
incentive to leave and the poor could not afford to depart their
homes to the south and east. The men and women of Berkshire
County, then, were twice sifted for homogeneity. Most had adequate means, but not great wealth. Almost all came from small
towns in southern and eastern New England. And all had arrived
recently enough in Berkshire to lack any local hereditary distinction.

The values and behavior fostered by social and economic homogeneity acted to preserve it. Traditions of deference had developed
far less than in the Connecticut River towns. Dalton citizens, for example, so valued their right to independent opinion that various minorities delayed selection of a permanent meetinghouse site for
nearly a quarter century. Likewise, local residents frowned on os-
tentatious display of wealth by successful farmers, merchants, and
manufacturers. Social distinctions between worker and owner
barely existed because few anticipated lifelong wage work. Most
men expected to be farmers like their fathers, although a growing
number, like Stephen Thatcher, readily exchanged one trade for
another. Henry Marsh and William Cole, sons of early Dalton landholding families, operated small stores and also briefly joined paper-making partnerships. Nathan Dillingham, tavern proprietor,
storekeeper, and potash manufacturer, also helped establish an
early Lee fulling mill. His original partner in the tavern, Cornelius
Bassett, was currently a mason, but he had earlier been a farmer and
a privateer and later joined Stephen Thatcher in operating a turning shop. Zenas Crane, the paper worker who sought to be a mill
owner, would fit easily among such men.[34]

Because southern New England became a cradle of American industry, we can surmise that Berkshire's people brought with them
their favorable attitudes toward small-scale manufacturing. Moreover, judging from later developments, the traditions local men and
women inherited from southern New England helped shape local

[34] Birdsall, *Berkshire Cultural History*, pp. 25–26, 28; Drew, *History of Dalton*, pp. 14–
16; United States Manuscript Population Census Schedules, 1820, Dalton; Hyde,
History of Lee, pp. 145, 154, 280, 282, 307, 314; Pierson, "Industrial Architecture,"
1:156; Smith, *Housatonic*, pp. 370–71. The Dalton meetinghouse squabble bears similarities to those of Hampshire County, where many local citizens had been born. Nobles, *Divisions Throughout the Whole*.

manufacturing as well as encourage it. In the ensuing industrialization of New England, Rhode Island, Connecticut, and southern
Massachusetts firms shared a common pattern distinguishing them
from the Boston-dominated industries of eastern Massachusetts,
the Connecticut River valley, and New Hampshire. Whereas the
mercantile capitalists of Boston could muster large initial investments, the manufacturers of southern New England had to reinvest
to grow. Like Rhode Island's Samuel Slater, these small industrialists relied on families for labor, whereas the Boston men recruited
single women to their boardinghouse mills. In contrast to Boston's
absentee investors, southern New England mill owners lived near
their establishments and took a personal interest in them.[35]

As it developed, Berkshire industry mirrored these southern
New England patterns, suggesting, in part, the influence of shared
values that southern New Englanders had carried to Berkshire
County in the eighteenth century. At the very least, local citizens
had a highly developed aversion to outside dominance of Berkshire
economic life, demonstrated in their strong and widespread support for Daniel Shays in the 1780s. Such feelings persisted. Five
years after the insurrection, Cornelius Bassett advised the newly or-
dained Alvan Hyde, "We have been very Shaysy here and you'll
have to be wise as a serpent to keep the peace among us." Zenas
Crane, who expected to live near and work in the mill he founded
and to prosper through reinvestment, shared the local preference
for economic independence. Like the rest of the local environment,
Berkshire's values gave him encouragement.[36]

The prospect of Berkshire County furnishing workers with the
requisite skills appeared less heartening. Crane knew from experience that even in eastern Massachusetts most paper mills employed
English, Scottish, or Irish immigrants at skilled tasks. After many

[35] Ware, *Early Cotton Manufacturers*, pp. 123, 199; Thomas R. Navin, *The Whitin Machine Works Since 1831: A Textile Machinery Company in an Industrial Village* (Cambridge, Mass., 1950), pp. 7–9; John William Lozier, "Taunton and Mason: Cotton
Machinery and Locomotive Manufacture in Taunton, Massachusetts, 1811–1861"
(Ph.D. diss., Ohio State University, 1978), pp. 1–22; Jonathan Prude, *The Coming of
Industrial Order: Town and Factory Life in Rural Massachusetts 1810–1860* (Cambridge,
1983).

[36] On the long tradition of resentment of outside economic influence in the county
see Taylor, *Western Massachusetts*. Drew, *History of Dalton*, p. 12; Hyde, *History of Lee*,
pp. 156–61, 214. Persistent similarities between Berkshire and Rhode Island factory
architecture reinforce the sense that underlying cultural affinities lay at the root of
Berkshire County's economic and industrial similarities to southern New England.
Pierson, "Industrial Architecture," 1:114–17, 140–41, 154, 172.

years of operation, mills to the east produced skilled journeymen
too slowly to meet employers' needs. Being so far from other mills
could only aggravate the problem for Crane. Fortunately, he knew
paper makers to be a peripatetic lot and he could count on fellow
workmen in Worcester to mention his mill to ambitious journeymen. At least one former Burbank employee, David Carson, arrived
at Crane's Dalton mill within a few years.[37]

Local men and women could be trained to perform less skilled
work, and like Stephen Thatcher, some were sufficiently tired of
farm labor to welcome alternative employment. But depending on
a rural community placed Crane at something of a disadvantage
here as well. Most traditional paper-making tasks required a modi-
cum of formal education: the ability to count, perform rudimentary
calculations, and jot down a few procedures or recipes. The weak
public schools of a comparatively poor, isolated, and indifferent region prepared potential workers poorly. In the early nineteenth
century many a local resident approximated Pittsfield resident
Oliver Wendell Holmes's characterization of a "virtuous rural citi-
zen as 'temperate in material things, and in things intellectual, totally abstinent.' "[38]

On the other hand, as training for mill employment, growing up
around manufacturing counted more than formal education. Here
Berkshire men and women probably held the advantage over people growing up in large eastern commercial towns. Much contemporary industry operated in rural areas because of its dependence
on raw materials and the limitations of transportation. To the gristmills and saw mills common in most rural areas, Berkshire's special
agricultural emphases and resource endowments had added chair
factories, fulling mills, shoe shops, tanneries, lime kilns, iron furnaces, and forges. Because paper mills used some power-driven machinery, Crane also stood to benefit from the skills local millwrights
had acquired in building and maintaining the many local waterwheels, transmission systems, mill races, and dams.[39]

REVIEWING his findings, Zenas Crane must have felt relatively certain that Berkshire County was a good place to build a paper mill.

[37] McGaw, "Sources and Impact," p. 28. David Carson's background is discussed in
Chapter 2.

[38] Birdsall, *Berkshire Cultural History*, pp. 8, 105–7.

[39] David Montgomery, "The Working Classes of the Pre-Industrial American City,
1780–1830," *LH* 9 (Winter 1968):4–5; Lemon, *Poor Man's Country*, p. 122. Before
1832 the many local histories of Berkshire County towns are the best sources of information on local industrial development.

The human environment seemed almost as ideal as the physical setting. Roads to the Hudson and ships to New York; local rivers and springs; the products of field, forest, mine, and quarry; the traditions, values, and abilities of local men and women—nearly everything he had found promised to aid his venture.

While supervising construction of his new mill, Crane heard news that presaged an even more hospitable environment for local manufacturing. Two other men had just decided to establish enterprises in the county. In 1800 Lemuel Pomeroy, Jr., moved his firearms shop from Northampton, where five generations of his family had made guns, to Pittsfield. He would soon be manufacturing large numbers of muskets under federal contract. The following year Englishman Arthur Scholfield introduced the machine carding of wool to Pittsfield, an important first step toward the county's emergence as a textile manufacturing center. Pioneers of nineteenth-century machine production techniques, textile and gun manufacturers fostered the growth of local machine shops and exemplified the advantages of mechanization, alterations of Berkshire's technological environment that ultimately influenced Zenas Crane's industry. But environment explains only part of paper making's subsequent development in the Berkshires. The technics and organization of Crane's craft exerted as great an influence.[40]

[40] A. Merwyn Carey, *American Firearms Makers* (New York, 1953), pp. 96–97; Birdsall, *Berkshire Cultural History*, pp. 30–31.

ZENAS CRANE'S BAGGAGE:
THE PAPER-MAKING
TRADITION, 1801–1820

When Zenas Crane moved to Dalton, he carried few material possessions with him. As the youngest of five sons and one whose father had died while he was still an infant, Crane owned only what his journeyman's wages had purchased. Once he had decided to set up a mill, he undoubtedly saved most of his earnings to finance the venture. Thus, he brought little over the mountains other than some household furnishings and the tools of his trade.

Nonetheless, he had managed to raise three or four thousand dollars to build and equip his mill and roughly six thousand dollars more as working capital. Henry Wiswell, a paper worker Crane may have met in Newton Lower Falls, contributed part of the money and joined Crane at the mill in Dalton. But most of the money probably came from a third partner, Daniel Gilbert. Chroniclers of the local industry record nothing about Gilbert beyond his name. He may have been the same man who had practiced law, engaged in politics, and invested in manufacturing near Crane's early home and had later turned out muskets under federal contract not far from Worcester.[1]

If so, Gilbert ranked as a prominent contemporary manufacturer and, at the age of seventy-two, brought many years of experience to his decision to back Crane. He would have valued the young man's knowledge of how to make paper and how to organize a paper mill. He also would have understood why later historians forgot his contribution, but recalled Crane's. Gilbert soon recouped his investment with interest and, so far as we know, never visited the mill he helped to found. He left no permanent mark on Berkshire County or on paper making. On the other hand, Crane's and Wiswell's experience dictated the shape of local paper manufacturing in 1801

[1] McGaw, "Sources and Impact," pp. 32–35; Deyrup, *Arms Makers*, p. 43; Carey, *Firearms Makers*, p. 44. That both Gilbert's and Crane's fathers had served in the Revolutionary army from neighboring towns southwest of Boston enhances the probability that the two manufacturers knew one another and that Crane felt free to ask Gilbert to back him.

and, in its fundamental processes, in 1885. Zenas Crane's baggage was more impressive than it appeared. He carried a complex paper-making tradition with him to the Berkshires.

Zenas Crane was only the first of several men to carry the paper industry's distinctive technical and social baggage to the county. In 1806 Samuel Church, a skilled paper maker from East Hartford, Connecticut, established the first paper mill in Lee, and in 1809 David Carson, who had originally learned paper making in Goshen, New York, arrived from Worcester "with only his trade and a change of linen." Over the next decade three more members of the Church family built mills in Lee. Local citizens recognized the value of these craftsmen's skills. During the Berkshire paper industry's first twenty years, the various local paper mill investors mentioned in Chapter 1 made sure to enlist one of these paper makers as a partner.[2]

Like these local investors, we will find our encounter with paper making more profitable if we first appreciate the knowledge that Carson, Wiswell, Crane, and the Churches brought with them. We can begin by examining the tools they used and the techniques they had mastered. We can also notice that they had learned certain traditions of work. Between 1801 and 1820, as each of these paper makers made the transition from worker to owner, he reproduced a familiar social system, including a complex division of labor, expectations about workers' behavior, and customary modes of interaction between owner and worker. Clearly, Crane and his fellows were not innovators. When they moved to Berkshire County, they simply replicated what they had learned in other paper mills.

TRADITIONAL PAPER MAKING

Paper making involves breaking down vegetable matter into cellulose fiber; forming it into a thin, wet sheet; drying it; and when it is destined for writing or printing, giving it a suitable surface. In the early nineteenth century paper makers performed each of these steps in a different section or room of the mill. In the rag room workers sorted and prepared the raw materials. In the beater room or engine room, power-driven machinery washed and broke down the rags into fiber. Craftsmen in the vat room formed the fiber into sheets of paper. Other men and women hung the sheets up to dry

[2] Snell, *Hurlbut's Papermaker Gentleman* 1 (January 1933):1; Hyde, *History of Lee*, p. 289; *VG*, 3/28/67, p. 2; 150th Anniversary Committee, *The One Hundred Fiftieth Anniversary of the Town of Dalton, Massachusetts* (Pittsfield, Mass., 1934), p. 52.

in the dry loft. In the size room, a workman applied a coating to make the sheets less absorbent. Finally, employees of the finishing room smoothed the paper and prepared it for shipping. To learn their trade, Crane, Carson, Wiswell, and Church had worked in each of these areas. They re-created traditional mill organization in the Berkshires.

Following the practice of mill owners in Newton Lower Falls, Worcester, East Hartford, and Goshen, Berkshire's earliest paper makers set up rag routes and sent teamsters along them regularly to collect and bring to the mill rags gathered by village storekeepers. By 1810, with three local mills in operation, Crane and Wiswell found it necessary to draw up a "rag rout" agreement. Crane and his new partner, Joseph Chamberlin, promised to confine their rag purchases to southern Berkshire, while Wiswell and Carson, partners in Dalton's other mill, acquired the right to northern Berkshire rags. Neither partnership included Lee on its route, suggesting a prior agreement to leave Samuel Church his home territory. Peddlers and post riders, who accepted rags in payment for their wares, also brought supplies to mill rag rooms in exchange for paper.[3]

On their arrival at the mill, a workman weighed the rags, noted their quality, and calculated their value. After recording this information, he opened the bundles or bales and thrashed the contents to remove loose dust and dirt, a process known as dusting. Other rag room attendants opened seams and shook out debris, clipped off fasteners, and cut out decayed sections. Then they cut the rags into uniform pieces two to four inches square. For all of these tasks they used long rag knives or scythes fixed on posts.[4]

Finally, rag room personnel sorted the rag pieces. Ideally they exercised great care, separating rags by type of fiber, color, and degree of cleanliness. All rags were either cotton or linen, traditional European paper fibers because of their ready availability and high cellulose content. The ease with which beaters later reduced rags to fiber depended on which fiber they contained and how coarse the weave. By separating rags according to these characteristics, discriminating rag sorters could shorten average beating time and prevent fiber loss through excessive beating. Both brought savings to the mill owners.[5]

[3] Rag Rout Agreement, 11/16/10, Crane Museum Display; Appendix A.

[4] Zenas Crane Daybook, 1817–25, CA; Zenas Crane Daybook, 1825–30, CA. A more detailed version of the ensuing discussion of the technology of early American paper making can be found in McGaw, "Sources and Impact," pp. 40–53.

[5] Cotton is 90 percent cellulose, and linen, 85 percent.

Sorting by color and cleanliness affected the paper's quality. In 1801 American paper mills still relied on bleaching by long exposure to sunlight or, more often, simply neglected bleaching. Most natural dyes of the era were anything but fast, although indigo withstood the action of sunlight. Workers sorted out blue rags for making blue writing paper or tobacco wrappers. They also reserved very dirty rags for cheaper grades, such as wrapping paper.

After sorting, workers carried the rags to the engine room. Processing here required much more skilled attendants and complex equipment than the cutting and sorting of the rag room. Rags had to be washed, broken down into individual fibers, and the fibers, in turn, cut and frayed so as to mesh in a smooth sheet. To perform these tasks, paper makers had devised power-driven mechanisms in the twelfth century and had substituted more sophisticated machinery in the seventeenth century. In 1801 rag processing remained the only mechanized stage of paper manufacturing and the sole reason paper makers called their establishments mills.

The machine preparing rag fiber in Crane and Wiswell's original mill was named a Hollander beater (Figure 2.1), in recognition of its Dutch origin. Depending on the task it carried out, workers referred to it as a washing, breaking, or beating engine, although in these early mills the same machine performed the three tasks in succession. Paper makers called the machine's skilled attendant an engineer, meaning a man who operated an engine. The beater consisted of an oval wooden tub. Attached to one side of its floor was a metal or stone bed plate set with knives. Over this revolved a roll made from a section of a tree trunk. Its surface contained about thirty metal bars or knives, varying in sharpness and arrangement with the task of the engine and the quality of the paper. The engineer filled the tub with water and rags, lowered the roll against the bed plate, and activated the engine, probably by connecting the roll shaft to the waterwheel shaft through a short belt. The rotation of the roll dragged the rags between knives and bed plate and lifted them over a backfall, down which they slid until drawn in again by the current the rotating roll created.[6]

Early beaters performed inefficiently and their crude construction precluded fine adjustment, but the engines used in 1885 re-

[6] In addition to being broken down by beating, clean wet rags were sprinkled with lime and allowed to stand for several days or weeks while they decomposed enough to break down more easily. For a discussion of the more primitive stampers that may have been used in one early Berkshire mill, see McGaw, "Sources and Impact," pp. 41–43.

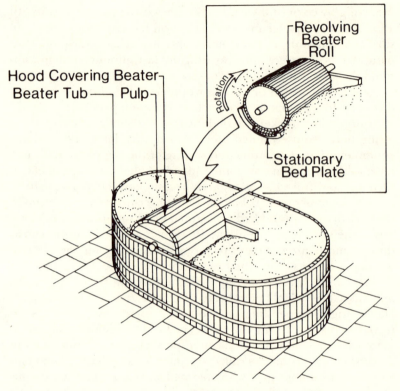

Fig. 2.1 Hollander beater.

mained essentially the same as those in Berkshire's first paper mill. Construction of early beaters by unspecialized millwrights using local materials accounted for most of the differences. The size of available trees dictated the dimensions of the beater roll. Millwrights mounted the roll shafts on wooden beams and provided for adjustment of the distance between roll and bed plate with a series of wooden wedges that the engineer slid between beam and shaft. Considering the slow pace of subsequent stages of paper making, inefficient beaters hardly constituted a problem for Crane, Wiswell,

---

* The use of the term "engineer" for a man operating a beater engine parallels other contemporary usages of the term to describe men who operated engines, including various military devices known as engines. This is the lineage from which the usage of engineer to denote a steam engine attendant or railroad engine driver derives. Later, when Berkshire paper mills installed steam engines, their attendants were known as steam engineers to distinguish them from "the engineer," the beater attendant. General paper industry histories do not indicate when the term was first used in the industry.

and Church. But primitive adjustment mechanisms made their engineer's skills critical.

During beating, the final stage in rag processing, the arrangement and thickness of roll and bed plate knives and the firmness of the roll against the bed plate determined the quality of the fiber and, ultimately, of the paper produced. Whether acquired in Massachusetts, Connecticut, or New York, Crane, Church, and Carson's trade secrets included knowledge of what knife arrangements yielded fine paper. Given these, they expected their engineers to arrive at appropriate beater settings. Constant wear on roll, bed plate, and knives made precise engine regulation inherently difficult. Rough beater construction simply aggravated the problem. Like his contemporaries in other skilled crafts, the engineer compensated with trained senses for inadequate tools. He appraised the consistency of the pulp by feeling it. He diluted some of it and studied it while pouring it from pan to pan. He listened to the rumble of the roll against the bed plate, sometimes magnifying its vibrations by setting a metal rod on the bed plate.

Ideally the rag pulp arriving in the vat room had been beaten to specifications for a particular paper. The longer the beating of the pulp, the greater the shrinkage, density, hardness, and translucency of the final product. The paper's folding, bursting, and tensile strength also varied directly with length of beating. Tearing strength declined with long processing in the engine, and paper made from such stock exhibited greater changes in size as humidity varied. Wiswell, who probably served as the first local beater engineer, balanced these qualities against one another, making him one of the mill's highly skilled workmen.

Most skilled was the vatman who presided over the next area of the mill. Initially, given their limited number, skilled paper makers such as Crane and Church served as their own vatmen. Within a few years, however, David Carson and other skilled vatmen arrived at the Dalton and Lee mills and took their places at the vat. After Carson arrived at Wiswell's mill in 1809, he worked over a rectangular or oval wooden vat measuring five feet across and standing waist high. He replenished his vat with spring water, drawn to the mill by wooden pipes, and with beaten rag fiber, or "stuff," carried by gravity flow from a wooden stuff chest where the engineer had stored it. Carson formed this dilute fiber solution into sheets on a hand-held mold (see Figure 2.2).[7]

7 As shown in Appendix A, the numerous changes in mill ownerships would, if chronicled fully, make this book twice the length and quite tedious. By 1809, Crane

Fig. 2.2 Vat room of Crane's Paper Mill. Scale model by Dard Hunter. *Left to right*: vatman holding paper mold over vat; coucher depositing wet paper on felt; layboy separating paper from felts. A stack of paper ready for pressing and the pole of the screw press appear in the foreground. Workers are attired in traditional paper makers' caps, folded from a sheet of paper. Courtesy of the Crane Museum.

Two molds of the same size rested on racks on the vat. Each mold consisted of a rectangular wooden frame. Within the frame were a number of parallel wooden, wedge-shaped ribs tapering toward the bottom. Skilled mold makers attached a coarse wire cloth to the top of this framework and covered that surface with a finer wire cloth. Two traditional types of wire covering had evolved. A fine woven brass screen with a smooth, clothlike surface produced smooth-surfaced "wove" paper. Molds for "laid" paper had a surface of brass

was engaged in commerce and in courting his wife; thus when Carson first arrived in the Berkshires he worked for Wiswell, who later became his partner. Local histories are contradictory or silent on Wiswell's fate after leaving paper making in 1812.

wires laid side by side and sewn together with several rows of perpendicular wire stitching. This pattern of wires appeared when the finished paper was held up to the light. Either kind of wire cloth could have a wire figure or series of wire letters attached, creating a watermark on the finished paper. Crane, Wiswell, Church, and Carson used such devices to distinguish their mills' products, and bankers sent them molds bearing banks' watermarks to use when making bank note paper.

As vatman, Carson placed a narrow wooden frame, called a deckle, on the upper rim of the paper mold. Holding mold and deckle firmly together at each end, he dipped the mold perpendicularly into the vat, flattened it, and raised it covered with a smooth, even layer of macerated fiber. The slight suction created by the wedge-shaped ribs drew water out the bottom of the mold, while the deckle kept the fiber from running over the edges. By tipping and flattening the mold at appropriate intervals, Carson created paper of various thicknesses. By shaking the mold from side to side and back and forth, he caused the fibers to intertwine, making sheets with equal tearing strength in both directions. He then removed the deckle, set the mold on a rack, and quickly withdrew his hands so as to avoid spotting the newly formed sheet with water. Years of observation and practice gave his movements their necessary precision and rapidity.

To rest after his repeated exertions, minimize damage to his hands, and give journeymen practice at the vat, Carson regularly traded places with the adjacent coucher. In this capacity he judged by the sheen of the paper's surface when enough water had drained and then carried the mold to a nearby trestle, a small frame with a board and wet felt on it. Holding the mold right hand to left side and left hand to right side, he placed it next to the trestle and, using a deft rocking motion, turned the mold over, pressed it against the felt, and deposited a thin, wet sheet of paper. After couching each sheet of paper, Carson set another felt on top of it until he had built up a stack of one hunded to two hundred sheets, known as a post. Then he carried the stack to a huge screw press and summoned all hands. Together the workmen applied sufficient pressure to squeeze most remaining water from the paper and felts.[8]

The damp, matted sheets of paper could now be separated from the felts without tearing. The layman or layboy accomplished this

[8] Coucher is pronounced *küch'ər*. A post varied from four to eight quires, depending on the size of the sheet of paper being made. A quire is twenty-five sheets and a ream is twenty quires.

task. When finished, he called all workers to the press again and they squeezed more water from the paper and from the stack of felts. The layboy returned the felts to the coucher and delivered the paper to the loftman.

The loftman slung the stack of damp paper over his shoulder and carried it upstairs to the dry loft. Here rounded wooden poles resting horizontally in wooden uprights ran the length of the room. Dry loft workers hung the paper over these poles, lifting it into place with T-shaped wooden devices. Vertical wooden shutters (Figure 2.3) admitted enough air to dry the paper gradually. When the loftman judged the paper to be dry enough, he and fellow loft workers removed the sheets, stacked them evenly, and carried them downstairs to the size room.[9]

Size was animal glue applied to writing paper so that it would not absorb ink. In the size room, or in one corner of the rag room, sat the large kettle used to cook animal hide, horn, and hoof, producing glue. Individual size makers developed different formulae for size, and like most contemporary chemical craftsmen, they guarded these as secrets. Size workers coated the paper by dipping bunches two to three inches thick into a vat full of hot size. Then they turned the sheets and dipped the uncoated edge. Finally, workers squeezed out excess size in the press and washed thicker deposits from the paper's edges. The loftman carried these sized sheets to the loft and hung them in a special, heated section.

In 1801 mills sometimes sold paper as it came from the dry loft, because the quill pens of the era could write on very rough surfaces. But even in Crane's first mill, finer grades of paper went to the finishing room, where workers smoothed them by pressing. Hot pressing gave the highest finish. Finishers filled the screw press full of numerous small stacks of interleaved paper and very smooth pasteboard, placing each stack between hot polished metal plates. They left the paper in the press overnight to smooth. The following morning, finishing room workers classified each sheet as perfect, seconds, or broken, counted it into quires or reams, trimmed it with a sharp knife or binder's plough, and wrapped it in dirty brown or gray wrapping paper made from the dregs of the vat.[10]

[9] The effect of more abundant wood in America is evident in the substitution of wooden poles for beeswax-coated rope in the drying loft, one of the few departures from the European tradition. Elsewhere around the mill where wood was one of the alternative materials from which to construct equipment, American mills generally chose wood.

[10] The binder's plough was a wooden tool similar to a woodworking plane with a

Fig. 2.3 Ream wrapper showing preindustrial Berkshire paper mill. Shown on a printed wrapper used to identify Crane's paper in the 1840s, this early mill features dry loft shutters on the top floors of the main building and wing (*left*). In the lower right foreground a tramping paper worker seeks employment. Courtesy of the Crane Museum.

The complexity of traditional hand processes suggests the challenge mechanizing the paper mill posed for nineteenth-century machine builders. By contrast, the simplicity of the one traditional paper machine, the Hollander beater, helps explain the wonder later machines evoked. Men and women who lived near, worked in, or owned nineteenth-century Berkshire paper mills grew accustomed to the rumble of the beating engine. Like other preindustrial power-driven equipment, it excited little comment. We can comprehend the absence of awe at these early machines by returning briefly to the beater room of Zenas Crane's mill.

Considering its achievements, it is hard to understand why contemporaries found the Hollander unremarkable. The machine transformed mere rags into paper fiber. Almost alone its operations determined the paper's character. Highly motivated later engineers have failed to devise a better machine for the purpose. But by looking carefully at the machine, it becomes easier to understand why contemporaries remained unimpressed. In evoking wonder, appearances count for much and almost everything about the Hollander appeared unimpressive.

Standing in Crane's engine room, watching the beating engine, a visitor would have grown bored quickly. Its simple, wooden construction hardly arrested attention and it shared with other preindustrial machines tediously simple, regular motions. As with the repetitive up-and-down motion of triphammer and fulling stocks or the monotonous circling of grindstones or tan bark grinder, a brief glance conveyed the continuous turning motion of the beater roll. Nor did the transmission of power involve any complex mechanism to enchant the eye or intrigue the mind, because the waterwheel drove early beater rolls directly. Adjusting the machine was equally straightforward.[11]

Few probably found the machine's transformation of the rags noteworthy either. To the trained engineer and his colleagues, this traditional machine was too familiar to excite comment. Indeed, as practitioners of a trade handed down from father to son, many of them had watched their grandfathers at work around identical ma-

---

knife set perpendicularly in the side of the stock. The ream of paper was held under a template and the binder's plough was run back and forth along the edges of the ream.

[11] For useful discussions of other preindustrial American machinery see Elizabeth Hitz, "A Technical and Business Revolution: American Woolens to 1832" (Ph.D. diss., New York University, 1978); Brooke Hindle, ed., *America's Wooden Age* (Tarrytown, N.Y., 1975); Ellsworth, *Craft to National Industry*; Paskoff, *Industrial Evolution*.

chines. Most paper mill workers had been acquainted with beaters since childhood. On the other hand, to the untrained eye of the visitor, the machine appeared to do little. Like the grinding of grain, rag grinding took place out of sight, hidden by a hood over the beater roll, and submerged beneath many gallons of water. Also, like most early machines, the beater operated quite slowly. Days elapsed before the rags became stuff. Gradual, invisible processes are not calculated to evoke wonder.

The leisurely pace of earlier and later steps in paper making permitted the slow speed of the Hollander. Because they used only one machine among many hand processes, owners of paper mills, like owners of fulling mills, tanneries, or gristmills, had little incentive to increase that machine's rate. The solitary situation of these early machines also helps account for the fact that contemporaries ignored them. Even simple machines when set in a series attracted attention, as did Oliver Evans's mechanized gristmill. One simple machine amidst a host of skilled paper workers escaped notice. In 1801 the craftsmen were far more impressive than the machine.

The Traditions of Work

In establishing paper making in Berkshire County, Zenas Crane brought more than skills, tools, and machine plans from the east. Paper mills organized work in distinctive ways, and he also transported these traditions of the workplace. Crane re-created familiar divisions of labor and assigned tasks to particular individuals in accordance with expectations shared throughout the industry. He and Carson apportioned wages among workers as they had seen the Burbanks do in Worcester. As paper workers themselves, they acknowledged the workers' prerogative to structure their day's work along customary lines. As a result, by the late 1820s and early 1830s, when mill owners, including Crane, Carson, and several of the Churches, installed the first new machines, owners, workers, and local citizens shared several assumptions about paper mill work. Rooted in more general cultural convictions, these assumptions readily earned local acceptance.

Like most contemporary manufacturing workers, nearly all paper mill employees possessed some skill. Nonetheless, the work force was highly differentiated. Tradition dictated division of labor along lines of sex and age. Crane, Wiswell, and Church simply reproduced those familiar patterns of specialization.

The tasks classified as women's work shared characteristics common to most feminine tasks. They did not require rapt attention. They could be interrupted and resumed without difficulty. They carried little risk of serious injury. These qualities also distinguished the many manufacturing tasks women performed at home, where work had to be compatible with simultaneous child tending. Shaped by traditional household work divisions, ingrained beliefs about women's abilities and preferences had helped determine which work mill owners assigned female workers.[12]

Although a few women assisted in the dry loft, mills employed most female paper workers in two areas: the rag room and the finishing room. They performed all rag cutting and sorting. Similarly, they assumed responsibility for sorting paper. They also prepared stacks of paper and pasteboard for hot pressing and counted the finished product into quires and reams. All of these tasks required that women exercise judgment, and some, such as the rapid hand counting of paper, called for considerable manual skill. None, however, took very long to master, and once learned, these jobs became rather monotonous. Fortunately, women worked in groups in the rag room and finishing room, allowing conversation to relieve the tedium.[13]

Most men's work, by contrast, required complex skills acquired during a long training period. When female sorters exercised judgment, they assigned rags or paper to one of a limited number of general categories. Male engineers and vatmen had to distinguish a range of finely graded differences, weigh mutually exclusive characteristics against one another, and cope with constantly changing combinations of circumstances. Even loftmen dealt with differing paper thicknesses, temperatures, and humidity levels yielding drying times ranging from four to ten days. Men also monopolized supervisory positions, taking charge of the finishing room and rag room. Overall management, accounting, and marketing fell to the owners of these early mills, also invariably men.[14]

Younger men generally performed the mill's less skilled tasks while learning more complex ones. The journeyman coucher stud-

[12] Judith K. Brown, "A Note on the Division of Labor by Sex," *American Anthropologist* 72 (October 1970):1073–78; Judith A. McGaw, "Historians and Women's Work: Insights and Oversights," in Valerie Gill Couch, ed., *Women and the Workplace: Conference Proceedings* (Norman, Okla., 1979), pp. 41–43.

[13] Judith A. McGaw, "Technological Change and Women's Work: Mechanization in the Berkshire Paper Industry, 1820–1885," in Martha Moore Trescott, ed., *Dynamos and Virgins Revisited: Women and Technological Change in History* (Metuchen, N.J., 1979), pp. 77–99.

[14] McGaw, "Sources and Impact," pp. 51, 60.

ied the adjacent vatman. The engineer's, loftman's, and size maker's assistants expected to be taught these crafts as they helped. Boys did menial work in all parts of the mill because indentures traditionally promised apprentices exposure to all stages of paper processing, but owners assigned most boys long stints as layboys. From such positions they familiarized themselves with the trades of vatman and coucher, trades most in demand because the average mill employed four skilled vat room workers, but only one skilled engine, size, and loft worker.[15]

The division of labor by age and sex meant that almost no paper worker faced a lifetime of unrewarding toil. Women and girls anticipated that marriage or childbirth would interrupt or terminate their careers. Boys and young men tolerated lowly tasks as apprentices and journeymen on their way to craftsman's status. Local farmers and their sons supplied most of the mill's intermittent demand for unskilled labor, such as wood cutting, cartage, and construction. The remaining tasks, those commanding respect and requiring ingenuity, were reserved for full-time adult male employees.[16]

Adult males also reaped the greatest financial rewards. In Dalton's first mill, Crane earned $8.00 or $9.00 a week as superintendent. He paid both the vatman and the coucher $3.50 a week and the engineer, $3.00. Adult male workers also received remuneration for boarding their employed children or wives. Women and girls received only $1.50 a week, including board. Boys' pay varied with the terms of their indentures. Some earned $0.60 a week plus board. Crane gave others weekly board and presented them with a new suit of clothes and $40.00 annually.[17]

For 1832 the first detailed census of manufactures makes it possible to compare paper workers' earnings with those of Berkshire men and women in other trades. Most male paper workers earned $0.90 to $1.00 a day by that time. At this rate they took home slightly more than the average worker in manufacturing, although less than skilled men in some textile mills and metalworking trades. Agricultural workers, still far more numerous in the county, earned substantially less at $0.75 a day. At $1.67½ a day, a few Dalton paper workers held the county's highest-paid manufacturing jobs.[18]

[15] Ibid., p. 60.

[16] Ibid.; Zenas Crane Daybook, 1817–23, CA; Zenas Crane Daybook, 1825–30, CA.

[17] Zenas Crane Daybook, 1817–23, CA; Zenas Crane Daybook, 1825–30, CA; McGaw, "Sources and Impact," p. 61.

[18] Louis McLane, Secretary of the Treasury, *Documents Relative to the Manufactures*

Female workers are more difficult to compare. At $0.31 a day, paper mill women earned less than women in any other trade. Other female manufacturing workers in the county averaged over $0.40 a day in 1832, but nearly seven-eighths of them worked in large, mechanized textile factories. Moreover, paper mill women worked much shorter hours, probably accounting for their lower pay.[19]

Male and female paper workers also differed in regularity of employment, differences that reflected underlying disparities in skill. Early mill owners could risk losing female employees because they could train replacements when needed. Skilled male employees or even young men with several years training behind them were less easy to come by. Crane's time book, in which he recorded each worker's daily presence or absence, suggests that he assured male workers of regular employment, but made no similar provision for female workers. It also reveals different seasonal work patterns for men and women. Crane hired fewer women in the winter months than during the rest of the year, whereas lowest male employment came in the spring and summer. These seasonal variations indicate that one or two of the mill's least skilled men probably moved back and forth between manufacturing and agricultural work or other casual labor. In the warm months, when plentiful outdoor work drew these men away, mills called in women workers to take their places, probably in the dry loft or finishing room.[20]

Seasonal layoffs, fluctuating demand for their services, and cultural expectations about work and marriage combined to reduce the average woman's stay in Crane's mill to about nineteen months by the years 1821 to 1834. Even if we include the small group of seasonal male workers, men averaged nearly two years in the mill. In fact, most men served far longer, but nearly one-third of the male work force lowered the average considerably by remaining three months or less.[21]

---

in the United States (Washington, D.C., 1833), part 1, pp. 126–59. Because only three paper machines had probably been installed by the time of the McLane report (although several others were installed during the year in which questioning took place) the information is probably a good reflection of the relative wages of paper workers at a time when hand production prevailed in most local manufacturing, with textile mills as a significant exception.

[19] Ibid.; Judith A. McGaw, " 'A Good Place to Work': Industrial Workers and Occupational Choice—The Case of Berkshire Women," *Journal of Interdisciplinary History* 10 (Fall 1979):243. It is also likely that wage figures quoted to McLane's investigators failed to include additional compensation for "over work," which paper mill women could generally count on.

[20] Zenas Crane Time Book, 1809–36, CA.

[21] Zenas Crane Time Book, 1809–36, CA. The comparable fractions of female

These data suggest that, despite the social and financial rewards and the continuing demand for their services, many male employees of hand paper mills experienced discontent. Their disappearance from mill time books leaves their ultimate response in doubt, but at least two strategies were available to some of them: becoming mill owners and tramping. Crane, Wiswell, Carson, and the Churches illustrate that the first option remained viable in early nineteenth-century America. But one-sixth of Crane's workers appeared in his time book only once, indicating that tramping was a common response.

Tramping meant moving from mill to mill, working briefly if work was available, and seeking out yet another mill if all jobs were filled. Paper-making tradition afforded workers this chance to better, or simply to change, their positions. It required that fellow craftsmen aid traveling paper workers with a meal, a bed for the night, a quire of broken paper, and a parting dram of spirits if no job was forthcoming. As a former paper worker, Zenas Crane honored this tradition, crediting the daybook accounts of those who boarded "trampers."[22]

What sparked the discontent that sent some paper workmen wandering and drove others to become mill owners? That both early Berkshire mill owners and many tramps were vatmen suggests part of the answer. Although vatmen were a proud lot and commanded respect in the mills and mill towns, their work entailed hardships and risks that experience prepared them to recognize and seek to avoid. The complex motion, repeated bending and lifting, and continuous exposure to water that the craft entailed strained a man's endurance. It also subjected him to inflammations of the muscular tissue, rheumatism, skin diseases, and loss of his fingernails. Tramping afforded a respite from the work and helped protect the worker's health. More terrifying than these routine maladies was the sudden loss of "stroke" that older vatmen sometimes experienced, a temporary or permanent inability to perform the shaking motion the job required. In addition to the desire for independence, seeing fellow craftsmen suddenly deprived of their skill and security must have helped motivate men such as Crane, Carson, and Church to become mill owners.[23]

---

workers spending three or fewer months on the job was two-sevenths. One-ninth worked for a month or less.

[22] Weston, "Paper Making," p. 19; Smith, *Zenas Crane*, pp. 26–27; Weeks, *History of Paper Manufacturing*, p. 146; Zenas Crane Daybook, 1817–25, CA, 5/1/19.

[23] Hunter, *Papermaking*, pp. 178–80; Armin Renker, "Some Curious Customs of

Workmen who chose to remain on the job could obtain some solace from liquor. On a typical workday spirits flowed almost as freely as the pure Berkshire spring water. Workers paused for grog at ten or eleven in the morning and again at four in the afternoon. The completion of any construction project around the mills required liberal doses of rum or brandy. One itemized bill for repairs at Crane's mill in 1823 totaled $2.65: $0.15 for shingle nails and nearly $2.50 for nine and a half quarts of rum. When work ended early, the men gathered at the local tavern.[24]

Work organization patterned on traditional practices gave workers the ability to arrange an early departure from work. Rather than working by the clock, the mill's principal employees customarily completed a set task. Vat room workmen, for example, completed twenty posts of paper and then quit for the day. This gave them some control over their pace and hours of work.[25]

On the other hand, workers periodically put in a very long day because the time required for key production processes, such as beating and drying, remained unpredictable. Workers might have to wait for stuff to fill the vat or for paper to finish. Other delays occurred when layboy, sizer, and finisher made competing demands on the screw press or when workers interrupted their regular tasks to power the press. As with work on the farm or in the craftsman's shop, then, the intensity of hand paper mill work fluctuated. Paper mill employees, like local farmers, generally began work at six and might not leave until sunset, but breaks for food and drink joined with routine delays to provide intermittent rest periods.

The work traditions Crane established assured his workers ready acceptance in the Dalton community. Male paper mill workers' task

Old-Time Papermaking in Germany," *PM* 30 (February 1961):9–10. Red hands and arms, and stooping backs were universal symptoms of being a vatman.

[24] "Paper Making in South Lee, Mass.," *SF* 2 (January 1929):2; Weston, "Paper Making," p. 19; Weeks, *History of Paper Manufacturing*, pp. 146–47; Zenas Crane Daybook, 1819–24, CA, flyleaf; Snell, *Hurlbut's Papermaker Gentleman* 1 (January 1933):4. Workers at the county's second paper mill, Samuel Church's in South Lee, even had a peach brandy distillery located next door. Scull, *Papermaking in the Berkshires*, p. 9.

The pattern of work and leisure discussed here and below has received considerable attention from historians of both British and American labor. See especially, E. P. Thompson, "Time, Work-Discipline, and Industrial Capitalism," *Past and Present* 38 (December 1967):56–97; Herbert G. Gutman, "Work, Culture and Society in Industrializing America," *AHR* 78 (June 1973):531–88; Bruce Laurie, " 'Nothing on Compulsion': Life Styles of Philadelphia Artisans, 1820–1850," *LH* 15 (1974):337–66.

[25] "Paper Making in South Lee," pp. 2–3; Weston, "Paper Making," p. 19; Weeks, *History of Paper Manufacturing*, pp. 146–47.

orientation, regular employment, high pay, and substantial skill commanded respect in the early Berkshire paper-making centers. Because women worked at tasks fundamentally like those performed at home, their employment also earned local sanction. The employment by Crane of Eliza, Sarah, and Henrietta Chamberlin, members of Dalton's leading landowning family, confirms the local acceptance of women's paper mill labor.[26]

The short social distance between worker and owner, another traditional aspect of the industry, made paper mill work even more respectable. Whatever their motives for becoming mill owners, the highly visible success of Crane, Carson, and the Churches had important implications for their workmen. As former paper workers, owners respected craftsmen and their traditions and were sensitive to real difficulties employees encountered on the job. They might socialize with workers after hours. A skilled paper worker could approach such a mill owner on rough terms of equality.[27]

Egalitarian relations remained especially appropriate as long as some mill workers anticipated eventually becoming local mill owners. In the years before 1827, when a Lee firm installed Berkshire's first paper machine, vatmen harbored such hopes with good reason. The examples of their employers supported the expectation that conscientious vatmen advanced to proprietorship, just as attentive layboys became couchers and vatmen. Skilled workers participated in all but two of the partnerships that erected twelve paper mills in Berkshire County by 1827. Because most local mills retained the two-vat form characteristic of New England, the industry grew only as men established additional small mills. This form of growth both guaranteed workers chances to invest in new ventures and kept capital requirements moderate enough that workers' savings counted for something. Moreover, the same traits encouraged in workmen—frugality and mastery of one's trade—also brought success as owners.[28]

[26] Zenas Crane Time Book, 1809–36, CA; Zenas Crane Daybook, 1819–24, CA; Zenas Crane Daybook, 1824–33, CA.

[27] A fuller discussion of the backgrounds of early mill owners appears in McGaw, "Sources and Impact," pp. 36–39.

[28] For a fuller discussion of capital requirements see McGaw, "Sources and Impact," pp. 32–33. See also ibid., pp. 401–2; Weeks, *History of Paper Manufacturing*, p. 110.

The first partnership that did not include a skilled paper maker was James Whiton & Sons, who may have intended to rely on a skilled employee for paper-making expertise. They bought Lee's third mill, built in 1819 by Luman Church and subsequently operated by Joseph and Leonard Church. Their brief tenure as mill propri-

Legal disabilities and exclusion from highly skilled jobs precluded female workers' aspiring to mill ownership. They might have hoped, however, to marry a prospective mill owner. In any event, women's paper mill employment proved no bar to marriage within the community and occasionally introduced them to prospective husbands. For example, Onor Cole, who spent three years in Crane's mill in the early 1820s, later married farmer Warren Holden, who frequently used his team to make deliveries at the rag room. Widow Hannah Bassett, who boarded workers and worked with her daughters in Crane's mill, married daughters Rebecca and Lucretia to Crane's nephews, Zenas and Charles, young men who also served in Crane's mill.[29]

Nor was the employment of Crane's nephews unusual. Their father, Stephen, owned a mill and he probably viewed their work as preparation for mill ownership. Zenas Crane arranged similar training for his sons, Marshal and J.B. Marshal began summer labor at age ten, worked half the year in the mill at twelve, and took a regular job at seventeen. J.B. appeared in the mill time book regularly at age twelve. Emeline Crane, daughter of Zenas's brother Nathan, also held a job in Crane's mill, indicating that her family considered mill work respectable even when not in preparation for ownership. Similarly, Thomas Hurlbut, a former paper worker who purchased Samuel Church's South Lee mill in 1822, employed his daughter

---

etors suggests that relying on employees' skills proved unsatisfactory. By contrast, all of the skilled paper makers stayed in business for at least ten years; Joseph, Leonard, and Luman Church owned mills for at least twenty years; and Crane and Carson remained in paper making for at least forty years. (See Appendix A.)

The other firm that did not include a skilled paper maker was that owned by the Laflins, including brothers Winthrop and Walter and their cousin, Cutler. They moved to Lee from Southwick, Massachusetts, in 1817 and entered paper making after local citizens grew outraged at the explosions that punctuated their careers operating local powder mills between 1817 and 1826. By 1826 their principal market for powder, Erie Canal construction, was also disappearing. In any event, the Laflins discontinued powder manufacture and invested their substantial resources in a Lee paper mill in 1826 and a second mill in 1827. Given their affluence, they were probably in a position to recruit and retain highly skilled employees. But at least Cutler, Walter, and Walter's two young sons took care to learn as much as possible about paper making. Cutler later went on to a career as a paper merchant and Walter, whose interests shifted to banking and insurance, played an active part as silent partner in his sons' enterprise. The Laflins stayed in the Berkshire paper industry a little more than ten years. Hyde, *History of Lee*, pp. 284, 291; *VG*, passim.

[29] Zenas Crane Time Book, 1809–36, CA; New England Historic Genealogical Society, *The Vital Records of Dalton, Massachusetts, to the Year 1850* (Boston, 1906), p. 55; Zenas Crane Daybook, 1825–30, CA; *Crane Family Record, 1648–1961* (Dalton, Mass., 1961), pp. 5–6.

Eliza in his mill. Indeed, Charles Crane's wife returned to the mill briefly after the birth of her first child. The presence of such workers further blurred the lines between employer and employed.[30]

Finally, just as the small, wooden early paper mills sat unobtrusively among the neighboring shops and barns, the arrival of their small work forces altered local communities little. Estimates of numbers employed in Berkshire's earliest paper mills range from six to eleven. By 1832 thirteen county paper mills reported an average of about twenty-two workers. Throughout the years of hand paper manufacturing, then, paper-making centers retained their rural character. In 1820, despite the town's two paper mills, a woolen mill, and numerous craftsmen's shops, Dalton census takers found 70 percent of those working engaged in agriculture.[31]

Small paper mill work forces meant that a mill owner such as Crane could know each of his workers and keep posted on their lives outside the mill. Thus, the established farming community did not need to worry about workers' potential deviance or dependency. In addition to permitting direct surveillance by the mill owner, the small size of traditional paper mill work forces enabled early mill proprietors to maintain family governance of workers' behavior. Most employees lived locally with their families. Crane easily arranged for the few exceptions to board in respectable households, including his own and that of his brother Nathan. In sum, traditional paper manufacture did not disturb or threaten the traditional farming society it entered.[32]

By 1885 machines had transformed the traditional craft of paper making and mill villages such as Dalton, yet with the knowledge he possessed in 1801, Zenas Crane would have recognized the later industry. Some stages of paper manufacture remained virtually unchanged. Mechanized procedures essentially mimicked earlier hand operations. The intrinsic character of product and process imposed constraints on machine builders as they had on craftsmen.

[30] *Crane Family Record*, pp. 5–8; Zenas Crane Time Book, 1809–36, CA; Zenas Crane Daybook, 1819–24, CA; Zenas Crane Daybook, 1824–33, CA; Owen & Hurlbut Blotter, 1824, HP, 4/24.

[31] *McLane Report*, part 1, pp. 145, 157–58; McGaw, "Sources and Impact," pp. 59–60; Records of the Bureau of the Census, Fourth Census (1820), Population Schedules, Dalton, Berkshire County, Massachusetts.

[32] Zenas Crane Daybook, 1817–25, CA; Zenas Crane Daybook, 1825–30, CA. For a discussion of similar housing and family governance of workers see Paul E. Johnson, *A Shopkeeper's Millennium: Society and Revivals in Rochester, N.Y. 1815–1834* (New York, 1978).

Given these underlying similarities of mill and factory, many of the assumptions about work that Crane brought with him also survived to influence the mechanized paper industry.

But if traditional practices determined much about the later industry, they explain little about why it changed. As with the geography of Berkshire County, Crane and his fellow mill owners took the technology of paper making as a given. Their craft tradition rested on imitation. Nonetheless, within thirty years of Crane's arrival, he and his fellows had become innovators. They rapidly installed one new machine after another. Their willingness and ability to innovate originated in the 1820s as they experimented within the framework of traditional hand manufacture.

CHAPTER 3

A DECADE OF PREPARATION:
THE 1820s

After their initial establishment, hand paper mills excited little curiosity among the men and women living in early nineteenth-century Berkshire County. Modest frame buildings, they differed from surrounding residences and barns chiefly in their location on a mill race and in the wooden waterwheels rumbling at their sides. Local residents could distinguish them from other power-driven mills only by the shutters of their second-story dry lofts. Early nineteenth-century mills remained so unobtrusive, most contemporaries no doubt passed them by without wondering about the work going on within. Historians have followed suit, largely disregarding what went on inside preindustrial mills. As a result, most studies of mechanization simply state that hand production methods were inadequate and explain a machine's introduction by contrasting its productivity with the limited output possible with traditional manufacturing techniques.

In broadest terms, of course, this approach does account for why mechanical innovation took place. In the case of the Berkshire paper industry, for example, after 1819 Zenas Crane and his colleagues found themselves drawn into a larger, regional economy oriented toward New York City. Both the New York market's magnitude and the higher prices offered there motivated mill owners to meet its demand. Responding, they attempted to increase output substantially and ultimately encountered limitations inherent in conventional technology. Paper-making machines finally overcame these restrictions on productivity.

Emphasizing the inadequacies of traditional techniques may explain why mechanization occurred, but it begs the equally important question of how it occurred. How did mill owners and workers become both willing and able to adopt mechanical solutions to production problems? How did they target particular production stages for early mechanization? By looking inside traditional Berkshire paper mills in the 1820s, I find that, before mechanization commenced, a series of less dramatic changes in hand manufacturing methods prepared manufacturers to adopt machines and workers to labor alongside them.

Incomplete mill records and unreliable early census schedules often render the development of the paper industry obscure before 1819 and hazy thereafter, but they show that Berkshire manufacturers were already experienced innovators when they decided to install paper-making machines in the late 1820s and early 1830s. In the decade before they introduced new mechanical technology, mill owners managed to expand output by increasing capital invested in fixed assets and inventory, by adopting new technology, and by modifying the organization of work in their mills. Mechanization, when it came, required the same sorts of behavior. It required mill owners to continue augmenting capital, accepting technological change, and reorganizing work.[1]

While new markets and new methods altered the workplace, the revivals and reform movements of the 1820s transformed mill owners and mill workers, preparing them for work in mechanized mills. As with changes in manufacturing methods, revival-induced changes in habit took place within a very traditional context. Berkshire's established Calvinist clergy fostered new habits of discipline, punctuality, and temperance by drawing employers and employees into orthodox Congregational churches. Ultimately these fruits of revitalized orthodoxy anticipated the unorthodox requirements of machine production. Discipline, punctuality, and temperance enabled workers to cope with more rigorous work schedules and equipped owners to rationalize operations and accumulate capital.

[1] Almost no mill records exist for the period before 1819. Rather than rely on local histories, which are often contradictory or, occasionally, so uniform as to suggest extensive borrowing from one another, this account of the industry's early development will focus on the years from 1819 to 1832. For this period a mill time book and a number of company daybooks are available. Because these were the years during which conditions fostering the 1827 decision to install the county's first paper-making machine developed, such an emphasis is especially appropriate.

Federal statistics for this period, used to supplement mill records, are far from satisfactory. At best the 1820 census enumerated only half of the establishments operating in the county at the time. The 1824 report of the Secretary of State on manufactures lists only one of the nine mills known to be operating before 1824 and supplies authorized capitalization only for a combined cotton and paper manufacturing firm, utterly unrepresentative of the county's other paper mills. The *McLane Report*, cited earlier, provides the fullest coverage of Berkshire manufactures, Massachusetts enumerators having been the most thorough. It probably missed only one Berkshire paper mill. As noted earlier, however, this 1832 document includes in composite statistics several mills already using machines. (See Chapter 2, n. 15.) U.S. Secretary of State, *Digest of Accounts of Manufacturing Establishments in the United States and of Their Manufactures* (Washington, D.C., 1823); U.S. Secretary of State, *Report of Such Articles Manufactured in the United States as Would Be Liable to Duties if Imported . . . with a Schedule of Factories Incorporated by State Laws* (Washington, D.C., 1824), pp. 15, 19, 27.

In several fundamental respects, then, the 1820s was a decade of preparation. We can see these preparations once we look beyond the deceptively familiar facades of preindustrial mills. Inside, hand paper makers were responding to new markets with new production methods. And the men who responded were becoming, in their hearts and habits, new men.

NEW MARKETS

Berkshire manufacturers had always carried on some trade with New York. After 1810 and especially after 1820, however, Berkshire County became part of an emerging economic region that produced primarily for New York City and consumed goods purchased in New York. The objective of Berkshire paper makers shifted from local production for local consumption to manufacture for a far larger, more specialized, and more discriminating market. The impact on the industry was profound. By 1820 maximum output of Berkshire's five paper mills amounted to only two-thirds of a ream for each person in the county. Although they might have supplied the county, paper makers had hardly exhausted local demand, which included that of adjoining counties in New York and New England. Under these circumstances, the sudden expansion of the industry's market exerted strong pressure to expand production.[2]

A series of improvements in the regional transportation network precipitated the reorientation toward the more distant urban market. After 1812 a macadam, all-weather road from Pittsfield to Albany, one of the nation's earliest, tied Berkshire more closely to Manhattan. Steamboats supplemented Hudson River sloops after 1807, initially shortening the trip from Albany to New York to thirty-four hours. By 1820 steamboats carried goods upstream at one-fifteenth and downstream at one-thirtieth of overland freight

[2] Diane Lindstrom, *Economic Development in the Philadelphia Region, 1810–1850* (New York, 1978), has provided a detailed demonstration of the importance of intraregional trade and specialization for the economic development of one major American region during the Industrial Revolution. She also makes a convincing case for the applicability of the "Eastern demand model" of economic development to the New York City region. While the timing of development in, dimensions of, and special character of the New York regional economy await detailed analysis, my argument follows the broad outlines of regional development delineated by Lindstrom, especially pp. 34–40, 48–51, 93–151. For purposes of comparison, Michael Merrill, "Cash Is Good to Eat: Self-Sufficiency and Exchange in the Rural Economy of the United States," *RHR* 7 (1977):42–71, offers some important observations concerning economies oriented toward local production for local consumption.

charges. Most freight continued to travel quickly enough by cheaper sailing vessels, but steamboats assured shorter trips and more predictable arrival times for Berkshire manufacturers with business in the metropolis. Steamboats also speeded and regularized communication between New York merchants and hinterland producers. After the Supreme Court struck down the Fulton-Livingston monopoly in 1824, intense competition lowered steamboat fares, making travel between New York and Albany considerably cheaper than travel between other American urban centers. Competition also reduced travel time to as little as ten hours by the late twenties. For Berkshire paper manufacturers this meant that men, commodities, and commercial information that had taken three to four days to reach New York in 1800 arrived in about twenty-four hours in 1830.[3]

Between 1820 and 1825 the completion of the Erie and Champlain canals brought northern and western New York into the New York City regional economy, opening the way for further division of labor between the city and its hinterland and within the hinterland. Berkshire farmers, for example, found themselves unable to compete with the newly cultivated grainfields to the north and west and shifted to dairy farming, sheep raising, and other specialties for which greater proximity to urban and industrial markets conferred advantages. Similarly, Berkshire mill owners concentrated on turning out goods they could make better than could urban manufacturers. By 1832 several industries favored by local conditions manufactured for sale in New York. A number of turning mills and several carriage makers, furnaces, and forges reaped advantages from the quality of locally abundant raw materials. Many tanneries, woolen mills, and clothiers processed local agricultural specialties to fill New York's needs. As elsewhere in New England, cotton mills proliferated, enjoying the benefits of Berkshire waterpower and of mechanics previously schooled in woolen textile technology. In fact, county machine shops competed successfully in the New York market for textile machinery.[4]

[3] Howard S. Russell, *A Long, Deep Furrow: Three Centuries of Farming in New England* (Hanover, 1976), p. 267; Herman E. Krooss, *American Economic Development: The Progress of a Business Civilization* (Englewood Cliffs, N.J., 1966), pp. 290–91; North, *Growth and Welfare*, p. 111; Allan R. Pred, *Urban Growth and the Circulation of Information: The United States System of Cities, 1790–1840* (Cambridge, Mass., 1973), pp. 144–47, 175–82, and passim; Albion, *New York Port*, pp. 143–44, 153, 158.

[4] This pattern of specialization parallels that described by Lindstrom for Philadelphia's eastern hinterland. Lindstrom, *Philadelphia Region*, pp. 122–29, 149; Albion, *New York Port*, pp. 86–87; Russell, *Long, Deep Furrow*, pp. 272, 284–85, 289–302; *McLane Report*, part 1, pp. 126–59. The New York orientation of Berkshire cotton

Within the enlarged New York region, the many assets Zenas Crane had identified in the Berkshires guaranteed established paper makers a competitive advantage and favored the location of additional paper mills in the county. New York's particular urban specialties, in turn, assured a ready market for paper. By the 1820s New York reigned as America's preeminent commercial center and contemporary commerce consumed most American paper. Counting houses recorded transactions on the strong, heavy paper of journals and ledgers. To provide a medium of exchange, banks required thin, watermarked paper, hot-pressed smooth enough to take the detailed impressions of bank note engravings. Their customers needed first-class printing or writing paper for the promissory notes and bills of exchange that lubricated trade. Handwritten correspondence on fine writing paper linked New York merchants to their distant British, Irish, and southern customers and agents, and together with growing numbers of newspapers, conveyed vital commercial information. Stimulated by commerce, the city's burgeoning printing industry consumed quantities of book, as well as news, paper. By 1832 New York merchants consigned paper to other American printing and commercial centers, such as Philadelphia, and included it in the cargoes they shipped to the American South.[5]

Despite the adequacy of existing local markets, both the magnitude and the commercial orientation of New York demand offered Berkshire paper manufacturers incentives to sell in Manhattan. Berkshire customers purchased a wide variety of papers, including much of the cheap, low-quality paper that retailers used to wrap hardware, sugar, and other goods. Local manufacturers also sought wrapping paper for their wares. Nor was writing paper sold to workers and other townspeople, or paper bound in books and sold as farmers' or craftsmen's ledgers, as fine as writing and ledger paper demanded by New York merchants. Manufacture for the urban market enabled Berkshire mills to specialize in high-quality paper. As Table 3.1 indicates, this specialization in fine paper, combined with greater New York demand, raised average New York prices well above local prices, far offsetting transportation costs and higher raw material and finishing expenses.[6]

---

textile manufacturers is suggested by the fact that only one reported Alabama as its source of raw cotton; the rest reported New York.

[5] Pred, *Urban Growth*, pp. 22–26, 79–81; Lindstrom, *Philadelphia Region*, pp. 49–51; *McLane Report*, part 1, p. 145.

[6] Zenas Crane Daybook, 1817–23, CA; Zenas Crane Daybook, 1825–30, CA. In general, higher-quality paper meant higher linen content, more uniform thickness

TABLE 3.1
AVERAGE PRICE PER REAM
ZENAS CRANE'S PAPER SALES, 1826–30

Year	New York Sales	Local Sales
1826	$4.05	$2.73
1827	4.11	3.25
1828	3.78	3.17
1829	3.43	3.17
1830	3.38	2.89

NOTE: Data on paper sales come from a detailed analysis of individual transactions in Zenas Crane Daybook, 1825–30, CA. Figures for 1830 are only available for the first ten months of the year. Comparison with time book figures of mill output indicates that most, but not all, sales were recorded in the daybook. Probably only those involving credit—all New York sales and the majority of local transactions—were noted. In 1819, when Zenas Crane Daybook, 1817–23, records no paper sales in New York, average price per ream of paper sold locally was $3.19, indicating that local prices were relatively uninfluenced by New York sales.

Specialization also probably permitted some economies of scale, further enhancing New York profits. This seems especially likely because New York orders were not only more uniform than local purchases, but also consistently larger. Both in 1819, before Crane sold much paper in New York, and in 1826–30, when his New York sales increased dramatically, only about 10 percent of his local transactions dispensed ten or more reams. Over half of his daybook entries for Berkshire sales recorded one ream or less. By contrast, a single paper merchant, Jonathan Seymour, handled all of Crane's New York business for the period. Shipments to him consistently exceeded ten reams, often numbering one hundred or more reams of a single kind of paper.[7]

---

of the sheets in a ream, few flaws or blemishes, greater smoothness, and whiter color for white paper or more consistent color for colored sheets. Greater care in sorting rags and paper, more pressing in the finishing room, and more consistent exercise of the vatman's skill could assure these characteristics. Fine paper also was stronger and more durable, reflecting careful treatment in the beating room.

[7] Because Crane's daybook recorded shipments of paper rather than orders, these figures probably understate the size of Seymour's orders. Zenas Crane Daybook, 1817–23, CA; Zenas Crane Daybook, 1825–30, CA. In 1819, 54.5 percent of local transactions dispensed a single ream or less; between 1826 and 1830 the comparable figure was 52.5 percent. In both periods 36.6 percent of local sales supplied customers with between one and ten reams. Ten or more ream transactions accounted for 8.9 percent of local sales in 1819 and 10.9 percent in the later period.

Manufacturing for New York probably ensured economies of scale by regularizing production, reducing inventory relative to output, and saving clerical time. Several features of New York orders must have lowered production costs. Skilled workers such as engineers, vatmen, loftmen, and size makers undoubtedly turned out more consistent sheets of paper more rapidly when working on large, uniform lots. Other workers performed operations required only on certain kinds of paper, such as hot pressing fine grades, sizing writing paper, or ruling ledger sheets. Mill owners could employ these workers more fully when mills specialized in fine paper. Owners could also more easily plan use of the dry loft and press as their product became more uniform. Elsewhere in the mill, selling fewer product lines might have reduced costs by enabling manufacturers to adjust supply to demand without maintaining so large an inventory. Finally, savings must have accrued as fewer, larger, more uniform accounts cut time invested in processing orders and keeping track of accounts receivable.

As they experienced these advantages, Berkshire paper manufacturers increasingly sought out New York customers. By 1832 thirteen local mills reported sending 65 percent of their output, or 46,000 reams of paper, to New York State. Even allowing for sales in Albany, Troy, and the adjacent rural area, Berkshire County must have made well over half of its paper for the New York City market. Mill owners listed 18,000 additional reams, over 25 percent of local production, as destined for Pennsylvania and the southern states, undoubtedly by way of New York. Local customers took less than 10 percent of the paper manufactured in the Berkshires, even if they consumed all of the 7,000 reams listed as sold in Massachusetts. In fact, they almost certainly used far less. Lee wall paper manufacturers purchased 4,000 of the reams sold locally, but disposed of all their paper hangings through merchants catering to affluent New York customers.[8]

Clearly, by 1832 Berkshire paper mills responded primarily to New York's demands. The timing and pace of the shift to serving New York elude precise determination, but the pattern of new mill

[8] Both the extant records of the Berkshire paper industry and the patterns of regional trade outlined by Lindstrom support the assertion that New York City consignments far outnumbered those to hinterland centers such as Albany.

Because the owners of the wall paper factory also owned two large paper mills, they may not have included paper sent for conversion to wall paper among their sales. In either case, total local consumption would fall below 10 percent of output. *McLane Report*, part 1, pp. 144–45, 156–57.

construction offers some clues. After completion of the county's fourth paper mill in 1809, paper makers built no additional mills during the ensuing decade of embargo, war, and postwar depression. Then, beginning in 1819, local men erected ten new paper-making establishments within a ten-year period. While more than tripling the number of mills, they multiplied the region's productive capacity by more than five, because two mills built in 1826–27 together manufactured nine times as much paper as a conventional two-vat mill.[9]

Judging from mill construction, then, the reorientation from local to regional market occurred in the course of the 1820s. Fragmentary sales information confirms this impression and indicates that growth in New York sales, like increases in productive capacity, accelerated in the last half of the decade. In 1819 Crane's daybook listed no sales in New York. In 1826 Crane named his newborn son Seymour, after his New York paper merchant, suggesting the importance he attached to his New York trade by that date. A two-month shutdown for repairs in 1826 and the inclusion of paper made in 1826 among paper finished in 1827 distort totals for those years individually, but Crane's shipments to New York already comprised nearly one-quarter (23.7 percent) of his output for the two-year period. His New York consignments as a percentage of paper manufactured rose to 30.5 percent in 1828, climbed to 46.5 percent in 1829, and remained near that figure at 42.2 percent in 1830.[10]

Less favorably located for attracting Pittsfield and Albany customers, paper manufacturers in Lee probably turned to New York earlier. The tripling of paper mills in the town between 1820 and 1824 shows more rapid growth than the Dalton industry experienced in the early twenties. Three mills built after 1825 account for nearly half of the town's 1832 capacity, however, so that Lee's production for New York also accelerated in the late twenties.[11]

Growing reliance on foreign raw materials reinforced ties to

9 "Paper Making in Lee Village," *SF* 2 (March 1929):1; McGaw, "Sources and Impact," pp. 34, 401–24. This estimated increase in productivity is a conservative one because it fails to take into account changes in existing mills and because information on capacity is not available for several of the mills built from 1819 through 1828, some of which may also have exceeded the conventional two-vat size.

10 This last percentage is distorted by substituting November and December 1829 sales figures for 1830 figures, because Zenas Crane Daybook, 1825–30, ends in early November 1830. The direction of the bias introduced is uncertain. Zenas Crane Time Book, 1809–36, CA; *Crane Family Record*, pp. 4–8.

11 "Paper Making in Lee Village," p. 1; McGaw, "Sources and Impact," pp. 34, 401–24.

New York and fostered rapidly mounting sales there. With expansion, the county paper industry quickly outran local rag supplies. Increasingly Berkshire mills made paper from rags that New York paper merchants collected elsewhere in the Northeast. Eventually America failed to generate enough rags and New York rag dealers turned to Europe for additional supplies. By 1832 Europe provided 75 percent of the Lee industry's nine-hundred-ton rag requirements. Of Dalton's more modest ninety tons, over 22 percent originated abroad. New York, with her extensive foreign trade, delivered such rags at close to domestic rag prices and her well-developed Irish trade, in particular, assured supplies of linen rags.[12]

New York rag purchases increased Berkshire mill owners' dependence on the New York paper market. Paper mills could pay for local rags, like other local commodities, through a system of more or less perpetual daybook accounts. Complex three- or four-way transactions by which, for example, Crane purchased rags from peddlers and country storekeepers; Pittsfield merchants bought paper from Crane; and peddlers, country storekeepers, and Crane's workers acquired goods from Pittsfield merchants meant that most accounts maintained a rough balance. Within the county, tradition and a scarcity of circulating medium encouraged tolerance of these networks of indebtedness. New York rag dealers, by contrast, demanded payment in notes or bills of exchange recognized in New York. Paper sales in New York granted Berkshire mill owners the right to draw on New York merchants to reimburse rag dealers and generated acceptable commercial paper. Paper consignments balanced rag accounts with paper merchants more directly.[13]

Just as trade with New York introduced new financial arrangements, the new market's terms compelled paper makers to institute novel manufacturing practices. As compared to local markets, New York's demand for larger quantities of finer paper had initially at-

[12] In Lee, where lower-quality rags may have sufficed and mills bought large quantities, prices for foreign and domestic rags were identical at five cents a pound. Dalton mills, using smaller quantities of rags on the average, paid five and a half cents a pound for domestic rags and six and a half cents for "foreigns." *McLane Report*, part 1, pp. 144–45, 156–57; Lindstrom, *Philadelphia Region*, pp. 35–36.

[13] W. T. Baxter, "Accounting in Colonial America," in A. C. Littleton, ed., *Studies in the History of Accounting* (Homewood, Ill., 1956), pp. 272–75, 282, 286–87, describes this "book-keeping barter." See also, Merrill, "Cash Is Good to Eat," pp. 54–59, 63, 65. Detailed analysis of Zenas Crane Daybook, 1817–23, CA, and Zenas Crane Daybook, 1825–30, CA, together with a reading of other Lee and Dalton daybooks of the period, substantiates the extensive use of bookkeeping barter in the Berkshire paper industry as late as 1834.

tracted Berkshire mill owners, but they soon discovered that production for New York forced unanticipated adjustments. On the
one hand, New York paper merchants had customers of their own
to satisfy and brooked no unpredictable delays in filling their large
orders. On the other hand, the New York market exhibited greater
seasonal variation and proved less predictable than the familiar
Berkshire market. Moreover, increasingly intense competition
among the growing number of paper producers enabled New York
merchants to insist that mill owners meet the new market's terms.
Coping with New York's demands made Berkshire's traditional paper industry innovative.

NEW METHODS

Historians have generally portrayed the adoption of machinery as
one of three possible ways to increase production in the early nineteenth century. Producers content with local markets could aug-
ment supply simply by adding more laborers performing conventional hand operations. To cope with the large-scale demand of
more distant markets, however, manufacturers either simplified
workers' tasks and recruited large numbers of new laborers through
the putting-out system or they substituted machines for skilled
workers. Surveying the transition from traditional to industrial
manufacturing in gross terms, this formulation adequately describes the alternatives, but with the benefit of hindsight, it makes
both the choices and the final outcome appear much more obvious
than they could have seemed to contemporary manufacturers.
Thus, in explaining the choice of mechanization, it beclouds the
process by which mill owners arrived at that choice.[14]

In the 1820s the Berkshire paper industry followed a more circuitous and gradual path to mechanization. Traditional manufacturers adopted a variety of techniques for enhancing productivity
before they embraced the alternative of mechanization. They multiplied output primarily by reinvesting in plant and stock, rather

[14] For example, Alfred D. Chandler, Jr., *The Visible Hand: The Managerial Revolution
in American Business* (Cambridge, Mass., 1977), pp. 53–55. Smith, *Harpers Ferry Armory*, pp. 83–84, has shown that, as in the putting-out system, simplifying workers'
tasks through the division of labor enabled at least one important factory to increase
production prior to mechanization. Two other important exceptions to this generalization are Ellsworth, *Craft to National Industry*, and Paskoff, *Industrial Evolution*. See
also, Gail Barbara Fowler, "Rhode Island Handloom Weavers and the Effects of
Technological Change, 1780–1840" (Ph.D. diss., University of Pennsylvania, 1984).

than by adding employees or purchasing machines. They expanded existing mills, erected new ones, modified traditional technology, and increased inventory. These changes were prompted not only by the size of the New York market, but also by its seasonality and competitiveness. The resulting increases in both fixed and working capital also helped manufacturers compensate for the relatively limited supply of skilled paper workers. In sum, a survey of innovation in traditional mills shows that hand paper mill owners had considerable preparation for mechanization. For at least a decade before mechanization, they had been developing increasingly capital-intensive methods of hand production.[15]

Table 3.2 demonstrates that, although firms manufacturing for large, remote markets invested their resources differently than did those serving local needs, by 1832 New York–oriented mills pursued diverse strategies to expand output. The generalization that manufacturers for local consumption relied more heavily on labor appears warranted. By contrast, textile mills had clearly chosen the alternative of adopting machines to increase labor productivity. Paper mills and other firms producing for the New York market had evolved a third strategy, relying on relatively greater commitment of their resources to inventory in the form of stock on hand, goods in process, and raw materials. Paper-making establishments, however, tied up relatively greater sums in real estate. Like the more heavily capitalized textile mills, they had increased production through investment in fixed assets.[16]

Expenditures on improvements at two Berkshire mills indicate some of the fixed capital investments paper makers considered most remunerative. In the mid-1820s both mills favored construction and repairs designed to lessen production delays. Crane's largest single outlay expanded beater capacity. At South Lee, Owen and Hurlbut added 247 feet of drying poles to their loft. Such investments reduced the likelihood that inadequate supplies of pulp and

[15] Although mills achieved increases in productivity prior to 1820, fragmentary records (nine months of production figures for two Dalton mills in 1809–10 and five months of figures for one Dalton mill in 1817) indicate that these increases were probably achieved simply by meeting traditional full employment standards for existing plant and equipment. Extrapolating full-year totals from partial-year figures, the two mills at work in 1809–10 appear to have operated respectively at less than half and at about two-thirds normal capacity (two thousand reams per vat per year). By 1817 one Dalton mill apparently operated at traditional full capacity. Zenas Crane Time Book, 1809–36, CA.

[16] Relatively greater investment in inventory also charactrized industries relying on the putting-out system.

TABLE 3.2

MEDIAN INVESTMENT IN PRODUCTIVE FACTORS AS A
PERCENTAGE OF VALUE OF MEDIAN ANNUAL OUTPUT,
BERKSHIRE COUNTY MANUFACTURERS, 1832

Manufacturers	Machinery	Annual Labor Cost	Real Estate	Stock on Hand and in Process	Raw Materials/ Annum
Producers for local markets	9.5	44.2	26.8	11.1	50.6
Textile mills	40.7	15.2	39.1	11.0	48.8
Paper mills	3.0	26.8	43.2	18.1	59.0
Other New York market firms	4.7	21.6	35.1	26.3	57.7

NOTE: Data derive from the *McLane Report* for Berkshire County. McLane's figures for daily wages have been multiplied by the number of persons employed at each rate, summed for each establishment, and multiplied by 308 days annual employment. As will become clear, this procedure probably results in overstatement of labor costs, especially for firms depending on New York's seasonal market.

Median figures have been employed because small numbers of firms with widely divergent assets tend to distort mean values. Aggregate data for several mills has simply been divided by the number of mills. Token values of $1 for tools and $10 for rent have been substituted where the response "none" was given in answer to queries about the value of machinery and tools and the response "rent" was recorded under real estate. Where labor, raw materials, or stock are not reported, those firms have been excluded from averages for that particular factor only. Almost all of these instances occur for shoemakers producing for local consumption. This would tend to inflate median figures for labor, raw materials, and stock in the "local consumption" category. For raw materials and stock, this possible distortion merely strengthens the argument. Slightly inflated labor figures do not detract from the argument because most shoemakers had no employees, but themselves supplied the labor that went unrecorded by McLane. Given the small size of their shops, this results in disproportionately greater underreporting of labor in these establishments than does the failure to report owner's labor in managing textile mills, paper mills, tanneries, and other establishments catering to the New York market. Real estate reported includes buildings and "fixtures," so there may be some overlap of real estate and machinery categories. It is likely, for example, that the low machinery and high real estate figures for paper mills result from inclusion of beaters as fixtures. Clothiers, by contrast, evidently considered fulling stocks to be machinery, rather than fixtures, accounting for the relatively higher investment in machinery by locally oriented firms.

paper would force vatmen, couchers, size workers, or finishers to suspend work. They did so at the cost of increasing the amount of stock in process as well as committing more resources to fixed capital.[17]

[17] Zenas Crane Daybook, 1825–30, CA, flyleaf; Owen & Hurlbut Blotter, 1824, HP. The fact that "Repairing the Press" and "the Engine Stopped" are among the few reasons given for the sharply curtailed production of Dalton's mills in 1809–10 also

Both mills also enhanced beater productivity by harnessing the Housatonic more effectively. Owen and Hurlbut either built a new dam or raised their old one. Crane reduced power loss from his existing fall by replacing the gudgeons on his waterwheel. Both investments probably reduced seasonal fluctuations because of low water in addition to increasing maximum power at the mill's disposal.[18]

Other mills lack construction records for these years, but their owners clearly reinvested and probably reduced delays at specific processing stages. Existing records at least provide evidence that most mill owners multiplied overall productive capacity, perhaps allowing one skilled vatman to monitor additional journeymen. Sometime between 1817 and 1821 Crane expanded his Dalton mill from a one-vat to a two-vat operation. Dalton's other mill installed a second vat after 1810, probably in the late teens or early twenties. Samuel Church had increased Lee's first mill from two to four vats by the time he sold it to Charles Owen and Thomas Hurlbut in 1822. In 1825 and 1826 Owen and Hurlbut tore down parts of another Lee paper mill, a converted gristmill, and enlarged the building. When compared to drawings of other manufacturing establishments, the illustration Dalton's 1831 surveyor used to represent local paper mills (Figure 3.1) suggests graphically that paper makers typically expanded output by adding to their mills bit by bit. In addition, a few mill owners, such as the Laflin brothers of Lee, constructed new mills on a grand scale. For the county as a whole, enlarged mills and improved mill fixtures made the average mill's fixed capitalization more than 20 percent greater in 1832 than in 1820.[19]

---

suggests that added investment in certain key pieces of equipment was essential to maintaining continuous production. Zenas Crane Time Book, 1809–36, CA.

[18] Owen & Hurlbut Blotter, 1825, HP; Zenas Crane Daybook, 1825–30, CA, flyleaf.

[19] Because hand paper makers normally indicated total mill capacity by specifying number of vats, recorded changes in vats per mill imply more general expansion of the establishment. Zenas Crane Time Book, 1809–36, CA; Owen & Hurlbut Blotter, 1825, HP; Hurlbut papers, 1820s, HP, May 1826; "Paper Making in South Lee, Mass.," p. 1; "Paper Making in Lee Village," p. 1; McLane Report, part 1, pp. 144, 156; 1820 Census. Average capitalization for the two mills recorded in 1820 was $6,000. Because those mills omitted are most likely to have been smaller ones, this probably overstates capital invested in 1820. To avoid any chance of inflating the 1832 figure by including the few paper-making machines in operation, only real estate and fixtures have been counted as capital in the second figure. The average for 1832 was $7,230.77. It seems certain, then, that these figures substantially underestimate increases in fixed capital.

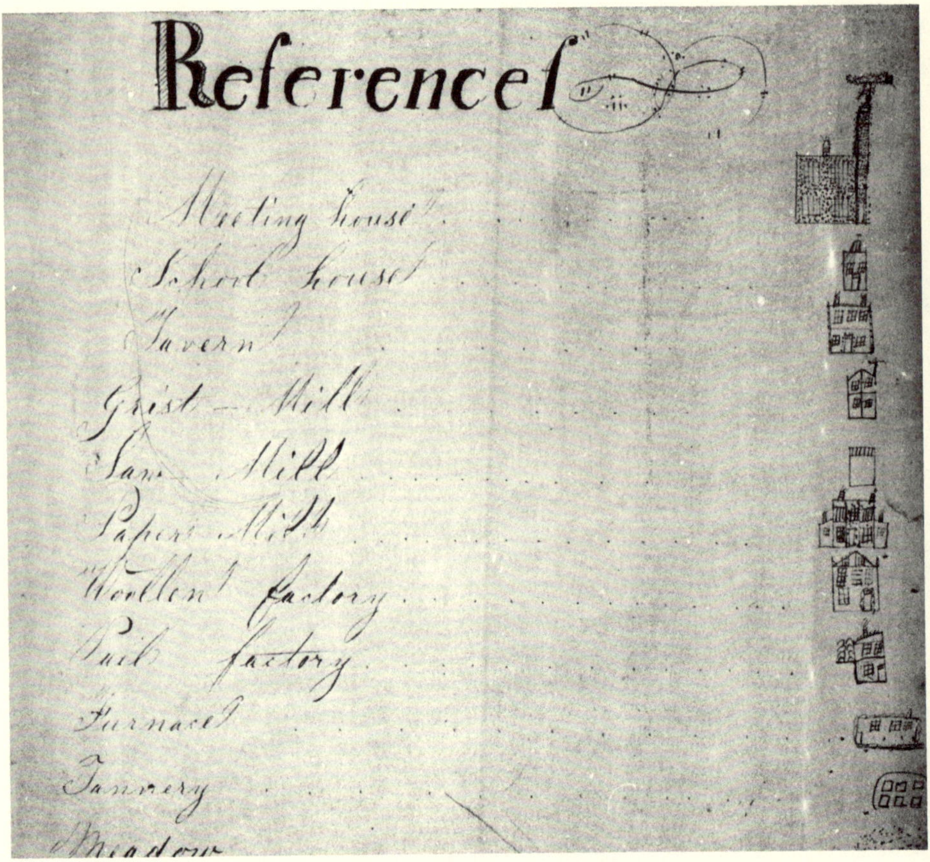

Fig. 3.1 Symbolic illustrations of Dalton manufacturing establishments and public buildings. Used as the key for Dalton's 1831 survey map, these symbols suggest the distinguishing feature of paper mills and the relative prominence of the church. (Map of Dalton, Ma., 27 October 1831/Massachusetts Archives, 1830 Series, V. 5: 16 No. 1856.) Courtesy of the Archives of the Commonwealth, Boston.

Established mill owners also expanded production by building or buying additional mills. Joseph and Leonard Church plowed back some of the profits of eleven years as paper makers when they bought a second Lee mill in 1819. David Carson, who had joined with Joseph Chamberlin and Henry Wiswell to build Dalton's second mill in 1809, had bought out his partners by 1816 and, in 1823, invested with Chamberlin in building another mill. Two years later Carson and Crane formed a partnership and purchased a mill in Lee. Also in the twenties, Crane, his vatman William Van Bergan, and East Lee manufacturer Stephen Thatcher built an additional Lee mill. By 1823 Owen & Hurlbut owned three mills in Lee, and after erecting their first mill in 1826, the Laflin brothers constructed a second in 1827.[20]

Building additional mills, enlarging existing mills, and adding equipment to reduce work delays were each responses to the magnitude of New York demand. Mill owners reacted to the seasonality of that demand primarily by increasing inventory. Winter ice limited most Hudson River shipments to the months of March through November. From November 1825 through October 1830, for example, Crane's accounts with Seymour, his New York paper merchant, show no paper shipped in 30 percent of the months. Seymour compensated by carrying a large inventory through the winter, but Crane footed the bill because Seymour reimbursed him only after he sold the paper. Crane's inventory in New York amounted to $2,791 by December 1828 and $4,754 a year later. These were substantial sums, and Crane invested yet more to store a large stock of rags at the mill each fall for processing during the winter. As rag inventory fell during his winter operations, he tied up increased capital in the growing stock of paper at the mill. Moreover, the timing of freezes and thaws varied from year to year. Thus, seasonal demand fluctuated far more sharply in some years, adding an unpredictable element that further raised inventory requirements. In sum, stock in process, paper and rags stored at the mill, and several thousand dollars worth of paper held in New York almost certainly raised investment in stock far above the $2,400 average that mill owners estimated in 1832.[21]

---

[20] McGaw, "Sources and Impact," pp. 34, 403, 415, 417–18, 423; "Dalton Conveyances" (bound volume of deeds), Crane Museum, passim; Zenas Crane Time Book, 1809–36, CA; Hyde, *History of Lee*, pp. 282–83.

[21] Zenas Crane Daybook, 1825–30, CA; *McLane Report*, part 1, pp. 144, 156. Crane's daybook also supplies quantitative evidence of the unpredictability of seasonal variation. From 1826 to 1830 annual coefficients of variation of Crane's monthly shipments to New York exhibit no consistent pattern. They were 0.79, 1.06, 0.88, 0.79, and 1.27. (The coefficient of variation describes the degree to which individual cases—each month's paper sales—differed from the average of all cases. Because it is the standard deviation divided by the mean, figures approaching or exceeding 1 express a relatively high degree of variance.)

As the figures in Table 3.1 indicate, manufacture for New York also subjected Berkshire paper mill owners to intense competition. Although the growth of the local paper industry lowered Berkshire paper prices as well, prices in the increasingly important New York market declined more precipitously. In 1832 the Ames brothers, competing Springfield manufacturers, summarized western Massachusetts paper makers' situation for Treasury Secretary McLane's investigators: "The price of our article has constantly declined since 1824, and, in addition to this, the consumers have demanded a much better article at the same price, and *home* competition has compelled the manufacturers to furnish it."[22]

Adopting new technology enabled Berkshire paper makers to lower costs while maintaining or enhancing quality. Bleaching represented the most important technical innovation of the period. Having observed the practice in Britain, in 1804 Joshua Gilpin conducted the first American chlorine bleaching of rags at his paper mill on the Brandywine. Lawrence Greatrake, an English paper maker who assisted Gilpin, summarized the financial significance of the process when he concluded that, after bleaching, "pulp from these [cheap, low-grade rags] may be worked . . . into the finest papers." Gilpin, like English paper manufacturers for some years to come, bleached with clorine gas, a process fraught with potential danger for paper workers. In 1799, however, a Scottish chemist, Charles Tennout, had produced calcium hypocholorite or bleaching powder. Berkshire paper makers probably relied on this safer whitening agent from the start, for there is no evidence that they constructed the more elaborate equipment gas bleaching required.[23]

Initial county use of chlorine bleach cannot be dated precisely. Crane's shipment of a bleach kettle to his partner, Stephen Thatcher, in 1824 provides the earliest indication of the practice, but Crane must certainly have adopted bleaching before Thatcher did. Daybook entries for "bleaching salts" begin in 1829 for both Crane and Carson, but earlier unitemized credits to county retailers might easily hide sales of bleaching powder. The purchase of nearly a ton of bleaching powder by the average county paper mill in 1832

[22] *McLane Report*, part 1, p. 96 (emphasis in the original). For a detailed analysis of the relationship between transportation, market prices, and technological change, see Uselding, *Studies in Technological Development*, pp. 149–64.

[23] Edelstein, "Papermaker Joshua Gilpin," pp. 3–12; Ferguson, *Early Engineering Reminiscences*, p. 128; Snell, *Hurlbut's Papermaker Gentleman* 2 (Fall 1934):17–18. Perhaps investment in this more elaborate equipment accounts for the persistence of gas bleaching in England noted by Sellers in 1832.

shows that the use of chlorine bleach was well established by that date. Whatever the precise date, bleaching helped Berkshire mill owners respond to price competition in New York. They relied on it increasingly to lower rag costs and assure whiter paper, answering New York's call for a cheaper, finer-looking product. Their greater relative investment in raw materials helps explain why paper mill owners adopted this method of reducing costs much earlier than did Berkshire textile mill proprietors.[24]

As with other chemical technologies of the era, successful bleaching depended on skill acquired through experience. Acid solutions can materially weaken cellulose fiber. Bleaching itself increased the acidity of the stock solution, and alum and oil of vitriol, used to speed the process, aggravated the problem. High temperatures and stock concentrations also hastened bleaching to the detriment of the paper's permanency. Antichlors, chemicals added to halt bleaching action, further heightened acidity. As Greatrake had noted after the first American bleaching of rags, "a thoughtful Steady person will be necysary [sic] to do it compleat [sic]." He also observed, however, that "the labor would be no more charge for 200 lbs than for 100 lbs. . . ." In fact, because whitening with bleaching salts took place in the beaters, it entailed no additional labor costs, although it increased the engineer's work and the mill's dependence on his skill. As was the case when they purchased more beaters, mills derived cost advantages from bleaching by employing the same skilled workman more fully.[25]

Another technological innovation of the 1820s held down costs by allowing each unskilled male rag duster to process more bales of

[24] Likewise, Gilpin's first use of the process antedated the first use of bleaching in American textile mills. Edelstein, "Papermaker Joshua Gilpin," pp. 3–4; Zenas Crane Daybook, 1824–33, CA, 8/16/24, 12/13/24; Zenas Crane Daybook, 1825–30, CA, 5/29/29; David Carson Daybook, 1828–34, CA, 9/14/31; McLane Report, part 1, pp. 126–59. No Berkshire textile mill reported use of bleaching powder in 1832.

Early American usage of the term "bleach" makes it possible that the bleaching kettles referred to were used to cleanse very dirty rags by boiling them with lime or caustic soda. The absence of contemporaneous references to these chemicals or to bleaching powder leaves the issue in doubt. For a fuller discussion of bleaching technology in the industry see McGaw, "Sources and Impact," pp. 194–98. Zenas Crane Time Book, 1809–36 denominates certain papers "bleached" as early as 1810. It is possible, then, that chlorine came into use even earlier, although these infrequent references may also refer to paper made from rags whitened by long exposure to sunlight.

[25] Also, of course, the use of bleach involved modest increases in stock expenditures. Edwin Sutermeister, The Story of Papermaking (Boston, 1954), pp. 19–20, 114–15, 119–20, 125; Edelstein, "Papermaker Joshua Gilpin," 11. Oil of vitriol is sulfuric acid. Antichlors include sodium thiosulfate and sodium sulfite. It is unclear whether mills used antichlors at this early date.

rags. As mills consumed larger quantities of rags, the task of shaking out debris grew more time-consuming, disproportionately so because urban and European rags contained more dirt than did "country" rags. Rather than hire more men to open bales and thrash their contents, mill owners installed dusters. Mill records afford only an oblique glimpse of this device. It evidently consisted of a large wire mesh container, but the wire comprised only about half of its $42 cost. Probably the remaining $21 paid for a simple mechanism to rotate the cage and toss the rags about, allowing debris to fall through the mesh into a metal pan below. Crane's daybook entry for a "tin duster pan" suggests as much. The duster drive could easily have been run off the beater shaft, leaving the rag room man only the task of engaging and disengaging the mechanism, loading and unloading the duster cage, and emptying the pan. Dusters probably came into use soon after New York sales began. Crane forwarded one to Thatcher at Lee in 1824.[26]

Additional technological changes may have occurred even earlier, but mill owners straining to raise output in the 1820s undoubtedly took fuller advantage of their potential for increasing the efficiency of skilled workmen and the quality of their product. Mechanical agitators, known as hogs, kept the fiber in the making vat evenly distributed through the water and eliminated intermittent hand stirring. Knotters excluded knots of twisted fiber from the vat, decreasing the number of lumpy sheets vatmen formed. A cutting press and cutting knife Crane purchased must have shortened time spent trimming by hand and resulted in better-trimmed edges. Simply adding another press reduced delays. It also potentially multiplied the work of the vatman by cutting several small sheets from a single large one, rather than depending upon a complex hand operation to fabricate each sheet.[27]

Such innovations helped manufacturers minimize one important constraint on expanding output by conventional means. Considering the sudden growth of the local paper industry and the long training skilled workers required, mills of the 1820s must have been hard pressed to find enough skilled workmen. Rapidly mounting wages paid to male employees after 1822 suggest as much. Under these circumstances most mill owners had to raise output with only the traditional complement of skilled craftsmen, and if Crane's mill

[26] Zenas Crane Daybook, 1824–33, CA, 8/16/24, 6/2/31; David Carson Daybook, 1828–34, CA, 10/26/31.

[27] McGaw, "Sources and Impact," p. 53; Zenas Crane Daybook, 1824–33, CA, 10/20/31; David Cogswell Account Book, 1821–23 CA.

is representative, they succeeded. Table 3.3 shows greater productivity as the decade progressed, despite relatively constant numbers of male workers. In general, the mill used progressively less skilled work time to make each ream of paper, and as a result, the cost of labor per ream fell.[28]

TABLE 3.3
LABOR AND OUTPUT, CRANE'S MILL, 1821–30

Year	Mean Monthly Employment		Reams Made	Male Days/Ream	Labor Cost/Ream	% Male Labor Cost/Ream
	Male	Female				
1821	10.08	8.58	3772	.78	$.97	80.10
1822	10.50	9.33	4082	.75	.94	79.40
1823	11.25	10.16	4597	.71	.90	79.14
1824	10.67	11.58	4314	.72	.95	75.94
1825	9.92	12.58	4430	.65	.89	72.98
1828	10.75	12.75	4581	.68	.92	74.28
1829	11.33	12.92	4779	.69	.92	75.28
1830	11.25	13.08	4753	.69	.92	74.66

NOTE: Data in the first three columns come from Zenas Crane Time Book, 1809–36, CA. Because a shutdown in 1826 distorts figures for 1826 and 1827 by reducing the female work force, adding short-term male construction workers, and causing marked fluctuations in output, these years have been omitted. Data for 1825 also appear to be somewhat aberrant. The figure for worker days per year results from multiplying mean monthly employment figures by the average number of days men and women worked monthly from January 1828 to September 1830 according to data from Zenas Crane Daybook, 1825–30. (Some distortion is introduced by the fact that on three occasions number of workdays per worker is given for a two-month period, and I have arbitrarily divided those days equally between the two months.) Because men averaged 24.30 days work per month, whereas women averaged 22.79 days, this calculation compensates for women's greater propensity for intermittent employment. Labor cost calculations assume 1832 Dalton pay rates. Because vatmen probably earned substantially more than the $1 cited as average pay for male workers in 1832, total male labor costs were probably somewhat higher. However, because the male work force grew slightly, neglecting the vatman's pay differential results in understatement of the relative decline in male labor costs.

[28] Growth in the supply of skilled labor probably derived principally from immigration from the British Isles. More rapid growth of demand for skilled labor, however, resulted in that inelasticity of labor supply which, as Uselding explains most clearly, better describes the early American situation than the amorphous term "scarce labor." Uselding, *Studies in Technological Development*, pp. 26–27, 67–68, 108; Herbert Heaton, "The Industrial Immigrant in the United States, 1783–1812," *Proceedings of the American Philosophical Society* 95 (October 1951):519–27. Nathan Rosenberg, "The Direction of Technological Change: Inducement Mechanisms and Focusing Devices," in idem, *Perspectives on Technology*, pp. 108–25 elucidates how such inelasticity probably directed innovative activity. McGaw, "Sources and Impact," p. 322.

Additional fixed capital, increased stock on hand and in process, and technological change each helped achieve this result. Dusters processed more rags, obviating delay in supplying the engine room. More waterpower, additional beaters, and chlorine bleach amplified the work of the engineer and assured continuous pulp supplies to the vatman. More pulp, hogs, knotters, and additional presses reduced delays and made the vatman, coucher, and layboy more productive. Expanded dry lofts occupied the loftman more fully and permitted continuous work by the size maker. Mill owners also increased capital invested to compensate for inelastic supplies of skilled labor when they built inventory over the winter months, maintaining full employment and maximum production despite the lack of a ready market.

Table 3.3 indicates another method paper mills of the 1820s used to reduce skilled labor requirements. Disproportionate increases in female employment constituted partial substitution of less skilled labor for skilled male workers. Mills probably employed more rag room women to guarantee continuous supplies to the beater, keeping the engineer fully employed. Production of finer paper also required more female finishers, a way of multiplying the productivity of the skilled male boss finisher. Similarly, additional women employed in the dry loft or at dipping sized paper augmented the output of skilled supervisors.

More elastic supplies of female labor also compensated in part for the increases in stock and inventory that full male employment necessitated. Both female employment and female "over work" consistently mounted in the spring, peaked in the summer, declined slightly in the fall, and plummeted in the winter. This employment pattern paralleled New York's seasonal demand. Although mills stored up the output of continuously employed skilled males, they evidently called in women to finish paper only as needed. Thus, they avoided investing the greater amounts of capital an inventory of finished paper would have required.[29]

Table 3.4 summarizes the consistently greater fluctuations in female employment in a mill producing for New York. Even when Crane disrupted regular work schedules in 1826 and 1827, he was more able to vary the number of women working and the amount of extra time they labored. Renewed regular production in 1828 reduced variation in male employment and "over work," but mill owners continued to shuttle women in and out of the work force as demand dictated.

[29] Zenas Crane Time Book, 1809–36, CA; Zenas Crane Daybook, 1825–30, CA.

TABLE 3.4

COEFFICIENTS OF VARIATION FOR MALE AND FEMALE WORK AND
"OVER WORK," CRANE'S MILL, 1826–30

Year	Male Work	Female Work	Male "Over Work"	Female "Over Work"
1826	.25	.27	.76	.78
1827	.26	.40	.76	1.01
1828	.09	.16	.57	.70
1829	.07	.24	.30	.77
1830	.09	.18	.37	.79

NOTE: The coefficients of variation for work represent the variability in number of workdays credited to males and females each month. For "over work," variability in total monthly "over work" pay has been computed. Because of the shutdown in 1826, that figure is for ten months only. The short year, 1830, has been artificially lengthened to twelve months by using data for the final months of 1829. Casual construction and teaming labor has been excluded insofar as possible. Zenas Crane Daybook, 1825–30, CA.

Women's employment fluctuated from day to day as well as from season to season. Whereas most men labored about the same number of days in any given period, women differed greatly in the number of days each worked in a particular month. Indeed, the greater irregularity of female employment grew more pronounced in the course of the 1820s. Even in 1821 women working for Crane remained home more days each month than did male employees. The mill time book indicates that women missed 8.6 percent of their potential workdays, although men missed only 5 percent. Between 1821 and 1830 men showed little change in their propensity to be absent, but female absences increased markedly. By 1830 women did not go to work 13.4 percent of the time, but men arrived at the mill all except 5.6 percent of the days. Moreover, during the same years male workers lowered the proportion of partial days they put in from 3.1 percent to 1.9 percent, while female partial day employment climbed from 2.0 to 4.1 percent.[30]

Whether women preferred intermittent employment or employers were simply more able to lay them off, in the course of the decade, women's less regular employment permitted greater freedom in scheduling their work, helping mill owners cope with irregular New York demand and diminishing flexibility in scheduling skilled male workers. Manufacturers found in the willingness of some women to work partial days or partial months the opportunity to ex-

[30] Zenas Crane Time Book, 1809–36, CA.

ercise more precise control over the level of unskilled employment by increasing or decreasing it in smaller increments. Coming at the same time that skilled employment levels grew more and more difficult to manipulate, mill owners might well have welcomed the rising numbers of part-time female workers.

On the other hand, mill proprietors could have placed a less agreeable interpretation on women's growing propensity to work irregularly. Having already added a large number of women to the work force, by the late 1820s mills probably drew in more marginal workers, women who would not or could not work regularly. Increasing absenteeism might have signaled the impending depletion of the pool of employable women. After all, county population had experienced only a modest 6 percent rise between 1800 and 1810 and between 1820 and 1830. In the intervening decade it had actually declined slightly. At the same time, women's paper mill employment grew by 340 percent from 1821 to 1832 alone. Seen in this context, Owen and Hurlbut's 1830 decision to declare an eight-hour day in their rag room, the place where most married women worked, suggests that by that date mill owners could expand unskilled employment only by adjusting work schedules to the special needs of female workers.[31]

Coping with a new market had certainly altered traditional paper manufacture by the late 1820s. In doing so it paved the way for mechanization. The final years of hand manufacture found the typical mill increasingly costly to build and run, and saw it operating at a far more hectic pace than had Crane's early mill. This "industrialized" style of production anticipated the paper-making machine and facilitated its adoption.

During the same years, innovative mill owners must have pinpointed where they most needed machines. By simply continuing the strategies of the 1820s—adding more beaters, presses, and loft space; improving power supplies; or employing more women—mill owners could further increase output at most stages of production. But once they had assured the vatman steady employment and an uninterrupted supply of pulp, mill owners could do little to aug-

[31] Time books, unfortunately, rarely specify whether an absence came at the insistence of employer or employee. While this makes interpretation of individual absences or the records of individual workers hazardous, it seems likely that both parties acquiesced in and gained some benefit from general arrangements that persisted over a number of years. Zenas Crane Time Book, 1809–36, CA; *McLane Report*, part 1, pp. 144–45, 156–57; Child, *Gazeteer*, part 1, p. 420; United States Census Office, *Report on the Statistics of Wages in Manufacturing Industries* (Washington, D.C., 1886), p. 276.

ment his output. By decade's end they must have looked especially
for an alternative way of forming pulp into sheets of paper. The mill
owners were ready to adopt machines.

New Men

While paper makers prepared their mills for machines, their experiences in the 1820s also prepared their minds. Judging from the
character of their innovations, in the course of the twenties mill
owners gradually grew accustomed to substituting capital for labor,
an attitude conducive to mechanization. Simultaneously, local social
and cultural institutions encouraged manufacturers and workers to
value discipline, punctuality, and temperance, traits necessary to intensified hand production and, later, to operating mechanized
mills. In Berkshire County, at least, local men and women adopted
these new values under the influence of traditonal religious revivals
orchestrated by the powerful orthodox clergy.

But the spectacular success of the revivals of the 1820s suggests
that mill owners and mill workers who were engaged in unprecedented efforts to increase production made a very receptive audience. Like most human beings, the people of Berkshire County
found coping with change and uncertainty an unsettling experience. In addition to the economic uncertainties and altered local agricultural and manufacturing strategies resulting from Berkshire's
incorporation into the new regional market, the decades preceding
paper mill mechanization brought to the county the unsettling experiences of embargo, war, depression, challenges to Federalist authority, and breakdown of early national era political organization.
Faced with pervasive change and uncertainty, Berkshire men and
women, like Americans elsewhere, responded wholeheartedly
when local clergymen offered in the Second Great Awakening a
new religious paradigm that endowed intensified, reorganized
work with profound meaning and looked beyond transient economic and political uncertainty to the transcendent promise of personal and social salvation through voluntary discipline. While
couched in comfortingly familiar Calvinist accents, revivalistic religion attracted local converts by reshaping traditional pieties into a
serviceable faith for a new age.[32]

[32] Brief overviews of the Second Great Awakening treating its relationship to contemporaneous social developments and to earlier religious practice and belief include: William G. McLoughlin, *Revivals, Awakenings, and Reform: An Essay on Religion
and Social Change in America, 1607–1977* (Chicago, 1978), pp. 98–140; Donald G.

Among Berkshire paper mill workers and owners, revived religious institutions also offered a vital and growing alternative to the moribund traditional institutions whose decline evoked so much anxiety among early nineteenth-century Americans. As was the case throughout the United States, the Second Great Awakening functioned as an "organizing process" for large numbers of unchurched men and women. Occasionally revivals appeared to encourage the very disorder that appeared so threatening in contemporary economic and political life, but undisciplined emotionalism generally served only as a temporary means to an end—widespread religious discipline organized within revitalized institutions. This was especially true in Berkshire County. From the 1790s through the 1820s the orthodox clergy there espoused the ordered revivalism of Jonathan Edwards's tradition and largely headed off rowdy itinerants and upstart Methodists.[33]

Among the most outspoken proponents of traditional revivalism were the Congregationalist clergymen of Berkshire's paper-making centers: Dr. Alvan Hyde of Lee and the Reverend Ebenezer Jennings of Dalton. During his more than forty years in the Lee pulpit, Hyde's activities made him "the most powerful moulding influence . . . in the town's history" and an authoritative religious voice in the county. Beginning in 1792, shortly after his ordination, "refreshing from the presence of the Lord" revived religion in Lee every six or seven years, increasing Hyde's church membership to among west-

Mathews, "The Second Great Awakening as an Organizing Process, 1780–1830: An Hypothesis," *AQ* 21 (Spring 1969):23–43; Perry Miller, "From the Covenant to the Revival," in James Ward Smith and A. Leland Jamison, eds., *The Shaping of American Religion* (Princeton, 1961), pp. 322–68.

Berkshire County's strong Calvinist tradition and dominant orthodox clergy make Miller's evolutionary interpretation of the revivals' relationship to contemporary social developments more convincing than the dialectical paradigm offered by Anthony F. C. Wallace, *Rockdale: The Growth of an American Village in the Early Industrial Revolution* (New York, 1978), pp. 296–397.

[33] David J. Rothman, *The Discovery of the Asylum: Social Order and Disorder in the New Republic* (Boston, 1971); Kasson, *Civilizing the Machine*, pp. 63–66; Birdsall, *Berkshire Cultural History*, pp. 63–67. Berkshire's Shaker communities provide the outstanding example of religious enthusiasm making way for rigorous discipline and greater order during the period.

Before the 1830s the strength of Berkshire's orthodox clergy, continued local predominance of manufacturing and agriculture, rather than commerce, and comparatively stable local population made Berkshire revivalism a communal endeavor orchestrated by the clergy, not "a shopkeeper's millennium" such as Paul E. Johnson depicts in Rochester, N.Y. After the mid-1830s, however, Berkshire religious activity increasingly reflected the perspective of middle-class mill owners, a development treated in Chapter 8.

ern Massachusetts' largest at his death in 1833. Similarly, several revivals punctuated Jennings's long pastorate, which extended from
1802 to 1834. By 1827 revivals had made Dalton the only town in
the county able to claim half its population as church members.[34]

Hyde expressed his commitment to disciplined revivalism most
succinctly in the words he later chose to describe a successful early
revival in Lee. "To the praise of sovereign grace," he noted in 1832,
"the work continued, with great *regularity.*" Hyde's description of his
midweek religious meetings as "very much thronged, and yet . . .
never noisy or irregular, nor continued to a late hour" suggests that
under his direction religious renewal proceeded in a manner that
complemented the increasingly full workdays in local mills. Periodically throughout his career, Hyde held nightly meetings in different parts of town, permitting laboring men and women to experience divine grace without traveling long distances on a work night.
Nine o'clock adjournments left ample sleep time for mill owners
and mill workers needing to arise early the next morning.[35]

Both Hyde and Jennings underscored their commitment to the
organizing function of revivals when they stressed the importance
of retaining regular church order during seasons of "refreshing."
Unlike the violent manifestations at Methodists' camp meetngs, "an
evident increase of solemnity in the church" signaled the approach
of a Berkshire revival. Hyde maintained traditional practices such
as days of fasting and prayer, careful explanation of church doctrine to potential members, and a waiting period of several months
before bringing the converted before the congregation for examination. He expressed as much pride in the infrequency of backslid-
ing as he did in the number of conversions. Jennings went so far as
to resign his pulpit rather than acquiesce in an outside evangelist's
use of extraordinary means to provoke conversions in his Dalton
church.[36]

[34] Smith, *History of Berkshire* 2:140; Alvan Hyde, *Memoir of Rev. Alvan Hyde, D.D. of
Lee, Mass.* (Boston, 1835), p. 359; H. Humphrey, *Old Age: A Discourse Delivered at the
Funeral of the Reverend Ebenezer Jennings of Dalton, February 8, 1859* (Pittsfield, Mass.,
1859), p. 13.

[35] Hyde, *Memoir,* pp. 53, 94, 135–36, 142, 151, 155, 162, 362.

[36] Ibid., pp. 96, 362, 366, 369–70; Smith, *History of Berkshire,* 1:649. In Lee, Hyde's
influence kept Methodism so weak as to be negligible before the mid-1830s. Dalton
Methodism, by contrast, was relatively strong for the Berkshires, but appears to have
differed little from Congregationalism, having arisen when a number of Dalton residents left the orthodox church to protest a relocation of the meetinghouse. Thus,
location of residence had more to do with determining early Methodist church membership than did conviction or social class.

By providing wholesome leisure-time activities and fostering habits of order and discipline, revivalism must have both abetted the intensification of work in the 1820s and prepared workers and owners for the machine's later demands. In this respect, the timing of local revivals was as propitious as their character. Widespread death from an epidemic that struck both Lee and Dalton in 1813 stimulated numerous conversions that year and smaller numbers each remaining year of the decade. Lee experienced another revival of major proportions in 1821, adding eighty-six members to the Congregational church. Dalton Congregational Church records indicate that the work of the spirit touched Dalton simultaneously. But in both communities, 1827 brought the most potent spiritual rekindling and the largest evangelical harvests. Thereafter, coinciding with years of rapid technological change in the paper industry, revivals became almost endemic. Shortly after the cessation of the 1827 revival, which continued for two years, renewed "effusions of the Spirit" struck the Lee congregation in 1831 and 1832. The year 1833 ushered in an extensive religious reawakening in both communities, continuing into the following year in Dalton at least.37

Such widespread and prolonged spiritual quickening must certainly have touched skilled male paper workers and mill owners, those most affected by intensified work and, later, mechanization. Contemporary Lee church records have been destroyed, but the memoirs of the Reverend Dr. Hyde give ample evidence that paper makers participated in the revival. The simple fact that 10 percent of the town's population joined the church between 1827 and 1832 supports such a belief. Further strengthening the supposition is Hyde's testimony that, unlike earlier reawakenings, which catered especially to juveniles, the revival of 1821 included "many young heads of families, and others in the midst of life . . . among the happy subjects." Both Jennings and Hyde noted the prominence of heads of families among 1827's harvest. Hyde elaborated further, commenting on the inclusion of "a number of our active, business men" and "not a few . . . from that class of people, who appeared to be far from righteousness," almost certainly a reference to the notoriously rowdy paper workers who congregated in Lee. Although incomplete, the preserved records of the Dalton Congregational Church provide more specific evidence that paper makers felt the call to Christ. Linked with incomplete employment records for

37 Hyde, *Memoir*, pp. 94, 96, 134–37, 142, 151–53, 155, 162, 358–71 passim; Humphrey, *Jennings*, p. 13; Records of the Dalton Congregational Church, Rollin H. Cooke Collection of Berkshire County Church Records, BA, p. 45.

Fig. 3.2 Interior, Dalton Congregational Church. Drawn from memory by Zenas Crane's son Seymour, this sketch captures the church and congregation as they looked shortly after the Second Great Awakening. Courtesy of the Crane Museum.

workers in only one of Dalton's three mills, they show five paper workers joining the church prior to 1827, five admitted in 1827, and twelve more added in 1833–34. The year 1827 also saw mill owner Joseph Chamberlin and boardinghouse keeper Mrs. Nathan Crane confess their faith, and in 1833 the church examined and admitted Zenas Crane. At least some paper makers must have remembered the late twenties and early thirties primarily as the time they "passed from death unto life" and only secondarily as the period when pa-per-making machines entered the mills.[38]

Moreover, the Awakening touched many who did not claim sal-vation. In Lee, Hyde made this certain by organizing a large church committee following the revival of 1821. Between 1822 and 1832 committee men and women repeatedly visited every family in town to "call the attention of the people to the neglected subject of vital religion." During their visits they "conversed with parents and chil-dren and domestics on the concerns of their souls, and their pros-pects for eternity, closing their interviews with prayer."[39]

When compared to depictions of other public buildings and of in-dustrial structures, the substantial size of the 1831 survey's symbolic representation of meetinghouses (Figure 3.1) conveys the same message. By that date revitalized churches overshadowed all of the towns' early social and economic institutions. They did so in part by inspiring local citizens to embody revivalistic values in new institu-tions.

Reform organizations, such as the Berkshire Society for Promot-ing Good Morals, founded in the wake of local revivals, spread evangelical influence beyond the churches. Reform associations fo-cused their efforts more exclusively on encouraging disciplined be-havior. They promoted strict Sabbath observance and chastised those who danced or swore. Their activities were quite in tune with the needs of paper makers in the 1820s. By scrutinizing workers' be-havior, guardians of public virtue fostered the disciplined habits re-organized mill work required. Equally important, they rewarded emerging middle-class virtues conducive to reinvestment and close management by mill owners.[40]

Supporting reformers, powerful local clergymen acted to enforce right behavior in their communities in addition to encouraging spir-itual rebirth in their parishes. Alvan Hyde, for example, visited and

[38] Child, *Gazeteer*, part 1, p. 420; Hyde, *Memoir*, pp. 358–71 passim; Humphrey, *Jennings*, p. 13; Zenas Crane Time Book, 1809–36, CA; Dalton Church Records, pp. 25–53. The incompleteness of both sets of records means that these figures can only indicate the presence of mill personnel among the converted, not their frequency. Compounding the incompleteness of the Congregational Church Records is the ab-sence of early records for the active band of Dalton Methodists. Again, the influence of religion on paper makers is merely hinted at by a report of David Carson's son among the members of the first Methodist Sunday school class, a class conducted by William Renne, a young paper worker, in 1826. Cora Hitt Smith, *A History of Dalton Methodism* (Pittsfield, Mass., 1927), p. 23.

[39] Hyde, *Memoir*, pp. 96, 368.

[40] Birdsall, *Berkshire Cultural History*, pp. 68–69.

lectured local citizens who missed either of his two lengthy Sunday services. By 1831 he had collected five hundred signed pledges not to violate the Sabbath, a reform that promoted ordered, regular habits as well as church attendance.[41]

Revivalism also spawned the temperance movement. Hyde recalled that as early as 1820 he had "witnessed a remarkable check to the progress of intemperance among my own people and throughout the land." In Lee, however, temperance reform began in earnest after Hyde's 1825 sermon celebrating "the wisdom of the Rechabites in their abstinence from wine and all intoxicating drinks." That sermon was published and widely disseminated and other such sermons followed. By 1829 Lee Congregationalists formally voted to abstain from ardent spirits and had used their informal influence to bar alcohol from local stores. Other community institutions joined the churches and moral reform societies in promoting temperance. In 1820, for example, the Berkshire Agricultural Society recommended the cultivation of hops and the home brewing of beer to replace that "pernicious poison, ardent spirits" on the farm.[42]

Embracing the new community standards, mill owners ceased supplying alcohol to their workers. At Crane's store, sales of rum, brandy, and whiskey, accounting for more than 11 percent of transactions in 1819, fell to 1.5 percent by the mid-1820s. By inspiring and enforcing temperance sentiment among workers, the mill owners, clergymen, and reformers probably abetted increased productivity through curtailing drinking on the job and reducing absenteeism, especially late arrival and early departure by male employees. More important, mill owners' efforts to promote temperance no doubt reinforced their personal commitment to the cause. Among mill owners temperance paid dividends: additional money to reinvest and additional time to devote to clearheaded managerial thinking, a new activity made necessary as these men gradually departed further and further from traditional operating and marketing practices. Over time, temperate behavior also conditioned their acceptance among local and regional members of the emerging middle class. Similar benefits of temperance accrued to aspiring mill owners among the industry's skilled workers.[43]

[41] Hyde, *History of Lee*, pp. 65–67, 204–7.

[42] Hyde, *Memoir*, pp. 142, 154; John Allen Krout, *The Origins of Prohibition* (New York, 1925), pp. 101–23; Hyde, *History of Lee*, pp. 48, 272; Josiah G. Holland, *A History of Western Massachusetts*, 2 vols. (Springfield, 1855), 1:398.

[43] Zenas Crane Daybook, 1817–25, CA; Zenas Crane Daybook, 1825–30, CA. For a fine study linking revivalism, reform, and the emergence of the middle class see

Nineteenth-century revivalists and reformers linked such right behavior to the prospect of personal or social salvation. Indeed, by the 1820s Berkshire's orthodox clergy differed from Edwards chiefly in deemphasizing past depravity in favor of future bliss. This, too, may have subtly abetted local industrial development by redirecting workers' and owners' thoughts from the certainties of the past to the possibilities of the future. As people grew accustomed to such an emphasis, they might be expected to seek and accept change rather than to fear and resist it.[44]

On the other hand, the revivalists of the 1820s and early 1830s probably struck such a responsive chord in part because they spoke a language their hearers already understood. Workers and owners engaged in unprecedented expansion of production must have come to the meetinghouse already looking forward rather than backward. Likewise, men and women who had already been rewarded for adopting more disciplined habits as owners and workers probably were more receptive to increased discipline at prayer and at play. Indeed, revivalistic discipline reinforced the home and work experiences of many local people, because paper mills were not the only places where men and women experienced a more mechanical pace. By the early 1820s the clock had entered local homes and machine production had commenced in several local industries.

Peddlers from Connecticut brought the wooden clock to Berkshire homes in about 1820. Inexpensive enough for skilled paper workers to afford, this device might awaken the family for the long Sunday drive to church or facilitate a more regular scheduling of work by enabling workers and owners to arrive at a prearranged hour and their wives to coordinate mealtimes with work breaks. As the first complex mechanisms commonly found in Berkshire homes, clocks made machines familiar and gave workers and owners a foretaste of their problems and possibilities.[45]

While they acquired the habit of living by clock time, Berkshire paper mill owners and workers had their initial exposure to industrial mechanization. Several years before paper-making machines became available, local textile mills and metalworking firms had already adopted complex mechanical technology. Two woolen mills,

Mary P. Ryan, *Cradle of the Middle Class: The Family in Oneida County, New York, 1790–1865* (Cambridge, 1981). For further discussion of the benefits accruing to Berkshire mill owners see Chapter 8.

[44] Miller, "From the Covenant to the Revival," pp. 361–67; Alice Felt Tyler, *Freedom's Ferment* (Minneapolis, 1944), pp. 308–50 passim.

[45] Hyde, *History of Lee*, p. 191.

a cotton factory, and a machine shop familiarized Lee paper workers with the new production techniques. Dalton paper workers knew of machines in the town's woolen mill and in the progressive woolen mills and firearms factory in nearby Pittsfield. Because county woolen mills supplied paper makers' felts, paper mill owners probably acquired their earliest familiarity with machine production when they visited the innovative Scholfield woolen factories to purchase supplies.[46]

EXPOSURE to machines and the acquisition of regular habits completed the preparation of Berkshire paper manufacturers, both workers and owners, for mechanized paper making. After a decade of change, the late 1820s found an expanding paper industry strongly tied to a growing New York market. Its mill owners already felt comfortable with innovation, already possessed a commitment to new technology and to more capital-intensive production methods. Its workers already knew either a more rushed and regular work pace or intermittent unemployment.

All of these developments antedated the machine. Yet later commentators regularly attributed each of these changes to the machine's influence. What was this new machine that so distorted men's view of their history?

[46] *McLane Report*, part 1, pp. 132–35, 144–45, 156–57; Zenas Crane Daybook, 1824–33.

PART II

THE MACHINE

CHAPTER 4

MECHANICAL PAPER MAKERS:
THE EVOLUTION
OF PAPER MACHINERY,
1799–1885

One day in 1880, the Honorable Byron Weston, paper mill owner and lieutenant governor of Massachusetts, seated himself at the desk in his Dalton home. Occasionally glancing out the window overlooking his mill, Weston reviewed the notes he had taken during conversations with some early Berkshire paper makers, American paper machinery inventors, and contemporary mill owners, and the letters he had received from others. Then, taking up his pen, he began his "History of Paper Making in Berkshire County, Massachusetts, U.S.A." After composing a brief description of Lee's first paper mill, Weston interrupted his narrative to impress on his reader the remarkable developments separating late nineteenth-century paper making from the industry in 1806. He wrote:

> Some idea of the progress made . . . at the mills may be had from the fact that a "four vat mill" of the hand era would produce about 400 pounds of paper per day. A modern *four engine mill*, with the same number of employees, . . . but with modern machinery, will make 2,000 pounds of very much better goods. . . . Ten thousand dollars was a large capital for a four vat hand mill; for a modern four-engine mill forty thousand dollars is sometimes too limited a sum.

Briefly stated, machines had effectively harnessed growing mill capitalization to expand output without adding workmen.[1]

Although he recorded the acts of mill owners and workers, Weston clearly gave mechanical paper makers credit for the major changes in nineteenth-century paper making. This accorded well with his personal experience. In the thirty-two years since he had begun his paper mill apprenticeship, Weston witnessed an apparent mechanical revolution. While growing up in Dalton in the 1830s,

[1] Weston, "Paper Making," passim; "History of Papermaking and Other Paper Makers," BWP.

Fig. 4.1 Byron Weston (1832–98), paper maker and
Berkshire paper industry historian.
Courtesy of Byron Weston Company.

and learning his craft in Lee, in nearby Saugerties and Ballston Spa,
New York, and in Hartford, Connecticut, in the 1840s and 1850s,
he had observed successive stages of mechanization. He had seen
hand paper making superseded by the cylinder machine and that
machine, in turn, give way to the superior Fourdrinier.

Despite the manifest accomplishments of machine builders, this
chapter, which summarizes the evolution of paper mill machinery,
and Chapter 6, which analyzes its adoption in Berkshire County,
find that mechanization transformed paper making more gradually
and less completely than Weston's summary suggests. Originally,
both the cylinder and the Fourdrinier paper-making machines were
quite limited mechanisms. Only after years of tinkering with them

Fig. 4.2 Weston's Defiance Mill. Weston's house appears
in the lower right foreground. Note also the teamster delivering rags.
Courtesy of the Byron Weston Company.

did they emerge as elaborate, multifunction contrivances capable of
operating without constant human intervention. Much of their development occurred in the twenty years between 1827, when the Laflin brothers installed Berkshire's first paper-making machine, and
1848, when Byron Weston began his apprenticeship. Thus, Weston
worked with relatively large, complex, impressive machines from
the start. Contrasted with hand technology, these machines seemed
revolutionary.

Weston also overstated the completeness of the mechanical revolution. Although the paper-making machine supplied incentives to
speed rag processing and paper finishing, mechanical technology
achieved only limited success at tasks other than fabricating sheets
of paper. Machines developed for finishing still required relatively
large numbers of attendants to help process the paper. Many hand
operations could not be replicated mechanically and continued to
be highly labor-intensive. Indeed, paper makers remained sufficiently skeptical of mechanical technology that they tried some apparently successful machines and subsequently set them aside for
traditional techniques.

The fact that little paper-making machinery originated in the

Berkshires also limited Weston's perspective on mechanization. The earliest, simplest paper-making machines introduced locally already embodied considerable time and money invested in their development elsewhere. Less satisfactory machines had been tried and scrapped or consigned to secondary roles before reaching western Massachusetts. To understand Berkshire mechanization we must first learn what options machine builders offered local mill owners by surveying mechanical invention and diffusion outside the county, in France, in Britain, and in America.[2]

THE PAPER-MAKING MACHINE

In the early nineteenth century, two different contrivances earned the name "paper-making machine." Each replaced the vatman, coucher, and layboy by forming damp sheets of paper from dilute pulp. The Fourdrinier paper-making machine appeared first. A Frenchman, Nicholas Louis Robert, patented the original Fourdrinier in 1799, the same year that Zenas Crane chose the site for Berkshire County's original paper mill. Eight years work by the ingenious British mechanic Bryan Donkin and a substantial investment by the Fourdrinier brothers, English stationers, intervened before a commercially feasible Fourdrinier emerged. Twenty years later, in 1827, Donkin's firm shipped two Fourdriniers to the United States. One, America's first, went into operation at the Saugerties, New York, mill where Byron Weston later began his paper-making career.[3]

Figures 4.3 and 4.4 depict the Fourdrinier as Weston knew it. Rag fiber, diluted to one part stock for every 199 parts water, entered the head box (A), where an agitator kept the fiber in suspension. Here the stock built up enough head to leave the box traveling at about the same speed as the wire surface of the machine. The stock flowed down a thin oilcloth or rubber apron onto the wire. The wire, like the surface of the paper mold, consisted of a woven brass mesh. When installed, its ends were sewn together to form a continuous

---

[2] Robert H. Clapperton, *The Paper-making Machine* (Oxford, 1967), provides a superb account of the evolution of the Fourdrinier paper-making machine in Britain. No adequate account of the evolution of American paper-making machinery exists. The following discussion does not attempt to fill that gap, but merely pieces together existing secondary literature and primary material found in Berkshire County collections and other archival sources consulted.

[3] Clapperton, *Paper-making Machine*, pp. 15–53 and passim; Hunter, *Papermaking*, pp. 268–356; "James McDonald," in "History of B.W. Co.," BWP.

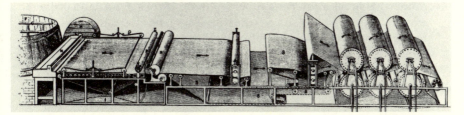

Fig. 4.3 Fourdrinier paper-making machine of 1856. From Clapperton, *The Paper-making Machine*.

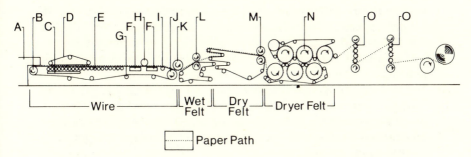

Fig. 4.4 Schematic diagram of Fourdrinier paper-making machine.

loop (extending from *B* to *J*). The machine imitated the movements of the vatman by shaking the moving wire from side to side, causing the rag fibers in the stock to intertwine. The forward progress of the wire and fiber substituted for the back-and-forth shake given by the vatman.[4]

From the breast roll (*B*) near the head box, the wire traveled over

[4] A summary description of the Fourdrinier in the nineteenth century is simply not possible. Not only was the machine continuously evolving, but also major innovations appeared briefly only to be forgotten for prolonged periods. Moreover, there was never a standard Fourdrinier machine. Rather, each machine was built to meet the customer's specifications and many machines underwent subsequent modification at the mills. Clapperton, *Paper-making Machine*, pp. 11–12; Sutermeister, *Papermaking*, p. 152. The following account will, therefore, describe the principal features of most nineteenth-century Fourdriniers. It will then describe the primary developments in the machine that were both invented and widely accepted prior to 1885.

Sutermeister, *Papermaking*, pp. 154–58; Clapperton, *Paper-making Machine*, pp. 45–53, 115–253, and passim. Standard wires were #60 and #70, with 2,301 and 3,519 holes per square inch, respectively.

numerous small supporting tube rolls or table rolls (*E*). All the while excess water drained through the wire into the white water trays (*C*) below. As with the paper mold, a deckle prevented stock from flowing over the edges of the wire. In the case of the machine, leather deckle straps (*D*) revolved above and against the wire at the same speed as the moving wire cloth. After the wire reached the wire return roll or bottom couch roll (*J*) it traveled beneath the machine, around adjustable stretch rolls (*G*), which held it taut, back to the breast roll.[5]

The gradually cohering wet web of rag fiber arrived with the wire at the couch rolls. The upper couch roll (*K*), covered with a wool cloth jacket, performed the task of the coucher. It picked up the wet web and transferred it to a woven woolen felt, know as the wet felt, which traveled at the same speed as the wire. Like the wire, the felt formed a continuous loop and adjustable rolls stretched it tight.[6]

The wet felt carried the web of paper between two rotating rolls held tightly together by a system of screws or weights and levers, known as the first press (*L*). Next, a dry felt picked up the paper and brought it through a second press (*M*). At the end of the dry felt the machine wound the damp paper on a reel. Workers in the early mechanized mills cut the reeled paper into sheets and carried it to a conventional loft for drying.[7]

The early Fourdrinier required almost incessant attention from its operators, the machine tender and the backtender. They had to maintain identical speeds in different sections or the web would tear or back up. Assuring uniform paper weight and consistent quality necessitated frequent scrutiny of the product and repeated adjustment of the machine. Only periodic human intervention kept wires and felts taut and prevented them from slipping to one side of the machine or the other. When felts clogged with fiber, machine at-

---

[5] Sutermeister, *Papermaking*, pp. 157–58; Clapperton, *Paper-making Machine*, pp. 45–53, 115–253, and passim. White water is the term for water that has been removed from the stock. It contained some rag fiber and, increasingly over the course of the nineteenth century, a variety of paper makers' chemicals. As early as the early nineteenth century, therefore, attempts were made to economize on fiber and chemicals by recycling the white water. The curved hood over the lifting device for accomplishing this appears in Figure 4.3 behind the head box. Recycling white water became an issue in America much later. See Chapter 7.

[6] Sutermeister, *Papermaking*, pp. 157, 160–61; Clapperton, *Paper-making Machine*, pp. 45–53, 115–53, and passim; J. Wallace Tower, "History and Other Data Relating to Fourdrinier Paper Making Machines 1799–1931," in "History of B.W. Co.," BWP.

[7] Sutermeister, *Papermaking*, pp. 160–61; Clapperton, *Paper-making Machine*, pp. 45–53, 115–53, and passim.

tendants had to remove and scrub them. They also had to detect and replace worn wires or felts before they left marks on the paper.[8]

Throughout the period before 1885, inventors subjected the Fourdrinier machine to a series of improvements almost as endless as the web of paper it fabricated. One of the earliest additions, patented in 1825, enabled the machine to produce laid paper. This device consisted of a spindle around which John and Christopher Phipps built a cylindrical framework supporting a cover of parallel wires sewn together with other, perpendicular wires. This revolving dandy roll (H) compressed the paper, which passed under it on the machine wire, and left a pattern similar to that on paper formed on a laid mold. Remarkably, it took fourteen years before William Joynson sewed letters and other devices on the surface of the roll, making possible the production of the first machine-made watermarked paper.[9]

The Phipps brothers claimed an auxiliary benefit from their dandy roll. It squeezed out a bit more water as it pressed down on the paper. That the results of such slight pressure attracted notice indicates that manufacturers seriously needed more effective measures to remove water from the paper, even on early, slow-moving machines. In answer, Canson, a Frenchman, developed the suction box (F). Placed just below the machine's surface, the suction box pulled additional water through the wire because a pump connected to the box maintained a partial vacuum in it. In 1836, ten years after Canson's original improvement, John Brown obtained the first English patent for a suction box.[10]

Earlier, in 1828, George Dickinson made an important contribution to the success of machine-made paper with the invention of the slice. A thin, flat board, the slice lay across the surface of the wire in front of the head box, barely allowing room for the pulp to pass under it. This simple expedient smoothed out the waves and bubbles, which had often left machine-made paper inferior to the handmade product.[11]

Machine-made paper continued to possess other imperfections, however. For example, the sheets possessed two distinct sides, one smoother than the other. This resulted because, unlike couchers, who pressed paper between two felts, paper-making machines car-

[8] Clapperton, *Paper-making Machine*, pp. 32, 193, 246; Byron Weston Letter Books, BWP, passim.

[9] Clapperton, *Paper-making Machine*, pp. 93, 113–14. Unless otherwise noted, the patentees mentioned here and elsewhere in this chapter are English.

[10] Ibid., pp. 96, 145.   [11] Ibid., pp. 101–2.

ried one side of the paper on the wet or dry felt, but exposed the other side directly to the smooth-surfaced upper press rolls. John Dickinson remedied this defect in 1829, when he contrived the reversing press. Before running the paper through a conventional second press, Dickinson transferred it back and forth between several felts, managing, as a result, to reverse the sides brought against felt and press roll. The immediate, widespread adoption of Dickinson's reversing press vanquished yet another objection to machine-made paper.[12]

Nearly forty-five years elapsed before Frenchman Gabriel Planche made the next major improvement in the Fourdrinier. His invention, the wire guide roll (*I*), considerably lightened the burdens of machine tending. It automatically counteracted the tendency of the wire to shift to the right or left. Machine builders readily adapted the device to guide the machine's wet and dry felts as well.[13]

Also in the 1870s, inventors developed the automatic felt washer, another boon to the machine tender. The innovators situated a shower so that water struck the felt during its passage beneath the machine's surface. After the shower had washed away any adherent pulp, a pair of squeeze rolls wrung excess water from the felt. Nonetheless, felts continued to require frequent, sometimes daily, removal for scouring.[14]

Although inventors quickly patented individual improvements that remedied defects in the Fourdrinier, no patents recorded the principal, incremental developments in the machine. Between 1807 and 1885 machine builders continually widened the machine and made it capable of operating more and more rapidly, permitting ever-increasing levels of production. Donkin's earliest machine had measured only 54 inches across; 1884 saw one machine at least 125 inches wide. Meanwhile, especially in America, operating speeds mounted, reaching 100 feet per minute by 1867 and 200 feet per minute by 1880. More rapid paper production, in turn, required a longer wire surface accommodating more suction boxes to remove water more quickly.[15]

Although this large, rapid Fourdrinier almost monopolizes contemporary paper production, nineteenth-century paper makers such as Byron Weston chose between it and the cylinder machine.

---

[12] Ibid., pp. 104, 107.   [13] Ibid., p. 193.   [14] Ibid., p. 246.
[15] Ibid., pp. 37, 245, 247; Sutermeister, *Papermaking*, p. 150. Here and elsewhere widths cited are widths of wires, following paper industry convention. Hereinafter, when a machine is simply referred to as a 54-inch machine, width is the dimension referred to.

John Dickinson developed this type of paper-making machine in England by 1809. By 1816 Thomas Gilpin of Wilmington, Delaware, had produced a similar machine, antedating the first American Fourdrinier by eleven years.[16]

Figure 4.5 portrays a cylinder machine. The device required stock about four times as dilute as the Fourdrinier's or about 799 parts water to one part pulp. The stock flowed into a vat (A) in which revolved a hollow, partially submerged cylinder (B) covered with wire cloth. The cylinder contained a V-shaped trough connected to a suction pump. The pump created a partial vacuum in the trough, causing rag fiber to cling to the cylinder's surface as it rose out of the stock. Water drained through the wire cloth surface to an outlet pipe connected to the suction pump. A revolving couch roll (C) pressed a wet felt (D) against the wire cylinder, removing the continuously forming web of paper. The paper traveled on this felt and on a subsequent dry felt through a first press (E) and second press to a reel, as in the analogous sections of the Fourdrinier.[17]

In the late teens and early twenties, several American paper makers, including John Ames of Springfield, Massachusetts, simplified the cylinder machine, eliminating the vacuum trough and substituting a lifting mechanism to maintain a higher water level outside the cylinder than inside it. Like the vacuum trough, this mechanism created enough pressure that water from the vat flowed into the cylinder with sufficient force to consolidate a film of fiber on the cylin-

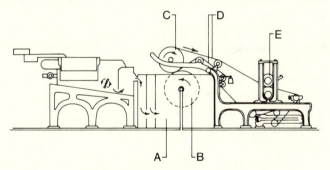

Fig. 4.5 Cylinder paper-making machine in elevation.

[16] Clapperton, *Paper-making Machine*, pp. 65–77, 323–24; H. B. Hancock and N. B. Wilkinson, "The Gilpins and Their Endless Papermaking Machine," *Pennsylvania Magazine of History and Biography* 81 (October 1957): 396–400, 402–4.

[17] Clapperton, *Paper-making Machine*, pp. 65–77; Sutermeister, *Papermaking*, pp. 165–67; Hancock and Wilkinson, "Gilpins," pp. 398, 403; Ferguson, *Early Engineering Reminiscences*, p. 98.

der's surface. The innovation made the cylinder paper machine much easier to build, greatly reducing its cost and encouraging its rapid and widespread adoption in American mills.[18]

From the mill owner's point of view, two principal characteristics distinguished the cylinder machine from the Fourdrinier. The cylinder machine cost much less and made inferior paper. The Fourdrinier's complex shaking mechanism accounted for both differences. It required meticulous construction and precise adjustment, raising the cost of building and of operating the machine. Its lengthy brass wire proved especially costly. Because the cheaper cylinder machine lacked a side-to-side shake, however, paper fibers did not intertwine on it so well as they did on the Fourdrinier. By revolving in the vat, the cylinder tended to lay most pulp fibers in the direction it rotated, creating paper that tore more readily in one direction than in the other.[19]

The primary change in the cylinder machine before 1885 was its adaptation for the production of two-, three-, and multi-ply paper and board, a capability that also distinguished it from the Fourdrinier. Machine builders accomplished this modification simply by adding more vats and making cylinders. Each cylinder transferred an endless sheet of paper to a separate couch roll. Then separate felts carried all sheets to a common set of press rolls, which united the sheets. Dickinson, who had developed the first cylinder machine, pioneered the two-vat cylinder, but Americans developed a multicylinder board machine in 1863, which the English adopted in the late nineteenth century.[20]

In the 1830s American paper manufacturers rapidly installed cylinder and, increasingly, Fourdrinier paper-making machines. By 1845, less than thirty years after the American debut of mechanized paper production, only two hand mills remained in operation. As in Berkshire mills, manufacturers throughout the nation had evidently found that an inadequate supply of skilled vat room workmen limited their efforts to increase output. Once the machine had

---

[18] Ferguson, *Early Engineering Reminiscences*, pp. 97–101, 104. Sellers reports on an unnamed Frenchman, owner of a New Jersey mill, who anticipated Ames's invention.

[19] Clapperton, *Paper-making Machine*, p. 137; Hunter, *Papermaking*, p. 276; Sutermeister, *Papermaking*, p. 167. Both differences account for the more widespread use of the cylinder in American than in British mills throughout the nineteenth century. For a fuller discussion, see McGaw, "Sources and Impact," pp. 81–82.

[20] Clapperton, *Paper-making Machine*, pp. 109, 214–15, 244; Sutermeister, *Papermaking*, 165–68.

speeded the fabrication of damp sheets of paper, however, pressure to increase output shifted to other steps in production.[21]

EXTENDING THE MACHINE

What early Berkshire manufacturers called a paper-making machine, Byron Weston considered only part of one. By 1880 machine builders had mechanized many additional paper-making processes and had integrated the new devices into the original cylinder and Fourdrinier. Because the newly mechanized tasks began with drying the paper, Weston and other mill owners called the newer portions of the machine the "dry end" and came to refer to the original machine as merely the "wet end" of the paper-making machine.

Accelerating one step in a serial production process such as paper making creates incentives to speed all other stages of manufacture, but not all receive equal attention from inventors. After the introduction of the paper-making machine, inventive activity focused on methods of drying paper. Before looking at the resulting mechanisms, it is worth considering why drying attracted particular attention. As noted in Chapter 2, loft drying times were unpredictable and varied greatly. Tasks of this character become early candidates for mechanization because they are most difficult to coordinate with machine production. In the case of paper drying, the alternative would have been to construct huge dry lofts and employ large numbers of loft workers, tying up capital and labor that mills would utilize fully only in poor drying weather.[22]

As a result, paper drying attracted inventors' attention almost from the start. By 1820 Thomas Bonsor Crompton had perfected and patented the most important paper drying machine. Figures 4.3 and 4.4 illustrate dryers operating on this principle. A dryer felt picked up the web of paper after the second press and carried it around a series of heated cylinders (N), holding it firmly against them. To keep the smooth-surfaced, cast-iron cylinders heated, pumps continually forced in steam and withdrew condensed water. Precision boring of the iron cylinders created a surface of uniform thickness, so that the steam heated the dryer evenly. To avoid damaging the web of paper, Crompton held the temperature of the initial cast-iron drum well below 212 degrees Fahrenheit and raised

[21] Ferguson, *Early Engineering Reminiscences*, p. 101; Hunter, *Papermaking*, pp. 360, 365.

[22] For a full discussion of this notion see Uselding, *Studies in Technological Development*, pp. 133–38. Rosenberg, "Direction of Technological Change," pp. 110–17.

the temperature of each successive drum. After traveling around four to six of these cylinders, each about four feet in diameter, the paper had dried.[23]

Crompton's original dryer used a common wet end felt of linen warp and cotton weft. Gradually, paper makers developed specialized dryer felts of heavy cotton duck. Cotton felts withstood heat better and played a central role in ensuring satisfactory drying. They held the paper taut to prevent its cockling or blistering. As the paper dried, the all-cotton felt maintained equal tension on its length and its width so that it did not curl or become more brittle in one direction.[24]

In succeeding years, mills continued to use steam dryers like Crompton's, with one modification. In 1823 Bryan Donkin sought to build his own dryer, but could imagine no good system very different from Crompton's. To avoid patent infringement, he rearranged Crompton's single tier of dryers into two tiers, as in Figures 4.3 and 4.4. Others generally adopted Donkin's arrangement, both because of his prestige as a machine builder and because his system saved floor space.[25]

In America, George Spafford of the South Windham, Connecticut, firm of Phelps and Spafford claimed that he invented the steam dryer in 1830. Because his firm had already imported and copied a Donkin Fourdrinier, it seems more likely that Spafford modeled his dryer on an English precursor. His claim, however, helps date the earliest American availability of steam dryers.[26]

The Worcester, Massachusetts, firm of machine builders Henry P. Howe and Isaac Goddard probably does deserve the credit they claimed for inventing the later, fire dryer. This iron cylinder measured ten feet in diameter and had a wood-burning stove suspended inside. A door in the cylinder's side afforded access for refueling. Cost of the cylinder, difficulty in regulating its heat, and lack of any

[23] Sutermeister, *Papermaking*, pp. 161–63; Clapperton, *Paper-making Machine*, pp. 81, 83, 86, 323. Considerable debate over the relative merits of cast-iron and copper drying cylinders took place in the early nineteenth century. Once mill owners had been convinced that inadequate rag processing, not iron machine parts, produced rust spots on paper, mills gave iron dryers preference because their heat could be regulated more readily. Ferguson, *Early Engineering Reminiscences*, pp. 101, 118, 123.

[24] Clapperton, *Paper-making Machine*, p. 86; Sutermeister, *Papermaking*, pp. 162–63; interview with Fred G. Crane, Jr., Vice-President for Research and Development, Crane & Co. Laboratory, Dalton, Mass., August 19, 1975.

[25] Clapperton, *Paper-making Machine*, p. 31.

[26] *A Century of Pioneering in the Paper Industry: 1828–1928* (South Windham, Conn., 1928), Introduction, pp. 1–3; Ferguson, *Early Engineering Reminiscences*, p. 101.

provision for raising the paper's temperature gradually all militated against its success. By 1849 the firm's successor, Goddard, Rice & Company, advised clients to purchase steam dryers instead.[27]

Despite the availability of the steam dryer, loft drying persisted through 1885 both in England and in America. Damage to paper from dryers with inadequate temperature regulation or loose dryer felts encouraged retention of traditional methods in some mills. But paper makers continued to use dry lofts principally because they continued to use animal size. They needed to exercise great care in machine drying this glue-coated paper to prevent cockling, sticking, or destroying the effectiveness of the size. To meet their needs, in 1839 Ransom and Millbourn patented a dryer that blew hot air against the surface of sized paper as it passed around sparred drums. Ten years later Amos and Clark discovered that sized paper could be dried on conventional steam dryers if, after partial drying, it ran through a trough of cold water. The cold-water bath eliminated cockles and preserved the sized paper's ability to bear ink well and erase readily. Makers of fine paper, however, maintained that neither alternative produced paper so fine as loft-dried.[28]

No similar fear discouraged makers of sized paper from adopting mechanized size application. John Dickinson built a machine that sized individual sheets of paper as early as 1817. Towgood and Smith added a web-sizing section to the paper-making machine in 1830. But Ransom and Millbourn's 1839 patent gave the sizing section of the paper-making machine its most widely accepted form. As shown in Figure 4.6, a copper cylinder (B) partially submerged in a size bath (A) drew the web of paper from the dryer through the size. Copper press rolls (C) squeezed excess size from the paper after it left the bath. Doctors (D) constantly scraped the press rolls to keep them clean. The sized paper either wound up on a reel (E) ready for loft drying or traveled through machine dryers.[29]

Whether it arrived at the end of the machine wet or dry, sized or unsized, mills ultimately divided most paper into individual sheets. Slitters first separated the machine-width roll of paper into several

[27] Weston, "Paper Making," pp. 20–21; "Letter from Rice, Barton & Fales, Inc.," *SF* 5 (November 1931): 4; Weeks, *History of Paper Manufacturing*, p. 135.

[28] Sutermeister, *Papermaking*, p. 178; Clapperton, *Paper-making Machine*, pp. 115–16, 156, 180–82; "American Industries No. 72: The Manufacture of Writing Paper," *SA* 44 (April 30, 1881):275. Thomas Gilpin had suggested a hot air dryer more than twenty years earlier, but there is no evidence that he ever constructed one. Ferguson, *Early Engineering Reminiscences*, p. 98.

[29] Clapperton, *Paper-making Machine*, pp. 83, 115–16, 154. For a more detailed discussion of sizing machinery see McGaw, "Sources and Impact," p. 86.

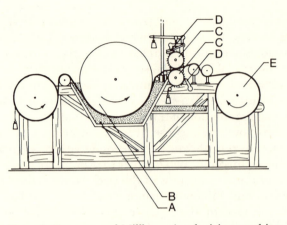

Fig. 4.6 Ransom and Millbourn's tub-sizing machine.

narrower rolls. Mill owners could adjust the revolving circular slitter blades on their shaft to cut rolls of various widths and to trim off uneven edges.[30]

Cutters next divided these narrower rolls into sheets. Although a bewildering variety of patent cutters emerged over the course of the nineteenth century, paper makers classified them either as stop cutters or as continuous cutters. The stop cutter required that the paper pause a moment, allowing a single guillotine-style knife to descend and cut it cleanly. By contrast, the continuous-feed cutter employed a revolving knife, which sheared the paper against a fixed bed knife. Early revolving paper cutters probably cut less perfectly than did stop cutters, but thanks to their continual improvement, these cutters' ability to keep pace with increasingly rapid papermaking machines ultimately gained them preference.[31]

Initially workers known as layboys caught and hand-stacked individual sheets as they dropped from the cutter. In 1843 Lemuel Wellman Wright patented the first mechanical layboy, a short felt that carried the paper from the cutter to a table. Three Americans filed for layboy patents in 1847: George L. Wright of Springfield, Massachusetts; J. C. Kneeland of Troy, New York; and James Brewer Crane of Dalton, Massachusetts, son of Berkshire's original paper maker. These simultaneous independent inventions suggest

[30] Sutermeister, *Papermaking*, pp. 183–84.
[31] Clapperton, *Paper-making Machine*, p. 246; Sutermeister, *Papermaking*, pp. 190–91. George Spafford claimed to have devised the first American continuous web cutter. *Century of Pioneering*, p. 3.

widespread recognition of the inadequacy of human layboys as machine speeds mounted in the 1840s. Crane's mechanical layboy consisted of a platform resting beneath the cutter. As the cutter knife revolved and cut a sheet, it transmitted its motion to the platform, which swung out to receive the new sheet on top of previous ones. Kneeland had priority over his competitors and eventually won patent office recognition for his claim of patent infringement because the revolving cutter activated all three layboys.[32]

After drying and cutting, paper processing depended on intended use and customer preference. To create the flat finish users of fine writing paper requested, many paper makers sent paper to the finishing room and pressed it between card boards, much as they had done before the paper-making machine. On other papers, especially printing paper, customers preferred a smoother, glazed finish. By the 1830s machine calenders administered this finish to paper in the web. The calender (Figure 4.4, O), a stack of revolving cast-iron rolls with very smooth surfaces, compacted the paper as it passed between the rolls, producing a hard, polished surface. To assure equal smoothness on both sides, paper might be run through two calender stacks.[33]

With the addition of dryers, sizers, slitters, cutters, and calenders, the paper-making machine became a very impressive example of the nineteenth-century machine builder's art. In marked contrast to the Hollander beater, it had all those characteristics calculated to inspire awe. Its size, complexity, and multiplicity of function moved Herman Melville to describe it as "inscrutable," employing the same adjective he applied to the Great White Whale. Even after years on the job, contemporary mill workers confess amazement at the machine's apparently instantaneous transmutation of waterlike pulp to solid paper. Nineteenth-century mill owners and workers, less inured to mechanized manufacturing, must have felt even greater wonder. But despite the immense prestige the paper-making ma-

[32] Clapperton, *Paper-making Machine*, p. 170; Weston, "Paper Making," p. 22; "Successful Paper Makers: Representative Industrial Leaders of the Times: Hon. Byron Weston of Dalton, Mass.," *Paper World* 1 (July 1880):7; "The Automatic Layboy, 1847–1848," CMF, 3/16/47, 8/14/47, 8/19/47, 3/3/48, 3/6/48, 8/8/48. One letter in the Crane & Co. files suggests that a fourth claimant, Hollingsworth, also bowed to Kneeland.

[33] "American Industries No. 72," p. 275; Sutermeister, *Papermaking*, pp. 163–64, 183; Clapperton, *Paper-making Machine*, pp. 118, 166, 246; "Alfred Hoxie," interview typescript, CMF, p. 10. The machine calender was descended from an earlier calender used in some hand paper mills. Henk Voorn, "A Short History of the Glazing of Paper," *PM* 27 (1958):8–10.

chine conferred on mechanical paper processing, and despite the
pressure it applied to speed and regularize other paper-making
tasks, nowhere else in the mill did mechanization succeed so well.

THE LIMITS OF MECHANIZATION

Having surveyed machine builders' accomplishments, let us now
consider their limitations. Once the machine had speeded the fabrication of dry sheets of paper, the rag room, the beater room, and
the finishing room experienced pressure to keep pace. Machines replaced some hand processes in these areas, but attempts at mechanization encountered intractable problems in the rag room, beater
room, and finishing room. Although inventors had devised machines to perform the difficult work of skilled vatmen, couchers,
and loftmen, they failed to duplicate mechanically the apparently
simpler occupations for which mills readily trained women.

Indeed, as in the machine room, which housed the paper-making
machine, technological change occurred most often and most successfully where jobs required greatest human skill. For example,
mills substituted the ruling machine for the skilled workman who
had hand-ruled various patterns on ledger, copybook, and writing
paper. In 1835 the English and American patent offices granted
patents for similar ruling devices. Each contained a series of metal
pens attached to metal ink boxes, which could be raised or lowered
by a lever and brought to bear upon sheets of paper traveling beneath the pens on an endless cloth belt. Seven years later, the foreman of the Ames mill, George L. Wright, simplified the operation
of the machine, reducing the required number of attendants from
four to two. By 1858 Robert McAlpine, an employee of Platner
& Smith's mill in Lee, had perfected a striker, which automatically
raised and lowered the pens, eliminating another attendant. Other
improvements included a simplified, specialized ruling pen (1857),
an automatic feed device (1878), and a method of simultaneously
ruling both sides of a sheet (1880). Ruling clearly could be mechanized, but the process was neither so quick nor so complete as the
mechanization of paper making.[34]

Also for the finishing room, as early as 1828 Philadelphia machine builder Coleman Sellers introduced a paper-cutting machine
to replace the hand-wielded binder's plough. It administered a final

[34] "The Ruling Machine," *Hurlbut's Papermaker Gentleman* 3 (Spring 1934):17–20;
VG, 10/14/58, p. 2.

trimming to finished reams, remedying the slight unevenness of the edges produced by the slitters and cutters, an unevenness that loft drying exaggerated. As Sellers's son, George Escol, explained to Bryan Donkin, the crucial component of the Sellers cutter was a press. By compacting the ream of paper before trimming, the press allowed a guillotine blade to slice through the paper "without any oblique or lateral motion."[35]

Other successful innovations speeded work in the engine room, province of the skilled engineer. One device, the bleach boiler (Figure 4.7), both reduced washing time in the Hollander and lessened required rag sorting. Bleach boilers removed dirt, grease, and some color from rags. Before sending dirty rags to the washing engine, rag workers placed several thousand pounds of them in these cylindrical or spherical containers and added water and caustic soda, or slaked lime and soda ash. Then they closed the boiler's doors and opened valves admitting steam at fifty pounds pressure per square inch. The boiler rotated, adding a tumbling action to the cleansing properties of steam and alkali. Together these agents loosened dirt, which had previously rendered the cheapest rags unfit for paper makers' use. As did chlorine bleach, then, bleach boilers lowered raw material costs without adding to labor expenses.[36]

In the engine room the Hollander remained the principal machine, essentially the same as in 1800. Machine builders gradually increased its size and efficiency and improved the precision with which it could be regulated. They accomplished this, in part, by constructing specialized breaking engines equipped with blunt roll bars and bed plate knives and separate beating engines supplied with sharper knives. They also introduced washers (Figure 4.8), eight-sided cylinders of fine wire cloth, which fitted inside the engine op-

[35] Sellers was forced to explain the device to Donkin, because it was unknown in England, despite its widespread replacement of the binder's plough in America. Ferguson, *Early Engineering Reminiscences*, pp. 119–21; Coleman Sellers Letter Book, 1828–34, APS, 12/24/28.

In some mills, machines for converting paper into various forms, such as bags, boxes, or envelopes, were also introduced during the period. Frequently, however, these operations were carried out by manufacturers called paper converters, who were not themselves engaged in paper making. They are beyond the scope of this study.

[36] Sutermeister, *Papermaking*, p. 21; "American Industries No. 72," p. 275. The name bleach boiler is a misnomer since washing, not bleaching, occurred in these machines. I have found no date assigned the earliest of these machines. One of Crane & Co.'s correspondents reported the device as novel in eastern Massachusetts in 1851. "Oscar Crane," CMF, 7/27/51.

Fig. 4.7 Rotary bleach boiler (*left*) and breaking engines (*right*), as illustrated in *Scientific American*'s April 30, 1881, article on the Owen Paper Company.

posite the rotating roll. Dirty water flowed out through the cloth and was discharged through an outlet pipe, but the wire covering prevented rag fiber from following. Continuous expulsion of dirt speeded washing, essentially enhancing the efficiency of existing technology. Washers originated in France in 1835.[37]

Whereas the paper-making machine had multiplied output yet required only two attendants, far fewer than had been employed at the numerous hand processes it superseded, single-function finishing machines speeded processing but reduced the mill's dependence on human operatives much less. Each trimming machine needed one attendant and ruling machines kept one or more busy. Other mechanical finishers each employed at least one person and one, the supercalender, required more skillful workers than had the hand operation it superseded.

By 1832 mills added supercalenders to give first-class printing paper an even more polished finish than the machine calender supplied. The device contained a smooth cast-iron roll at either end of the calender stack and had two cotton or paper rolls in between. Paper makers used cotton rolls on coated paper and paper rolls on plain paper. Calender makers built up these softer rolls by winding cotton or paper on a shaft under heavy pressure and then fastening the ends with steel heads.[38]

[37] "American Industries No. 72," p. 275; Sutermeister, *Papermaking*, pp. 21–22, 131-32, 140–41; Hunter, *Papermaking*, pp. 358–59; Brown & Weston and Byron Weston Letter Book, 1866–67, BWP, 3/5/66.

[38] Coleman Sellers Letter Book, 1828–34, APS, passim; Clapperton, *Paper-making*

Fig. 4.8 Hollander beater with washer (*upper left*).
Courtesy of the Crane Museum.

Initially supercalenders required two attendants: one to feed in
paper a sheet at a time and one to remove each sheet. By the 1870s
and 1880s Rice, Barton & Fales of Worcester, Massachusetts, offered supercalenders that automatically fed the paper through,
either in the web or in single sheets, but these devices still required
one full-time attendant. Paper broke easily under the heavy pressure supercalenders applied. Unless stopped immediately, the supercalender quickly damaged its soft paper or cotton rolls by running against the slight unevenness caused by even a single scrap of
broken paper. Successful calender operation depended on workers'
skill as well as attentiveness. Calender girls had to judge the moisture content of the paper because, if too dry, paper failed to take a

---

Machine, p. 246; Sutermeister, *Papermaking*, pp. 183–86. In their correspondence
and other records, mill owners and machine builders generally referred to both machine calenders and supercalenders simply as calenders. In general, such references
are probably to supercalenders. Hereinafter "calenders" will refer to supercalenders.
Initially calenders were made so as to allow heating of the iron rolls, in evident imitation of the earlier process of hot pressing. This feature was found to be unnecessary almost immediately. For a photograph showing supercalenders see Figure 10.3.

high finish, whereas too much moisture resulted in a burned appearance. Skillful calender attendants also achieved the required finish with a minimum number of passes through the rolls, because each pass produced more damaged paper. In addition, the skilled boss finisher had to adjust both calenders and ruling machines every time they processed a different kind of paper.[39]

Less skilled workers could create various surfaces on the paper with a plater. This later device consisted of two revolving rolls. The attendant placed a sheet of paper between sheets of appropriate material and ran the sheets through the rolls. For an extremely smooth glazed finish, paper makers used polished metal plates. Zinc plates, on the other hand, left a satin finish on the paper. In either case, considerable hand labor accompanied use of the machine.[40]

Stamping machines, another finishing room device, impressed a raised design by lowering a steel die bearing the maker's or customer's name and emblem against the paper's upper-left-hand corner. The Ames mill in Springfield had introduced this contrivance to western Massachusetts by 1841. Again, as with other finishing equipment, stamping machines occupied an attendant fulltime at feeding and withdrawing paper.[41]

Knowing that considerable hand labor accompanied machine finishing, it is less surprising to discover that other finishing processes withstood any attempts at mechanization. Throughout the nineteenth century sorting and counting remained tedious hand operations. Sorting involved scanning both sides of each sheet for dirt, wrinkles, tears, or defective edges. Unsalable paper, known as "broke," returned to the beaters for reprocessing. The sorter classified the remaining paper as either perfect or seconds, the mill's standards or the customer's preferences predetermining the percentage falling into each class. Careful hand sorting was a costly process and mill owners reserved it for their better papers, but even lower grades received a more cursory scanning and sorting at the layboy.[42]

[39] Coleman Sellers Letter Book, 1828–34, APS, 12/28/33; Sutermeister, *Papermaking*, pp. 187–88; "Crane, Martin and Co. Successor to Crane, Wilson and Co. 1857–1858," CMF, 1/5/57.

[40] "American Industries No. 72," p. 275; "Alfred Hoxie," interview typescript, CMF, p. 10. For a photograph showing a plater see Figure 9.6.

[41] "American Industries No. 72," pp. 274–75; "George L. Wright to Owen & Hurlbut," *Hurlbut's Papermaker Gentleman* 3 (Fall 1935); "A History of the Bay State Mill," "Crane & Co. Historical Articles," CMF, p. 7.

[42] Sutermeister, *Papermaking*, pp. 191–92; Byron Weston Letter Books, passim. Sometimes more numerous sorters' classifications were employed. Laflin, "Address to Writing Paper Makers," CMF, p. 8.

Workers also counted paper by hand. With practice, an operative could quickly and accurately count out a 480-sheet ream. Holding it with the left hand, the worker fanned out the stack of paper by bending it in a gentle S-shaped curve. Then he or she inserted a finger of the right hand after every fourth sheet, turning back sixteen sheets each time. Thirty hand insertions completed a ream.[43]

Mills retained hand sorting and counting because these operations involved the worker's eye as well as his or her hand. The mechanical genius of nineteenth-century technology could replicate complex manual tasks, but could not duplicate visual skills. Only twentieth-century electronic technology has partially superseded human scanning in the paper mill.[44]

The fate of two final innovations designed for the rag room and the beater room illustrate the limits of mechanization even more clearly. Mill owners did not accord either the mechanical rag cutter or the stock refiner, a proposed alternative to the beater, anything approaching the universal welcome granted the paper-making machine. Some mills made only limited use of the new devices and others utterly rejected them.

Mechanical rag cutters could not perform the tasks of opening seams or removing buttons, hooks, and spoiled sections of cloth, because these operations involved both visual and manual skills. When used, rag cutters assumed the more routinized task of reducing rags to two- to four-inch squares. Rag-cutting machines consisted of one or more moving knives shearing against bed knives. By 1879 machine shops equipped them with automatic feed mechanisms and arranged them sequentially to cut rags in one direction and then transfer the rags to a second machine, which cut them perpendicularly to produce squares. As late as 1885, however, manufacturers of fine paper judged that rag room women turned out more uniform squares and employed women in preference to machines. In addition, as Chapter 7 will describe, after the 1860s few except fine paper makers continued to use rag fiber exclusively. Thus, the market for mechanical rag cutters remained limited.[45]

[43] Brown & Weston Letter Book, 1865–66, BWP, 11/30/65; Sutermeister, *Papermaking*, p. 192. The author has had the good fortune to observe and talk with a worker at Crane & Co.'s Bay State Mill who still possesses the skill of hand counting. She maintained that her work was more accurate than that of the new electronic counters in the mill. Her performance, despite not practicing the skill regularly, was remarkably quick.

[44] Ralph Kendall, interview and tour of the Bay State Mill, Dalton, Mass., July 17, 1975.

[45] "American Industries No. 72," p. 275; Sutermeister, *Papermaking*, p. 21; "Machinery, Engineering, and Chemistry, 1866–1871," CMF, 2/8/70.

As a case study in the limits of mechanization, the attempt to re-place the Hollander with the stock refiner is even more illuminat-ing. Hollanders took up much floor space, used large amounts of power, were difficult to adjust precisely, and did not deliver a con-tinuous flow of pulp. These liabilities became more apparent as mills installed more and more beaters to supply faster, wider paper-making machines. In 1858 Joseph Jordan and Thomas Eustace of Hartford, Connecticut, responded by developing their stock re-finer, generally known as the Jordan refiner or Jordan (Figure 4.9). The Jordan consisted of a conical plug (*B*) studded with knives, which revolved inside a conical casing (*A*) lined with knives. Stock entered through the inlet pipe (*G*) at the narrow end of the Jordan. Chemicals could be added through a second inlet pipe (*I*). The Jor-dan's knives cut and frayed the fiber in the stock as it passed through the refiner. Stock then exited through an outlet pipe (*H*).[46]

Although the Jordan met most of their objections to the beater, few nineteenth-century mill owners adopted it. Experience had convinced paper makers that only long, slow beating in the Hol-lander adequately prepared paper stock. They employed the Jor-dan, if at all, merely to finish stock already beaten and to even out differences between pulp from different batches. Another refiner, invented by paper maker J. Kingsland of New Jersey in 1856, en-joyed a brief popularity, but unlike the Jordan, it was not designed to replace the beater, merely to take half-beaten stock and complete its preparation for the machine. Moreover, Cyrus Currier and Sons of Newark, its sole fabricator, found that its four disks, which re-volved simultaneously within a casing, were difficult to machine precisely enough with existing machine tools. For the remainder of the nineteenth century, therefore, those mills purchasing refiners usually bought Jordans.[47]

As we have seen, the limited success of refiners and rag cutters, the continuation of hand counting and sorting, and the use of rela-tively labor-intensive machines such as supercalenders, stampers, rulers, and platers can each be explained by the requirements of the particular process involved. But they can also be understood in more general terms. Mill owners evidently felt less need for ma-chine technology in the rag room, the beater room, and the finish-

---

[46] Sutermeister, *Papermaking*, pp. 134–36; Clapperton, *Paper-making Machine*, pp. 197, 237; *Century of Pioneering*, pp. 5–6; Jones, *Jones Story*, p. 6; *VG* 5/28/57, p. 2.

[47] "Alfred Hoxie," interview typescript, CMF, p. 4; Sutermeister, *Papermaking*, p. 136; Jones, *Jones Story*, p. 6. In the twentieth century, some mills eliminated Holland-ers and began to rely solely on refiners.

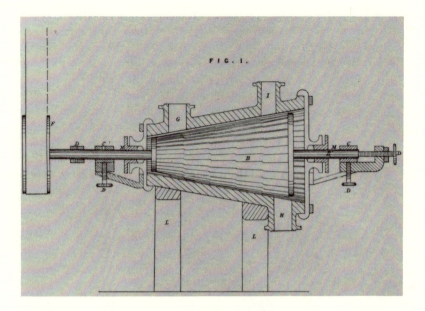

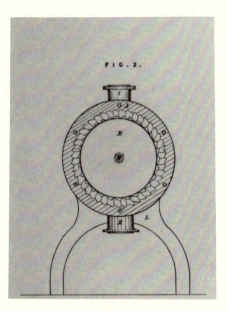

Fig. 4.9 Jordan refiner (side section and end section).
From Clapperton, *The Paper-making Machine*.

ing room—those areas of the mill where traditional technology had succeeded best at expanding mill output in the 1820s. After mechanization, the rag room, beater room, and finishing room all continued to be spared the problem of inelastic labor supply, which had fostered mechanization in the vat room. In the beater room, each mill already employed an engineer. He could tend all the additional engines mechanized mills needed, especially as fewer, larger engines replaced more numerous smaller ones. In the finishing room and rag room, women remained willing to work cheaply and irregularly. Because demand for finished paper continued to fluctuate, mills may have invested more sensibly when they relied on expensive labor-intensive methods. More costly on an hourly basis, intermittent manual labor tied up far less total capital than would partially employed machines or large inventories built up by continuous machine operation. Moreover, where processing varied with the product, as it did in the finishing room, mill owners might understandably have preferred workers capable of several different tasks to inflexible fixed capital.

ON THE WHOLE, then, nineteenth-century machine builders seem to have served the paper maker rather well. They perfected a large, complex, paper-making machine so that paper production could increase more rapidly than did the supply of skilled workmen, and they constructed a host of subsidiary machines that multiplied the output of most other workers as well. American paper production grew from about $3 million worth in 1820 to almost $49 million worth in 1870, indicating that the industry successfully recruited enough hand workers to perform those processes remaining unmechanized.[48]

The accomplishments of paper machine inventors are, however, only a part of the story of mechanization. What enabled mill owners scattered about in rural areas to discover the machines, assess the machines' worth, and raise the requisite capital? Until we know how mill owners managed the transition to machine production, we will not fully understand why Americans embraced the machine so readily. Because mill owners were numerous and their problems diverse, we will follow Weston's example and confine our attention to Berkshire County.

[48] Smith, *History of Papermaking*, pp. 20, 83.

CHAPTER 5

THE COMMUNITY OF
MECHANIZERS:
BERKSHIRE PAPER
MILL OWNERS,
1827–1857

Beginning in 1827 Berkshire mill owners installed most of the new paper-processing mechanisms just discussed. Later I will describe the mechanization of Berkshire paper making, analyze the patterns of machine purchase, and generalize about why the county provided an especially hospitable climate for machines. But such a retrospective and summary description necessarily conveys a sense of order and clarity utterly lacking in the contemporary mill owner's experience.

To understand the emergent mechanical order, we need first to consider the disorderly human experience that created it. The men who mechanized Berkshire paper mills faced innumerable individual decisions. They made their choices amidst the turbulence of a technologically and economically chaotic era. Many failed. Few survived without considerable determination and sustained assistance from friends, associates, or family members.

Who were these remarkable human agents of mechanization? How did they learn about new machines, decide whether or not to buy them, and raise the necessary capital? Between 1827 and 1857 mill owners formed a gradually coalescing community of entrepreneurs whose informal cooperation, business sense, and technical expertise made continuous mechanization possible. Because the men who owned mills during these three decades made the initial decisions to acquire paper-making machines and devised ways to operate mechanized mills, their activities command our attention here. Moreover, as the years of innovation drew to a close, the panic of 1857 ushered in a prolonged depression in the paper industry, clearing the way for a subsequent generation of mill owners, a generation that took mechanized paper making for granted. Their story will be told later.

Between 1827 and 1857 the market for paper continued to ex-

pand as a growing rail network facilitated Berkshire paper makers'
trade with New York and created links to additional urban markets.
These developments provided incentive for 136 men to invest in 50
local paper mills, 37 of the plants newly constructed or converted to
paper making from other purposes. To understand how mill owners managed to mechanize, we must first examine the closely related
growth of the industry and its market, establishing the increasingly
competitive climate in which they made their decisions. Against this
backdrop we can see why paper makers sought out machines and
how their training and friendships abetted their attempts to assess
rapidly changing technology. Finally, to learn how mill owners successfully solved the problem of capital accumulation, we can examine how they applied the business tools at their disposal, analyzing
contemporary accounting procedures as the lens through which
they viewed investment decisions and partnership as the most common technique for pooling resources. Each of these perspectives on
mill owners' decisions reinforces a single conclusion: mechanization
was not easy but it made good business sense, and manufacturers
were prepared to recognize that fact and act on that recognition.[1]

New Markets and New Mills

Between 1832, shortly after machines were introduced locally, and
1855, shortly before the depression curtailed production, the number of Berkshire mills enumerated in the census grew from thirteen
to thirty-five. Machines simultaneously raised the average mill's output to over three times its 1832 level. Although the average ream of
paper sold for 10 percent less than it had in 1832, by 1855 Berkshire
mills valued their output at nearly $1 million, almost seven and a
half times the comparable 1832 figure.[2]

[1] Appendix A provides a detailed time line for all Berkshire mills from 1801 to
1885, including their often frequent changes in ownership.

[2] *McLane Report*, part 1, pp. 144–45, 156–57; Francis DeWitt, *Statistical Information
Relating to Certain Branches of Industry in Massachusetts for the Year Ending June 1, 1855*
(Boston, 1856), pp. 20–63.

My count (fig. 6.1) finds forty-one mills in 1855. The lower number enumerated
by the census reflects the fact that census takers missed the mills in Becket, Lenox,
and Tyringham (two mills); and they omitted two mills that were built in 1855. One
mill in Otis was reported "idle." Because no figures were entered for this mill, I have
omitted it from my calculations. As usual, census figures are not strictly comparable.
In 1855 most mills reported output in pounds, whereas McLane's figures are in
reams. Estimating the weight of the average ream high, at twenty pounds, I have converted 1855 figures to reams, thus minimizing increases in output and giving paper
prices per ream an upward bias.

During the same years, the market for Berkshire paper grew rapidly enough to absorb this burgeoning output and to motivate mill owners to invest in new mills and machines. Market expansion resulted from improved transportation that combined with mechanization to reduce paper prices. Most important was the inception of rail service, which both lowered the transportation costs mill owners had to pass on to established customers and enlarged the region to which they could ship paper at reasonable prices. As we shall see, new mill construction followed closely the opening of new rail lines. Also stimulating the market for paper were a host of simultaneous developments, ranging from changes in the postal rate structure to improved domestic lighting, which lengthened the time available for reading. One of these developments, the growth of journalism, not only increased demand for paper, but also gave mill owners easier access to vital technical and business information.

Berkshire manufacturers credited the railroad for much of their expanded market. Paper mill owners repeatedly testified to their belief in the railroad's importance by investing their time, money, and political influence to promote new lines. As early as 1826 paper manufacturers joined other local citizens in petitioning the state assembly for a railroad. Two years later a railway survey calculated that Lee teamsters alone carted four tons of paper to the Hudson each year, underscoring paper makers' potential savings. This teaming cost about $3,000, and when combined with a somewhat larger sum spent to haul back rags and supplies to make the paper, it totaled more than fifteen cents on a twenty-pound ream of paper. It also added as much as a day to the time orders took to reach New York customers.[3]

Nonetheless, ten years elapsed before local railroads began operating, speeding shipments and travel to New York and lowering their cost. Only after the state of New York began constructing a railroad from Hudson City through the mountain pass to the state line did the Massachusetts legislature appropriate funds to extend

[3] Zenas Crane Investment and Mortgage Record, CA, 5/12/37; Smith, *Housatonic*, p. 270; Alvin F. Harlow, *Steelways of New England* (New York, 1946), p. 48; "David Barnard," interview typescript, CMF, p. 3.

Although periodic fluctuations occurred, the cost of shipping freight from Dalton to Albany, Troy, or Hudson City in the 1820s and 1830s amounted to about .375 cents per hundred pounds. Since the cost of transportation to Pittsfield, Adams, Williamstown, and Hancock was the same, it seems likely that this figure was standard for trips within a certain radius, and I have used it to compute costs from Lee to Hudson City. Zenas Crane Daybook, 1824–29, CA; David Carson Daybook, 1828–34, CA; Zenas Crane Journal, 1825–30, CA; Zenas Crane Journal, 1829–41, CA.

the line three miles to West Stockbridge village. In 1838 this rail connection lowered paper mills' teaming expenses by two-thirds.[4]

Three years later, on August 4, 1841, the superintendent of Crane & Co.'s Old Red Mill inscribed important local news alongside routine records of workers' hours and the mill's paper output. "First Locomotive on the Western Railroad in Dalton," he noted, capitalizing all of the important words. The completion of this line to Boston gave Berkshire paper mill owners their first inexpensive winter route to a seaport and their first fast passenger service to the hub of New England commerce. Five years later the Western completed a connecting line to Adams and North Adams.[5]

Mill owners quickly capitalized on improved transportation to Boston. In 1839 and 1840, when shipments to Boston still traveled slowly or circuitously, the Chamberlin family received three-quarters of Dalton's Defiance Mill's orders from New York customers and less than one-quarter from New England. Between 1844 and 1847 the railroad enabled George Platner and Elizur Smith of Lee, who operated the same Dalton mill, to ship about one-third of their orders to New England, reducing New York's share to about one-half. Likewise, whereas Zenas Crane had sold virtually all of his paper in New York, between 1844 and 1849 Z. M. and J. B. Crane, his sons, recorded more than twice as many New England as New York orders. L. L. Brown of Adams, whose mill began operating in 1849, boarded the train with his first lot of paper and personally displayed it to Boston paper merchants. He evidently received a warm welcome. Between 1853 and 1855 L. L. Brown & Co. sold to New England paper merchants three times as frequently as to New Yorkers.[6]

For the county as a whole, however, trade with New York remained preeminent. In 1847 an all-season route to the metropolis opened when Connecticut's Housatonic Railroad extended its track to West Stockbridge. Three years later, in 1851, the Pittsfield and Stockbridge Railroad linked the Housatonic Railroad to the Western and gave Lee and Lenox paper makers local railroad depots. Their experience motivated Lee's leading paper makers during the 1860s and 1870s to seek state support for two additional railroads, designed to provide convenient freight service for the many paper

---

[4] Smith, *Housatonic*, p. 270; Crane & Co. Journal, 1840–, CA.

[5] Crane & Co. Time Book, 1836–48, CA, 8/4/41; Child, *Gazeteer*, part 1, pp. 55–58; Smith, *Housatonic*, pp. 271–75.

[6] Ledger of the Aetna, Housatonic, and Defiance Mill, 1839–47, BWP; Crane & Co. Ledger, 1844–49, CA; Blaine S. Britton, *The History of Paper Merchandising in New York City* (New York, 1939), p. 56; L. L. Brown & Co. Ledger, 1853–55, LLBP.

mills in East and South Lee, Tyringham, and Mill River, but to no avail. The county's rail network (Figure 5.1) was completed in 1875, when twenty years of work on the Hoosac Tunnel culminated in the opening of the Troy and Greenfield Railroad through northern Berkshire.[7]

Railroads helped expand Berkshire markets for paper by reducing the prices mill owners had to charge to cover their costs. In addition to eliminating expensive horse-drawn wagon cartage, steady improvements in rail service and competition between lines lowered freight charges. Whereas mill owners paid eight to twenty-four cents per ton mile in the 1840s, by 1865 their freight rate had fallen to four and a half cents. More immediate and substantial savings accrued to manufacturers as railroads eliminated the expense of building inventories at commission houses and at the mills in anticipation of each snowbound winter. In fact, improved transportation combined with machine production and telegraphic communication to reduce inventory requirements throughout the year. By 1848 the *New York Journal of Commerce* could report to its readers:

> We were informed a few days since, by a large paper dealer in New York, that it was not uncommon for him to have in his warehouse, and sell at nine o'clock in the morning, paper which was in *rags* a hundred and fifty miles from New York at nine o'clock of the previous morning. . . . The telegraph enables New York merchants to order paper in Massachusetts at any moment, and receive the returns, manufactured, and even ruled, by almost the next steamer.[8]

New paper mill construction offers tangible evidence that good rail service motivated mill owners to invest. Berkshire paper makers built sixteen new mills between 1848 and 1857, the first decade after most towns had railroad depots. By comparison, they had opened nine new establishments from 1827 through 1837 and eleven from 1838 through 1847. Among the new entrants was Lee wagon builder Samuel A. Hulbert, the leading promoter of the Pittsfield

---

[7] Hyde, *History of Lee*, pp. 266–70; Child, *Gazeteer*, part 1, pp. 55–58; Smith, *Housatonic*, pp. 271–75.

Lee paper manufacturers even succeeded in getting town voters to subscribe to the stock of these railroads. The active role of paper manufacturers in promoting these and other, more successful, railroads and in continuing to serve on their boards is chronicled in great detail in the local press.

[8] William T. Davis, ed., *The New England States: Their Constitutional, Judicial, Educational, Professional and Industrial History*, 4 vols. (Boston, 1897), 4:1813; Weeks, *History of Paper Manufacturing*, p. 194.

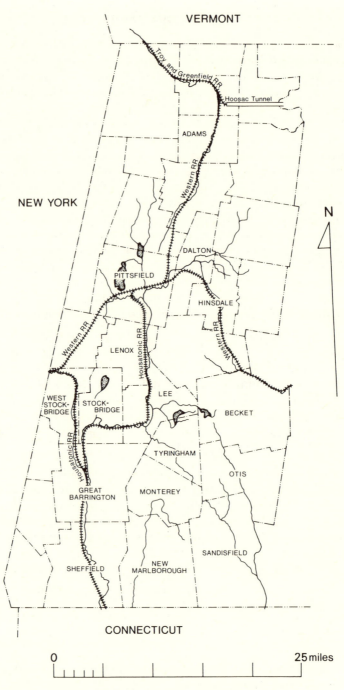

Fig. 5.1 Berkshire County railroad network.

and Stockbridge Railroad. He invested in a Lee paper mill the same year his railroad linked Lee to New York, acting on his conviction that railroads ensured local industrial growth. Four years later a credit reporter for R. G. Dun & Co. characterized the Lee paper industry of the early railroad era when he reported of Chaffee and Baird, Lee jewelers, "They have the Lee Mania & have purchased a paper mill." Established paper manufacturers such as the Cranes of Dalton, Owen and Hurlbut of South Lee, Platner and Smith of Lee, and Benton and Garfield of East Lee all built additional mills in the 1850s. While mills proliferated in older paper-making towns, paper manufacture also spread to Adams, Housatonic, Otis, Sandisfield, Stockbridge, and West Stockbridge after 1848. During the same years, as Figure 5.2 suggests, railroads permitted mill owners to enlarge existing mills.[9]

Stimulated by the railroad, New York and Boston's rapidly growing commerce assured expanded markets for Berkshire's traditional product, fine writing paper. Also, after 1850 revised postage rates based on weight, rather than number of sheets, boosted consumer demand for thin writing paper and created a market for envelopes. More important, cheaper machine-made, railroad-borne paper combined with improved printing technology to foster popular journalism, creating a new paper-buying constituency to support the new mills. By 1833 Napier presses, manufactured by Hoe & Company of New York, had reduced printing costs sufficiently that New York publishers introduced the penny press to Jacksonian Americans. Shortly thereafter, the use of steam power lowered printing costs further and popular journalism spread to Philadelphia, Boston, and Baltimore. But it especially flourished in New York, where editors founded a dozen penny dailies between 1833 and 1837. Abetting the concentration of journalism in major metropolitan centers was Hoe's 1847 "lightning" press which quadrupled the output of the original Napier, but cost between $20,000 and $25,000. Lowered postal rates for newspapers also subsidized the huge circulations of the urban dailies. New York dailies, including the *Herald*, the world's largest, with a circulation of 77,000 in 1860, and New York weeklies, including the *Tribune*, with a circulation of 200,000, bought their paper in Lee, fueling the "Lee Mania"

[9] See Appendix A; Hyde, *History of Lee*, pp. 266–67; R. G. Dun & Co. Ledgers, Dun and Bradstreet Collection, BL, 3:139. Dun's handwritten credit reports routinely employ abbreviations, generally omitting vowels (e.g., "gd" for good). Rather than bracket the many omitted letters that I have filled in, quotations here and elsewhere from the Dun records simply spell out the words.

Fig. 5.2 Carsons' paper wrapper of 1849. This ream wrapper symbolically links the enlarged Old Berkshire Mill and its paper-making machine to the local railroad. Courtesy of the Crane Museum.

for building paper mills and purchasing paper-making machines.[10]

At the same time, the American population grew rapidly. Moreover, public education fostered literacy and better-lighted homes facilitated evening reading so that the market for books and periodicals grew more rapidly than did the population. Stimulated by

[10] Pred, *Urban Growth*, passim; Samuel Carter III, *Cyrus Field: Man of Two Worlds* (New York, 1968), p. 77; Frank Luther Mott, *American Journalism: A History of Newspapers in the United States through 260 Years: 1690–1950* (New York, 1959), pp. 220–52, 303–6, 314–16; WPA Guide, 143; Hyde, *History of Lee*, p. 290.

democratic politics, reform crusades, and sensational reporting, Americans supported both urban dailies and smaller newspapers throughout the country, tripling the number between 1833 and 1860. In Berkshire County, for example, twelve newspapers were published in the 1840s, whereas six had sufficed in the 1820s. Likewise, books proliferated. Between 1820 and 1850 the number of new American novels doubled every ten years and gross receipts of the book trade multiplied five times. Magazine journalism offered an equally fast-growing market. Periodicals other than newspapers multiplied six times between 1825 and 1850.[11]

The expanded and increasingly specialized journalism that paid for investments in paper-making machines simultaneously supplied mill owners with information they needed when deciding to buy machines. The subscription list maintained by Z. M. and J. B. Crane in 1848, for example, kept them abreast of technical improvements, business conditions, and the legal and political climate. From New York came the *Scientific American*, with its regular descriptions of newly patented machines, and the *New York Journal of Commerce*, which specialized in Wall Street reports and merchants' activities. The *Bankers Magazine and State Financial Register*, published in the same city, offered news of special concern to bank note paper makers, kept paper manufacturers posted on the period's frequent financial crises, and occasionally even noticed improved paper-making technology, such as dandy rolls for watermarking bank note paper. The Cranes also took the *New York Legal Observer*, which reported the numerous court cases defining business law in nineteenth-century America. To balance the Democratic *Journal of Commerce*, the brothers read New York's largest political newspaper, Thurlow Weed's *Albany Evening Journal*. As businessmen affected by Massachusetts legislation and Boston markets, they also bought New England's leading Whig newspaper, the *Boston Semi-Weekly Atlas*. Finally, because they lived in a predominantly agricultural nation and because they, like many local mill owners, operated a farm to feed the company's draft horses, they purchased the *Boston Cultivator*.[12]

[11] Child, *Gazeteer*, part 1, pp. 58–66; Mary Kelley, *Private Woman, Public Stage: Literary Domesticity in Nineteenth-Century America* (New York, 1984), pp. 10–12; Frank Luther Mott, *A History of American Magazines, 1741–1850* (Cambridge, Mass., 1939), pp. 341–42.

[12] They also subscribed to several local newspapers and to several magazines for their wives and children. "Magazines—Newspapers—Periodicals, 1845–1859," CMF; File 8, CMF, 7/14/53. I have relied on Mott for a summary of periodical content. The Cranes' subscription lists in other years were similar, except for increasing

Essentially these magazines and newspapers gave hinterland manufacturers, such as Berkshire paper makers, access to the vastly superior informational networks that developed in early nineteenth-century New York and, to a lesser degree, Boston and Albany. Berkshire mill owners' more frequent visits to their urban customers, made possible by the railroads, must have functioned similarly. Indeed, if Harrison Smith of Lee is representative, mill owners found it easier to convey technical information orally. Writing in 1853, Smith prefaced a dye formula with the apology "I should have given it to you before now but I expected to come up that way and I can talk about colors better than I can write."[13]

Unfortunately, the oral transmission of information has left little historical evidence, but scattered clues in mill owners' correspondence indicate that urban sales trips helped manufacturers obtain technical information. For example, the Laflins' 1834 inquiry about Coleman Sellers's calender rolls gave a New York return address, suggesting that they learned about the Philadelphian's innovation while visiting New York clients. Information traveled from Philadelphia to New York far more rapidly and frequently than to any other American city or town, making news from America's earliest paper-making center readily available in New York. Similarly, an 1859 letter shows that New York encounters between Massachusetts mechanics and mill owners could result in machine purchases. Z. M. Crane notified the Worcester firm of Goddard, Rice & Co., "You may proceed to make the rag boiler as Mr. Goddard gave me the terms for in New York the other day." One can also imagine paper manufacturers from different regions meeting one another at New York paper warehouses or hotels and swapping technical information. Mill owners' letters relaying information that "I promised you" evidently followed earlier conversations. In addition, paper merchants probably overheard manufacturers' discussions and passed on technical and business news to their regular suppliers. Like paper merchant Cyrus W. Field, many were equipped by paper mill work experience to perform such a role.[14]

---

numbers of antislavery and Republican publications. L. L. Brown Company records for the entire period 1849–85 document similar periodical subscriptions. For the year 1871 Byron Weston's receipts show a variety of newspapers and trade publications as well as the *Journal of Chemistry*, the *American Agriculturalist*, the *Congregationalist*, and *Harpers*. Correspondence to Byron Weston, 1871, BWP.

[13] Pred, *Urban Growth*, pp. 202–4, 239–71; McGaw, "Sources and Impact," pp. 173–74; File 566, CMF, 4/19/53.

[14] Coleman Sellers Letter Book, 1828–34, APS, 4/28/34; Pred, *Urban Growth*, passim; File 278, CMF, 1/5/59. References to New York visits and meeting other mill

Between 1827 and 1857, then, railroads lowered the cost of doing business with New York and Boston, and urban commerce and journalism gave Berkshire mill owners ample incentive to expand paper production. At the same time, the concentration of paper sales and of publishing in New York and a few other cities speeded the diffusion of commercial and technical information, lowering the risks of business decision making. These developments encouraged mechanization, but did not bring it about. Ultimately the transformation of the paper industry depended on the mill owners.

MUTUALLY MADE MEN

The men and women who gathered in the Lee Congregational Church on May 24, 1855, certainly appreciated the benefits that the railroad, the paper-making machine, and the new journalism had conferred on the town. In contrast to the community of farmers who had gathered to raise the church fifty-five years earlier, the congregation included large numbers of paper workers and paper mill owners, together with the machinists, construction workers, and tradesmen who supplied them with goods and services. Seated prominently among the local church members were the leading beneficiaries of the New York market—the members of the recently organized Association of Berkshire Manufacturers.[15]

Their success had costs as well as benefits. On this occasion the Reverend Nahum Gale did not mount the pulpit to offer thanks for the manifest blessings of the machine age. Members of the manufacturers' association had gathered to mourn the death of their first president, forty-four-year-old paper maker George Platner, and they listened solemnly as Gale reminded them of the risks accompanying the new technology. "Presume not on length of days," he warned.

> The burdens of business life are increased by the intense activity, the unsettled policy, and the rapid changes of our young, and, it must be confessed, too reckless country. Casualties are multiplied. The burning steamer, and the crashing car, are fearfully common.[16]

---

owners are scattered throughout the extensive mill owner correspondence in the Byron Weston Papers and the Crane Museum Files. Carter, *Cyrus Field*, pp. 47–50, 53–54, 58–59, 77; "Cyrus W. Field," CMF; Britton, *Paper Merchandising*, passim.

[15] Hyde, *History of Lee*, pp. 230–31; the Rev. Nahum Gale, *Remarks at the Funeral of George W. Platner, Esq., at Lee, May 24, 1855* (Pittsfield, Mass., 1855), p. 3.

[16] Gale, *Funeral Remarks*, p. 15.

Many a paper mill owner would have agreed wholeheartedly. The decades since 1827 had been both a time of opportunity and a time of trial. Financial panics punctuated the years between 1827 and 1857, periodically dulling the market for paper. Although the rapidly growing paper market had encouraged 136 men to invest in paper mills, only 70, slightly more than half, managed to own a mill for as long as ten years. Even of those 70, 8 failed or suspended payment on their debts during the period. Although Berkshire mill owners had access to more and better information, they extended credit to distant and unfamiliar customers and they relied heavily on rapidly changing machine technology. Both entailed risks that paper makers could not anticipate. Because improved transportation had prompted their risk taking, Gale's choice of the steamboat and the railroad to symbolize the dangers inherent in contemporary business life must have struck some listeners as especially appropriate.[17]

As fate would have it, 1855 was a propitious time for Gale to issue his warning, but an unlikely time for him to capture the manufacturers' attention. In 1855 prosperity hid the fact that some apparently successful paper mill owners were among those reckless men Gale cautioned. For example, most prominent among those gathered to honor their brother paper maker was Elizur Smith (Figure 5.3), Platner's partner and also owner, with Platner's widow, Adeline, of six Lee paper mills. Credit reporters later characterized Smith as "a bold operator" who "runs great risks." With "a change in the tide," they noted, he "might be swamped."[18]

The tide turned in 1857. The national financial panic spread to

[17] See Appendix A. I have maximized the number of men who managed to own a mill for at least ten years by including men who owned mills for fewer than ten years between 1827 and 1857, but who had owned mills before 1827 or continued to own mills after 1857, a method that also assures that all mill owners were at equal risk of failure even if they purchased their mill late in the period. As long as an individual owned one mill for any ten-year period beginning or ending between 1827 and 1857 he has been deemed a success. Because it is difficult to determine when mills were in operation, at least a few of these "successful" mill owners probably owned an operating mill for less than ten years. In a few instances, information on the dates at which mills were built or changed hands is contradictory. In these cases, I have estimated length of ownership by taking the maximum number of years a mill owner might have owned the mill and the minimum number of years of ownership and averaging the two figures. Finally, George Platner's widow, Adeline, was the only female mill owner during the period. She continued in partnership with Smith for five years only because her husband's will required it and she took no active part in the business. Thus, I will consistently refer to the "men" who owned mills and employ masculine pronouns.

[18] R. G. Dun & Co. Ledgers, 3:272.

Fig. 5.3 Elizur Smith (1812–89). Smith owned
six early mechanized mills, failed in 1857, and became
Lee's most successful paper maker after 1865.
Courtesy of Lee Library.

the Berkshires as readily as had national prosperity and lingered as
what was commonly called "the depression in the writing paper
trade." The firm of Platner & Smith failed in 1857. Another Lee mill
remained closed from the previous year, and owners of seven additional mills failed, suspended payment, or shut down perma-
nently between 1857 and 1861. Only nine of the town's twenty-two
mills remained solvent and open throughout these years. In the
county as a whole, three mills stood locked as 1857 dawned and
twenty more failed, shut down, or suspended payment within five
years, totaling exactly half of all Berkshire paper mills.[19]

What made paper manufacturers in the years between 1827 and

[19] Laflin, "Address to Writing Paper Maker's," CMF, p. 1; Appendix A.

1857 able to seize the opportunities offered by expanding markets and willing to run the risks of depending on rapidly changing machine technology and a jerry-built credit system? The following pages find the answer not in the mill owners' skills and assets, but in their kin and associates. The unsettled conditions of these decades called forth a new breed of mill owner. Unlike their predecessors of the handmade paper era, who had prospered by demonstrating personal paper-making skill, the men who enlarged and mechanized the paper industry were not self-made men. They worked hard and saved their money, but they could turn for help to a host of family members and friends. Nor were they the highly competitive individuals conjured up by classical economic theory. They survived primarily because they could enlist and retain the experience and capital of other men—their brother mill owners.

Before turning to the survivors and their strategies for survival, let me emphasize, as did the Reverend Mr. Gale, that, whatever a man's intellectual, financial, or social assets, luck or providence played a part in his success or failure. Credit reporters repeatedly acknowledged this truth when they began assessing paper makers' prospects during these decades. In 1848, for example, the report on Ezra Heath and Joshua Boss, proprietors of Tyringham's Bay State Mill, noted their modest capital, apparent industriousness, and limited experience. It concluded, they "are hard pressed, if the times are favorable they will go through." Unfortunately, European political and economic turmoil disrupted American commercial centers that year. Heath and Boss failed. Certainly limited capital and inexperience in paper making did not help, but the failure of Heath and Boss resulted primarily from their having entered the business in 1846, several years before the prolonged economic recovery that lasted into the mid-fifties. By contrast, Orton Heath of East Lee, with equally modest capital and limited waterpower, survived for fifteen years despite the fact that he "had a very unfortunate affair with a woman other than his wife," with the result that "he left the state" and needed "others [to] transact business" for him. Heath, however, had the good luck to have entered paper making in 1849. Cushioned by six years of prosperity, his hasty flight in 1855 did not prove his undoing.[20]

Statistical evidence makes the same statement in more general terms. Between 1827 and 1857 the mechanizing paper industry's

[20] R. G. Dun & Co. Ledgers, 3:240, 142; Douglass C. North, *The Economic Growth of the United States, 1790–1860* (Englewood Cliffs, N.J., 1961), pp. 208–9.

tremendous opportunities attracted numerous new investors, some with experience, some with capital, but many with neither. At the same time, the growing industry's enormous technical and economic risks made every man's success uncertain. Under these conditions, if we apply a statistical test, Lambda$_b$, which measures our ability to guess an outcome—success or failure—once we know whether or not an individual possessed various skills, assets, or associates, we find that even the best predictors listed in Table 5.1 yield relatively modest success probabilities. Data on commercial experience, outside manufacturing experience, and financial resources do not even show statistically significant differences in the success of the men who possessed them. In sum, as long as papermaking technology, capital requirements, paper and raw material prices, and customers' financial responsibility remained unpredictable, mill owners' greatest assets conferred only modest advantages. No man could be certain of success and no man's chances could be utterly discounted.[21]

Personal paper-making skill remained important, but became less essential to success after mills began installing machines. Before 1827 eight of the nine mill owners who had trained as paper makers remained in business ten or more years, making them nearly three times (2.87) as likely to succeed as men without paper mill training. Between 1827 and 1857, trained paper makers who owned mills succeeded 78 percent of the time, but 50 percent of those with no such training also succeeded. Thus, possession of paper-making skill made a man only half again (1.56 times) more likely to succeed. Skilled paper mill owners remained about as common during mechanization as before it (37 percent versus 40 percent), so their relative abundance does not explain their diminished achievement.[22]

Knowledge of paper making was, nonetheless, the only preparation that reduced a man's chances of failing. Neither commercial training nor general manufacturing experience enhanced a paper

[21] Throughout the ensuing discussion I will define success as staying in business for ten or more years (see n. 17 for method of calculation). No definition of success is ideal for this tempestuous financial era. Declaring bankruptcy and closing temporarily are less satisfactory measures of failure than is brief total life span, because a number of the county's long-term successes experienced such reverses, and renegotiating indebtedness after failure was fairly common in this era of jerry-built credit systems. Therefore, defining success as longevity seems most satisfactory. It also focuses attention on the group of men who made far more of the machine purchase decisions. Nonetheless, a few individuals who died or left the Berkshires to become successful mill owners elsewhere are inevitably included among the failures.

[22] See Appendix B.

TABLE 5.1
PAPER MILL OWNERS, 1827–57: EXPERIENCE, ASSETS,
ASSOCIATES, AND SUCCESS

Attribute	% Successful with Attribute	% Successful without Attribute	Lambda$_b$	Level of Significance (Chi square)
Paper mill experience	78	50	.00	.01
Commercial experience	64	59	.00	.70
Other manufacturing experience	55	62	.00	.70
Financial resources	62	54	.00	.50
Paper mill trained partners	70	42	.14	.01
Commercially trained partners	66	47	.04	.10
Relatives owning paper mills	69	42	.09	.02

NOTE: Appendix B summarizes the sources and liabilities of the information on which this table is based. It also supplies the more detailed numeric data on which statistical tests were performed and numbers of mill owners for whom data concerning a particular attribute was not available.

Lambda$_b$ is a statistic that measures our ability to guess an outcome (success or failure) once we know whether or not an individual possessed a particular attribute. Its potential values range from 1 (perfect prediction) to 0 (no predictive value).

The Chi square test indicates whether we can reject the null hypothesis (that there was no difference between men with and without a particular characteristic). Values presented here are the levels at which the null hypothesis can be rejected. For example, a difference significant at the .01 level indicates that the distribution would occur by chance less than one time in one hundred, so that it seems safe to reject the null hypothesis, whereas significance levels of .5 and .7 indicate that the distribution would occur nearly 50 and 70 percent of the time, thus we are in a poor position to reject the null hypothesis.

mill owners' probability of success. About two-fifths (39 percent) of paper manufacturers between 1827 and 1857 had worked in general stores, banks, paper warehouses, or other commercial institutions. By comparison, only one-fifth (22 percent) of hand mill owners had previous commercial training. The change reflected both the growing number of local commercial establishments and the increased call for accounting and marketing skills in mechanizing mills. As Table 5.1 indicates, however, those with skill in commerce succeeded only slightly more frequently (1.08 times) than those without.[23]

As in the hand paper-making days, relatively few men who owned mills between 1827 and 1857 turned from other manufactures to making paper. Men with prior manufacturing experience made up one-quarter (27 percent) of hand mill owners and one-fifth (21 percent) of the mechanizers. Table 5.1 suggests that their knowledge of machine building, tanning, cotton and woolen manufacture, or powder mill operation did not increase their probability of success. They were slightly more likely to fail (1.13 times) than those without other manufacturing experience. In at least some instances, expectations derived from success in a markedly different enterprise may have contributed to failure as a paper maker. Heath and Boss, for example, had operated a rake factory that also manufactured spools. Conditioned to supplying local textile mills and farmers, these men were probably ill-prepared to adjust to a treacherous commercial market.[24]

Just as they did not require training in manufacturing or commerce, the men who successfully mechanized the Berkshire paper industry did not have to be rich. Mill capitalization mounted gradually and averaged only $28,147 by 1855. Credit reporters frequently mentioned that successful mill owners "began years ago on very small means, and by hard work and industry became wealthy" (Caleb Benton and Harrison Garfield of Lee) or that a paper maker "earn[ed] his food by the sweat of his brow—. . . made all his money by his own labor" (John Carroll of New Marlborough).[25]

Quantitative evidence tells the same tale. Two-fifths of all mill owners in the period began with "little or nothing," to borrow a favorite phrase of credit reporters. Only one-fourth (26 percent) had wealthy families behind them. One-third (33 percent) had accumulated capital in real estate or substantial business ventures before investing in paper mills. All three groups met remarkably similar fates as mill owners. Although those with family financial backing had most success and those with no resources had least, men from wealthy families avoided failure only slightly (1.2 times) more often than those with no initial capital.[26]

[23] See Appendix B.

[24] R. G. Dun & Co. Ledgers, 3:240; Eloise Myers, *A Hinterland Settlement* (n.p., n.d.), p. 30.

[25] *Massachusetts Census, 1855*, pp. 21–63; R. G. Dun & Co. Ledgers, 3:131, 160, 162.

[26] See Appendix B for a detailed breakdown of successful and unsuccessful owners by known financial assets. The distinction between those with capital and those with

All this confirms what Jacksonian Americans frequently argued: that a man did not need wealth or experience to succeed. But the careers of Berkshire paper manufacturers do not support another contemporary conviction: that a man could succeed with little more than hard work and clean living. Although a mill owner's partners or relatives did not assure his success, we shall see that virtually no manufacturer lasted ten years without the advantage of advice from mill-owning relatives or partners trained in commerce or paper making. By contrast, men with all three sources of information almost always succeeded. The reason lies in the distinctive economic and technological climate prevailing in antebellum America. Whereas volatile business and technical conditions rendered experience and wealth relatively unimportant, they made good current business and technical information crucial. Faced with rapidly changing machines and markets, the mill owner who maximized his access to timely information had the best chance of succeeding, for the paper maker whose associates supplied numerous and perceptive assessments of new machines, potential customers, and trends in paper and rag prices ran less risk of erring in daily decision making.

Between 1827 and 1857, successful mill owners acquired more and better technical and business reports by associating with other paper manufacturers. First, when they lacked experience themselves, they sought partners trained in paper making. Skilled paper maker partners could supply informed assessments of new machines. They also maintained ties with mentors and former co-workers experienced in paper manufacture and attuned to new technical developments in the industry. Second, when they lacked commercial training, mill owners selected partners with commercial experience. This assured them better information from company accounts, an informed perspective on developing markets, and continuing lines of communication to mentors and former co-workers in the commercial community. Finally, Berkshire paper manufacturers often had relatives who owned paper mills and they exchanged frequent, candid reports of technology and business with their kinsmen. A look at each of these networks reveals how they lowered a manufacturer's risk of failure.

So many new men entered the paper industry after 1826 that a

---

little or nothing is generally borrowed from credit reporters. Where specific property is mentioned, small commercial establishments and personal residences have been considered worth little or nothing. Occasional valuations confirm this assessment.

large number lacked paper-making experience. In Lee, the local newspaper reported that "for many years" Caleb Benton, who bought his mill in 1831, "and two other gentlemen were the only resident manufacturers who were practical paper makers." Nonetheless, only a minority of paper mill owners risked manufacturing without the aid of skilled associates. Although slightly more than one-third (37 percent) of all paper mill owners started out with mill training, a larger group benefited from their skill. Two-thirds of all mill owners belonged to partnerships that included at least one experienced man.[27]

Many initially unskilled mill owners achieved technical proficiency under the tutelage of skilled partners. For example, in 1824 Stephen Thatcher, former farm laborer, turnpike laborer and overseer, and wire and chair manufacturer, invested in a Lee paper mill with Zenas Crane and Crane's skilled employee William Van Bergan. Van Bergan, who probably received a working interest, must have gone to Lee to superintend operations, for his name disappears from Crane's time book in 1824 and he received cash in 1826 that Crane debited to Stephen Thatcher and Company. By 1827 Thatcher had learned enough to continue on his own. He bought out his partners and Van Bergan returned to work for Crane. A few years later, Thatcher brought his inexperienced son-in-law, Jared Ingersoll, into the business. After attaining proficiency under Thatcher, Ingersoll went on to participate in several other paper mill partnerships in Lee and Tyringham and to a subsequent career selling paper mill sizing. Later, Byron Weston's correspondence identified additional unskilled investors who remained dependent on their skilled partners for mill supervision and assessment of new technology.[28]

Having a skilled partner enhanced a mill owner's prospects of staying in business. Men who formed partnerships that included trained paper makers succeeded one and two-thirds times as frequently as men who lacked skilled partners. In fact, this figure probably understates the advantages of associating with skilled men. At least some mill owners succeeded without skilled partners by hiring highly skilled associates. For example, in 1856 Becket farmer Prentiss Chaffee hired Ashbel Childs, an experienced paper maker, both

[27] VG, 3/1/66, p. 2.

[28] Hyde, History of Lee, pp. 282–83; Zenas Crane Time Book, 1809–36, CA; Zenas Crane Journal, 1825–30, CA, 1/8/26, 10/17/26; Brown & Weston Letter Book, 1863–64, BWP, 12/1/63, 12/5/63, 12/15/63; Byron Weston Letter Book, 1867–68, BWP, 4/13/68, 9/16/68.

to superintend the mill and to transfer his knowledge to Chaffee's son, George. George Chaffee later assumed Childs's position. As a result, although Prentiss Chaffee lacked both mill training and skilled partners, he operated a Lee paper mill for twenty-five years.[29]

In a period of rapidly changing technology, but nascent technical journalism, men with paper-making experience gave their partners or employers access to the best source of current technical information—other paper makers. They corresponded with or visited former employers and former fellow employees, exchanging news of technical and economic developments. Because machine shops produced various versions of paper mill machines between 1827 and 1857, the more different machines a mill owner had good current assessments of, the more he reduced his risks of choosing a less satisfactory model. Moreover, because paper-making machinery still required considerable human intervention to make it operate properly, mills whose owners could discuss operating problems with and solicit advice from many other mill owners and workers must have run much more efficiently.[30]

Most experienced Berkshire paper mill owners had trained or worked locally so that they had a large number of ties to former employers and co-workers at readily accessible Berkshire County mills. Lee mill owners Ira Van Bergan and William Van Bergan, Adams mill owner L. L. Brown, Dalton mill owner James Wilson, and Pittsfield mill owner Thomas Colt all had trained in Crane family mills. John Carroll, who owned and operated two New Marlborough mills, and Harrison Smith, owner of a Lee mill, had probably either apprenticed with or worked for the Cranes. Lee mill owners Caleb Benton, Matthew Field, George W. Linn, Joseph Kroh, S. S. May, and Elizur Smith had all trained or labored in Lee paper mills. Linn had also gained experience in a Tyringham mill and in a mill in Ancram, New York, operated by George Platner and Platner's brother. George W. West had learned his trade in one Tyringham mill before buying shares in another Tyringham mill and in a Lee mill. Platner and Smith had employed and probably trained Robert McDowell

[29] See Appendix B; Hyde, *History of Lee*, p. 297; *VG*, 3/2/71, p. 2; Appendix A. In 1872 George Chaffee joined with two Lee druggists in a successful partnership at the Glendale (Stockbridge) paper mill. His father, Prentiss, had evidently mastered paper making by that time. He continued on his own until 1881.

[30] Collections of paper mill correspondence in Berkshire archives contain extensive evidence of communications networks between mill owners, including those between former employer and employee and former fellow workers. Chapter 6 offers a number of references to such correspondence, as do the ensuing paragraphs.

before he joined a Monterey paper mill partnership. In addition, ten paper mill owners' sons had learned the business in their fathers' mills before becoming mill owners themselves.[31]

Experienced paper makers transmitted a variety of information through their informal communications networks. For example, in 1851 Oscar Crane, a paper worker employed by a Gardner, Massachusetts, mill, wrote to the Carson brothers, whose father he had known during his apprenticeship in Dalton. He reported that he had heard about their new Fourdrinier from mutual friends in the paper machine manufacturing center of Worcester. He had experience with the machine and he offered his services in getting the new contrivance running properly. He then relayed the local technical news: "There is nothing new here excepting a Cylinder Bleach and they don't like it—and some machines for cleaning stock that does the thing right up." Thomas Colt, who probably had worked in Dalton, but acquired much of his experience while renting the Cranes' Ballston Spa, New York, mill, penned a number of lengthy and discursive letters indicating that he swapped information with both the Cranes and the Carsons. For example, in 1849 he wrote to Zenas Marshal Crane:

> *Driving* the mill without deteriorating the quality of the paper. Isn't this the secret of making manufacturing profitable?
>
> Excuse me if I trouble you too much. But it gives me pleasure to tell you of the bright *streaks*, since I have told you of so many dark ones. It seems to me that if any Paper Mill is making money, ours must be. Don't ask how much, for I have a great dread of *counting chickens before they are hatched*.

He also acknowledged his dependence on Dalton mill owners for machines and technical information:

> And about the Ruling Machine. Had we better wait for Ames' movements with your patent. We have 6 or 7 reams between

[31] See Appendix B. Although R. G. Dun & Co. records and other sources cited in Appendix B frequently inform the reader that an individual trained in a paper mill, the name or even the location of the mill is rarely reported. Thus, available information probably understates the density of the network of ties. Excluding mill owners' sons, we know the training grounds or former workplaces of nineteen men. Other than the fifteen who worked or trained in the Berkshires, one trained in Winsted, Connecticut, one in Goshen, New York, and one in Worcester, Massachusetts. Another trained in Scotland. In addition, some mill owners who worked or trained in the Berkshires also worked or trained in one or more additional mills. This was true for at least eight, six of whom had previously worked in mills in nearby counties.

calender and ruling machine, the latter running 18 hours a
day. You can judge how badly we want a new machine that will
do the work faster.

I want too to have you send us *as soon as possible* that machine
for turning rolls in the calender. Tom Carson says it worked
well. . . . Tom told me he would lend me the turning tool he had
made. Don't forget that.

Later, after Colt bought a Pittsfield mill a few miles downstream
from the Carsons and Cranes, he probably discussed new technology with them directly.[32]

Naturally, far less evidence remains of the frequent oral communication between former employees and employers who lived in
Berkshire County. Seymour Crane, youngest of Zenas's sons, reported from Ballston Spa that L. L. Brown had visited the mill
there, evidently with the intention of buying it. As a Berkshire resident, it seems likely that Brown originally learned of the New York
mill when talking with his former mentors in Dalton. Likewise, because Lee mill owner S. S. May began his local career as Walter Laflin's foreman, Laflin, retired and living in Pittsfield, probably
acquainted May with the Herkimer, New York, mill that May eventually purchased from Laflin's sons, Byron and Addison. Harrison
Smith explicitly noted that he was relaying a chemical formula because his former employers, the Cranes, had requested it
when visiting his Lee mill. Additional evidence that mill owners
visited one another to acquire technical information appears in
Chapter 6.[33]

In Lee, where mill owners could not avoid meeting former employers and employees on the busy streets, candid oral assessment
of new machines must have been especially common. Mill-trained
paper manufacturers also met their mentors at church, because two
out of three successful mill owners attended Congregational
churches. Although the rigid Sabbatarianism of early mechanizers
may have precluded Sunday discussions of technology, later mill
owners probably compared notes on machines after services ended

[32] Z. M. Crane File, CMF, 7/27/51; File 496, CMF, 4/4/49 and passim. Emphasis in
original.

[33] File 490, CMF, 4/20/49; R. G. Dun & Co. Ledgers, 3:130; *VG*, 2/16/71, p. 2;
Alfred L. Holman, *Laflin Genealogy* (Chicago, 1930), pp. 56, 82; File 278, CMF, 1/5/
59; Appendix B. Even in the 1830s Sabbath-conscious Caroline Laflin felt free to
write love letters to her fiancé, Zenas Marshal Crane, on Sundays, so it seems likely
that some mill owners felt free to discuss business on the Sabbath, at least later in the
period.

and early manufacturers may at least have arranged to meet on Monday. Similarly, ordinations and county Congregational conventions offered occasions for mill owners to visit former acquaintances operating mills elsewhere in the Berkshires. As noted earlier, they also saw one another in New York. In sum, the proximity of most mill owners to their former employers and co-workers created a genuine community of paper makers. Partnerships that included men trained in paper mills gained access to that community.[34]

Although no equivalent community existed among Berkshire men with commercial skills, most mill owners, especially successful ones, made certain that one member of their firm had commercial training. Some of the period's most successful partnerships consisted of only two men: one supervising the manufacturing end of the business while the other tended to marketing and finance. For example, in the twenty-six-year Benton and Garfield partnership, Harrison Garfield drew on his superior education and his earlier meat market experience to supervise sales and purchases, while mill-trained Caleb Benton oversaw production in their four mills. Two other long-term partners, Charles M. Owen and Thomas Hurlbut, both had experience in small stores, but Hurlbut alone had paper mill training. Owen was also far more gregarious and for forty years he specialized in traveling for the company, while Hurlbut superintended their three mills. Likewise, both members of the era's largest firm, Platner & Smith, had experience in commerce and academy educations. But Smith's work for a paper manufacturing concern prepared him to oversee their six mills, while Platner assumed primary responsibility for company finances during their twenty-two-year partnership.[35]

The long duration of these partnerships suggests that good financial accounting and marketing helped enable firms to weather the unpredictable years between 1827 and 1857. Statistical evidence affirms that mill owners generally recognized the increasing need for commercial training. Although less than two-fifths (39 percent) of contemporary mill owners had such training, almost seven-tenths (68 percent) formed partnerships that included men with back-

[34] Appendix B. Data on religious affiliation is available for thirty-three successful mill owners. One was an Episcopalian, one a Baptist, two were Universalists, seven Methodists, and twenty-two Congregationalists. Data on five failures finds three Congregationalists, one Methodist, and one free thinker/spiritualist.

[35] VG, 3/1/66, p. 2; 2/2/71, p. 2; 2/9/71, p. 2; 2/23/71, p. 2; Hyde, History of Lee, p. 295; Scull, Hurlbut, pp. 11, 14; Gale, Funeral Remarks, p. 23; In Memoriam, Hon. Elizur Smith: Funeral Services, Resolutions, Extracts from the Press (Lee, Mass., 1889), p. 23.

grounds in commerce. On the average, access to commercial skill paid off. Two-thirds (66 percent) of the men who had commercial training or commercially trained partners succeeded. More than half (53 percent) of those without failed. In other words, those assured of commercial skills succeeded 1.4 times as frequently as those without them.[36]

Because a mill owner's reputation as credit-worthy and his ability to extend credit judiciously often determined his chances of surviving a financial panic, it is possible to speculate that men with commercial experience tied themselves and their partners into informational networks as essential as those that prior mill training created. In a few cases, commercial ties clearly gave Berkshire mill owners improved access to vital information. For example, in his more than thirty years managing his two Becket mills, Edwin C. Bulkley benefited from his apprenticeship as a clerk for a paper wholesaler. His expertise enabled him to join William C. Dunton in establishing a New York paper merchandising firm, an enterprise they continued to operate throughout their careers as Berkshire paper manufacturers. The partners' commercial activities guaranteed excellent current information about paper customers' credit-worthiness and raw material suppliers' reliability, as well as frequent communication with other paper mill owners. Similarly, Orton Heath's friendship and temporary employment with the New York paper merchants Sturges and Steele helped tide his mill over the crisis his extramarital entanglement created.[37]

Thomas Colt offers another example of success through commercial ties. The son of a leading county banker and state bank examiner, Colt became a director of the Pittsfield National Bank two years after buying his Pittsfield mill. His knowledge of finance and considerable familiarity with local and regional institutions of credit almost certainly contributed to his twenty-two-year success as a paper maker. Similar advantages probably accrued to the ten mill owners who trained in their fathers' mills and learned early how to negotiate with urban paper merchants and keep the company books.[38]

[36] See Appendix B. On accounting methods during the era see Judith A. McGaw, "Accounting for Innovation: Technological Change and Business Practice in the Berkshire County Paper Industry," *T&C* 26 (October 1985).

[37] Britton, *Paper Merchandising*, p. 14; R. G. Dun & Co. Ledgers, 3:290. Bulkley & Dunton's paper merchandising firm also benefited from the partners' experience as mill owners, for the firm increasingly specialized in paper mill supplies.

[38] Child, *Gazeteer*, 1:285; R. G. Dun & Co. Ledgers, 3:189. Colt later became the bank's vice-president. His banking position led to his selection to the boards of numerous county financial, transportation, and manufacturing concerns. *VG*, passim.

Most paper manufacturers, however, gained their commercial experience in modest local retail establishments. Without knowing what careers their fellow clerks and proprietors subsequently followed, it is impossible to estimate the importance of their networks of information. Probably all that many brought to paper mill partnerships was a talent for face-to-face bargaining and a knowledge of double-entry bookkeeping. As competition intensified, their ability to negotiate with customers and suppliers assumed increased importance, and as transactions with distant and unfamiliar paper merchants came to predominate, their bookkeeping skills became more useful.[39]

Business partners had economic incentive to share technical and commercial skills and information, but kinship created an even more reliable bond for most nineteenth-century businessmen. Thus, for many Berkshire paper manufacturers, relatives who also owned paper mills constituted an important asset. Some family members lent financial aid by forming partnerships with one another or by bequeathing family mills. The expertise and outside information relatives made available to each other were equally significant.[40]

Berkshire mill owners between 1827 and 1857 included three sons of Zenas Crane, three of David Carson, one of Charles M. Owen, one of Stephen Thatcher, and two of Warren Wheeler, a New Marlborough paper manufacturer. Each of these sons had the advantage of mastering the paper business, in both its technical and commercial aspects, while working in his father's mill. Later, these sons assumed increasing responsibility for mill supervision and marketing trips, repaying their aging fathers with information as well as with their energy. Nephews and sons-in-law developed similar relationships with uncles and fathers-in-law.[41]

The relationship could also be reversed, with younger family members contributing the initial paper-making expertise. Textile

[39] One indication that firms with commercial skills learned through their extensive commercial communications networks is a letter Owen & Hurlbut sent to other writing paper manufacturers suggesting, in 1852, that discussions of overproduction were in order. Owen had been marketing paper in New York for thirty years by that date, longer than any other Berkshire manufacturer, and this probably accounts for his identification of the need for action five years earlier than most paper manufacturers acknowledged it. File 420, CMF, 6/1/52.

[40] Johnson, *Shopkeeper's Millennium*, pp. 25–31. Clyde and Sally Griffen, "Family and Business in a Small City: Poughkeepsie, New York, 1850–1880," *JUH* 1 (May 1975):316–37, make clear that reliance on family members continued into the late nineteenth century, albeit in a somewhat different form.

[41] See Appendices A and B.

manufacturers Daniel and William Jenks, for example, entered a paper-making partnership with their nephew, L. L. Brown, after Brown had mastered the craft. Similarly, George Chaffee shared his paper mill education with his father, Prentiss.[42]

Tied by affection as well as by shared paper-making experience, family members maintained communication networks akin to those between mill owners and former apprentices; as one brother-in-law phrased it in 1847, I am "yours in the bonds of paper making." Such written correspondence reflected a geographic dispersal that gave kin networks knowledge of innovations in other towns or states. Brothers, cousins, or brothers-in-law often owned mills in different Berkshire towns, and also formed partnerships or operated additional mills within the same town. By the late 1840s, as good Berkshire mill sites grew scarce, younger relatives of county mill owners increasingly ventured into the rapidly growing New York State paper industry. Walter Laflin's sons moved to Herkimer; two of David Carson's sons, David and William, relocated to Newburgh; Lindley Murray and Seymour Crane owned or operated mills in Ballston Spa and Saratoga; and their brother-in-law, J. D. Weston, had a mill at Saugerties. Winthrop Laflin also bought a Saugerties mill. Adjacent Hampshire County, Massachusetts, offered additional paper mill sites. Both Elizur Smith's and George Platner's brothers operated mills there and Matthew Field's brother, Cyrus, owned a share of one. Figure 5.4 illustrates the resulting extensive kin networks of Berkshire mill owners both inside and outside the county.[43]

Relatives maintained a level of communication that was more sustained and more detailed than that between former apprentices and their mentors or former co-workers. Because relatives frequently operated mills within easy travel of one another, most family discussions of paper making went unrecorded. The extensive Crane family correspondence documents the commonness of face-to-face interaction even between mill owners in upstate New York and their Berkshire kin. J. D. Weston's 1847 plea to his brother-in-law—"Marshall, I wish you would come down as soon as convenient"—sounds a recurrent theme. For example, an 1849 letter to Dalton from Seymour Crane in Ballston Spa requested: "If Marshall is

[42] See Appendices A and B.

[43] File 497, CMF, 9/2/47. If anything, this discussion understates the density of the network of relatives, because evidence about family ties is not available for many men who owned mills in the period. However, because most family ties between mill owners were between blood relatives, rather than between relatives by marriage, the number of relatives within Berkshire County is probably roughly accurate.

home tell him to come out soon. Murray [brother Lindley Murray of nearby Saratoga] is very anxious to know about his conclusions, etc. He ought to decide something soon so that he can go into business [at the Saratoga Mill]." Similarly, Seymour Crane's cryptic message to his brothers in 1849—"If you learn any thing about the thing let me know"—evidently refers to inside information better left to oral transmission. That same year Addison Laflin reported to his cousin Z. M. Crane, "Father is here [from Pittsfield] & altho' some things go wrong we are doing very well. . . ."—evidence that other paper maker relatives visited and aided one another.[44]

Relatives also tendered advice at a distance. In 1848 Seymour Crane acknowledged: "Murry [sic] gave me Z.M.'s [letter]. We will steep all of the pulp hereafter. . . . We will have to let one of the engines stand more or less for want of water—but then, we won't lose anything by that as we get each one off much quicker than when we wash and beat together." Later, after a lengthy report of technical and commercial plans, he responded to Z.M.'s personal advice: "Marshall writes about my boarding at the village and being [at] the mill. I leave for the mill every morning *right after* breakfast, and stay until five or six—never leave before five and generally *nearer* six— You need not fear about my not being there or not seeing to things." Two years later Seymour replied to continued brotherly advice: "Yours of the 4th came to hand this morning . . . —I gave you particulars of every thing I could think of—That Blower Shaft is no more unsafe than what is occasioned by running upon wooden bearings. The[y] are constantly watched and kept well oiled." Brother Lindley Murray also acknowledged the value of long-distance assistance: "I have had the cutter nearly to pieces in endeavoring to make it cut more square and even. I tried first what Z.M. suggested. I think it cuts better than it did & do not despair of having it eventually right."[45]

Family members who owned paper mills supplemented their technical and managerial counsel with commercial information and advice. Murray Crane, now of Ballston Spa, reported to Z.M. and J.B. in 1860:

> Wednesday I am expecting to go to New York. It is proposed to me by the other tissue makers Hogan & Kenada to advance on the price of our paper. . . . We are to meet in New York next

[44] File 497, CMF, 9/21/47; File 490, CMF, 4/25/49, 3/24/49.

[45] File 489, CMF, 7/4/48; File 490, CMF, 2/4/50; File 452, CMF, 11/22/52. See also File 448, CMF, 7/29/50, and additional letters in each of these files.

FIG. 5.4 Family Ties among Berkshire Paper Mill Owners:
A Partial Portrait

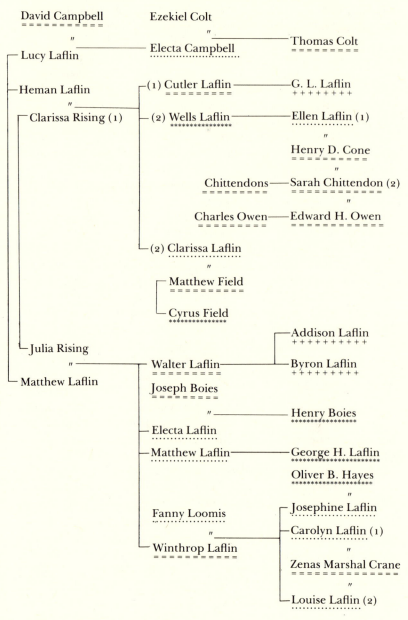

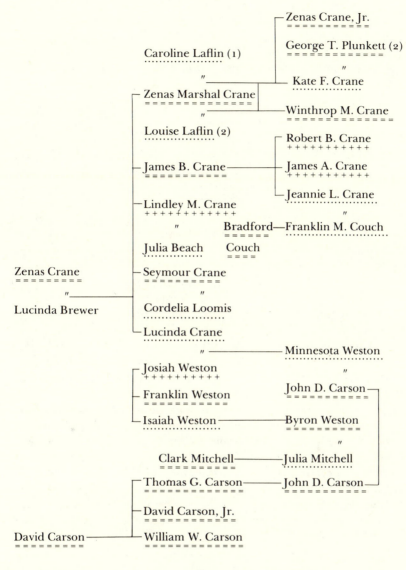

The numerals (1) and (2) indicate that an individual is a first or second spouse, or distinguish offspring of a first and second marriage. Except among the first generation, spouses are shown only when they also owned paper mills or came from paper makers' families. Likewise, mill owners' offspring are included only when they remained connected with the industry.

Thursday to fix a uniform price on the paper and to all so [sic] agree on size and weight, all of which I see no objection to except advancing the price and that objection is—will it not invite others to go into the business. I would like your opinion, write me fully.[46]

The figures presented in Table 5.1 reflect both the obvious benefits of receiving sage counsel and inside information and the less obvious advantages to the adviser of acquiring added experience at a different mill. Nearly seven out of ten (69 percent) mill owners with mill-owning relatives succeeded, whereas less than half (45 percent) of those without family in the business did so. In other words, those with paper-making relatives succeeded half again (1.53 times) as frequently as those without. Moreover, considering only those mill owners who had mill-owning relatives, successful mill owners were supported by more family members funneling them current technical and business information. They averaged 3.29 relatives in the business. Men who failed averaged only 2.24.[47]

If ties to the paper-making and commercial communities through relatives or partners raised an individual's probability of success, links to more than one of these networks multiplied the data he received and further lowered his risk of making bad decisions. Table 5.2 demonstrates as much. Individuals with access to all three networks succeeded almost 85 percent of the time, making them three and one-third times (3.36) more likely to succeed than those with no evident informal sources of information. In fact, it is doubtful that either of the two men who stayed in business despite limited outside advice should be considered a success. One, John Manser, operated a small, unmechanized mill. The other, Perry Green Comstock, survived by operating his mill seasonally with his underemployed farmhands and by producing low-cost, low-quality products such as cardboard boxes for stovepipe hats. Excepting these two mavericks, then, no manufacturer lasted ten years without ties to skilled paper makers, commercially trained men, or mill-owning relatives.[48]

Nonetheless, the data in Table 5.2 caution us that even mill own-

[46] File 453, CMF, 4/27/60. In an era before well-established credit reporting agencies, relatives probably also gave one another commercial support by keeping one another's names and, therefore, credit clear. For example, A. H. Laflin wrote to his cousin, Marshal Crane, in 1849: "Your friend Mr. Moore of Saquoit is doing 'all he knows' to injure us. He has reported sundry statements which reflect most unfavorably upon our prospects. I don't know him. I am exceedingly surprised the manufacturers here in this section [upstate New York] feel so." File 771, CMF, 6/2/49.

[47] See Appendix B.   [48] See Appendix B.

TABLE 5.2
MILL OWNERS' TIES TO INFORMATIONAL NETWORKS,
1827–57

	Successes	Failures	% Successful
Ties to all three	27	5	84
Ties to two	24	18	57
Ties to one	9	8	52
Ties to none	2	8	20
Insufficient information	8	27	—

Lambda$_b$ = .15; level of statistical significance, .01 (Chi square)

ers who maximized their associations with other paper mill owners ran the risk of failure. Paper manufacturing in the dynamic years between 1827 and 1857 was always financially treacherous. Now that we know how mill owners acquired knowledge of new machines and markets, we need to examine why they willingly reinvested their profits.

ACCOUNTING METHODS AND INVESTMENT STRATEGIES

Although an average 1855 paper mill capitalization of $28,147 appears modest by our standards, it meant that paper makers had multiplied their mills' assets at least two and one-half to three and two-thirds times since 1832. In fact, 1855 census figures include several small hand mills, so capital invested in most establishments mounted more dramatically. Furthermore, a number of firms had acquired several mills, so assets per firm grew even faster. Recalling the earlier substantial increases in mill capitalization described in Chapter 3 and embodied in 1832 figures, capital accumulation after 1832 becomes even more impressive. Mill owners achieved this rapid growth in assets primarily by maintaining high rates of reinvestment.[49]

[49] *Massachusetts Census, 1855*, pp. 20–63; *McLane Report*, part 1, pp. 144–45, 156–57. The 1855 figure is what mill owners reported as "capital." What they meant by this term is not entirely clear. If, as seems likely, they included only real estate, machinery, and tools, the figure was 3.67 times the comparable 1832 figure. If their 1855 reports included stock on hand and in process, the 1855 total was 2.57 times the 1832 total.

Such rapid and sustained capital accumulation is a most impressive and distinctive feature of early industrialization. The twentieth-century experience of developing nations has underscored the complexity and difficulty of the feat. Thus, understanding mechanization requires that we consider how and why early nineteenth-century paper makers came to reinvest at high levels. By examining accounting practices and partnership data we can reconstruct the mill owners' perspective on capital accumulation at two distinct stages: First, how did mill owners assess their costs and options in the 1820s, when sustained capital accumulation began? Second, how did they evaluate and preserve their mills' assets in the 1830s, 1840s, and 1850s, when reinvestment became habitual?

Even before the 1820s, some mill owners had acquired the habit of plowing back their profits. This was especially the case for former paper workers who initially needed outside backing, but ultimately sought financial independence. For example, paper worker David Carson twice garnered support from Joseph Chamberlin, a member of Dalton's leading landholding family, and Zenas Crane entered short-term partnerships with several of the Chamberlins as well as with his initial backer, Daniel Gilbert. By the early 1820s, however, both Crane and Carson had bought out their partners and become sole proprietors of mills. They had raised the requisite capital by saving their wages and their shares of mill profits.

When paper making became increasingly profitable in the 1820s, mill owners theoretically had three options: they could increase their consumption, invest their profits in other ventures, or reinvest by expanding and improving their paper mills or buying new ones. In fact, paper manufacturers immediately rejected the first two options. The Calvinist tradition, contemporaneous revivalism, and the economic homogeneity of the population discouraged conspicuous consumption. Mill owners continued to work long hours and to reside near their mills in houses similar to those of their workers. Religious affairs, politics, and business travel kept them busy when not at home or at the mill. At the time, alternative business investments appeared more risky than paper making, primarily because most mill owners lacked experience with other manufactures. Paper making had taught them the importance of technical knowledge to manufacturing success and they could bring such knowledge only to the paper industry. In the years before improved transportation made paper industry growth feasible, they invested only occasionally and briefly in other local industry, putting most profits into real estate near their mills. By the 1820s, when paper production could begin expanding, the local textile industry was still recovering from a severe postwar depression and New England agriculture promised slim returns, making alternative investments even less attractive.[50]

Given their preference for paper industry investments, an analysis of paper mill accounting practices in the 1820s sheds light on the alacrity with which mill owners substituted capital for labor both before and during mechanization. In particular, it helps explain the well-known difference of opinion between nineteenth-century manufacturers and twentieth-century economic historians over factor substitution. With the wisdom of hindsight, economic historians have pointed out the difficulty of substituting capital for labor in the early nineteenth century, especially in America, where capital remained as scarce as labor. By contrast, contemporaries habitually spoke of machine technology as an obvious response to American labor scarcity, ignoring the problem of scarce capital.[51]

Manufacturers' accounts for the years before mechanization suggest how they came to see capital as far more plentiful than labor. During the 1820s paper mill accounting practices supplied little information about either fixed or working capital invested. As a result, manufacturers had no real sense of how much they were plowing back into their businesses. By contrast, they kept full and detailed records of mounting labor costs. Inadequate capital accounting does not explain why manufacturers reinvested; the dearth of acceptable alternatives prompted that decision. But given their decision to invest in paper mills, the absence of capital accounting does help explain why they viewed it as easy to substitute scarce capital for inelastic supplies of skilled labor.

As noted in Chapter 3, the New York paper trade was very profitable in the 1820s, so that mill owners could readily finance increases in fixed and working capital. Their accounting, however, did not reflect the amounts they were investing. Paper manufactur-

---

[50] McGaw, "Sources and Impact," pp. 36–39; Hyde, *History of Lee*, pp. 284–85, 290. On the dearth of alternative opportunities see Zevin, *Manufacturing in Early New England*, pp. 4–5, 15.

[51] A considerable body of literature deals with this debate, but see especially Nathan Rosenberg, "Anglo-American Wage Differences in the 1820's," in idem, *Perspectives on Technology*, pp. 50–58; Rosenberg, "Direction of Technological Change," pp. 108–25; Uselding, *Studies in Technological Development*, pp. 26–27, 67–68, 108. For "classic" statements of the debate see H. J. Habakkuk, *American and British Technology in the Nineteenth Century: The Search for Labour-Saving Inventions* (Cambridge, 1962); and Peter Temin, "Labor Scarcity and the Problem of American Industrial Efficiency in the 1850s," *JEH* 26 (September 1966):277–98.

ers, like other contemporary industrialists, used conventional double-entry bookkeeping. Devised for merchants, this system was suited to record and summarize the complex networks of indebtedness created by numerous credit sales and purchases. It met these needs admirably. But merchants employed little fixed capital, and so they did not have to account for it. Following early American mercantile procedures, paper mill owners of the 1820s did not depreciate fixed assets, such as buildings, waterwheels, or rag engines. Mill owners took account of fixed capital only when they built new mills, repaired existing ones, or installed new rag beaters or waterwheels. They treated such increases in fixed capital as operating expenses, not as capital improvements requiring long-term planning for replacement. No annual appraisal of fixed capital forced mill owners to recognize mounting investment in buildings and tools during the twenties. Paper makers certainly had a general sense that they were putting more money into plant and equipment, but so many of the improvements were incremental that they probably underestimated their total investment.[52]

Moreover, as shown in Chapter 3, during the 1820s working capital grew far more rapidly than fixed capital. It was also far more difficult to assess informally. Manufacturers' accounting procedures provided little help because they failed to acknowledge inventory. Mill owners did not adjust for the changing market value of paper and rag stocks. Their records supply no evidence that they even conducted periodic physical inventories. New York paper merchants occasionally rendered accounts of paper held on consignment, but these reports of increasing New York inventory arrived very infrequently. Manufacturers' regular presence in their mills certainly gave them a general awareness of stock on hand, but much of the increase in working capital came in the less obvious form of

---

[52] Sidney Pollard, *The Genesis of Modern Management: A Study of the Industrial Revolution in Great Britain* (Cambridge, Mass., 1965), pp. 226–49; Michael Chatfield, *A History of Accounting Thought* (Huntington, N.Y., 1977), pp. 97, 103; David Solomons, "The Historical Development of Costing," in idem, *Studies in Costing* (London, 1952), pp. 8–12, 16–17; S. Paul Garner, *Evolution of Cost Accounting to 1925* (University, Ala., 1976), pp. 1–90; B. S. Yamey, "Scientific Bookkeeping and the Rise of Capitalism," *EHR*, Second Series, 1 (1949):99–113; W. T. Baxter, "Accounting in Colonial America."

These and subsequent generalizations about paper mill accounting practice in the 1820s are based on a thorough examination aided by computerized data manipulation of Zenas Crane daybooks, 1817–23; 1819–2(?); 1824–33; 1824–29; 1825–30; and Zenas Crane Time Book, 1809–36, CA; David Carson Daybook, 1828–34, CA; Owen & Hurlbut Blotter, 1824, HP; Owen & Hurlbut Blotter, 1825, HP.

stock in process or on consignment. As a result, mill owners had little sense of the extent to which inventory grew in the twenties. For example, in 1831 the average mill owner estimated his stock on hand and in process at only about $3,000. A few years earlier one fairly typical mill's records showed that a fraction of its stock, that on consignment, amounted to $4,800, indicating that the 1831 estimates were ridiculously low.[53]

Paper manufacturers, like most of their contemporaries in the 1820s, failed to strike periodic balances or to calculate profit, further obscuring rapidly mounting capitalization. Judging from their books, paper makers did not misrepresent the facts when they reported to Treasury Department investigators in 1831 that their rate of profit was "altogether uncertain, and unknown." Except for mill owners' modest personal expenses, all earnings remained in the business to be reinvested in plant, equipment, and inventory. Since their personal and business accounts ran together in their books, mill owners did not need to decide in advance what proportion of their profits they would reinvest. They automatically reinvested all that they did not consume.[54]

In general, then, accounting practice in the 1820s ignored capitalization. In the same years, the time book, the only specialized account kept, both reflected and heightened manufacturers' preoccupation with mounting labor costs. Because they had been trained to make paper rather than to manage a business enterprise, many of the mill owners of the twenties probably grasped the costs of raw materials and the price of labor better than the costs of fixed and working capital, even without consulting their books. Available technology offered little chance to reduce rag costs. By default, mill owners must have identified labor as the cost they could control. Time books, which required daily recording and monthly summation of the increasing labor they employed, inevitably reinforced mill owners' conviction that they must reduce labor costs. By contrast, infrequently acknowledged capital costs could rise much more rapidly without attracting equal attention or eliciting equal concern.[55]

[53] Consignment inventories for two years appear in Zenas Crane Daybook, 1825–30. Because they include only paper held by the mill's leading New York customer, they clearly understate total inventory at the mill and on consignment, suggesting that mill owners underestimated inventory substantially. Estimates for 1831 are from *McLane Report*, part 1, pp. 144–45, 156–57.

[54] *McLane Report*, part 1, p. 146.

[55] McGaw, "Sources and Impact," pp. 36–39.

These characteristics of their accounting help explain why paper makers, like other early nineteenth-century manufacturers, invariably described the choice of "laborsaving" machine technology as an obvious one, despite the reality that both capital and labor were scarce in America. By the time machines became available, Berkshire paper mill owners had exhausted the possibilities for expanding output with conventional technology. Whatever their novel aspects, machines essentially mimicked the activities of workers making paper by hand. Owners with paper mill training could observe and judge the comparative speed, regularity, expense, and paper-forming ability of man and machine. Once satisfied that machines made acceptable paper, the decision to buy them could not have been difficult. On the other hand, as economic historians have argued, raising the capital to purchase machines should have been harder than contemporaries acknowledged. Yet, on the eve of mechanization, high profits and limited capital accounting combined to minimize mill owners' sense of their high rates of reinvestment and rapid capital accumulation. Simultaneously, full records of work and wages made any reduction in labor costs highly visible. Viewed through these lenses, mechanization looked easy.

After the 1820s Berkshire mill owners, who had embraced work discipline and forsworn dissipation during the Second Great Awakening, had every reason to continue reinvesting most of their profits. Increasingly intense competition, rapidly improving technology, and the opportunity to expand markets dramatically by lowering costs provided additional incentives. The lament of one paper manufacturer in 1850 strongly implies that mill owners simply felt compelled to reinvest: "All we paper makers say, 'all our profits go for improvements.' "[56]

As capitalization mounted, preserving existing assets became as important as continued reinvestment. Under these circumstances, mill owners who formed stable partnerships with other men, especially relatives, had significant advantages. Men who maintained longstanding partnerships, such as Platner and Smith, Owen and Hurlbut, and Benton and Garfield, kept both men's profits and assets in the business. Similarly, a man who brought his sons or nephews into the business, or who formed partnerships with his brothers or cousins, avoided dividing family resources. Berkshire manufacturers clearly adopted this approach, for male blood relatives made up the vast majority (89 percent) of mill owners' kin who owned pa-

[56] *McLane Report*, part 1, p. 97; File 295, CMF, 9/4/50.

per mills, an investment strategy that served primarily to keep family money in the industry. Relatives by marriage, who brought new money into the business, represented a distinct minority.[57]

As Table 5.3 indicates, family partnerships also helped preserve paper mill capital by cementing bonds between partners. In the chaotic years between 1827 and 1857, partnerships shifted almost kaleidoscopically as men without paper-making experience moved into and out of the industry. Under these conditions, men who had

TABLE 5.3
LONGEVITY OF PARTNERSHIPS BY COMPOSITION, 1827–57

Composition	Less than 2 Years	2 to 10 Years	10 or More Years
Sole proprietorships	6 (23%)	12 (46%)	8 (31%)
Partnerships of relatives	4 (23)	8 (47)	5 (29)
Mixed partnerships of relatives and nonrelatives	5 (42)	5 (41)	2 (17)
Partnerships of nonrelatives	15 (30)	27 (61)	7 (14)

NOTE: Data are for partnerships created after 1826 and before 1858. Thus, firms that existed during these years, but had been founded earlier, are omitted. Also omitted are two firms whose names are known, but whose composition cannot be ascertained. Whenever any individual entered or left a partnership, the resulting partnership is considered a new one. Many individuals persisted in the industry much longer than the partnerships to which they belonged. The only exception to this general rule is when an employee was given a working interest. This has not been considered as creating a new partnership.

[57] Johnson, *Shopkeeper's Millennium*, p. 26, finds that the opposite was true of the frequency of different types of family ties in Rochester, New York. The difference undoubtedly rests, as Johnson suggests, on the much higher level of geographic mobility among the Rochester businessmen. By contrast, the vast majority of Berkshire paper mill owners whose birthplace is known were born in the Berkshires. Family relationship had, of course, formed the basis for bringing together the men who forwarded the early American textile industry. Robert K. Lamb, "The Entrepreneur and the Community," in William Miller, ed., *Men in Business* (New York, 1952), pp. 102–3, 117–19. Family concerns continued longer in the paper industry. Even in Holyoke, "the most important paper companies were scarcely more than family concerns." Green, *Holyoke*, pp. 87, 92. Evidence from other Berkshire industries supports the generalization that family ownership persisted longest in industries such as paper making, characterized by moderate capital requirements and comparatively skilled work forces. Family partnerships and family corporations were common in the local woolen industry, the other major local industry with these characteristics. In more heavily capitalized and routinized local cotton manufacturing, by contrast, family concerns played a distinctly minor role. Child, *Gazeteer*, part 1, passim.

enough capital to establish sole proprietorships and men who combined with relatives had the advantage of being far more likely to keep all of their original investment and most of their profits in the paper industry for ten years or more. They achieved this degree of permanence more than twice as frequently as did partnerships of unrelated individuals. Combinations of relatives also more successfully avoided the problem of seeking out reliable partners every year or two than did firms including unrelated men.

In fact, by assigning partnerships to a few longevity categories, Table 5.3 understates the advantages of joining with relatives. Average longevity figures underscore the economic usefulness of family ties. The mean life span of partnerships in which members were unrelated was 5.48 years, that of mixed partnerships 6.3 years, and that of sole proprietorships 8.46 years, whereas partnerships of relatives lasted 10.75 years on the average. Nor are these figures unduly influenced by a few extremely long-lived or short-lived combinations. The median life of partnerships of unrelated individuals, mixed partnerships, and sole proprietorships was 4.0, 3.5, and 5.5 years, respectively. Partnerships of relatives had a median life of 8.5 years.[58]

Even these figures understate the stabilizing influence of blood ties, because long-term partnerships of relatives sometimes persisted through the comings and goings of other partners. The two longest-lived business relationships begun in this period pooled the resources of two brothers, although they attracted other investors for varying periods. After successfully establishing himself in an East Lee paper mill in 1837, Sylvester S. May convinced his brother, Edward, to sell his woolen mill in nearby Granby and buy out Sylvester's partner, Jared Ingersoll. The brothers became partners in 1840 and acquired additional mills in 1845 and 1851. Although they had plenty of land on which to build single-family houses, they reinforced their business ties by building a huge double house, large enough for both families, on land near their mills. They amicably lived and worked together for forty-six years, until Sylvester's death. Similarly, Zenas Marshal and James Brewer Crane cooper-

[58] Even these figures understate the difference somewhat, because the exact month in which partnerships were begun and ended is rarely known and, therefore, the initial and terminal year have been counted as full years. This especially inflates life-span figures at the lower end of the spectrum. For example, a partnership begun in December 1834 and lasting a little over a month would be counted as having lasted two years, nearly twenty-four times its actual length. A longer-lived partnership would be inflated by only a modest percentage as a result of adding a similar span to its length.

ated successfully for forty-five years, continuing their father's mill and investing their inheritance and profits in three additional local mills.[59]

Equally important in preserving mills' assets were improved accounting methods introduced by commercially trained partners. Like most nineteenth-century factories, paper mills remained small enough that they did not require enormous amounts of fixed capital. Instead, mill owners' most pressing problem was to keep track of the greatly increased working capital required by mechanized mills. As manufacturers installed more and more efficient machines, they increased paper output and raw material consumption far more rapidly than investment in machines. Simultaneously, instead of dealing with a few New York wholesalers, as had mill owners of the 1820s, Berkshire paper makers after 1827 sold to larger numbers of paper merchants and publishers both in New York and in other metropolitan areas. This multiplied working capital tied up in accounts receivable and in inventory held on consignment.[60]

From the start of mechanization, working capital grew, at the very least, as rapidly as did fixed capital. Indeed, although precise figures are unobtainable and available estimates are not always strictly comparable, the evidence suggests that, despite rapid acquisition of machines in the 1830s and 1840s, inventory and accounts receivable grew from two to four times as quickly as fixed assets. By 1846, for example, the Dalton firm of Crane & Co. valued two mills and their machinery at only $14,000, whereas their accounts receivable amounted to nearly $9,000 and inventory tied up more than $20,000.[61]

Greatly expanded working capital called the skills of commercially trained partners into service. Successful mill owners' most substantial new business problems in the years after 1827 included keeping abreast of accounts receivable and accounts payable and

59 Hyde, *History of Lee*, p. 298; R. G. Dun & Co. Ledgers, 6:369; Appendix A.

60 McGaw, "Sources and Impact," pp. 132–44, 169–73, 244–58; McGaw, "Accounting for Innovation."

61 *McLane Report*, part 1, pp. 156–57; Crane & Co. Inventories File, CMF, 4/1/46. The first, conservative calculation assumes that manufacturers underestimated stock by one-half in 1831. This should more than compensate for the tendency to underestimate working capital discussed above. Nonmanufacturing real estate has been included in the first two calculations for 1846 on the assumption that it was also included in McLane's estimates. If not, the figures simply understate my point. Accounts receivable have been omitted, because McLane's figure is for stock on hand and in process, not overall working capital. All the evidence indicates that, had McLane's figures permitted a comparison that included accounts receivable, the relative increase in working capital invested would be greater still.

maintaining an adequate, but not excessive, inventory. Conventional mercantile accounting could help with each of these problems. Especially after rail transport permitted relative inventory reductions, mills with commercially trained partners probably tied up less working capital than those without.

By the 1840s and 1850s the urgent need to account for augmented working capital had prompted Berkshire mill owners to adopt the full range of available commercial accounting procedures. Only two types of mill account books survive from the 1820s: time books, in which mill owners listed workers and their work; and daybooks, in which they recorded company store transactions, paper shipments, mill expenses, and personal disbursements as they occurred, and recorded mill payroll, board, and rents on a monthly basis. In some cases check or slash marks next to entries suggest that proprietors posted original entries from these single-entry daybooks to double-entry ledgers since lost. But there is no indication that they balanced accounts regularly, maintained any subsidiary accounts, or conducted inventories. By contrast, in the years after mechanization, they kept their daybooks, journals, and ledgers with greater care, closing them annually, striking monthly balances, and developing a growing array of balance sheet accounts. Separate company store daybooks and rent books removed retail and housing expenditures and profits from the manufacturing accounts. Together, these changes gave mill owners better expense, raw material, and labor cost records as their mounting scale of operations made informal assessment more difficult. New subsidiary books emerged to deal with mill owners' special concerns—accounts receivable, accounts payable, and inventory. Bill books provided convenient summaries of payables and receivables. Merchandise books detailed original terms of paper sales and permitted mill owners to spot overdue accounts at a glance. Receipt books served as the mill's record of actual weight of rags received, allowing mill owners to verify invoices. Mill owners with commercial training also began to prepare quarterly inventories and weekly tallies of paper output and supplies consumed, enabling proprietors to judge whether inventory was adequate or excessive. Finally, manufacturers adopted formulae for charging interest on receivables, enhancing the probability that their working capital would be profitably employed.[62]

[62] McGaw, "Accounting for Innovation," offers additional evidence of manufacturers' recognition of the value of mercantile accounting.

Nineteen ledgers, journals, and daybooks in the L. L. Brown Papers provide the fullest documentation for this summary, but see the Bibliography for a full listing of

SPURRED by rapidly expanding markets for paper, yet repeatedly chastened by unpredictable economic and technological change, the men who survived as paper mill owners and made most of the decisions to mechanize the industry succeeded primarily because they chose partners well and learned how to cooperate. By selecting associates who had paper mill and commercial training and by calling on relatives for advice, they could base their machine purchase decisions on better and more plentiful technical and business information, substantially lowering their risk of making poor choices. Initially, in fact, because they had good information about new paper machines and new paper markets, but limited information about profits or alternative investments, mill owners readily invested their profits to purchase machines. Later, stable partnerships and kinship ties both supplied and preserved sufficient capital to buy machines and to operate mechanized mills.

In sum, once machine builders made their wares available in Berkshire County, they encountered mill owners extremely well prepared to appreciate and afford paper mill machinery. The cooperative network of paper mill owners explains a great deal about the rapid and successful mechanization of the local industry. Keeping this community of decision makers in mind, we can now examine the general patterns of paper mill mechanization and the local conditions that shaped those patterns.

---

paper industry records consulted. Also, Crane & Co. Inventories File, CMF; Owen & Hurlbut Quarterly Reports, HP. Preserved records are generally those of the county's more successful firms and their accounting practices may not be representative of less successful operations. In addition, all record collections are incomplete, so it is impossible to tell whether even successful firms adopted all of these procedures. However, given the extensive communication among successful mill owners, practices found useful in one mill probably found their way into others rather quickly.

CHAPTER 6

LOCAL CONDITIONS AND
MECHANIZATION:
MACHINES IN THE
BERKSHIRES,
1827–1885

Sounding a theme characteristic of nineteenth-century historical writing, Byron Weston emphasized "progress . . . at the mills" in his history of Berkshire paper making. Unfortunately, this approach led him to chronicle technological advances, rather than to explain technological innovation and diffusion. Like many later historians who have depicted mechanization as the triumphant march of invention, Weston assumed that, once invented, superior technology inevitably prevailed. Why mechanization proceeded as it did in the Berkshire paper industry simply did not occur to him as a meaningful historical question.[1]

Taking a different approach, this chapter describes county patterns of machine purchase and analyzes the determinants of those patterns. Although Weston's history offers little help in explaining technological change, his observations, when combined with information from his business records and a host of other nineteenth-century documents, show that invention did not ensure a new paper machine's adoption. Berkshire mechanization, although generally rapid, varied from mill to mill, and often remained incomplete.

While the availability of new machines and mill owners' ability and willingness to buy them made mechanization possible, five characteristics of the Berkshire paper industry interacted to promote rapid, but selective, diffusion of new technology. The timing of most Berkshire mill construction coincided roughly with the availability of machines, encouraging early mechanization. The location of Berkshire mills abetted early machine purchase by giving paper manufacturers access to a number of machine builders. The

---

[1] For a discussion of a similar predisposition among economists see Nathan Rosenberg, "Problems in the Economists' Conceptualization of Technological Innovation," in idem, *Perspectives on Technology*, pp. 61–84, especially pp. 75–77.

concentration of paper making in the region enabled mill owners to scrutinize machines before deciding to buy them and opened up alternatives such as purchasing used machines or sharing machines. The relative cost of the new machines and their rising absolute prices also fostered selective acquisition. Likewise, local specialization, most commonly in fine paper, led mill owners to invest heavily in some machines, while eschewing others. To understand the mechanization of Berkshire paper making we need to consider each of these factors in turn.

Timing

In 1880 the trade journal *Paper World* published a biographical sketch of Byron Weston. Its author attributed much of Weston's success to good timing. "[H]e commenced his life's labor at a most favorable time for practical development and growth, . . . a time from whence were dated some of the most important changes, improvements, and developments . . . in the history of paper making." A similar theme underlies the achievements of the Berkshire paper industry. In general, Berkshire paper mill owners mechanized readily because they had not had time to invest either money or reputation in older processes. Having commenced operations after 1800, even Berkshire's initial hand paper-making establishment lacked a longstanding commitment to traditional methods. Most local hand mills originated amidst the innovations of the 1820s, innovations that prepared them to adopt machines. As shown in Chapter 5, the renewed mill building of the twenties heralded a period of new paper mill construction, which continued into the mid-fifties. Thus, the vast majority of the region's paper firms opened their doors after local mills already employed paper-making machines.[2]

Figure 6.1 shows that the sustained and rapid growth of the Berkshire paper industry occurred late enough that most mill owners considered the adoption of paper-making machines early in their histories, when innovation came easiest. Increased mill construction in the 1820s coincided with the first local discussions of paper machinery, both developments being responses to the emerging New York market. Because machines overcame the final constraint on meeting New York demand, they encouraged paper makers to erect even more mills in succeeding decades. All but one of the thirty-

[2] "Successful Paper Makers," p. 7.

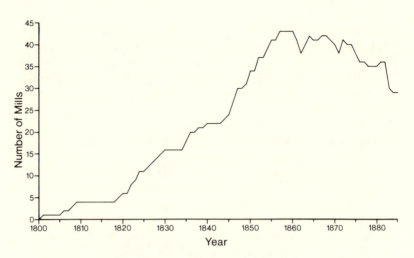

Fig. 6.1 Number of paper mills in Berkshire County, 1801–85.

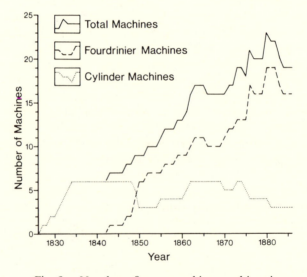

Fig. 6.2 Number of paper-making machines in
Berkshire County, 1827–86.

nine mills built after 1827, when machine production began, housed machines from the start. The few older mills unable to make the transition rapidly closed their doors.[3]

Berkshire's comparatively late development as the leading American paper-making region conferred a distinct technological advantage. The fate of the industry in eastern Pennsylvania, early national leader in paper production, documents the benefits of late entry by contrast. Despite geographic assets equal or superior to those of the Berkshires, the many established hand mills of Pennsylvania failed to make the transition to machine production. Unable to compete, the industry relinquished leadership to Berkshire County and then virtually died out, reviving only much later.[4]

Comparatively late mill construction also enabled Berkshire mill owners to buy superior machinery earlier. Figure 6.2 offers one outstanding case in point by comparing local ownership of Fourdrinier and cylinder machines. In 1827 two Lee mills installed the county's first cylinder machines. American machine builders had yet to construct a Fourdrinier, so that these mills had little choice but to purchase cylinders. Until 1843, when Zenas Crane and Sons purchased Berkshire's earliest Fourdrinier, American "shaking machines" remained scarce enough that most local mills probably considered the cylinder their only option. More than half of the county's mills began operation after the Fourdrinier's local debut, however, giving them the choice of installing such machines at the outset. Evidently most decided to do so, because after Crane adopted this superior paper-making machine, almost all Berkshire mill owners purchasing machines bought Fourdriniers.[5]

The comparative frequencies of the two paper-making machines in Berkshire and in other American paper-making regions under-

[3] The last of the old hand paper mills, the Manser Mill in Monterey, closed sometime before 1855. A small mill producing bank note paper was built in Lee in 1855 and may have relied on hand production for its specialty. L. L. Brown revived the production of handmade paper in 1881 and continued to operate a two-vat hand department in one mill until 1907, but this was primarily a promotional venture, as discussed in Chapter 8. Appendix A; Weston, "Paper Making," p. 9; Hunter, *Papermaking*, p. 372.

[4] Appendix C discusses the sources and limitations of data summarized in Figure 6.1. Smith, *History of Papermaking*, pp. 22–24, 88–89.

[5] For seven of the Berkshire mills built after the 1843 local inception of Fourdrinier paper production, the initial machines are known. One mill engaged in hand paper making, one employed a cylinder, and five commenced operations with Fourdriniers. *Century of Pioneering*, pp. 1–3. See Appendix C for sources and limitations of data summarized in Figure 6.2.

score the importance of timing. Because so many Berkshire mill owners built late enough to choose the Fourdrinier, these machines became much more common in Berkshire County than in the nation as a whole. As late as 1882 Fourdriniers comprised only 39 percent of American paper machines, but they made up more than 44 percent of the known machines in Berkshire as early as 1849. By 1882 that percentage had risen to 77 percent.[6]

Comparison of Berkshire machines with those of Holyoke, Massachusetts, successor to Lee as America's "Paper City," confirms that regions developing later adopted superior machines earlier. Holyoke's paper industry commenced only in 1853, and the Fourdrinier dominated the city's mills from the outset. By 1873, 84 percent of Holyoke machines were Fourdriniers, and by 1897, 95 percent. Berkshire mills' less complete conversion to Fourdriniers suggests that manufacturers who started with cylinder machines moved more slowly to install Fourdriniers. Unwillingness to relinquish the painfully acquired benefits of familiarity with their machines and inability to justify the substantial added investment probably combined to account for their hesitancy.[7]

Largely because their markets did not warrant earlier mechanization, Berkshire mill owners' initial machine purchases lagged eighteen years behind the first American cylinder and fourteen years behind the first American Fourdrinier. Thereafter, mill owners evinced increasing eagerness to install novel technology. Fragmentary mill records before 1860 do not consistently document innovations, but owners added improvements to their paper machines, such as the slice and the dandy roll, no later than ten to fifteen years after the Fourdrinier's local introduction. After 1860 more complete mill records reveal owners' very early willingness to adopt paper machine improvements. For example, in 1863 and 1865 Crane & Co., the firm managed by two of Zenas Crane's sons, expressed interest in having its couch and press rolls covered with rubber. This improvement, designed to eliminate troublesome rust spots, received its initial patent only in 1864.[8]

Berkshire mills also quickly adopted machinery developed for preceding and succeeding stages of production. By the late 1850s, before Berkshire County relinquished paper-making leadership to

    [6] See Appendix C. Clapperton, *Paper-making Machine*, p. 247.

    [7] Weeks, *History of Paper Manufacturing*, pp. 244, 284; Green, *Holyoke*, p. 88.

    [8] L. L. Brown & Co. Journal, 1856, LLBP, 10/56; Carson & Brown Ledger, 1849–53, CA, 3/21/51; "Machinery, Engineering, and Chemistry, 1854–1865," CMF, 8/18/63, 11/15/65.

Holyoke, at least some local mill owners had installed each available mechanical device. Berkshire mill owners may have taken fifteen to twenty years after the first European patents to introduce a few machines, such as cylinder washers and sizing machines. They adopted most machinery much more quickly. Zenas Crane installed steam dryers four years after their first production in an American machine shop, and David Carson ordered a stamping machine within ten years of its American debut at Springfield. Platner & Smith had a Kingsland refiner in operation the year after its invention. Owen & Hurlbut and the Laflin brothers sent Coleman Sellers two of the earliest orders for his pioneering supercalenders. Finally, various Berkshire mills employed ruling machines, machine calenders, and layboys at about the same time as their inventors filed for patents.[9]

As was the case with Byron Weston, then, the Berkshire County paper industry reaped the rewards of good timing. Berkshire mill owners readily incorporated the most improved machinery into their mills from the start simply because they started late. Even those mills that antedated the paper-making machine remained relatively new when machinery became available, not wedded to a long tradition of hand production as were the mills of Pennsylvania. But timing accounts only in part for the early acceptance of machinery in the Berkshires. Location also played a significant role.

LOCATION

"[T]o John Ames of Springfield more than to any other one paper maker, is the [paper] trade indebted for its improvement and advancement," wrote Byron Weston in his history. He credited Ames with inventing the cylinder paper-making machine, steam dryer, cylinder washer, sizing machine, knotter, calender, and trimming press. Although none of these devices originated with Ames, from a Berkshire paper mill owner's perspective Ames deserved the recognition Weston accorded him. The Springfield paper maker bor-

---

[9] L. L. Brown Daybook, 1853–54, LLBP, 10/53; Owen & Hurlbut Receipt Book, 1843–46, HP, 3/46; Zenas Crane Time Book, 1809–36, CA, 10/34; Carson & Brown Ledger, 1849–53, CA, 9/3/49, 9/29/50; "Paper Making in South Lee, Mass.," p. 6; "The Automatic Layboy, 1847–1848," CMF; "The Automatic Layboy, 1849–1858," CMF; "Machinery, Engineering, and Chemistry, 1854–1865," CMF, 12/22/60; Brown & Weston Letter Book, 1863–64, BWP, 2/24/64; VG, 5/28/57, p. 2; Coleman Sellers Letter Book, 1828–34, APS, 12/28/33, 1/13/34, 4/28/34, and passim. The earliest references to specific machines in paper company records undoubtedly understate the case for early acceptance of innovations because several of the earliest references are orders for parts for machines already in operation.

rowed and improved upon a number of early paper mechanisms. Because the successful transfer of early machine technology depended heavily on the machine builder's proximity to the machine user, the presence of the imitative Ames in Springfield made the superior creativity of more distant inventors available to early Berkshire mills. Following Ames, numerous regional and local machine builders promoted and sustained Berkshire mechanization.[10]

The 1827 introduction of the cylinder machine in Berkshire County owed most to Ames. He patented his version of the device in 1822 and subsequently became New England's first paper-making machine builder. At least two of the earliest Berkshire mills to buy paper-making machines purchased them from Ames. The sources of other early machines remain unknown, but they, too, probably originated in Ames's shop. Nearby Worcester is another possible source. There, the Burbanks, mentors of David Carson and Zenas Crane, made further improvements on the cylinder. At the very least, their commitment to mechanized paper making must have helped legitimize the machine for Dalton mill owners.[11]

Berkshire County's location near machine builders also helps explain the local predominance of the Fourdrinier. Soon after American production of the machine commenced, local mill owners found themselves situated near several pioneering paper machine shops. The first American Fourdrinier, built by Phelps and Spafford of South Windham, Connecticut, initiated a long line of machines made by that firm and its successor, Smith, Winchester & Company. The other early American Fourdrinier builder, located in Worcester, was Howe & Goddard, later Goddard, Rice & Company, and Rice, Barton, & Fales. Berkshire mill owners could readily visit either machine maker to study machinery, and the shops could deliver orders and dispatch men to assemble them with equal ease.[12]

Later, two additional leading Fourdrinier builders set up shop in

[10] Weston, "Paper Making," pp. 5, 21; Weeks, *History of Paper Manufacturing*, pp. 124, 176; Nathan Rosenberg, "Economic Development and the Transfer of Technology: Some Historical Perspectives" and "Factors Affecting the Diffusion of Technology," in idem, *Perspectives on Technology*, pp. 163–68, 199–202.

[11] "Fire Destroys Crane & Co.'s Red Mill, December 16, 1870," CMF; "Paper Making in South Lee, Mass.," p. 6; Weeks, *History of Paper Manufacturing*, p. 176. Carson Brothers also got a ruling machine and slitters from the Ameses' shop. Carson & Brown Ledger, 1849–53, 4/29/50.

[12] Weeks, *History of Paper Manufacturing*, p. 180; *Century of Pioneering*, passim. Frequent references to both of these machine builders occur in the L. L. Brown, Crane & Co., and Byron Weston records.

John L. Severance (Seaverns), a French paper machinery designer who emigrated

Massachusetts, close enough to supply machines to Berkshire paper makers. In 1857 the Lowell Machine Shop started selling paper machinery and within two years found two Berkshire buyers for Fourdriniers. Six years later the Holyoke Machine Company began to serve the growing paper industry at Holyoke. Save for local machine shops, Holyoke Machine remained Berkshire County's nearest Fourdrinier builder. Major Fourdrinier machine manufacturers emerged more slowly in other sections of the country, so that Berkshire paper mills retained their locational advantage. In addition to good timing, then, favorable location permitted Berkshire mills to purchase the superior Fourdrinier machine much more easily than could most American mills.[13]

The same generalization applies to other machines. The early and widespread acceptance of the layboy in Berkshire County clearly resulted from its local origin. J. B. Crane developed one of the first layboys, and Crane & Co. built and marketed his invention. Because they knew Berkshire mill owners personally, when the Cranes wrote describing the advantages of the layboy, their letters carried more weight than did machinery prospectuses from strangers. Favored by propinquity, local mill owners could easily visit the Cranes' mill to watch layboys perform and, after purchasing them, could expect ready assistance with the many problems mills usually encountered with new machines. Not surprisingly, then, of the sixteen machines the Cranes sold outside Dalton, nine went to Berkshire County firms. Two other orders came from relatives of Berkshire paper makers with paper mills in Herkimer, New York, and Ware, Massachusetts. Crane & Co. installed all of their remaining layboys in neighboring counties.[14]

---

to the United States in the 1840s, was also accessible to Berkshire mill owners. He was first associated with a machine shop in Lawrence, Massachusetts, then moved to Worcester, operating on his own and in association with Rice, Barton, & Fales. During his Worcester years he served several Berkshire paper mills. See, for example, "Machinery, Engineering, and Chemistry, 1854–1865," CMF, 10/10/65; Letters to Byron Weston, 1867, BWP, 1/2/67; "Letter from Walter E. Bellows, Secretary to Mr. Barton, Rice, Barton, & Fales, Inc.," SF 5 (March 1932):14.

[13] George Sweet Gibb, *The Saco-Lowell Shops: Textile Machinery Building in New England, 1813–1949* (Cambridge, Mass., 1950), p. 194; Paper Machinery Memoranda, vol. RA-1, Saco-Lowell Machine Shops Records, BL, 3/1/59, 6/21/59; Green, *Holyoke*, p. 80; Clapperton, *Paper-making Machine*, pp. 345–53.

[14] "The Automatic Layboy, 1847–1848," CMF; "The Automatic Layboy, 1849–1858," CMF. Additional layboys were installed in Dalton, probably quite early, but since no correspondence was necessary in selling these layboys, no records remain. "Alfred Hoxie," interview typescript, CMF, p. 9; "Philo Brownson and Edwin Brownson," interview typescript, CMF, p. 2.

Similarly, paper makers and machine builders in nearby towns made innovations available to Berkshire mill owners earlier than to more distant paper manufacturers. Wright's perfection of the ruling machine in Springfield encouraged rapid adoption of that device in the Berkshires. Firms in South Windham, Connecticut, and Brattleboro, Vermont, produced, respectively, the first American Fourdrinier and cylinder machines to include steam dryers, helping to explain Zenas Crane's early acquisition of a dryer. The origin of fire dryers in Worcester and of Jordon refiners in Hartford and South Windham made Berkshire mill owners aware of these machines from the start. Later, when Berkshire paper makers decided to produce their own envelopes, they found envelope machines already for sale in Springfield.[15]

By contrast, the problems encountered by the Laflin brothers after ordering an early calender from Coleman Sellers & Sons of Philadelphia illustrate vividly why proximity to machine shops expedited machine purchases. Sellers notified the Laflins in late April of 1834 that he had shipped their machine and promised to forward "particular directions how to put it up." Ten days later extremely detailed directions followed, illustrated by six diagrams. Nonetheless, on June 21 Sellers advised the Laflins "to pack up the paper rolls and ship them immediately to us and if the iron ones have in any way been injured, them also." By operating the machine after improper assembly, they had damaged it. Sellers acknowledged the root of the problem when he added, "We would in all cases prefer sending a man to put them into operation, but that [would] y[ie]ld so small a profit that we [c]ould not afford it. . . ." Delays postponed the return of the repaired portions from Philadelphia until early September, six months later than the Laflins had wanted the machine delivered.[16]

If, as the Sellers-Laflin case suggests, dealing with nearby machine shops expedited both the start-up of new machines and their repair, Berkshire mills experienced progressively fewer delays as more and more machine builders set up shop locally over the course of the century. Shops serving the paper industry especially congregated along East Lee's Greenwater Stream, where they obtained adequate power for their intermittent use, but did not compete for sites with local paper mills, which increasingly located along more

[15] Carson & Brown Ledger, 1849–53, CA, 4/29/50; Ferguson, *Early Engineering Reminiscences*, p. 101; Michael H. Frisch, *Town into City: Springfield, Massachusetts, and the Meaning of Community, 1840–1880* (Cambridge, Mass., 1972), p. 82; William G. O'Connell, interview, Dalton, Mass., July 21, 1975.

[16] Coleman Sellers Letter Book, 1828–34, APS, 4/28/34, 5/8/34, 6/21/34, 8/28/34.

powerful and reliable water courses. As early as the 1820s two general metalworking establishments fabricated parts for paper machinery in East Lee. Blacksmith Cornelius Barlow made a variety of edge tools, including Hollander roll bars, and Beach & Royce built wool-carding machines and supplied metal parts for paper mills. By the 1840s, with the proliferation of paper mills and paper machines in Lee, these shops specialized in paper mill equipment. Henry Murray and John Dowd, who succeeded the aging Barlow, had added the manufacture and repair of trimmer and cutter knives to the engine roll bar and bed plate business. Meanwhile, former journeyman Edward P. Tanner bought out Beach & Royce, which had entered textile manufacture. By 1848 Tanner offered mill owners a complete line of paper-making machinery, including both Fourdrinier and cylinder machines. Two new East Lee firms also catered exclusively to the paper-making trade. John McLaughlin, an Irish immigrant who had learned his trade in Beach & Royce's shop, had gone into business making and repairing calender rolls. For Hollanders, waterwheels, and other wooden equipment, paper mills hired E. D. Jones, an Otis native who had trained in an Ohio wheelwright's shop. In 1848 Jones returned to the Berkshires and arranged to work out of Bradford Couch's East Lee carpenter and millwright's shop. The skills of these local machine builders compounded the advantages of Berkshire mills' location.[17]

As paper mills grew in number, size, and mechanical sophistication, East Lee machine builders expanded their operations. By the 1860s E. D. Jones had purchased the Couch establishment and functioned as a contractor and engineer as well as a machine builder. He turned out beaters, dusters, waterwheels, and shafting in his shop; subcontracted metal equipment; and assembled complete paper mills. In 1866 he decided that further expansion required location on a railroad. He moved to Pittsfield, where he operated a foundry and a boiler works, contracted to build entire mills both in the Berkshires and outside the county, and turned out as many as thirty-four Hollanders in six months. His journeymen, Henry Couch and Freeland Oakley, purchased his East Lee shop and continued on a more modest scale, building beaters, dusters, and waterwheels with their two planers, two buzz saws, and jigsaw. By contrast, Jones doubted that shop training would suffice to manage his burgeoning enterprise, and he packed off his son to M.I.T.[18]

[17] Jones, *Jones Story*, pp. 3–4; Hyde, *History of Lee*, pp. 286–87, 301.
[18] As noted in Chapter 7, Jones also helped introduce hydraulic turbines in the Berkshires. Jones, *Jones Story*, pp. 6–7, 9–12; McGaw, "Sources and Impact," p. 148.

Jones's former neighbors also expanded their businesses. By the 1870s Dowd, now in partnership with his brother Rex, supplied paper mill edge tools to mills throughout the county. John Mc-Laughlin built a foundry alongside his machine shop, expediting his completion of calender roll orders, and he added a saw mill to supply lumber to build beaters. He evidently enlarged his machine shop as well, for he promised to receive, repair, and return calenders in a single day. E. P. Tanner also set up a foundry and enlarged his machine shop, becoming the village's most substantial machine builder, with average annual sales of $100,000 by the 1870s. By 1885 his establishment, shown in Figure 6.3, employed thirty men and made everything from Hollanders to dryers.[19]

In addition to these specialist shops, 1860 found six Berkshire machine shops and foundries doing some paper mill work, and 1885 saw twice that number. Eight of them clustered in the industrial centers of Pittsfield, North Adams, and Adams, where they could also serve textile mills, shoe factories, and other manufacturers. Because much of the county remained rural, some of these diversified firms produced agricultural implements, stump pullers, and saw mill machinery as well. County paper mills' regular patronage of the various county machine shops testifies to the continuing importance of ready communication between shop and mill after the shop's initial task of diffusing machine technology had given way to its more mundane responsibility for improving, replacing, and repairing previously accepted equipment.[20]

Both the development of local machine shops and the regional concentration of leading machine makers must have progressively lowered the expense of owning machines in the Berkshires. The growing size of paper-making machines made transportation charges alone an important consideration. More important, proper installation and maintenance saved money by preventing damage to the equipment and to the paper it made. Nearby machine shops could more easily provide these services. Proximity also reduced

In 1887 young Edward Jones first employed his education by setting up a system of engineering records. By contrast, his father had been trained to sketch plans on a board, which was later planed and reused.

[19] Rex Dowd subsequently moved to Wisconsin and set up a similar establishment, while John Dowd's son joined his father as a partner. Hyde, *History of Lee*, pp. 287–88, 301; Child, *Gazeteer*, part 1, p. 201. McGaw, "Sources and Impact," pp. 147–49, cites the extensive correspondence between East Lee shops and mills in Dalton and Adams.

[20] Child, *Gazeteer*, part 2, passim; Jones, *Jones Story*, p. 10; McGaw, "Sources and Impact," pp. 150–51.

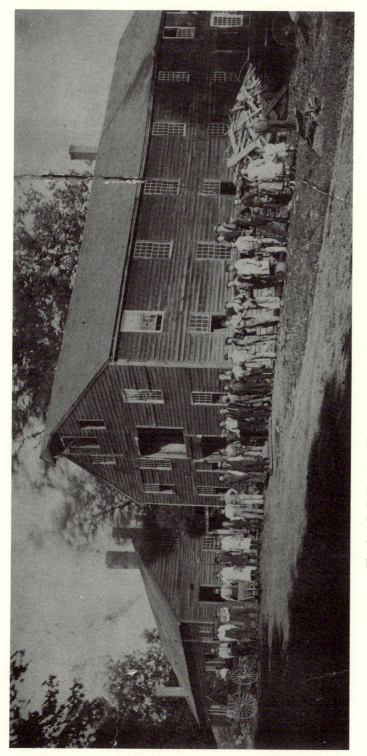

Fig. 6.3 E. P. Tanner, his workmen, and his East Lee machine shop. Shown here in about 1870, this was the county's leading paper-making machine shop. Courtesy of Lee Library.

"down time" at the mills while machines traveled to the shop for repairs or mill owners awaited spare parts, an increasingly important consideration as the various machines' operations became more fully integrated.

As with timing, then, location fostered Berkshire mechanization. Numerous regional and local shops introduced machines early, assured their initial successful operation, and contributed to their ongoing profitability. By contrast, the other factors influencing mechanization sometimes delayed or discouraged mechanical innovation. Concentration, cost, and quality each promoted selectivity.

CONCENTRATION

Of course, we cannot really separate the various factors affecting mechanization. Concentration and location are especially interrelated. The growing number of county paper machine shops, an important aspect of the Berkshire industry's locational advantage, could hardly have existed without the local concentration of paper mills. Local machine-building firms needed different machine tools to make and repair paper machines than to make local textile mill equipment. This was true as early as 1834. Shops could justify investment in specialized machine tools only after numerous paper mills had assured adequate demand. In the interim, however, the concentration of even a few paper mills in the county conferred some of the same locational advantages as having machine shops nearby. When several Berkshire paper firms ordered simultaneously from a distant shop, it became economical for the shop to send a skilled workman to assemble new devices properly. Coleman Sellers, for example, sent his son, Charles, to Lee in late 1834 to set up calenders for both Owen & Hurlbut and the Laflins.[21]

By drawing skilled machinists to the region, concentration abetted mechanization. On balance, however, concentration permitted a cautious approach to technological innovation. It gave mill owners a chance to see machines at work in other mills, fostering mechanization only after machines demonstrated their superiority. Similarly, it gave mill owners the opportunity to pick and choose among rival contrivances. It also made used machines available locally, allowing some mill owners to mechanize without incurring the risks of innovation or the cost of new machines. Mill owners with many

---

[21] Coleman Sellers Letter Book, 1828–34, APS, 7/2/34, 7/14/34.

neighboring mills could also reduce their investment in machines by sharing some machines with mills in the vicinity.

In cases where a machine had obvious advantages, the concentration of mills within the narrow geographic confines of Berkshire County stimulated technological diffusion. Most mill owners could assess new machinery at neighboring mills before committing themselves to its purchase. Especially in the early years of mechanical paper making, seeing a new machine in operation probably reassured more tradition-bound mill owners that the machine did, in fact, live up to its claims.

In later years, when machine makers believed their product demonstrably better, they took advantage of the concentration of mills in the Berkshires to document their contentions. For example, in 1882 Cranston & Co. of Brooklyn, New York, wrote to Crane & Co. recommending their paper cutter and advising Crane that L. L. Brown operated two of their machines at his Adams mill, where Crane could easily examine them. Similarly, in 1865, when the Cranes asked Isaac Goddard of Worcester about Goddard's new engine, he simply directed them to a neighboring mill by replying, "You had better see Colt's new Engine and get at its practical working from him."[22]

When several mechanical alternatives existed, the large number of local mills allowed the paper maker to study different machines and select the one best adapted to his needs. For example, when Crane & Co. needed a new paper-making machine, Isaac Goddard arranged to meet the Cranes in Lee to show them two different machines he built. Byron Weston, bewildered by the variety of paper cutters, solicited the opinion of fellow paper maker R. W. Wilson. After stating his preferences, Wilson listed which cutters several local mills used and advised, "I think I would see the different cutters and you could then tell better what to do." Essentially, the proximity of a number of local mills gave all Berkshire manufacturers the chance to discover the advantages of a superior machine as early as any one of them did.[23]

The large number of local mills also created a supply of used machinery. As machine prices mounted after the Civil War, this guaranteed smaller, less affluent mills the chance to obtain improved machinery earlier than they might otherwise have done. Byron

[22] "Machinery, Engineering, and Chemistry, 1879–1886," CMF, 4/10/82; "Machinery, Engineering, and Chemistry, 1854–1865," CMF, 10/13/65.
[23] "Machinery, Engineering, and Chemistry, 1854–1865," CMF, 1/2/59; Letters to Byron Weston, 1867, BWP, 9/16/67.

Weston and Crane & Co. both purchased used equipment from the county's leading firm, the Smith Paper Company of Lee. Weston bought a larger trimming press, and Weston and Crane both replaced old screw presses with Smith's used hydraulic presses.[24]

While giving some mills an intermediate option between outdated technology and the latest advance, the used-machinery market simultaneously encouraged innovation by permitting mill owners to buy new equipment, assured that they could realize something on their old machines. Smith's sales to Weston and Crane helped pay for newer presses. Similarly, after spending nearly $10,000 for a new Fourdrinier in 1872, Byron Weston offered his old machine for sale at $2,000.[25]

The used-machinery market permitted financially troubled mill owners to cut back production or change specializations and liquidate machinery they no longer needed. The local concentration of mills guaranteed a buyer if the price fell low enough. Such transactions benefited both parties. In 1879, for example, the hard-pressed Adams Paper Company sold Zenas Crane, Jr., a relatively new trimmer at a price well below that of a new one.[26]

Concentration also enabled neighboring mills to share a machine that neither used constantly. Generally one mill paid fees to the other, lowering both mills' fixed capital outlays. Such arrangements had ample precedent. Even in hand paper-making days, mills had rented different sizes of molds from one another, rather than each purchase a complete set. After mechanization, mill records show, for example, that in 1849 Platner & Smith of Lee shipped its paper to the Henry Chamberlin & Co. mill in Dalton for calendering. Likewise, Byron Weston relied on Crane & Co. to press his paper in the 1860s, before he owned a hydraulic press. Irregularly used machine tools might even be purchased jointly, as when Byron Weston pooled resources with the neighboring Bartlett and Cutting partnership and bought a calender lathe. As the number of firms operating more than one mill rose from one in 1830 to two in the following decade, four in 1850, nine by 1860, and eleven by 1880, the

[24] Byron Weston Letter Book, 1868–69, BWP, 3/31/69, 5/17/69, 5/31/69; "Machinery, Engineering, and Chemistry, 1866–1871," CMF, 12/29/69, 1/5/70. The Smith Paper Company press was offered to Crane & Co. by a firm in adjacent Litchfield County, Connecticut, which had bought it from Smith two months earlier. See also, Zenas Crane, Jr., Journal, 1879–81, CA, 11/3/79.

[25] William Bond Wheelwright, "Paper Making Since 1863: A Chronicle of Byron Weston Company and Paper Making in Berkshire County" (1938), BWP, p. 33; Byron Weston Letter Book, 1873–74, BWP, 9/2/73, 10/9/73.

[26] Zenas Crane, Jr., Journal, 1879–81, CA, 11/4/79.

practice of several mills sharing machinery must have grown even more common. After 1875, for example, the four Smith Paper Company mills made joint use of tools in the company machine shop.[27]

In sum, concentration helped to promote selective mechanization at Berkshire paper mills. It made the Berkshire paper maker receptive to the best technology by enabling him to examine and identify superior machines at other local mills. It allowed him to finance these new machines by selling old equipment locally. At the same time, the concentration of mills in the Berkshires gave the mill owner the chance to identify and avoid purchasing less satisfactory new machines. He could also make innovation less risky and less expensive by buying used equipment or by sharing machinery costs. The increasing frequency with which mill owners chose these alternatives points to a fourth major factor informing technological decisions—cost.

COST

In general, cost, like concentration, location, and timing, favored mechanization. Machines cost far more than hand tools, but reduced production expenses disproportionately. Originally, then, mill owners rushed to buy them. As machine builders improved on and extended paper-making machines, however, they continually raised their prices. The substantial initial investment later machines required made mill owners debate longer before buying, especially because improvements promised far less dramatic cost reductions than had the initial shift from hand to machine production.

Machine paper making cost far less than hand paper making, primarily because it lowered wage bills. The first American paper machine eliminated the jobs of ten men and five boys, saving the Gilpins between $6,000 and $12,000 a year. By comparison, the cost of a paper-making machine must have appeared negligible. Early American Fourdriniers sold for about $2,000 and simpler cylinder machines for even less. Closer to the Berkshires, as early as 1832 the Ames brothers reported to Treasury Department investigators that their manufacturing costs "had diminished since 1824 from 6 to 10

[27] The number of individuals owning shares of more than one mill also increased. Unfortunately, given contemporary cost accounting, the last kind of machine sharing has left little evidence. Zenas Crane Daybook, 1825–30, CA; Henry Chamberlin & Co. Ledger, BWP, 4/4/49; Byron Weston Letter Book, 1868–69, BWP; McGaw, "Sources and Impact," pp. 151–52; R. G. Dun & Co. Ledgers, 5:55.

per cent. . . . [I]t is principally to be attributed to the improvement in machinery," they explained.[28]

But the Ames brothers emphasized that while machines had lowered costs, "home competition has compelled the manufacturers to furnish [a much better article at the same price]; and this competition will continue to cause the price to decline." Byron Weston's retrospective analysis confirmed their prediction. Among the principal changes in Berkshire paper making between 1806 and 1880, he noted that whereas "the price of the old hand-made paper was from 40 to 50 cents a pound; the price of our modern machine-made paper is from 15 to 25 cents." As Weston's figures and the Ameses' testimony make clear, intense competition forced mill owners to pass on much of the machine's cost reduction to consumers. Falling prices either convinced hesitant mill owners to buy machines or drove them out of business. By 1850 James Willcox, a leading Pennsylvania paper maker, estimated that, neglecting only interest on machine purchases and the expense of repairs, machine production cost eight times less than hand paper making.[29]

Proprietors of mechanized mills, however, found it increasingly difficult to exclude the expense of repairs from their calculations. Repair bills further diminished the proportion of the machine's savings that mill owners realized in profit. Whereas in 1826 a major overhaul of Zenas Crane's hand mill had totaled only $197, routine maintenance expenditures in a mechanized mill quickly dwarfed that figure. Each paper-making machine had three different felts, which mill owners had to replace about every two months. Fourdriniers' wires needed equally frequent changes. Felts and wires remained expensive, in part because Americans continued to depend on imports long after they had become self-sufficient in paper machine manufacture. Paper machinery also contained numerous cutting blades needing costly professional sharpening and calender rolls requiring regular turning.[30]

Added to these routine maintenance costs, mills contended with

[28] Hancock and Wilkinson, "Gilpins," p. 401; *Century of Pioneering*, p. 4; *McLane Report*, part 1, pp. 96–97. Cost of imported machines probably delayed the introduction of the Fourdrinier machine. The first of these cost $30,000.

[29] *McLane Report*, part 1, p. 96; Weston, "Paper Making"; Weeks, *History of Paper Manufacturing*, p. 192.

[30] Zenas Crane Daybook, 1825–30, CA, rear endsheet. A detailed discussion of mill maintenance and repairs, including costs and frequency of various items needing replacement and changes in these figures over time, is provided in McGaw, "Sources and Impact," pp. 138–44.

mounting repair bills. Table 6.1 indicates that by the 1870s such expenses had assumed formidable proportions. Moreover, judging from these summary totals derived from L. L. Brown's detailed records, repair costs remained difficult to forecast as late as 1885. With annual repair bills varying by as much as $13,000, paper-making firms understandably debated longer before making financial commitments to new machines.

Simultaneously, as machines became more complete, more efficient, and larger, their purchase prices rose. L. L. Brown paid $4,000 for a Fourdrinier with dryer, sizing machine, cutter, and slitters in 1859. In 1872 one machine shop asked $5,600 of Crane & Co. for a similarly equipped cylinder machine, and Byron Weston spent $9,993 for a new Fourdrinier. By the 1880s shops quoted local mills prices of between $8,231 and $13,300 for a new Fourdrinier. Over time, then, cost became a factor working against the purchase of a new paper-making machine. The eventual savings might be great, but the necessity of raising so much capital and the competing expense of repairs and maintenance led growing numbers of mills to retain their old machines. The early development of good paper-making machines encouraged this practice. As Byron Weston observed:

> The machinery of 1850 brought the paper through all its stages to the "lay off," precisely as it does in this year of our Lord, 1880. The machinery may not have been so effective or convenient to run, but the paper-engine, and making process, has

TABLE 6.1
ANNUAL EXPENDITURES ON REPAIRS: L. L. BROWN'S UPPER
AND LOWER MILLS, ADAMS, 1873–85

Year	Amount	Year	Amount
1873	$10,823.19	1880	$ 5,551.60
1874	9,875.43	1881	11,973.14
1875	14,784.59	1882	15,754.54
1876	5,635.59	1883	13,400.97
1877	9,252.83	1884	6,704.73
1878	7,655.93	1885	2,707.54
1879	5,596.19		

NOTE: Figures include routine repairs discussed above. Compiled from L. L. Brown Journals, 1872–74, 1874–77, 1877–80, 1880–84, 1884–88, LLBP.

not changed in its work, and it then made as clean and perfect paper as the products of the present mills.[31]

Under these circumstances the used-machinery market developed into more than a local exchange. Machine shops took old machines in trade to promote sales of new machinery. The Lowell Machine Shop, for example, credited Carson Bros. & Co. for their used machine in 1859, billing the firm only the $1,600 difference in value for their new machine. Smith, Winchester & Co. offered Crane & Co. a secondhand sixty-three-inch Fourdrinier with machine calender for $5,700, after Crane's disastrous mill fire in 1869. By the same year dealers specializing in used machinery had emerged. One gave Crane several choices, ranging from a thirty-six-inch cylinder with two making vats, a sizing machine, a layboy, and a cutter for $600, to a two-year-old fifty-six-inch Fourdrinier with dryers, calender, and cutter for $5,500.[32]

Similar cost calculations preceded the decision to purchase other types of paper machinery. Most machines saved so much money over hand production that cost favored their initial adoption. But once mills owned adequate machinery, rising prices of new machines discouraged rapid replacement. For example, no mill could manage financially without some form of machine drying. In 1873 the English correspondent of one Lee paper mill owner noted from his personal experience that loft drying "is far the most expensive, so much so as to be inapplicable to any but the very best class papers." By 1869, however, a four-cylinder dryer cost $1,200 and a six-cylinder one, $2,000, enough so that one Berkshire paper mill used an outmoded fire dryer into the 1870s.[33]

Mills could be induced to substitute one machine for another

[31] Paper Machinery Memoranda, BL, 6/21/59; "Machinery, Engineering, and Chemistry, 1866–1871," CMF, 5/14/72; Wheelwright, "Paper Making Since 1863," BWP, p. 33; L. L. Brown Journal, 1884–88, LLBP, 12/84; "History of the Defiance Mill," History of the B. W. Co. File, BWP, p. 16; Weston, "Paper Making," p. 22. In 1832 Sellers found the Donkin Fourdrinier so perfect "that in the 54 subsequent years no essential changes have been made, and now the great bulk of the paper of the world is produced on machines substantially as they came from his brain and hands at that early period." Because he also referred to Donkin as "the most advanced mechanical engineer of the time," however, Weston's date of 1850 may be more appropriate for the machines used in the Berkshire paper industry. Ferguson, *Early Engineering Reminiscences*, p. 130.

[32] Paper Machinery Memoranda, BL, 3/1/59; "Fire Destroys Crane & Co.'s Old Stone Mill, 1869," CMF, 11/2/69, 12/24/69.

[33] "Miscellaneous Letters," HP, 8/7/73; "Fire Destroys Crane & Co.'s Old Stone Mill, 1869," CMF, 12/29/69; Weston, "Paper Making," p. 21.

when the newer machine greatly reduced operating expenses. This was the case with the partial replacement of the calender by the plater. Although the calender remained necessary for highly glazed finishes, the amount of paper damaged by the calender could be very costly. On one order Byron Weston even calculated that he lost money. Out of 125 reams run through the calender twice, only 100 emerged unscathed. Mills substituted platers for all but highly glazed surfaces because the plater made less "broke." Likewise, Platner and Smith found in high operating costs ample reason to innovate. They explained their willingness to experiment with a Kingsland refiner by noting that it used one-third less power than a Hollander performing the same work.[34]

Where older processes incurred smaller, or at least less obvious, expenses than did loft drying, calendering, or beating, the high cost of machines might convince manufacturers to retain equipment of a type used in hand paper mills. At prices of $720 to $950, a hydraulic press represented a significant investment. Because screw presses performed the same task adequately, many mills employed them long after the hydraulic press became an option. One old man who began working for Crane & Co. in 1881 recalled a scene that might have taken place in Zenas Crane's original mill:

> The paper that was between these form boards was put in the press (an old screw press), that would be screwed down just as hard as possible. They would secure these presses, and then along toward night after they had got all the presses full, one of the men from the finishing room would go around the mill and call out "Press!" The men would know that they were to go in the finishing room. They would hitch a little "jack" on to it. We had a long pole with an eye on the end of it, and we would stick one end of that pole into the hole in the screw press. Then at the upper end of the room there was a windlass with a big rope an inch in diameter, and a hook on the end of it. They would take that and pull it out, and hang it on to the eye of the pole. A man would then start and put it around just as far as he could and back. It was a slow process. In those days it was hard work—a whole lot of it, and slow.[35]

[34] Brown & Weston Letter Book, 1864–65, BWP, 3/17/65; "Philo Brownson and Edwin Brownson," interview typescript, CMF, p. 6; *VG*, 5/28/57, p. 2.

[35] Paper Machinery Memoranda, BL, 8/4/60; "Machinery, Engineering, and Chemistry, 1854–1865," CMF, 1/8/63, 9/25/63; L. L. Brown Paper Company Journal, 1877–80, LLBP, 1/80; "Alfred Hoxie," interview typescript, CMF, pp. 10–11.

Hollander beaters, which remained essentially unchanged throughout the nineteenth century, offer a less extreme example of high cost promoting technological conservatism. As beaters increased in size, speed, and efficiency, prices quoted to Berkshire mill owners rose from $450 in 1853 to $1,400 in 1872 and $2,604 in 1882. At the same time, machine shops could not predict with much precision the number of pounds of rags their engines would process or the efficiency with which they would operate, giving the mill owner little incentive to replace his old, familiar beaters. Not surprisingly, mill owners proceeded cautiously when deciding to purchase new Hollanders. Byron Weston, for example, wrote to E. D. Jones:

> You can make a rough sketch of the Engines and Drainers and how the engines will be driven and make an estimate of what *you will build them for all in running* order.
>
> We must know what the whole thing is to cost us before we make a start. Then we can tell whether we will attempt it this season or not.
>
> . . . When we are ready we shall give the job to the one who will do it *best* and *cheapest*.[36]

Mill owners typically purchased new beaters only to increase capacity, placing them in service beside older ones. Because old engines gradually wore down and their wooden linings eventually began to decay, Hollanders periodically underwent extensive repairs, giving mills many of the advantages of owning new beaters without equivalent expense. Workmen installed new timber linings and replaced bed plates and rolls. Indicative of the thoroughness of such alterations, Zenas Crane spent $160 on engine repairs as early as 1826, and in 1854 L. L. Brown paid over $500 for new beater parts. Similar cases of making extensive repairs, rather than replacing an old machine, include Crane & Co. ordering new vats and couch rolls for its cylinder machine and Zenas Crane, Jr., lengthening his old bleach boiler.[37]

[36] Emphasis in original. L. L. Brown & Co. Daybook, 1853–54, LLBP; "Machinery, Engineering, and Chemistry, 1866–1871," CMF, 5/8/72; L. L. Brown Paper Company Journal, 1880–84, LLBP, 1/82; "Machinery, Engineering, and Chemistry, 1854–1866," CMF, 10/10/65; Sutermeister, *Papermaking*, p. 132; Brown & Weston Letter Book, 1864–65, BWP, 2/20/65.

[37] Byron Weston Letter Book, 1867, BWP, 8/4/67; Letters to Byron Weston, 1867, BWP, 5/23/67; Zenas Crane Journal, 1825–30, CA; L. L. Brown & Co. Daybook, 1853–54, LLBP, 7/54; "Machinery, Engineering, and Chemistry, 1854–1865," CMF, 8/5/63; Zenas Crane, Jr., Journal, 1879–81, CA, 8/1/80.

In general, then, cost initially fostered innovation but ultimately came to slow its pace. The initial cost of newly developed machines, though substantially higher than that of hand tools, totaled far less than the wages saved, so the rapid acceptance of novel machines made good economic sense. Later, high prices for improved but not pathbreaking machinery convinced mill owners to keep old but adequate equipment in operation. Cost also encouraged technical compromises, such as renovating old machines or purchasing used ones.

Considered in combination, cost, concentration, location, and timing still fall short of delineating the final pattern of machine use in Berkshire paper mills. All four factors generally promoted uniformity among Berkshire's various paper-making establishments. Yet different mills in fact came to own different combinations of machines. Specialization, a factor that sometimes overrode all others, accounts for most technological variation.

SPECIALIZATION

As machinery became increasingly costly, specialization offered mill owners the chance to hold down their investment in fixed capital. Making many diverse products required many different machines, whereas concentrating on a smaller variety reduced the number of machines a mill needed. Given the advantages of Berkshire County's pure spring water and its proximity to the New York market for fine ledger, writing, and bank note paper, an increasing percentage of local mill owners equipped their mills to turn out fine paper exclusively. In general, this specialization made paper makers cautious about adopting new machines whose impact on paper quality remained undetermined. It also directed the efforts of the county's few paper machinery inventors toward perfecting fine paper equipment. Not all local manufacturers chose to make fine paper, however, and those making cheaper products more willingly risked lowering quality to cut costs.

County paper mills had departed from the traditional practice of manufacturing all grades of paper as early as the 1820s, when they entered the New York market. After mechanization, both rising machine prices and the economic advantages of operating specialized machines continuously, enforced greater specialization. For example, when Byron Weston and his partner, Charles O. Brown, bought Dalton's Defiance Mill in 1864, they acquired a mill already equipped for fine paper making. Brown replied to a customer's request for lesser grades of paper, "Our mill is not adapted to make cheap paper and we hope to put out first class paper exclusively." With this goal in mind, the partners invested in improved presses, calenders, and trimming knives, because fine paper making entailed more finishing. By 1867 experience had convinced Weston that enough potential customers existed to support a narrower specialty, first-class ledger paper. He bought out his partner, who disagreed, introduced chlorine bleaching to prepare the necessary linen rags, improved his ruling machine, rebuilt his beaters, and installed a new Fourdrinier. In Adams in 1849 L. L. Brown also decided to make only fine ledger paper, and he equipped his two mills for its production at the outset.[38]

Other mill owners' activities paralleled Weston's and Brown's. They concentrated on making particular fine papers and bought only the finishing equipment the product required. If ruling machines distinguished ledger paper mills, envelope machines and platers characterized stationery manufactories, and calenders identified fine printing paper makers. Likewise, specialized products called for appropriate beater rolls and bed plates. Despite these variations, however, all fine paper mills exhibited certain technological similarities.

Makers of fine paper often rejected innovations, invariably explaining their behavior by arguing that new techniques yielded an inferior product. Lacking testing facilities, their convictions rested almost exclusively upon tradition and experience, reinforced by a few adverse results obtained with new machines. Without objective evidence, such as microscopic analysis of the quality of paper produced by different techniques in different eras, it is not possible to assess how realistic manufacturers' objections were. In some cases, skepticism about a machine probably delayed its adoption even after its earlier shortcomings had been corrected. On the other hand, since their market depended on maintaining high quality and they had no reliable method for analyzing the results of some new techniques, fine paper makers' cautious attitudes toward new machines appear reasonable.

On occasion their beliefs certainly proved powerful deterrents to

[38] Brown & Weston Letter Book, 1863–64, BWP, 6/20/64; "History of the Defiance Mill," History of the B. W. Co. File, BWP, p. 3; Brown & Weston Letter Book, 1864–65, BWP, 1/23/65, 1/25/65, 11/29/64; Byron Weston Letter Book, 1867, BWP, 5/67; Wheelwright, "Paper Making Since 1863," BWP, pp. 33–34; Joseph Addison Wilk, "A History of Adams, Massachusetts" (Ph.D. diss., University of Ottawa, 1945), p. 157.

mechanization, as the persistence of loft drying illustrates. By the late nineteenth century, dry lofts remained only in fine paper mills. Between 1873 and 1889 Barlow and Bancroft conducted insurance surveys at nineteen Berkshire paper mills. They reported on drying methods in thirteen. All six of the mills making fine writing, bond, bank note, and ledger paper dried sized paper in steam-heated lofts. The six mills making manila, news, book, and common writing paper dried their paper on machines. A final mill, making collar paper, used both methods, probably reflecting production of two grades of paper.[39]

Crane & Co. tersely summed up the attitude of fine paper makers toward machine drying in a letter to a paper dealer: "If you put our papers on the same basis with papers that are dried over hot cylinders, then we can't talk." More discursively, they explained their beliefs to a new client, the United States government. Concerning enclosed samples of bank note paper, they wrote:

> . . . this paper is a double sized loft dried paper, which, while it will not print quite as readily as Machine dried paper, possess much better sizing qualities, is much stronger and will wear very much longer—We have facilities for making it either way i.e. Loft dried or Machine dried but our experience tells us that the former is much better, and that it is the only way to properly dry a Bank Note paper as by that process the paper is from three to four days drying and by the other about as many minutes which as you can readily see must and does burn the fiber and kill the sizing qualities. . . . —Owing to the paper being dried by machinery in a few moments as stated it is smoother, lies a little flatter, and is softer and perhaps will print a trifle better, but on the other hand the Loft dried paper, if properly made will hold any impression it takes much better than if dried by the other process.

Evidently the Cranes succeeded in convincing the government. Only in the 1950s did the Bureau of Printing and Engraving agree to accept machine-dried paper.[40]

---

[39] C. A. Barlow and J. M. Bancroft, "Special Insurance Surveys of Manufacturing Risks in the United States," BL, nos. 9790, 4166, 4169, 4593, 2978, 4868, 5236, 4396, 5878, 3836, 4167, 4170, 4300. Loft drying was probably confined to drying sized paper, although the insurance surveys do not make this distinction. After making, the paper was probably machine dried, then sized, and then loft dried.

[40] Crane & Co. Letter Book, 1874, CA, 8/12/74; "First Government Contract," CMF, 4/9/79; Irving Witham, Plant Engineer, Crane & Co., interview and tour of

Fine paper makers also suspected that mechanical rag cutters lowered paper quality. David Carson voiced his concern in 1847, shortly before his retirement, when he asked another mill owner "whether the machine cleans [the rags] as well as formerly when they were dressed by girls." Of the nineteen local paper mills Barlow and Bancroft surveyed, eleven of twelve making lesser grades of paper employed rag cutters. The exception reported using a cutter occasionally. The seven fine paper mills contrasted sharply. Four did all rag cutting by hand, one relied on hand cutting almost exclusively, one combined the two methods, and one used a cutter. The mill owner who rarely used his cutter had evidently found its performance disappointing. A year after its installation, the superintendent noted in his time book: "We started Rag cutter August 7, 1872. We did not start the cutter again since that day by Order of Z. M. Crane."[41]

Manufacturers making high-quality paper avoided some rag-processing and sheet-forming innovations as well. Fine paper mills insisted on using clean white rags, rather than using rotary bleach boilers. Of nine such machines known to be operating in the county, fine paper mills housed only two. Similarly, because fine paper makers believed stock had to be beaten slowly over prolonged periods, none of the five refiners in Berkshire mills before 1885 was located in a fine paper mill. Later, when one Dalton mill purchased a Jordan, Zenas Crane, Jr., disputed the wisdom of the decision, maintaining that the machine would impair the quality of the mill's product. Fine paper mills also normally retained traditional beaters lined with wood. Common paper mills, more concerned with cost than with quality, introduced more durable iron beater linings, despite the possibility of rust contamination. In addition, fine paper mills exhibited technological conservatism by running their machines more slowly and by retaining and even reintroducing hand paper making for some products. Their customers supported these deci-

---

Wahconah Mill, August 19, 1975. Earlier, in 1867, Byron Weston even disparaged the idea of heating dry lofts. Byron Weston Letter Book, 1867, BWP, 6/14/67. The fact that some customers doubted that there was a significant difference between machine- and loft-dried paper is revealed in a letter to the Hurlbut Paper Company from a customer. He asks that, to settle a debate between himself and a retail customer, one of the mill owners examine the enclosed two sheets of paper and label them as either loft or machine dried. "1880" File, HP, 3/31/82.

[41] Harrison Elliott, "A Century Ago an Eminent Author Looked upon Paper and Paper Making," *PM* 21 (1952):58; Barlow and Bancroft, "Insurance Surveys," nos. 4166, 4169, 4593, 2878, 4868, 6696, 5236, 3016, 4396, 6103, 5878, 3836, 4167, 4170, 8258, 8257, 8256, 6553, 4300; Crane & Co. Time Book, 1863–76, CA, 8/2/73.

sions. Bankers, for example, willingly paid some mills high prices for handmade bank note paper as late as the 1850s because they believed it was stronger.[42]

Although fine paper makers showed reluctance to introduce dryers, rag cutters, bleach boilers, and Jordans, their peculiar needs encouraged some innovation. The early and rapid acceptance of the Fourdrinier in the Berkshires and at Holyoke, also a fine paper center, owed much to fine paper mill owners' preference for a machine that formed a more perfect sheet. Indeed, they may have had little choice. Crane's bank note paper customers, at least, repeatedly specified Fourdrinier paper, preferring its greater strength and its uniform shrinkage, because, for multicolored printing, they had to dampen each sheet repeatedly. That Fourdrinier ownership abetted specialization is clear in the case of Crane & Co. They began making bond paper by machine one year after they set up Dalton's first Fourdrinier.[43]

Mechanized sizing and watermarking also especially characterized fine paper mills. In fact, mechanized sizing reflected their technological conservatism. As Chapter 7 will discuss, fine paper companies delayed the introduction of rosin or internal sizing, a method of sizing stock in the beaters. The chemistry of sizing remained poorly understood and size played a crucial role in keeping writing paper from absorbing ink and in making it erase well, so that Berkshire's fine writing and ledger paper makers understandably clung to known and trusted sizing techniques. Of necessity, then, machines to apply traditional animal size played a prominent role in fine paper mills. Similarly, the dandy roll, used to impress watermarks on paper, appeared in fine paper mills exclusively. Only such

[42] Brown & Weston Letter Book, 1864–65, BWP, 1/25/65; WPA Guide, p. 269; Barlow and Bancroft, "Insurance Surveys," nos. 4170, 8257, 8256, 4266, 4593, 6696, 4396, 4167; Smith Paper Company Test Records, 1875–, SP; Zenas Crane, Jr., Journal, 1879–81, CA, 10/1/80; "Alfred Hoxie," interview typescript, CMF, p. 4; McGaw, "Sources and Impact," pp. 124–25; "The (The Perry Green) Comstock Paper Mill," SF 3 (March 1930): 10; Weston, "Paper Making," p. 15; "Thomas J. Bolton," interview typescript, CMF, p. 5; Coleman Sellers Letter Book, 1828–34, APS; File 15, CMF, 1/12/49; File 86, CMF, 7/13/46, 1/19/50.

[43] Green, Holyoke, p. 88. Sources of data on machines are listed in Appendix C. Information on type of product is scattered throughout local histories, Weston's history, articles in SF, company records, and the Barlow and Bancroft insurance surveys. File 23, CMF, 4/28/60; File 27, CMF, 9/19/63; File 29, CMF, 4/9/64, 9/19/64; File 35, CMF, 10/28/70; File 170, CMF, 1/5/47.
The fact that the cylinder machine continued to predominate in the mills of Columbia County, New York, where inferior grades of paper were made, reinforces this point. Smith, History of Papermaking, p. 94.

mills and their customers had reason to identify their paper with distinctive markings.[44]

Machines especially suited to fine paper mills figured disproportionately in local inventive activity. Berkshire paper machine patentees generally worked in paper mills, rather than in machine shops, encouraging their concentration on devices for fine paper making. Of fourteen identifiable local paper machinery patents, nine catered to fine paper mills. As improved paper clamp, a layboy, and a trimmer all met the needs of mills selling paper in sheets, as did fine paper mills. News, book, and common printing paper makers, by contrast, sold paper in rolls for use in web presses. Two ruling machine improvements, two sizing machine improvements, and a device to mix color with pulp emerged from other minds preoccupied with the fine paper industry's problems. A final innovation, Z. M. Crane's development of threaded bank note paper, served the interests of even more specialized producers.[45]

[44] Sutermeister, *Papermaking*, p. 145. References to size machines appear scattered through Owen & Hurlbut Receipt Book, 1843–46, HP; L. L. Brown Daybook, 1853–54, LLBP; L. L. Brown & Co. Journal, 1856, LLBP; L. L. Brown Paper Company Daybook, 1874–76, LLBP; L. L. Brown Paper Company Journal, 1876–79, LLBP; L. L. Brown Paper Company Daybook, 1881–85, LLBP; L. L. Brown Paper Company Journal, 1880–84, LLBP; Brown & Weston Letter Book, 1865–66, BWP; Byron Weston Letter Book, 1867, BWP; "Fire Destroys Crane & Co.'s Old Stone Mill, 1869," CMF; "Byron Weston," CMF; Crane & Co. Time Book, 1863–76, CA; "Machinery, Engineering, and Chemistry, 1866–1871," CMF; Zenas Crane, Jr., Journal, 1879–81, CA.

On dandy rolls see also Carson & Brown Ledger, 1849–53, CA; "L. L. Brown Records of Business Transactions, 1862–1863," LLBP; Brown & Weston Letter Book, 1863–64, BWP; Letters to Byron Weston, 1867, BWP; Byron Weston Letter Book, 1867–68, BWP; Byron Weston Letter Book, 1868–69, BWP; Byron Weston Letter Book, 1874–75, BWP; Crane & Co. Letter Book, 1874, CA; "Machinery, Engineering, and Chemistry, 1879–1886," CMF.

[45] *General Index to Patents, 1790–1873*, Record Group 241, Records of the Patent Office, Microcopy GR16, NA, 1005–15; *General Index of the Official Gazette and Monthly Volumes of Patents of the Unites States Patent Office*, annual vols. 1874–85, NA. The index covering 1790–1873 lists the town of residence of the inventor and, therefore, all Berkshire patents have probably been located. For subsequent years the index omits this information, so some Berkshire patents, those by individuals not readily traceable to local mills and machine shops, may have been missed.

Of the fourteen local improvements, nine originated in paper mills, two were claimed by machine shop personnel, and three were the products of workmen whose affiliation is unclear. Five other innovations are mentioned in Weston, "Paper Making," pp. 20–22, and Munsell, *Chronology*, pp. 75–76, 96, although they do not appear in patent office records. As with patented improvements, most, if not all, originated in paper mills and four of the five were especially suited to fine paper mills. For a somewhat fuller discussion of inventive activity in the region see McGaw, "Sources

Despite the Berkshire industry's prominent commitment to fine paper making, many county mills chose other markets, and their machinery differed accordingly. A few paper mill products, such as the local manufacture of paper for twine, bonnets, industrial belting, and collars, lasted only as long as temporary fads or Civil War shortages. Each left distinctive mechanical contrivances behind. The manufacture of news paper, on the other hand, had a long local history. Unlike the fine paper market, where customers would bear the cost of expensive hand processing, the nineteenth-century news paper market emerged because of low prices. As a result, mills designed to produce news paper offer a sharp contrast to fine paper mills.[46]

Conscious of cost more than of quality, news paper mill owners welcomed the very technology fine paper manufacturers rejected. They installed rag cutters, steam dryers, stock refiners, and bleach boilers early. The importance of cost in the news paper market also guaranteed customers for the larger, faster, paper-making machines that fine paper makers found exorbitantly priced and unnecessary. Local news paper makers operated on a large enough scale to muster the requisite capital, and they dealt in a competitive enough market to value even slight operating cost reductions.

Not surprisingly, Berkshire news paper mills consistently set the pace in mechanizing. The Laflin brothers, who supplied paper for the first issue of Horace Greeley's *New York Tribune*, bought Berkshire's first paper-making machine. By the late nineteenth century, their successor, the Smith Paper Company, delivered a thousand dollars worth of newsprint a day to the *New York Herald*. To retain this business and meet an occasional rush order from James Gordon Bennett for a thousand tons, the firm led local mills in adding improved machinery and acquired its own machine shop to minimize delays.[47]

ALTHOUGH fine paper mills and newsprint mills illustrate very different technological approaches to paper making, it is important to recall that the same basic factors shaped these divergent approaches

---

and Impact," pp. 76, 153–54. See also the discussion in Chapter 9 of workers' innovations as described in the local newspaper.

[46] For a fuller discussion of other local specializations see McGaw, "Sources and Impact," pp. 119, 129–31.

[47] Barlow and Bancroft, "Insurance Surveys," passim; McGaw, "Sources and Impact," pp. 118–19, 128–29, 151. From 1857 to 1885 the *Valley Gleaner* published frequent reports of new machines installed by Smith.

and that, in general, these factors promoted rapid and continuous mechanization. Once machines became an option, all local mills hurried to install them, abetted by Berkshire mills' comparatively recent construction, their proximity to machine shops and to demonstration machines in other local mills, and their owners' willingness to invest modest sums in machines to realize greater savings in wages. Over time, however, rising machine prices and different market constraints made fine paper makers increasingly reluctant mechanizers and newsprint manufacturers especially avid ones. In the years after 1860 their divergent interests in cheapness or quality made their technological histories increasingly distinct.

PART III

AFTER THE MACHINE

CHAPTER 7

THE MILL TOWNS TRANSFORMED:
TECHNOLOGICAL CHANGE
AFTER MECHANIZATION,
1857–1885

January 23, 1857, began as a rather typical Berkshire winter night, bitterly cold and windy. Then, at 1:30 A.M., the Lee Congregational Church bell began ringing unexpectedly, awakening the sleeping citizens and startling those paper mill hands working night tour. In response, members of the recently organized volunteer fire company, including both paper mill workers and mill owners, rushed out into the bitter night. They dragged the new "Water Witch" fire engine to a spot opposite the blazing block of stores at the south end of Main Street and began pumping with all their might. But hostile nature frustrated their combined efforts. Howling winds fanned the blaze. Intense cold froze the water as it fell.[1]

The fire still burned brightly when the new town clock, one hundred feet away in the old church steeple, struck three. Shortly thereafter, as the assembled citizens watched with horror, a gust of wind picked up a flaming shingle from the business block and deposited it on the cupola above the clock and bell. The fire fighters had no way to reach the tower, no way to douse the flames. Several minutes later the clock and the bell plummetted to the earth. By 5:00 A.M. nothing remained of the church except two or three cords of charred wood. The rest was ashes. The imposing fifty-six-year-old landmark, where many local citizens had worshipped and most had gathered annually for the town meeting, no longer stood at the center of town life.[2]

The fiery destruction of the Lee Congregational Church can serve as a convenient symbol for the transformation of the paper mill towns after 1857. Like the citizens of Lee in January 1857, Berkshire paper makers suffered a rude awakening in the years after mechanization. Although their machines were running

---

[1] Hyde, *History of Lee*, p. 273; Col. William Weingar, "Notes on the History of Lee," LLHR; *VG*, passim.

[2] Hyde, *History of Lee*, pp. 230–35.

smoothly, alarming new problems drew them outside the mills and forced them to confront their limitations in the face of nature. Berkshire's resources, so long deemed inexhaustible, now appeared inadequate. Chronic shortages of fiber, fuel, process water, and waterpower recurrently plagued mill owners. Moreover, familiar but uncontrollable natural forces aggravated their situation. Local rivers periodically froze, flooded, or dried up, and between 1857 and 1885 twenty-six devastating fires reduced local mills to ashes and their costly machines to scrap. Berkshire County's three oldest mills—Zenas Crane's original mill, the Church brothers' first Lee mill, and David Carson's Old Red Mill—all disappeared from the local landscape.[3]

Just as the fire began in the business block but created a baffling dilemma when it spread without warning to the church tower, so the new production dilemmas mill owners faced after mechanization resulted directly and unexpectedly from the mechanical productivity they had wrought. And like the volunteer fire company, mill owners found their impressive technological preparation insufficient when confronting unanticipated new problems. Initially, like the firemen vainly pumping water into the howling wind, mill owners tried to mitigate the impending crisis by repeating familiar behaviors: they sought out more rags, fuel, sizing, and springs; built more dams; and expanded existing mill structures. Ultimately, however, they found that traditional solutions fell short when addressing novel problems.

With substantial investments at stake, mill owners managed to solve the problems of scarce resources, inadequate power, and devastating fire. But unlike mechanization, the new technological solutions they adopted brought to the mill towns physical changes as dramatic as the old church's destruction. Berkshire paper makers pioneered the American manufacture of wood pulp newsprint, but at the cost of deforesting local hillsides. They introduced new chemicals to economize on traditional raw materials, but understood their use so poorly that they frequently polluted local rivers. After flooding hundreds of acres to increase waterpower, they supplemented waterwheels with steam engines, burned up more of the local forests, and exhausted steam and smoke into the village air. Finally, they constructed enormous new fire-resistant buildings to concentrate production and replace mills that had burned. These imposing structures dominated the local landscape, their steam

[3] See Appendix A. Lee's earliest mill was torn down during these years; the two Dalton mills burned.

whistles replaced the church bell as the loudest local voice, and their numerous workers crowded the once quiet village streets. By 1885 the mill towns had been transformed.

FROM RAGS TO WOOD PULP

The most pressing problem mill owners confronted after mechanizing was a growing shortage of rags. Throughout its history in the Western world, paper making had meant fabricating sheets of interwoven cotton and linen fibers. The general use of these materials in clothing and bedding had assured their availability to mill owners. Machines, with their augmented paper-making capacity, quickly increased the demand for rags beyond the readily accessible supply. Manufacturers pursued two lines of response: maximizing the supply of rags and adopting new fibers. Initially, Berkshire mill owners solved the problem by getting rags from more distant sources, using inferior grades of rags, and monitoring raw material costs more closely. Despite their efforts, soaring rag prices threatened to curtail the growth of paper markets that existed only because machines had made paper cheap.

A second approach was to use non-rag fiber. Just as inelastic skilled labor supplies had motivated machine builders to devise mechanized paper makers, so a worldwide rag shortage induced inventive minds to examine alternative fibers. Because the Berkshire paper industry had achieved national prominence, advocates of new fibers often approached local mill owners to conduct experiments or otherwise invest in a new fiber's development. In the years after 1857, however, mill owners could not afford to risk money or productive capacity on untested fibers. They adopted new raw materials only after they saw some evidence of a fiber's probable commercial success. As rag prices soared, they made paper from straw, hemp, jute, and esparto grass. All had been tested successfully at paper mills outside the Berkshires, but each fiber still had significant liabilities. After outside investors assumed the risks of wood pulp production, therefore, Berkshire mill owners agreed to initiate commerical-scale manufacture of wood pulp newsprint in America.

The earliest solution to the rag shortage was to obtain additional rags abroad. Although Zenas Crane had used foreign rags as early as 1822 and Berkshire mills bought large quantities of "foreigns" ten years later, rag imports expanded most dramatically following the mechanization of local paper mills. Between 1837 and 1872 the dollar value of American rag imports increased 26 percent a year on the average. Most local mill owners continued to buy foreign rags through New York warehouses, as Zenas Crane had done. Beginning in 1871, however, the county's leading mill owner, Elizur Smith, demonstrated the importance he attached to a continuous supply of European rags by contracting directly for $20,000 worth a month.[4]

Berkshire paper manufacturers valued European rags as much for their quality as for their quantity. By 1850 an American paper maker noted ruefully, "The article of cotton has here almost entirely superseded the use of linen for wearing apparel and when much worn and reduced to rags becomes a very tender substance; in fact, scarcely able to support its weight when made into paper." Mill owners sometimes supplemented limp cotton rags with more expensive raw cotton, but the strongest, finest paper still required linen. In the years following mechanization, fine paper makers found linen rags especially difficult to acquire. Like their American contemporaries, citizens of industrialized northern and western Europe increasingly wore cotton clothing. For a time, desperate shortages of linen rags moved rag dealers to such bizarre expedients as importing exhumed Egyptian mummies solely for their wrappings. In the long run, rag dealers opened up rag markets in southern and eastern Europe, concentrating on Italy in particular.[5]

In addition to searching out foreign rag supplies, rag wholesalers rapidly organized the burgeoning rag trade. By the late 1830s and early 1840s they had abandoned earlier rough classifications of

[4] Zenas Crane Daybook, 1817–23, CA, 2/22/22; Smith, *History of Papermaking*, pp. 124–25; R. G. Dun & Co. Ledgers, 5:52. Although less data is available on pounds of rags imported, figures for 1846–57 suggest that increased expenditures generally reflect increases in quantities imported. Munsell, *Chronology*, pp. 88–119 passim.

These and subsequent generalizations on sources, costs, and quality of rag supplies are based on references in David Carson Daybook, 1828–34, CA; "1830s" and "1850s" Files, HP; Owen & Hurlbut Receipt Book, 1843–46, HP; Zenas Crane Journal, 1825–41, CA; Zenas Crane Daybook, 1817–33, CA; Crane & Co. Ledger, 1844–49, CA; Zenas Crane & Sons Record, 1840–42, CA; Carson & Brown Ledger, 1849–53, CA; Zenas Crane, Jr., Journal, 1879–81, CA; Crane & Co. Journal, 1840–, CA; Brown & Weston and Byron Weston letter books, 1863–68; 1873–75, BWP; Ledger of the Aetna, Housatonic, and Defiance Mill, 1834–47, BWP; L. L. Brown & Co. Daybook, 1853–54, LLBP; Byron Weston Miscellaneous Records, BWP; Letters to Byron Weston, 1867, BWP, 4/18/67; Byron Weston Letter Book, 1868–69, BWP, 12/23/68, 2/3/69, 2/5/69; Crane & Co. Letter Book, 1874, CA, 7/2/74, 7/8/74, 7/23/74, 7/24/74, 8/5/74, 8/10/74; "Byron Weston," CMF, 10/27/64; "Crane Brothers," CMF, 7/2/79, 11/15/72, 11/22/72, 2/18/75.

[5] Weeks, *History of Paper Manufacturing*, p. 219; Munsell, *Chronology*, pp. 88–109, 286–87.

stock by color, fiber, and grade (#1 or #2, common or fine). Instead, they introduced a series of trademarks, indicating much more precise grades. These expedited the increasingly specialized mill owner's task of ordering appropriate rags and controlling rag supplies.[6]

By enabling mill owners to specify precise grades of rags, dealers also helped the mill owner minimize growing rag costs. The Smith Paper Company, which made cheap papers such as news, could order only the cheapest grades, grades that Elizur Smith could not economically cull out for himself. By the 1870s, for example, Smith purchased muss, a mixture of lower-grade cotton rags and threads; dustings, the smaller bits and pieces of stock that other mills shook out at the duster; collar cuttings and shavings, the refuse of paper collar mills; used wrapping paper; and non-rag fiber. Rag dealers lowered fine paper makers' raw material costs primarily by guaranteeing them a market for refuse rags, threads, lint, and trimmer shavings. As a result of this market and of precise grading, Byron Weston calculated that his net loss from sorting out unacceptable rags had fallen to 2.8 percent by 1885. Alternatively, rag dealers offered fine paper makers the option of eliminating sorting costs entirely by purchasing new white rags, scraps that dealers bought from shirt makers. Most of Berkshire's fine paper makers availed themselves of this option, at least for their finest papers.[7]

Although they depended on rag merchants to open new markets and to organize the rag trade, Berkshire mill owners worked personally to control rag costs by scrutinizing the rags they puchased and by analyzing rag consumption. They carefully studied rags at neighboring mills or requested samples before buying in quantity, because, despite grading, dealers' wares varied. "If you have any

[6] "American Industries No. 72," p. 275. Rag merchants were frequently general paper merchants, wholesaling paper and supplying chemicals as well as dealing in rags. See, for example, Carter, *Cyrus Field*, p. 64.

[7] Smith Paper Company Test Records, 1875–, SP; Byron Weston Letter Book, 1867, BWP, 4/15/67, 5/15/67, 8/27/67; "Crane Brothers," CMF, 10/27/64, 1/25/65, 2/16/65, 11/15/72, 7/2/79; Letters to Byron Weston, 1867, BWP, 4/18/67, 5/8/67; Byron Weston Letter Book, 1873–74, BWP; Zenas Crane Journal, 1829–41, CA; Carson & Brown Ledger, 1849–53, CA; Zenas Crane Daybook, 1819–24, CA; Crane & Co. Journal, 1840–, CA; Crane & Co. Ledger, 1844–49, CA; Zenas Crane Daybook, 1824–29, CA; Zenas Crane Journal, 1825–30, CA; Zenas Crane Daybook, 1824–33, CA; Zenas Crane, Jr., Journal, 1879–81, CA, 2/14/79, 3/1/79, 3/31/79; "T. G. & W. W. Carson," CMF, 1845–46 account; Owen & Hurlbut Blotter, 1823–24, HP, May entries; Brown & Weston Letter Book, 1863–64, BWP, 1/27/64; Ledger of the Aetna, Housatonic, and Defiance Mill, 1839–47, BWP; Byron Weston Miscellaneous Records, BWP; L. L. Brown & Co. Daybook, 1853–54, LLBP, 4/53; Ledger of Henry Chamberlin & Co., BWP.

A #1 shirt cuttings please send us sample ton of them . . . ," wrote
Crane & Co. in 1874. Once satisfied, they ordered more rags, re-
minding the dealer to maintain quality. "Have you any more *good
cuttings?*" they inquired. "If you have send us *two* or *three* ton *as good
as the last you sent us.*" Even after identifying an acceptable dealer,
manufacturers found that eternal vigilance was the price of the very
best rags. "The last *cuttings* you sent us, were, some of them *very*
poor—but as they were so few we did not deduct but hope you will
see that the next you send us are all *right*," the Cranes cautioned one
supplier. They notified another, "We charge you back 3¢ *pr lb* on
475 lb of poor cuttings."[8]

Faced with rising rag costs, mill owners kept a close eye on every
shipment's weight and price as well. For example, Byron Weston
sent off a bill to a supplier whose rag invoice overstated his shipment. Weston explained: "The bales fall short from 1 to 7 lb. each.—
Your scale must be out of the way—. . . . I looked to this weighing
myself and don't think we are wrong." Several years later he demanded of another supplier, "Send me a copy of my order for rags
at 14 3/4¢—I haven't paid that in a year—. . . and don't believe I
ordered it."[9]

As noted earlier, after mechanization mill owners began keeping
receipt books and conducting inventories, accounting practices that
gave them a clearer picture of raw material expenses. To help them
control and compensate for mounting rag prices, they also instituted cost accounting, the first evidence of managerial accounting in
the industry. The elaborate and extremely advanced standard costing methods devised by Elizur Smith to promote efficient use of raw
materials will be discussed in Chapter 8. Less remarkable, but
equally important, were fine paper makers' calculations of actual
production costs, allowing them to pass rising raw material costs on
to their customers. Addison Laflin deserves primary credit for the
adoption of cost accounting in the industry. In 1862 he delivered a
forceful address before the new Writing Paper Maker's Association,
arguing that three decades of sustained technological and economic
change had so outmoded traditional pricing policies that writing paper manufacturers frequently sold paper for less than it cost to
make. He attributed the continuing depression in the industry not

[8] Brown & Weston Letter Book, 1865–66, BWP, 1/26/66, 3/30/66; Crane & Co. Letter Book, 1874, CA, 7/21/74, 8/7/74, 9/12/74.

[9] Brown & Weston Letter Book, 1863–64, BWP, 4/6/64; Byron Weston Letter
Book, 1868–69, BWP, 12/23/68, 2/5/69.

simply to overproduction, but to "ignorance of the cost of production and a general under-estimate thereof."[10]

When heeding Laflin's counsel to study actual costs closely, Berkshire mill owners concentrated especially on rapidly rising rag costs.
Byron Weston left detailed records of his procedures. He weighed
new cuttings on receipt and then took samples, dried them thoroughly, and weighed them again to determine weight loss attributable to moisture content. Then he washed the samples to remove all
starch, dried them, and weighed them again to determine how
much fiber a pound of cuttings actually contained. For old rags,
Weston also calculated net loss through dusting, sorting, bleaching,
and washing. All this enabled him to compute real rag costs per
pound of paper.[11]

Paper makers' particular concern with rag costs stemmed both
from rapidly increasing rag prices and from the fact that, whatever
their current price, rags comprised the paper mill's single greatest
expense. By 1866 Byron Weston found his average rag costs for one
hundred pounds of paper had reached $19.89. Labor, his next larg-
est outlay, totaled only $5.04. Even in 1881, after rag prices had
fallen, Weston calculated that rag purchases constituted 43 percent
of all his expenditures, including capital improvements. Similarly,
in 1883 the Bureau of Statistics of Labor reported that, of the market value of paper made in Massachusetts, stock accounted for
63.29 percent, whereas labor made up only 15.51 percent and interest and expenses only 14.06 percent.[12]

Despite all the efforts of mill owners and rag dealers, rag prices
advanced rapidly, especially after 1857. New rag sources, a reorganized rag trade, and mill owner surveillance all helped control
price increases until the 1850s. Thereafter, Berkshire mill owners,
who had paid at most eight to ten cents a pound between 1830 and
1855, found themselves paying eighteen to twenty cents a pound.

[10] Whereas financial accounting, such as the mercantile procedures described in
Chapter 5, is designed to summarize a firm's economic condition, cost accounting en-
compasses procedures developed to aid internal management decision making and
promote operating efficiency. Laflin, "Address," CMF.

[11] Byron Weston Miscellaneous Records, BWP.

[12] Ibid., pp. 22, 297; Commonwealth of Massachusetts, *Fourteenth Annual Report of
the Bureau of Statistics of Labor* (Boston, 1883), pp. 358–59.

By way of comparison, raw materials made up 53.45 percent of the value of cotton
goods produced in the state, 60.99 percent of the value of woolens, 51.39 percent of
the value of wooden ware, and 46.89 percent of the value of machines. BSL, *Fourteenth Annual Report*, pp. 356–61.

Minimum prices also rose from one to two cents before 1855 to three to six cents in subsequent decades. Byron Weston's rag costs averaged about fourteen and a half cents a pound in the late 1860s. Maximum rag prices returned to the eight-cent-per-pound level only in the late 1870s, reflecting lessened demand following the successful development of alternative fibers.[13]

After they instituted cost-finding techniques, fine paper makers such as Weston, the Cranes, and L. L. Brown could afford to pay high prices for rags, because they could pass costs on to their customers. By contrast, makers of news paper, book paper, and cheap writing paper, such as Elizur Smith and John Carroll, could not raise prices much without forfeiting some of their market. Addressing their problems, a bevy of would-be inventors mounted a wide-ranging quest for alternatives to rag pulp.

The need for a satisfactory substitute fiber achieved wide enough recognition that many men without paper-making experience devoted some thought to the matter. A number of them wrote to Berkshire mill owners, offering to share the fantastic fortune their fiber guaranteed, if only the mill owner would help to develop it. Before wood pulp became commercially successful, local mill owners received unsolicited suggestions of arrowroot pulp (1848), an unnamed fiber from the Pacific (1854), a mysterious vegetable fiber that "no acid or any known agent save fire can destroy or affect" (1860), asbestos (1860), and the wildflower Life Everlasting (1862). Later correspondents proposed wild cane (1869), milkweed (1870), an unidentified fiber from Honduras (1881), and another imported from Japan (1884). An 1863 correspondent who insisted on keeping his promising fiber secret, expressed the unwritten assumption of all these aspiring millionaires when he wrote, "At this time of high prices of stock I suppose all manufacturers would be ready to try any new plan which promised to decrease the price of paper stock." The writer failed to recognize that the problem was not simply one of identifying a fiber that could be macerated and formed into sheets. By 1772 Jacob Christian Schäffer had successfully made a few sheets of paper from hemp, bark, straw, cabbage stocks, cattails, thistles, cornhusks, wasps' nests, and many other vegetable fi-

[13] Nonetheless, the greatly augmented production of the mechanized paper mill kept total rag bills high. Whereas Zenas Crane had spent less than $2,000 on rags in 1822, Byron Weston spent almost $90,000 in 1881. Zenas Crane Daybook, 1817–23, CA; Zenas Crane Daybook, 1819–24, CA; Byron Weston Letter Book, 1866–67, BWP; Byron Weston Miscellaneous Records, BWP, pp. 22–23, 297. See n. 4 for sources of rag price data summarized.

bers and several individuals had experimented with asbestos as early as 1684.[14]

Men more familiar with paper making recognized three additional considerations as equally important. First, successful commercial production of paper from a new fiber would require a period of experimentation and might involve additional fixed capital. Already hard pressed to buy and operate increasingly large, expensive machines, paper manufacturers could afford neither. Second, to warrant investment in its development, a new fiber had to be more abundant than rags and far cheaper. Finally, even at lower prices, paper customers would be reluctant to buy a markedly inferior product. Indeed, a ready market depended on the new product resembling rag paper closely. These financial and commercial constraints narrowed the field of viable alternatives to hemp, jute, straw, esparto, and wood.[15]

Lyman Hollingsworth of South Braintree, Massachusetts, originated the use of hemp in 1837, when he substituted old rag-bale ropes for the rags he could not afford. He found that hemp possessed important similarities to rags. Like linen its fiber is about 80 percent cellulose and it is very strong. Probably this explains paper maker Hollingsworth's relatively quick adaptation of rag paper technology to hemp, indicated by his 1843 patent of the product. It also explains why Berkshire paper makers most frequently turned to hemp as an alternative. After machine production commenced, at least ten different local mills, including three of Smith's, made yellow-tinted manila paper from hemp. At least five other mills, including two of Smith's, made a similar paper, also often called manila, from jute butts. Nonetheless, hemp had two drawbacks that restricted its use. It cost more than the cheapest rag fiber, in part because it had to be shipped from the southeastern part of the nation. More important, paper manufacturers could not bleach it white enough to contrast sharply with black ink, as most paper customers preferred.[16]

[14] "Other Fibers," CMF, 7/13/48, 3/22/60, 11/10/60, 2/4/63, 11/19/70, 12/6/84; SF 3 (January 1930):11; File 491, CMF, 1/2/69; File 252, CMF, 9/3/81; Weeks, *History of Paper Manufacturing*, p. 211; Library of Congress, *Papermaking: Art and Craft* (Washington, D.C., 1968), p. 68.

[15] Laflin of Herkimer also experimented with hop vines and the U.S. Department of Agriculture tried to promote cornhusk paper, but these alternatives had many of the same liabilities as straw and lacked several of its virtues. VG, 1/8/63, p. 2; 4/9/63, p. 4; 9/8/64, pp. 1–2.

[16] Sutermeister, *Papermaking*, pp. 28–29; Library of Congress, *Papermaking*, p. 69; Barlow and Bancroft, "Insurance Surveys," nos. 4166, 6103, 4170; Weston, "Paper

Next to hemp, more Berkshire mills made paper from straw than from any other alternative fiber. In 1828 William Magaw of Meadville, Pennsylvania, patented a chemical process to reduce straw to cellulose fiber. The following year, aided by Pennsylvania mill owner George Shryock, he produced straw paper commercially. He successfully converted straw into either a bleached, white writing and printing paper, or a coarse yellow board. As with hemp, Berkshire paper manufacturers willingly adopted the new fiber once others had developed it. They began using straw at least as early as 1837. Between that time and 1885, no less than seven mills made straw paper, including John Carroll's New Marlborough mill, where Carroll produced huge rolls of it for sale to the *New York Times*.[17]

Straw had the advantage of being a waste product of local grain cultivation, making it much cheaper than hemp. Unlike hemp or rag, however, its cellulose content amounts to only 35 percent. In addition, grains are annual crops, so that a mill acquired an entire year's straw supply at one time. Both of these characteristics required straw mills to have huge storage capacities. Purchasing chemical digesters to remove straw's noncellulose content further increased their fixed capital investments. Moreover, straw paper had two undesirable characteristics. As a field crop, straw inevitably contained an admixture of dirt and weeds, which mills making cheap paper could not economically cull out. These impurities vitiated many sheets of straw paper. In addition, because straw's cellulose fibers are short, straw paper makers had to add some rag fiber for strength, and even so, their paper lacked rag paper's durability.[18]

The use of esparto grass provides another example of Berkshire mill owners' willingness to experiment with fiber technology previously developed with other men's capital. An English paper maker, Thomas Routledge, had made a fine, white esparto grass paper by 1857. British paper makers adopted esparto enthusiastically and eventually imported large quantities of the grass from its native

Making," pp. 13, 15; "Paper Making in Monterey, Mass.," p. 2; Child, *Gazeteer*, part 1, p. 385; "Paper Making in Lee Village," pp. 2, 9; "Paper Making in East Lee, Mass.," p. 2; "Charles Smith West," *SF* 5 (March 1932):9; "The Civil War and the Post War Period," CMF, 3/31/63.

[17] Library of Congress, *Papermaking*, pp. 69–70; Munsell, *Chronology*, pp. 62–65; Sutermeister, *Papermaking*, p. 26; Smith, *Housatonic*, p. 248; Barlow and Bancroft, "Insurance Surveys," no. 4396; "Paper Making in Gt. Barrington and Stockbridge," p. 8; "Paper Making in East Lee, Mass.," pp. 3–4; "New Marlboro's 150th Anniversary and Old Home Day," *The Berkshire Courier*, 8/19/1909, p. 6; *VG*, 8/28/73, p. 2.

[18] Field, *History of Berkshire*, p. 86; Sutermeister, *Papermaking*, pp. 24–27; Hunter, *Papermaking*, pp. 295–96.

North Africa and Spain. Twelve years after Routledge, the Smith
Paper Company made the first American esparto paper, but esparto
never approached its British popularity in this country. As the *Berkshire Courier* noted, it produced "a beautifully white and fibrous
pulp," so fine, in fact, that in 1873 one of the Hurlbut brothers of
Lee traveled abroad to investigate its possibilities for the Hurlbuts'
fine paper mills. By that time, however, rag prices had fallen
enough to weaken fine paper makers' incentive to try alternatives.
On the other hand, newsprint manufacturers, such as Smith,
quickly rejected esparto as too expensive. After paying to transport
it across the Atlantic, Smith found "the cost of beating and bleaching it by the only process known" made it almost as expensive as
"other material just as good." Given that, even when adopting
proven fibers, mill owners inevitably bore the cost of a shake-down
period while beater engineers and paper-making machine tenders
adjusted their procedures to a new fiber, Smith needed more substantial cost advantages to warrant continuing with esparto. Simultaneously, America's cheap, abundant wood supply gave ground
wood fiber all the cost advantage Smith could have asked.[19]

Inspired by the obvious example of the wasp, speculation that paper might be made from wood pulp occurred as early as 1719. By
1765 Schäffer, working in Germany, had produced paper from several woods, a feat repeated by Matthias Koops in England in 1800.
With the impetus of the paper-machine-induced rag shortage, attempts to develop wood as a paper fiber multiplied. Among the ex-
perimenters was a German weaver named Friedrich Keller, who
patented a wood-grinding machine in 1840. Six years later a paper
maker, Heinrich Voelter, joined in perfecting the machine. Keller
and Voelter began commercial production of wood pulp paper in
Voelter's Saxony mill in 1847.[20]

Keller's device consisted of a revolving grindstone with three
metal pockets arranged perpendicular to the stone's edge. Workers
placed logs in these pockets so that the length of the log rested
against the revolving stone. After the worker closed the pocket, hydraulic pressure plates pushed the log against the stone, causing the
grinder to tear off bits of wood several fibers thick. A stream of cold
water running across the stone's face cooled the stone and carried
off the fiber.[21]

Although Keller and Voelter's grinder achieved the earliest com-

[19] Hunter, *Papermaking*, p. 363; "Esparto Grass," SF 3 (December 1929):6; "Miscellaneous Letters," HP, 6/10/73.

[20] Hunter, *Papermaking*, pp. 280–81; Sutermeister, *Papermaking*, pp. 49–50.

[21] Sutermeister, *Papermaking*, pp. 50–51.

mercial success, it was far from the only attempt to produce wood pulp mechanically. Charles Fenerty, an innovative Nova Scotian, made the first attempt to manufacture North American ground wood paper and succeeded shortly after Keller's initial patent. Canadian paper mill owners rejected the product, however, and left Fenerty without the financing to develop his process.[22]

The vast forest resources of North America encouraged other inventors to persist. In 1856 an Albany, New York, friend of the Cranes sent them a sample of bass wood paper, asking whether they would like to help finance a wood pulp manufacturing venture. The proprietors projected enormous profits because they could make the pulp for one-quarter cent per pound, but they reckoned without the fact that quality was an equally relevant consideration. The enclosed sample looks like matted ground wood—not paper. The Cranes' correspondent acknowledged its inadequacies when he added, "Perhaps if you do not want the capital stock you would like a 100 tons of *singed, speckled or streaked paper stock.*" Seven years later the Lee newspaper reported a meeting of Boston investors to consider a very similar product. Lacking a commercially acceptable fiber, neither venture came to fruition.[23]

By the late 1850s the rapidly rising price of rags and the lack of a truly satisfactory substitute prompted wood pulp experiments in the Berkshires. In 1857 Elizur Smith made the first local trial of ground wood on a commercial scale. He prepared the fiber according to Keller and Voelter's principles, but with a grinder that had not been perfected. The machine ground slowly and the resulting product was unduly expensive and too coarse for printing paper. With bankruptcy looming, Smith lacked the resources to invest in developing the process. He simply abandoned it.[24]

Several years later, in 1863, wood pulp received a trial in northern Berkshire. P. A. Chadbourne, a professor at Williams College, a popular lecturer on natural history, and a fervent promoter of Berkshire economic development, had invented a process similar to Keller and Voelter's. He prevailed upon the nearest mill owner, L. L. Brown, to try making paper from his pulp. As a fine ledger paper maker, Brown probably conducted the experiment as a personal favor and would have had little interest in pursuing the matter. In any case, Chadbourne's process could never have competed with Keller-Voelter grinders. He added a chemical processing stage,

[22] Hunter, *Papermaking*, pp. 281–82.
[23] "Other Fibers," CMF, 5/17/56; *VG*, 2/12/63, p. 2.
[24] Hunter, *Papermaking*, p. 283.

which must have increased the cost, and he separated the wood fibers by rasping logs with files, a method that consumed enormous amounts of power.[25]

The numerous unsuccessful efforts to produce ground wood suggest that what set Keller and Voelter apart was sufficient capital to underwrite the development of their machine. The story of how wood pulp paper finally achieved commercial success in America underscores the importance of a substantial initial investment. The tale begins in South America, where Alberto Pagenstecher, a railway engineer from Wiesbaden, Germany, had accumulated a considerable fortune in railway construction. Seeking profitable investments, he wrote to his nephew, Albrecht, in New York. Albrecht had recently learned from piano manufacturer Theodore Steinway that German manufacturers had successfully made paper from wood. He wrote to a third Pagenstecher, brother Rudolph, who had stayed in Germany, and asked him to investigate the process.[26]

Rudolph reported favorably and the three Pagenstechers; Steinway; Louis Prang, an art dealer who was Voelter's American agent; and Professor Ferdinand Hoffman organized an American company to manufacture ground wood and Keller-Voelter grinders. They hired Frederick Wurtzbach, a skilled woodworker and creative mechanic from Magdesprung, to accompany the first grinders to America and set them in operation. He brought along five experienced German grinder operators to ensure successful transfer of the process. Undoubtedly because of the county's leadership in paper making and its proximity to New York, the promoters chose a site in Berkshire County, in the Stockbridge village of Curtisville. Wurtzbach, his men, and the grinders (Figure 7.1) arrived in December 1866, and by March 5, 1867, they had produced usable pulp. On the night of March 17, 1867, Wurtzbach shipped the first lot of pulp to the Smith Paper Company. The following day Wellington Smith personally supervised production of the first commercially successful American ground wood paper.[27]

[25] *VG*, 12/25/62, p. 2; 2/19/63, p. 2; 3/23/71, p. 2; and passim; Munsell, *Chronology*, p. 141; "L. L. Brown Records of Business Transactions, 1862–1863," LLBP, 3/11/63; Weeks, *History of Paper Manufacturing*, p. 226.

[26] Jones, *Jones Story*, p. 8; Wurtzbach, "Curtisville," SL; Hunter, *Papermaking*, p. 283.

[27] Wurtzbach, "Curtisville," SL; Earl H. Johnson, ed., *Mechanical Pulping Manual* (New York, 1960), p. 2; Jones, *Jones Story*, p. 8; Hunter, *Papermaking*, pp. 283–84; Smith, *History of Papermaking*, pp. 132–33.

Other attempts at wood pulp production continued. A month after Smith's success, Byron Weston wrote to one supplier that his father-in-law, who operated the

Fig. 7.1 Model of wood pulp grinder brought from Frederick Wurtzbach
from Germany to Curtisville. Courtesy of Stockbridge Library.

The Smiths expressed their delight in finally having a cheap alternative to rags by taking the Curtisville mill's entire first-year output, but many paper makers rejected ground wood as "inferior
stock" and encyclopedias advised the American public how to detect
this adulterant in their paper. Such resistance was not unreasona-
ble. Ground wood lacked many of the desirable qualities of rag fiber. In addition to the cellulose, which comprises about 60 percent
of wood, wood contains about 23 to 30 percent lignin. Ground wood
pulp retained the lignin, unlike more recent sulfate and sulfite
wood pulps, from which the lignin has been removed chemically.
The presence of lignin, the shortness of ground wood fibers, and
the absence from wood fibers of the smaller branching fibers that
intertwine in rag paper, combined to make ground wood even less
durable than straw paper. Like straw paper, ground wood paper

adjacent mill, was "on Book Paper and cannot make the test of wood pulp now . . .
we don't want to pay over 4¢ dry weight for it and we will make the test regularly and
send word to you as soon as we can get an order of Book paper made." He also reported hearing of the Smith Paper Company's use of wood pulp from one of his employees. Byron Weston Letter Book, 1867, BWP, 4/25/67.

had to contain an admixture of rag fiber, and even so, it became yellow after exposure to light and it tore easily.[28]

Nonetheless, ground wood pulp's assets ensured its eventual widespread use as newsprint. Most important was its cheapness. From an initial cost of eight cents a pound, its price fell quickly to five cents, four cents, and before 1900, one cent. Water drained more rapidly from ground wood than from rag stock, enabling machines making wood pulp paper to run more rapidly, further reducing costs. Moreover, by removing little of the noncellulose content of the wood, the grinding process produced a much higher yield per ton of raw material than could be derived from straw. Finally, newspaper publishers discovered that ground wood paper possessed good printing qualities. All of these advantages meant that, after some initial hesitation, makers of news paper adopted ground wood. News paper prices declined from twenty-five cents a pound in the early 1860s to two cents a pound in 1897. Combined with Joseph Pulitzer's "new journalism," these prices stimulated rapid expansion of the newsprint market.[29]

Having pioneered its use, Berkshire mill owners increased their purchases of wood pulp. The half ton a day manufactured at the first Curtisville mill in 1867 did not satisfy local mills' demand. The following year Lewis Beach and James H. Royce adapted their unsuccessful Lee textile mill to ground wood pulp production. At Curtisville, Benjamin Barker converted his failing textile mill to a pulp mill, the Pagenstechers erected an additional mill, and F. Burghardt built a fourth pulp mill. The Pagenstechers established a third mill at nearby Luzerne, New York. Once committed to ground wood, even paper makers risked investing in the new process. By 1876 the Smith Paper Company operated two pulp mills at Lenoxdale, one a converted glass factory and the other newly constructed. Together, by 1885, the Smith mills ground up thirty to forty cords of wood each week, making twenty-five tons of pulp.[30]

---

[28] Weeks, *History of Paper Manufacturing*, p. 235; Smith, *History of Papermaking*, p. 133; Hunter, *Papermaking*, pp. 283, 295; William B. Dick, *Dick's Encyclopedia of Practical Receipts and Processes* (New York, n.d.), p. 195; Sutermeister, *Papermaking*, pp. 19, 53–55; "Typescript of Address Delivered October 30, 1927, by Courtesy of *The Industrial Digest* Over Station WRNY, New York City," "History of the B.W. Co.," BWP, p. 1.

[29] Hunter, *Papermaking*, pp. 283, 285; Weeks, *History of Paper Manufacturing*, p. 236; "Typescript of Radio Address," BWP, p. 1; Sutermeister, *Papermaking*, p. 53; Mott, *American Journalism*, pp. 430–45, 498.

[30] Weeks, *History of Paper Manufacturing*, pp. 236–38; "Paper Making in East Lee, Mass.," p. 9; Hyde, *History of Lee*, pp. 286–87; Wurtzbach, "Curtisville," SL; L. L. Bar-

After the first imported grinders established their efficacy, Berkshire machine shops at Curtisville turned out growing numbers of American-built Keller-Voelter grinders, facilitating the dissemination of ground-wood technology. The Pagenstecher interests, which rented out the grinders on a royalty basis, contracted with Curtisville machinist and iron founder Erastus Burghardt to build the machines. His shop eventually employed fifty-five skilled workers, drawn principally from the ironworking center of Troy, New York. In the same village the Barker machine shop and foundry manufactured a competing machine invented by Barker. Together the pulp mills and the machine shops transformed a peaceful rural backwater into a bustling industrial community.[31]

Because the early American ground-wood industry concentrated in the Berkshires, Berkshire men contributed substantially to the rapid improvement of ground-wood technology. Between 1869 and 1877 county residents received eleven patents for improvements in wood pulp production. Skilled machinists instituted most of the changes in wood grinders. The Burghardts received three patents and Barker, four. Several of these refinements improved the pulp by ensuring longer fibers and sifting out splints. Another substituted an emery wheel for the grindstone, eliminating time lost in sharpening. Others made the grinders cheaper and easier to operate, Barker claiming by 1875 that "a delicate female or other attendant with little strength can maintain the proper action in a considerable number . . . without severe labour."[32]

The bustle associated with the early years of ground wood in Berkshire County proved extremely brief. By the 1880s the small pulp mills of Curtisville could no longer compete, and they closed their doors. Frederick Wurtzbach left to manage the Smiths' pulp mills and Curtisville relapsed into rural quietude. Even in Lee (Figure 7.2), the ground wood furor was inevitably short-lived. Berkshire forests had met the fuel and building needs of county residents for more than a century. Suitable trees in the region took sixty to eighty years to mature. Thus, farmers cutting trees for the local pulp mills rapidly depleted forests throughout the county. As early as 1869 Barker and Pagenstecher contemplated bringing poplar from Luzerne, New York, because it was much cheaper. The pulp

ker, "History of the Barker Mill," SL; VG, 10/29/68, p. 2; "Paper Making in Lee Village," p. 8.

[31] Wurtzbach, "Curtisville," SL; Barker, "Barker Mill," SL.

[32] *General Index to Patents*, pp. 1013–15; *Monthly Volumes of Patents, 1875*, p. 111; *1877*, p. 104; VG, 1/25/72, p. 2; 2/8/72, p. 2; and passim; Hunter, *Papermaking*, p. 285.

Fig. 7.2 Lee in 1868, center of American ground-wood paper making.
No longer the densely forested region Zenas Crane viewed, the north end
of Lee was already crowded with paper mills (*left center*), a service shop
(*foreground*), and Irish workmen's houses. Courtesy of Lee Library.

industry gradually relocated to regions endowed with untapped
forests, and lacking the advantage of cheap local pulp, one large
Smith Paper Company mill closed in 1891.[33]

By 1885, then, Berkshire mill owners, abetted by outside investors, had solved the problem of rag scarcity by redefining paper
from intertwined rag fiber to interwoven vegetable fiber. In the
process, they had ravaged forests throughout the county, making
the mill towns less attractive places to live. Moreover, the shift to
new fiber undercut the county's longstanding geographic advantages as a paper-making region and subjected citizens of paper and
pulp mill towns to growing economic uncertainty. Simultaneously,
straw paper manufacturers helped make the mill towns' environment less pleasant by dumping chemical wastes in local rivers. By

[33] Wurtzbach, "Curtisville," SL; Sutermeister, *Papermaking*, p. 31; "Paper Making
in Lee Village," p. 2; WPA Guide, p. 144; *VG*, 4/22/69, p. 2. Probably because of these
problems, there is no evidence of chemical wood pulp production in Berkshire
County before 1886, and chemical pulping processes are, therefore, not treated
here. For a brief account of contemporaneous chemical pulp innovation and production in Pennsylvania see Weeks, *History of Paper Manufacturing*, pp. 226–30. It
should be noted, in anticipation of the following section on paper chemistry, that the
chemical water and air pollution popularly associated with the twentieth-century paper industry is preeminently that of chemical wood pulp plants, not paper mills.

1885, however, pollution from pulp digesters was only one chemical among many.

CHEAP CHEMICALS AND DEAR WATER

The substitution of wood pulp for rags was the most dramatic technological consequence of paper mill mechanization, but it was certainly not the only one. Raw material shortages also motivated paper makers to experiment with a host of chemicals. Even in Zenas Crane's day, a new chemical technology, chlorine bleaching, had enabled mills to make white paper from cheap, previously unusable stock. After mechanization, manufacturers had introduced alkaline cleansing solutions to render additional stock acceptable. Gradually, they added or applied dyes, pigments, and coatings to hide remaining flaws. Later, finding animal hides for sizing as difficult to obtain as rags, some mill owners adopted rosin sizing as a cheap and acceptable alternative. Paper makers in mechanized mills also added fillers, such as clay, to their paper, another example of substituting cheap chemicals for increasingly expensive traditional materials.

The new chemical technology caused one obvious change in the mill towns: it polluted the water. As the succeeding discussion of the several new chemicals will show, paper makers polluted primarily out of ignorance. Most contemporary chemical processes remained far from exact, products of trial and error passed from one man to another as recipes. Manufacturers did not even understand the chemical properties of cellulose sufficiently to avoid damaging their paper through injudicious application of harsh chemicals. Given the mill owners' ignorance and the low chemical prices that blunted their impulse to economize, paper mill process water contained more and more excess chemicals. Accustomed to inexhaustible supplies of pure water and to using rivers as waste water conduits, paper makers did not recycle chemical-laden water, but dumped it into adjacent rivers. Only belatedly did they begin to recognize the scarcity of pure water and the economic need to alter traditional operating procedures.

Chlorine bleaching, which mill owners had practiced for several decades by 1857, illustrates the primitive state of industrial chemistry. After mechanization, when manufacturers introduced cheaper stock, bleaching assumed increased importance. Through the power of bleach and the cleansing action of alkaline bleach boiler detergents, one paper maker noted, "calicoes, worn-out sail, refuse

tarred-rope, hemp, bagging, and cotton-waste, . . . which hereto-
fore had been considered only applicable for the manufacture of
coarse wrapping papers, have . . . entered largely into the composition of news and coarse printing papers." He might also have
added straw to the list. Yet despite mills' greater dependence on
bleach and their long experience with it, as late as the 1860s and
1870s mill owners had not standardized the process. Byron Weston,
for example, recorded two different formulae. One mixed sulfuric
acid, soda ash, and a solution of bleaching powder. The other added
solutions of caustic soda and alum to a bleaching powder solution.
During the same period the Owen Paper Company of Housatonic
employed a solution of bleaching powder alone.[34]

If Weston, a fine ledger paper maker, risked damaging his rag fiber by adding acid and alum to speed bleaching, cost-conscious
makers of cheap paper must have made liberal use of acid and alum
to shorten processing time. Severe damage sometimes resulted. Elizur Smith, for example, made some paper that "turned yellow and
brittle three hours after it was made and before it left the mill it was
as yellow as safron [sic] and so brittle it would crack in two by once

[34] James M. Wilcox cited in Weeks, *History of Paper Manufacturing*, p. 192; Byron
Weston Miscellaneous Records, BWP, p. 29; Byron Weston Letter Book, 1866–67,
BWP, 7/24/66; "American Industries No. 72," p. 275. Soda ash was the term gener-
ally employed for commercial anhydrous sodium carbonate. Caustic soda is the com-
mon name for sodium hydroxide. Alum is the common name for sulfates of alumi-
num with sodium, potassium, or ammonium. Paper makers also used aluminum
sulfate and referred to it as alum. Clark and Crossley, *Elements of Chemistry*, p. 57.
These and succeeding generalizations concerning the use of various chemicals in
Berkshire paper mills summarize data found in Smith Paper Company Test Records,
SP; Quarterly Reports, 1859, HP; Zenas Crane, Jr., Journal, 1879–81, CA; Owen &
Hurlbut Blotter, 1824, HP; L. L. Brown & Co. Daybook, 1853–54, LLBP; L. L.
Brown & Co. Journal, 1856–57, LLBP; L. L. Brown Paper Company Journal, 1877–
80, LLBP; L. L. Brown & Co. Journal, 1867–71, LLBP; Ledger of the Aetna, Hou-
satonic, and Defiance Mill, 1839–47, BWP; Crane & Co. Journal, 1840–, CA; Zenas
Crane Journal, 1829–41, CA; Zenas Crane Daybook, 1824–29, CA; Carson & Brown
Ledger, 1849–53, CA; L. L. Brown Paper Company Daybook, 1874–76, LLBP; L. L.
Brown Paper Company Daybook, 1870–81, LLBP; Ledger of Henry Chamberlin &
Co., BWP; Byron Weston Letter Book, 1867–68, BWP; Crane & Co. Ledger, 1844–
49, CA; "Byron Weston—Mill Owner," BWP, sample sheet of yellow paper; "T. G. &
W. W. Carson," CMF, 1/19/46, 7/9/55; bills and receipts, 1867, BWP, 3/11/67; "Ma-
chinery, Engineering, and Chemistry, 1879–1886," CMF, 2/1/81, 1/2/82; Brown &
Weston Letter Book, 1864–65, BWP, 6/21/65; Brown & Weston and Byron Weston
Letter Book, 1866–67, BWP, 12/1/66, 12/4/66, 12/15/66, 12/17/66, 1/7/67; Byron
Weston Letter Book, 1867, BWP, 6/7/67; Byron Weston Letter Book, 1874–75, BWP,
1/9/75; Crane & Co. Letter Book, 1874, CA, 7/7/74, 7/29/74; Munsell, *Chronology*, p.
72; "New Marlboro's 150th Anniversary," p. 6; Zenas Crane Journal, 1825–30, CA,
5/29/29 and passim.

folding. . . ." Byron Weston, who had trained under Smith, attributed this condition to improper bleaching, among other things. In
another letter, Weston chose the phrase "bleached to death" to describe papers that were tender, easily broken, and yellowing. Paper
makers who understood the effects of harsh chemicals so poorly
that they damaged their paper were unprepared to exercise caution
when they disposed of acidic solutions. They simply drained the
bleaches into local rivers. Indeed, because they did not view water as
a scarce resource, they used large amounts of it to flush lingering
traces of bleach from the stock.[35]

Cheaper and less detrimental to fiber than acid bleaches were the
alkaline solutions bleach boilers used to remove grease and dirt
from paper stock. Slaked lime, the most common detergent, cost
less than one cent per pound in 1869. The price of lime fell
throughout the period, as did the price of most chemicals used in
the industry. In 1880 Zenas Crane, Jr., used 560 barrels of lime,
each costing less than eighty-eight cents. Because it was so cheap
and because excessive alkalinity posed no threat to cellulose fiber,
paper manufacturers had little incentive to economize on lime.
Rather, they had every reason to use excessive amounts to assure
thorough cleansing. Together with the tar, dirt, and grease removed from the rags, that excess ran into the rivers.[36]

Water pollution accompanying the use of dyes and pigments was
more varied in hue but probably less detrimental to river life. Coloring agents enhanced the appearance of fine paper and masked
many of the defects of low-quality products, permitting mill owners
to charge higher prices relative to their raw material costs. After
mechanization increased output, the use of color also multiplied the
variety of wares mill owners could vend. By the late 1840s at the latest Berkshire engineers had begun adding the pigments ultrama-

---

[35] Brown & Weston Letter Book, 1865–66, BWP, 3/2/66, 3/9/66. For a discussion of
the injurious effects of acidic solutions on cellulose see Chapter 3.

[36] "Rag Preparation," *Hurlbut's Papermaker Gentleman* 2 (Spring 1934):21; "George
C. Maynard," interview typescript, CMF, p. 3; Byron Weston Miscellaneous Records,
BWP, p. 300; Zenas Crane, Jr., Journal, 1879–81, CA, 1880 passim.

Undoubtedly the location of four lime kilns in Cheshire, North Adams, and West
Stockbridge, three of them producing thirty thousand barrels a year, aided local paper makers by keeping freight bills on this bulky item low. Child, *Gazeteer*, part 2, pp.
67, 114, 385. Similar to alkaline washing was the de-inking of old newspapers, practiced by at least one local mill and inquired about by another. The papers were added
to a boiling solution of soda ash and boiled for about ten hours, then rinsed with
clean, cold water. "Paper Making in Tyringham, Mass.," *SF* 1 (June 1928):12; "Crane
Brothers," CMF, 12/16/73.

rine and smalt to stock in their beaters. Used in small quantities, these substances offset the yellow hue that lingered in rag stock even after bleaching, giving paper the bluish tinge buyers perceived as white. As customers acquired a taste for colored papers, Berkshire paper makers introduced dyes, such as indigo and copperas, and pigments, such as umbers, oxides, and chrome yellow. They exchanged information and recorded in mill ledgers and machine tenders' books numerous and various recipes for preparing dyes and pigments. By 1868 several local mills had tried aniline dyes, first created only twelve years earlier. Whether they used aniline, natural dyes, or pigments, paper makers made extra demands on their water supply. They had to shut down and wash all their equipment whenever they changed the color of the paper they made. Wash and process water containing coloring agents ran directly into the Housatonic, the Hoosic, and their tributaries, although the relatively high cost of dyes and pigments discouraged waste. Ultramarine, the most commonly used, cost ninety cents a pound in 1850 and between fifty-two and fifty-six cents a pound in the late 1860s, and it was not among the most expensive.[37]

In the wake of mechanization, mill owners also adopted coating, another chemical technique for coloring paper and rendering cheap fiber more acceptable. Coating combined a pigment with an adhesive, which attached the pigment to the paper's surface. Prior to 1885 the pigment was generally a fine white clay and the adhesive, animal glue. Originally developed as a base for printing wallpaper patterns, glazed coated paper had a smoother surface than uncoated paper and took better impressions of lithographs, woodcuts, and after 1882 halftones, an important consideration in the increasingly sophisticated New York publishing and newspaper markets. When applied to ground wood papers, coating prevented their rapid deterioration. Thus, like bleach, dyes, and lime, coating gave cheaper fiber more potential uses.[38]

[37] Arthur C. Drehfield, "Ultramarine Blue," SF 3 (December 1929):5. In addition to general sources on chemicals (n. 34), use of pigments and dyes is documented especially in Byron Weston Miscellaneous Records, BWP, p. 101; Michael Maher, Machine Tender's Book, CMF; Hunter, Papermaking, p. 362; Sutermeister, Papermaking, p. 114. Mills arrived at their color formulae by repeatedly altering them until they suited customers, for whom they were specially prepared. Crane & Co. Letter Book, 1874, CA, 7/30/74; Carter, Cyrus Field, p. 58.

[38] Sutermeister, Papermaking, pp. 169–71, 55. There is only limited evidence of paper coating in Berkshire mills. Clay purchases, such as Crane & Co.'s 1864 order for 2,042 pounds from the nearby Sheffield China Clay Co., are suggestive but not definitive because the clay may also have been used as a filler. File 399, CMF, 12/22/64.

Similarly, the replacement of glue or animal size by rosin or vegetable size helped compensate for mounting raw material costs. As
paper production expanded, mill owners' difficulty in obtaining
good hides for animal size paralleled their difficulty in finding
enough rags. As early as the late 1840s Berkshire paper mills imported hides from as far away as the East Indies. By 1859 Owen and
Hurlbut calculated that they imported about 60 percent of their raw
size. Prices of hides rose accordingly.[39]

In 1806 German paper makers had demonstrated the feasibility
of rosin sizing. They added a solution of rosin soap to the pulp in
the beaters and precipitated it upon the fiber by adding alum. From
Germany the process traveled quickly to Dutch and French paper
mills, but in England the powerful and well-remunerated foremen
of sizing rooms successfully delayed its general adoption until 1840.
Thus, unlike most new paper mill technologies, but like the paper-
cheapening Keller-Voelter grinder, rosin sizing came to American
paper mills directly from Germany. As with many important new
paper technologies, it arrived in the person of an immigrant paper
maker, in this case Joseph Krah. After Krah reached New York in
1830, many mill owners vied for his services, but Harrison Garfield
finally lured him to his East Lee mill.[40]

Garfield, a fine paper maker, was unusual in adopting rosin size
early. Those most anxious to substitute rosin or "engine sizing"
were common writing paper makers, whose product required size
but whose market demanded a low price. Fine paper makers had
the luxury of passing on high costs as long as they could convince
customers that animal-sized paper was superior. For example, Byron Weston wrote to one hotelkeeper in 1869, "This is as cheap as I
can show and is cheap enough and any good hotel should have as
good as that instead of the Engine sized soft stuff they often have."
By 1875 Weston admitted that paper sized with rosin would erase
better, but he also claimed that such paper "will grow yellow and
tender by age." Although rosin sizing has slightly detrimental ef-

---

L. L. Brown & Co. used cotton calender rolls, designed for use with coated paper.
Several mills made wall paper, which was necessarily coated. Other mills sent their
paper to paper converters for coating. Zenas Crane, Jr., Journal, 1879–81, CA, 12/
11/79, 12/20/79, 12/22/79, 3/8/80.

[39] "Paper Sizing," pp. 4–6; Sutermeister, *Papermaking*, p. 173; Carter, *Cyrus Field*,
p. 64; Ledger of the Aetna, Housatonic, and Defiance Mill, 1839–47, BWP, 1/4/47;
Quarterly Reports, 1859, HP. Owen & Hurlbut also found that in 1859 the firm used
between thirteen and nineteen pounds of raw size material for every hundred
pounds of rags.

[40] "Paper Sizing," pp. 4–6.

fects on the strength and longevity of paper, Weston's comments suggest, rather, the excessive use of alum. Perhaps he learned as much, for later in the same decade he, L. L. Brown, and the Cranes, all fine paper makers, joined their neighbors in using rosin size. H. D. Cone of the Owen Paper Company rejected the innovation, however, and all fine paper makers continued to apply animal size to many papers.[41]

Notwithstanding the eventual widespread adoption of rosin sizing, no one in the industry fully comprehended the chemistry behind the process. Beater engineers furnished rosin to the Hollanders in combination with caustic soda or some other alkali, alum, and, frequently, starch. They believed that the alkali, the alum, or the starch made up part of the size. Actually, rosin alone operated as the sizing agent, but because a variety of interrelated factors affected the rosin's behavior, different mills arrived empirically at widely different formulae. For example, Byron Weston's three recipes, gleaned from different sources in the 1870s, had alkali-to-rosin ratios of one-to-four, one-to-five, and six-to-eleven. Because caustic soda, alum, and starch all remained relatively cheap, the principal adverse consequence of rule-of-thumb rosin sizing was environmental.[42]

As was the case when they searched for a new paper fiber, paper manufacturers experimented with a number of alternatives to animal size before settling on rosin. Byron Weston acquired two recipes for shellac size, which promised to resist ink's penetration and waterproof the paper at the same time. He also recorded size recipes based on gum arabic and starch. Elizur Smith, who made printing paper requiring little sizing, depended on starch, starch and flour, and, eventually, flour alone as his sizing agents in the late 1870s and early 1880s. During the same years the Old Turkey Mill

[41] Byron Weston Letter Book, 1868–69, BWP, 1/8/69; Byron Weston Letter Book, 1874–75, BWP, 3/17/75; Sutermeister, *Papermaking*, pp. 145–46; Crane & Co. Letter Book, 1874, CA, 9/74; Byron Weston Miscellaneous Records, BWP, 47, 101–2; L. L. Brown Paper Company Journal, 1877–80, LLBP; "American Industries No. 72," p. 275; "Alfred Hoxie," interview typescript, CMF, p. 3; Green, *Holyoke*, p. 153. Weston's conservatism and that of other fine pape makers reflected the prejudices of their customers as well. Weston inquired of one, "Would you advise my putting vegetable or Engine sizing into my papers to make them erase better—some are doing it but Binders allways [sic] have been opposed to Engine sized paper."

[42] "Paper Sizing," pp. 4–5; Sutermeister, *Papermaking*, p. 145; Byron Weston Miscellaneous Records, BWP, pp. 47, 101–2. In 1878 a German scholar finally demonstrated convincingly that free rosin was the sizing agent, but there is no evidence that contemporary American paper makers knew of the German scholarship.

at Tyringham experimented with sour buttermilk size, thus pioneering the use of casein, later widely used as an adhesive for paper coating. In the long run, however, mill owners decided that none of the alternatives possessed so many desirable features as rosin.[43]

A final chemical technique for reducing raw material costs was the addition of fillers, such as clay. Initially, because clay increased the weight of the paper more than its bulk, fine paper makers and their customers regarded it as an adulterant. Reflecting this attitude, the *Scientific American*, in its 1881 study of H. D. Cone's mill, noted, "He has continuously made it a specialty to manufacture only first class paper, . . . without any of the adulteration and make-weights in the shape of clay, china clay, kaolin, and other substances used in cheap paper."[44]

Makers of printing paper such as Elizur Smith, on the other hand, came to value fillers not only for their relatively low cost, but also for the opacity, finish, and printing qualities they gave to paper. While stock prices remained high, Smith clearly used clay principally for its cheapness. Between 1872 and 1876 he filled his beaters with up to one-third as much clay as stock. Between 1878 and 1881, by which time stock prices had fallen, Smith sought to determine the optimal amount of clay. He varied his beater loads by adding from 28 to 6 percent as much clay as stock. By 1884 and 1885 he settled on a range of between 4 and 16 percent. Priced at about half a cent per pound, fine white clay, available locally in Sheffield and New Marlborough, still made Smith's papers cheaper, but by using more moderate amounts he avoided greatly weakening his papers.[45]

Paper mills elsewhere in the nation used chalk and talc as fillers, although Berkshire mills have left little evidence that they did so. Several Dalton mills employed calcium sulfate, sold under the trade name of pearl hardening, as a filler. Calcium sulfate is transparent and water soluble, making its contribution either to opacity or to economy questionable. Much of it undoubtedly ended up in the Housatonic. Its common use as a filler reveals, once again, the primitive chemical knowledge of nineteenth-century Berkshire mill owners.[46]

[43] Byron Weston Miscellaneous Records, BWP, pp. 28, 100; Smith Paper Company Test Records, SP; "J. W. Boyd," *SF* 2 (February 1929):10.

[44] Sutermeister, *Papermaking*, p. 142; "American Industries No. 72," p. 276.

[45] Sutermeister, *Papermaking*, p. 142; Smith Paper Company Test Records, SP; Hadley K. Turner, *A History of New Marlborough* (Great Barrington, Mass., 1944), p. 45.

[46] Sutermeister, *Papermaking*, pp. 143–44; Zenas Crane, Jr., Journal, 1879–81, CA;

Although Berkshire mill owners remained ignorant about most chemicals and their effect on local rivers, experience had driven home the necessity of chemically pure process water. As with rags and animal size, however, supplies of this essential resource grew increasingly costly as demand for it outran the readily accessible supply. In comparison with hand processing, paper machines required enormous quantities of water, as did ancillary processes that the machine fostered. Bleach boilers and dryers employed it in the form of steam, pulp grinders functioned only with a steady stream of water, and most chemicals were applied in solution and removed by flushing with water.

As early as 1847 the descendents of Zenas Crane and David Carson emphasized the heightened economic importance of pure water by wrangling over a spring. D. Carson & Sons wrote to the Cranes: "We would like to repair the Cold Spring this week while you are not using the water. Will you come over and see how it will be best to put it in good shape?" Replied Z. M. and J. B. Crane:

> We think it will be unnecessary for us to call up to see about repairing the Cold Spring. As we have before intimated we cannot consent that you should take away part of the spring. . . . The spring having been paid for by us we cannot consent to yield any part of what you know is so valuable to us. You would take the course we do. What would our property be worth without it?

Similarly, in 1886 E. and S. May of East Lee ranked the filling of their spring as their most serious flood damage, listing it ahead of a damaged bridge, roads, and tenements.[47]

Mill owners sought to meet their increased water requirements by finding additional springs, just as they had previously tapped new sources of rags and size. In the years before 1880, for example, Crane & Co. employed at least one man solely to hunt for springs and to dig ditches and lay pipe from springs to the mills. By 1865 Byron Weston had constructed a bridge over the Housatonic to carry log pipes to mountain springs on the other side. Two years later Weston extended a water pipeline from 250 rods to 858 so as

---

Byron Weston Letter Book, 1874–75, BWP, 3/21/75; Byron Weston Letter Book, 1867, BWP, 4/1/67; Byron Weston Miscellaneous Records, BWP, p. 21.

47 "T. G. & W. W. Carson," CMF, 8/2/47; *A Complete Account of the Terrible Disaster at East Lee on Tuesday, April 20th, 1886, with the Impressive Funeral Obsequies, Full Testimony at the Inquest, A List of Contributions for the Relief Fund, Etc., Etc.* (Lee, Mass., 1886), p. 7.

to reach an additional spring. Other expedients included purchasing pure water from better endowed neighbors or from the town.[48]

An expensive but increasingly common alternative was drilling artesian wells. By 1885 in Dalton alone, nine artesian wells sent water to the mills, and drillers actively sought more. Even spending substantial sums on drilling, however, did not guarantee spring water. In the late 1850s and early 1860s, for example, the *Valley Gleaner* reported regularly on the Hurlbuts' search for an artesian well, but eventually speculated that they would "succeed in reaching China without finding a supply" of water. The Hurlbuts finally abandoned the project. Experiences such as theirs made the economic importance of pure water increasingly clear and by the 1880s a few mills installed save-alls to return process water from the paper machine's suction boxes to its stuff chest.[49]

In sum, mechanized paper making had two major chemical consequences. It encouraged mills to adopt chemical techniques that reduced raw material costs: alkaline cleansing, rosin sizing, coating, dyeing, and adding fillers. But because paper chemistry remained more art than science, cheap chemicals used in excess found their way into local rivers, making drinking, bathing, and fishing less healthy and adding unaesthetic odor, color, and cloudiness to the once-sparkling water. Ironically, however, the mechanization that promoted the use of paper-damaging and water-polluting chemicals ultimately enhanced the mill owners' appreciation of the economic value of pure water. Such contradictions merely underscore that, while paper machinery had attained maturity, paper chemistry remained in its infancy.

[48] "David Barnard," interview typescript, CMF, pp. 1, 5; Brown & Weston Letter Book, 1864–65, BWP, 7/11/65; Byron Weston Miscellaneous Records, BWP, p. 14; L. L. Brown & Co. Ledger, 1853–55, LLBP, Spring Water Account; L. L. Brown Paper Company Daybook, 1874–76, LLBP; L. L. Brown Paper Company Daybook, 1876–79, LLBP; L. L. Brown Paper Company Daybook, 1881–85, LLBP; "Machinery, Engineering, and Chemistry, 1854–1865," CMF, 10/17/65; Brown & Weston Letter Book, 1865–66, BWP, 10/20/65; Child, *Gazeteer*, part 1, p. 130.

[49] Toucey, "Artesian Wells," CMF; "Thomas J. Bolton," interview typescript, CMF, p. 5; "The Present Day Defiance Mill," BWP, p. 5; "Lithograph of the Honorable Byron Weston's Mills," clipping from *U.S. Paper Maker*, "History of the B.W. Co.," BWP; R. G. Dun & Co. Ledgers, 3:73; Ralph M. Snell, "Government Paper Making: The Manufacture of Bank, Bill and Bond Paper," typescript adapted from *Paper World* (June 1881):3–5, "Crane & Co. Historical Articles," CMF, p. 1; Brown & Weston Letter Book, 1863–64, BWP, 3/17/64, 7/21/64; Wilkes, "Old Berkshire Mill," CMF, p. 6; *VG*, 1/27/59, p. 2; 3/24/59, p. 2; 4/14/59, p. 2; 6/2/59, p. 2; 9/29/59, p. 2; 11/1/60, p. 2; 11/15/60, p. 2; 8/21/62, p. 1; "American Industries No. 72," p. 275.

Waterwheels, Reservoirs, and
Steam Engines

At the same time that owners of mechanized mills found pure water, animal size, and rags in short supply, they also learned the limitations of the abundant waterpower that Zenas Crane had once surveyed. As paper-making machines came to require more and more power, mill owners found it increasingly difficult to operate them continuously, as economy dictated. Recurrent production delays during dry summer seasons, spring floods, and severe winters frustrated them. Mill owners initially solved the problem of seasonally insufficient waterpower by tapping additional waterpower, just as they sought out more springs, more rags, and more hides. They increased the power they derived from existing dams by installing more efficient overshot waterwheels and hydraulic turbines, and they increased overall waterpower resources by constructing large, cooperatively financed reservoirs. Because New England climate and terrain created abundant potential waterpower and because cheap land in depopulated hill towns kept reservoir construction inexpensive, Berkshire paper manufacturers had little incentive to exchange waterwheels for steam engines. Only in the 1880s did falling coal prices and the increasing size and concentration of mills make auxiliary steam engines an attractive solution to periodic waterpower shortages. By 1885 towering chimneys, shrieking whistles, and belching coal smoke made local citizens uncomfortably aware of the new steam technology, but the following year's disastrous flood taught them the hazards of unregulated reservoir construction and underscored the advantages of steam.

The simplest and earliest response to growing power requirements was to install more efficient waterwheels. The Berkshire paper industry's early power needs had been so modest that most mills had used undershot waterwheels, delivering only a small fraction of potential waterpower. When millwright E. D. Jones set up shop in 1845, he found that most mills had adopted more efficient overshot wheels to generate the power required by paper-making machines and increasingly numerous beaters. Initially, Jones helped local paper makers capture more power by building them larger overshot wheels. One, thirty feet in diameter with a seven-foot face, proved efficient and sturdy enough to power East Lee paper machinery into the twentieth century.[50]

[50] Pierson, "Industrial Architecture," 1:8; Jones, *Jones Story*, pp. 4–5.

Whatever wheels they employed, occasional low water had troubled Berkshire manufacturers as early as 1820, causing some to insert in their contracts the clause "unless prevented by low water." By the late 1850s and the 1860s, the introduction of paper-making machines and the proliferation of rag engines had transformed the paper industry into an especially heavy power user. The problem of low water became endemic. In 1864, a year of severe drought, most mills ran only half time from June to October. The next year local rivers delivered adequate early summer power, but by August Byron Weston notified customers: "We run on 'half-time.' This was decreed by a 'higher power' than any Manufacturer's Association." Later, a cold and snowless winter followed a dry fall and Weston "feared the 'old river' would all turn to ice," terminating his already limited operations. He experienced similar problems in the winter of 1867. Again in 1873, 1874, and 1875 Weston repeatedly apologized for orders delayed by low water.[51]

High water also interrupted production because backwater stopped the overshot wheels as effectively as did lack of water. In February of 1857, for example, the newly established *Valley Gleaner* reported, "Business is nearly suspended, at present in South Lee, in consequence of high water and trouble from ice; and some of Messrs. Platner and Smith's works are unable to do duty for the same reason." Two years later the newspaper reported that the Housatonic had never been so high and that all "the mills on the stream were obliged to stop." Dalton mills left evidence that high water interrupted production in 1833, 1843, 1844, 1864, 1865, 1867, and 1869, and they must have experienced brief stoppages in other years as well. Moreover, local dams were the work of local craftsmen working by rule-of-thumb and using whatever materials came to hand. For example, when the county seat moved to Pittsfield, the citizens of Lenox tore down the old jail and built a dam with the material. After years of withstanding floods, such structures frequently succumbed to spring freshets, occasioning lengthy production delays.[52]

[51] "1820s," HP, 10/22/29; R. G. Dun & Co. Ledgers, 3:199; Green, *Holyoke*, pp. 56, 73; *VG*, 7/21/64, p. 2; Brown & Weston Letter Book, 1863–64, BWP; Brown & Weston Letter Book, 1864–65, BWP, 8/7/65, 8/17/65, 8/18/65; Brown & Weston Letter Book, 1865–66, BWP; "Windsor and Ashmere Reservoir Associations, 1866–1886," CMF, 1/17/66; Byron Weston Letter Book, 1867, BWP, 12/21/67; Byron Weston Letter Book, 1874–75, BWP, 2/4/75, 3/1/75; "Philo Brownson and Edwin Brownson," interview typescript, CMF, p. 3.

[52] *VG*, 2/19/57, p. 2; 3/17/59, p. 2; 6/30/59, p. 2; 7/14/59, p. 2; Zenas Crane Time Book, 1809–36, CA, 10/2/33–10/9/33; Crane & Co. Time Book, 1836–48, CA, 5/1/

By the 1850s the hydraulic turbine offered a solution to many of the problems mechanized mills experienced with conventional waterwheels. Turbines operated completely submerged so that backwater did not stop them. More compact than conventional wheels, they cost much less. The *Gleaner* reported in 1867 that when W. H. Blauvelt & Co. of East Lee replaced its thirty-foot wooden wheel with "a little iron [turbine] which one man can carry in his arms," the new wheel cost less than $400, whereas the old one could not have been built anew for $6,000. Turbines also saved money in the long run because their iron construction made them more durable. And after experiments by Boyden and Francis in the 1840s and 1850s and improvements by Swain and Leffel in the 1860s, turbines operated more efficiently than did waterwheels, allowing manufacturers in the Berkshires to extract more power from falls that were generally small- or medium-sized.[53]

Hydraulic turbines had to be manufactured by men with metalworking capabilities, so that the woodworking millwrights who had constructed the county's waterwheels could not supply the new contrivances. This initially inhibited their local introduction, although Berkshire paper makers received reports on turbines as early as

---

43–5/2/43, 10/19/44, 12/23/44, 5/11/48; Brown & Weston Letter Book, 1864–65, BWP, 3/16/65, 3/17/65, 3/20/65; Byron Weston Letter Book, 1867, BWP, 4/20/67, 4/25/67; Smith, *Housatonic*, p. 380; typescript diary of Oliver Bliss Hayes, "Crane & Co. Historical Articles," CMF, 10/4/69; R. G. Dun & Co. Ledgers, 2:73, 288; Brown & Weston Letter Book, 1863–64, BWP, 7/7/64.

One exception to the general rule of local dam construction was the dam on the Housatonic in Dalton where jutting ledges of rock pinched the stream, creating a powerful flow of water during spring freshets that had quickly washed out a number of dams. Finally, an outsider was brought in to construct a dam. Local residents would not concede the superior engineering skill of the outside expert and they so irritated the man with predictions that his dam, too, would not survive the spring freshets that, upon finishing, he announced publicly, "There was a dam that was built to stand and that he defied God himself to wash it away." The dam stood for many years and this striking achievement, coupled with the lasting impression made by the builder's blasphemy, gave the name "Defiance" to the adjacent mill. 150th Anniversary Committee, *History of Dalton*, p. 57. The belief in the superiority of the "common sense, old fashioned dams of this vicinity" over "the more scientific and expensive ones in . . . the eastern part of the state" persisted among Berkshire mill owners in 1885. *Complete Account of the Terrible Disaster at East Lee*, p. 31.

53 Hunter, *Waterpower*, pp. 292–388, provides a fine overview of the characteristics, development, and marketing of the turbine. See also, Louis C. Hunter, "Water Power in the Century of the Steam Engine," in Hindle, *America's Wooden Age*, p. 161; Edwin T. Layton, "Scientific Technology, 1845–1900: The Hydraulic Turbine and the Origins of American Industrial Research," *T&C* 20 (January 1979):67–82; *VG*, 7/25/67, p. 2.

1847. After 1855, however, large companies began to market standardized turbines. L. L. Brown purchased one for his new stone mill in 1859. Shortly thereafter E. D. Jones became an agent for James Leffel & Co., the leading American turbine manufacturer of the 1860s and 1870s. The local availability of Leffel's turbine, coinciding with the severe 1864 drought and the greater power requirements of fully mechanized mills, motivated Berkshire mill owners to substitute water turbines for overshot wheels. The shift generally occurred in the late 1860s and early 1870s. For example, in 1868 the Smith Paper Company had E. D. Jones install six new Leffels alongside the one they already owned. By 1872 Smith used a total of twenty-one.[54]

Jones's influence, Smith's example, and the fact that Leffel manufactured the vast majority of contemporary turbines led the majority of Berkshire turbine purchasers to buy Leffels. Nonetheless, mill owners spent considerable time studying the merits of different wheels, clipping out newspaper reports of tests, visiting other mills to observe various turbines, and after 1870 probably traveling to the new testing flume at Holyoke. Several mill owners finally chose Swain's turbine over Leffel's, undoubtedly because they accepted Swain's claim that his turbine delivered more power from a limited source. By 1885 at least one local mill had purchased McCormick's Hercules turbine, which had been developed ten years earlier to extract even more power from a limited flow of water.[55]

Even when operating with water turbines, however, seasonal droughts continued to interrupt production. In response, Berkshire mill owners stored up waterpower for use in dry sesons by constructing reservoirs. Where there were only a few mills on a stream and the same men owned several mills, a single company sometimes undertook such a project. E. and S. May developed Lake May in the

[54] Hunter, "Water Power," pp. 184–85; Layton, "Scientific Technology," pp. 82–87; *VG*, 9/15/59, p. 2; 10/29/68, p. 2; 12/24/68, p. 2; 8/26/69, p. 2; 8/15/72, p; 2; 11/18/72, p. 2; 3/7/76, p. 2; Jones, *Jones Story*, p. 5; "Fire Destroys Crane & Co.'s Old Stone Mill," CMF, 11/12/69; "Machinery, Engineering, and Chemistry, 1866–1871," CMF, 6/26/72, 2/16/72; L. L. Brown & Co. Journal, 1867–71, LLBP, 2/71, 6/71; Byron Weston Letter Book, 1874–75, BWP, 11/23/74; "Machinery, Engineering, and Chemistry, 1854–1865," CMF, 3/16/59, 4/20/65, 10/25/65.

[55] "Fire Destroys Crane & Co.'s Old Stone Mill," CMF, 11/12/69; "Machinery, Engineering, and Chemistry, 1854–1865," CMF, 3/16/59, 10/25/65, 4/20/65; "Machinery, Engineering, and Chemistry, 1866–1871," CMF, 2/21/72, 6/26/72; L. L. Brown & Co. Journal, 1867–71, LLBP, 2/71, 6/71; Byron Weston Letter Book, 1874–75, BWP, 11/23/74; Crane & Co. Time Book, 1863–76, CA, rear endsheet; "Machinery, Engineering, and Chemistry, 1879–1886," CMF, 8/28/85.

1850s, and Bulkley, Dunton, and Company constructed a large reservoir in Becket later in the century.[56]

Substantial reservoirs regulating the flow of water into the county's major rivers, the Hoosic and the Housatonic, cost more than a single company could afford and necessarily affected all the mills along these rivers. Mill owners banded together to create reservoirs in these cases. The earliest such venture coincided with the rapid growth and mechanization of the paper industry. In 1848 Hinsdale and Dalton manufacturers joined to construct a dam to raise the water fourteen feet in a Hinsdale pond that fed one Housatonic tributary. But cooperation broke down when Dalton manufacturers objected to expenditures that had exceeded what they had originally agreed to subscribe.[57]

The dry summers of the 1860s and mounting power requirements of the 1870s inspired larger and more successful cooperative reservoir associations. In 1860 the L. L. Brown Paper Company and other Adams manufacturers formed the Adams and Cheshire Reservoir Company, initially flooding 125 acres and doubling their Hoosic waterpower at a cost of $20,000. They had added two additional dams by 1874. Paper makers, textile mill owners, saw mill proprietors, and other manufacturers in Hinsdale, Dalton, Pittsfield, Lenox, and Lee all depended on the Housatonic River. They combined to form the county's largest associations and built the Windsor and Ashmere reservoirs. The Windsor Reservoir, begun by the proprietors of the earlier Hinsdale Reservoir as an immediate response to the 1864 drought, consisted of a thirty-five-foot dam flooding a hundred acres and cost $10,000. Continuing low-water periods prompted formation of the Ashmere Reservoir Association. Between 1871 and 1879 fourteen companies contributed more than $50,000 for dam construction and land purchases, seven paper companies providing over half or about $4,000 each. Simultaneously, in the years after 1873 several small mill and machine shop owners in East Lee pooled their resources to build the Mud Pond dam in Becket, regulating water on the tiny Greenwater Stream at a cost of $1,550, more than any of these small firms could have afforded.[58]

[56] *Complete Account of the Terrible Disaster at East Lee*, p. 30; Edward Church Smith and Philip Mack Smith, *The History of the Town of Middlefield* (Menasha, Wis., 1924), p. 87.

[57] "T. G. & W. W. Carson," CMF, 6/1/48.

[58] *VG*, 8/30/60, p. 2; L. L. Brown & Co. Ledger, 1867–84, LLBP, Adams & Cheshire Reservoir Account; L. L. Brown Paper Company Journal, 1874–77, 1884–88, LLBP;

As in the earlier Hinsdale Reservoir Association, leaders of these loose associations experienced difficulty maintaining cooperation. Disagreements occurred frequently over expenditures, land purchases, and selection of dam builders. These problems, however, occupied only the initial construction phase. Recurrent questions such as who should assume responsibility for the association's affairs and how water should be allocated proved far more divisive. For example, paper maker Charles O. Brown, treasurer of the Windsor Reservoir Association, finally wrote to association president and fellow paper maker Thomas Colt: "I do not know but it is right and fair for you to call meetings of the association and as its head and chief man, uniformally [sic] of late, absent yourself from them: but I cannot now see it. . . . I cannot go on this loose and uncertain way." Given mills' different needs, decisions to draw water from the reservoirs provoked even greater controversy. Byron Weston, for example, objected that the Carson Paper Company was "drawing off too fast and the result will be the same as last winter. Then as now a freshet of water ran by me the fore part of the season and we were left high and dry the later part." Although mill owners willingly organized to assure a more uniform flow of water, the actual terms of that flow remained difficult to work out.[59]

Even worse, without continuing organization and financial commitment, individual contributors neglected essential dam maintenance and inspection. In the case of the East Lee–Mud Pond project, lack of organization brought disaster upon the local community.

Brown & Weston Letter Book, 1863–64, BWP, 9/27/64; "Carson & Brown," CMF, 10/15/79; "Windsor and Ashmere Reservoir Associations, 1866–1886," CMF, 9/21/71 and passim; Jones, *Jones Story*, pp. 5, 9; *Complete Account of the Terrible Disaster at East Lee*, pp. 6, 25. Previously these East Lee mills had had to arrange to operate in sequence since their power was used up in a few hours of operation.

[59] Byron Weston Letter Book, 1867–68, BWP, 6/6/68, 6/27/68, 7/25/68; Letters to Byron Weston, 1867, BWP, 1/15/67; Byron Weston Letter Book, 1874–75, BWP, 10/7/74; Brown & Weston Letter Book, 1863–64, BWP, 11/21/64; Brown & Weston Letter Book, 1864–65, BWP, 11/29/64, 12/3/64, 12/16/64, 12/17/64, 6/9/65, 6/15/65; Brown & Weston Letter Book, 1865–66, BWP, 1/20/66, 12/30/65; Brown & Weston and Byron Weston Letter Book, 1866–67, BWP, 8/13/66. Such disagreements were not unlike those that occurred between parties above and below each other on the same stream. Mills with too little waterpower might use up their mill pond and then shut down to let it refill, leaving their successors on the stream without water. On the other hand, a succeeding mill might allow water in its pond to rise so high as to back up on preceding mills. "Crane, Martin, and Company Successor to Crane, Wilson, and Company, 1857–1858," CMF, 6/9/57; "John Bottomly Mill," *SF* 4 (Index):3; "Paper Making in Monterey, Mass.," p. 2; Byron Weston Letter Book, 1874–75, BWP, 10/26/74.

Eleven manufacturers participated in the project, some contributing labor, others cash. But they elected no officers and established no association. They merely gathered at Hamblin's general store from time to time and offered suggestions. As the years passed no one assumed responsibility for the dam. In 1886, thirteen years after the dam's construction, the impounded water broke free, killing several residents of East Lee and causing more than $80,000 in property damages to mill owners alone (Figures 7.3 and 7.4). At the subsequent inquest, local manufacturers could not even agree about who had contributed to the dam's construction.[60]

The disagreements and disorganization tolerated by members of these cooperative associations suggest the strong preference local mill owners had for familiar, relatively cheap waterpower. Their attitude typified that of American paper makers. As compared to other manufacturers, who relied primarily on steam power by 1869, paper mill owners still depended on water for 77 percent of their power in 1869 and for 66 percent of it in 1889. Not until 1919 did American paper makers generate less than half of their power from falling water. That paper makers took longer than other American manufacturers to install steam engines resulted from a combination of characteristics that the Berkshire industry shared. Paper mills were concentrated in New England, where waterpower remained abundant and cheap. Fourdrinier paper machines needed an extremely uniform flow of power, something that early steam engines did not always deliver. Most important, paper makers needed to stay in relatively rural areas to assure themselves pure water, so that they were not attracted by the fact that steam power permitted concentration in cities. Instead, inexpensive rural land made reservoir construction possible. As a result, although the feasibility of steam power had been demonstrated in a local paper mill as early as 1851, by 1875 only a little over one-third of the local mills supplemented waterpower with steam power. The great increase in the use of steam came only in the following decade, after reservoir construction had come to a halt. By 1885 at least twenty-four of the county's twenty-nine mills employed some steam power.[61]

[60] *Complete Account of the Terrible Disaster at East Lee*, pp. 1–9, 25, 27–28.

[61] Allen H. Fenichel, "Growth and Diffusion of Power in Manufacturing, 1838–1919," in National Bureau of Economic Research, *Output, Employment, and Productivity in the United States After 1800* (New York, 1966), pp. 477–78; Jeremy Atack, Fred Bateman, and Thomas Weiss, "The Regional Diffusion and Adoption of the Steam Engine in American Manufacturing," *JEH* (1980): 302–3; "The Present Day Defiance Mill," BWP, p. 3; R. G. Dun & Co. Ledgers, 4:376, 504; 5:56; Barlow and Ban-

Fig. 7.3 Decker & Sabin Paper Mill after the 1886 flood.
Already financially troubled (see Chapter 8), the mill never reopened.
Courtesy of Lee Library.

Fig. 7.4 East Lee flood damage, 1886. The remains of the former
Couch & Oakley millwright shop appear in the foreground of this view of
the village's main street. Courtesy of Lee Library.

In addition to growing waterpower shortages, two factors encouraged paper makers to install auxiliary steam engines. First, in the 1850s and 1860s paper mill owners gained experience with steam boilers when generating steam for bleach boilers and dryers. Thus, by the 1870s they had already worked out many of the problems associated with the new power source. Then in 1875 the arrival of a competing railroad line in the Berkshires reduced freight rates and lowered coal costs, an important consideration as wood grew scarce.[62]

The use of steam engines further altered the mill towns. Reliance solely on waterpower had limited the size and concentration of mills, but steam power enabled paper manufacturers to build large new mills and concentrate them in Lee and Dalton. In so doing, steam power reinforced the influence of the railroad, which made manufacturing in outlying villages increasingly unprofitable. The new mills announced the age of steam by replacing their "beautifully toned bells" with shrieking steam whistles, summoning their workers with a harsh new insistence and shattering the solitude of

---

croft, "Insurance Surveys," nos. 2978, 3016, 4166, 4167, 4169, 4170, 4300, 4396, 4593, 4868, 5236, 5878, 6103, 6553, 6696, 8256, 8257, 8258, 9790, 9878; Child, *Gazeteer*, part 1, p. 375; part 2, pp. 138, 142, 150, 154, 157, 419; Byron Weston Miscellaneous Records, BWP, p. 297; Zenas Crane, Jr., Journal, 1879–81, CA, 9/27/79, 10/4/79; L. L. Brown & Co. Journal, 1856–57, LLBP; "Machinery, Engineering, and Chemistry, 1879–1886," CMF, 8/29/81, 10/12/82, 4/23/83, 9/22/84; "Crane Brothers," CMF, 5/18/77; Crane & Co. Time Book, 1863–76, CA, rear endsheet; *Paper World* 1 (November 1880):24; Crane & Co. Letter Book, 1874, CA, 7/23/74; Carson & Brown Ledger, 1849–54, CA, 5/20/51; L. L. Brown & Co. Daybook, 1853–54, LLBP, 6/54; Wilkes, "Old Berkshire Mill," CMF, 6; "Alfred Hoxie," interview typescript, CMF, p. 2; "Bay State Mill," CMF, p. 14; typescript of *Pittsfield Sun* account of Old Stone Mill fire, 10/28/69, CMF; "Machinery, Engineering, and Chemistry, 1854–1865," CMF, 9/13/54; Weston, "Paper Making," pp. 11, 15.

The great increase in numbers of steam engines in these years may be in part an artifact of the greater abundance of industry sources reporting steam engines for the decade 1876–85. Industry sources indicate far more steam engines than do federal manuscript census data, Massachusetts census reports, or reports of the Massachusetts Bureau of Statistics of Labor, probably because these government investigations were interested in the mill's regular power source and thus missed auxiliary steam engines.

[62] Hunter, "Water Power," pp. 172–73; R. G. Dun & Co. Ledgers, 6:544; Pierson, "Industrial Architecture," 1:247; Byron Weston Miscellaneous Records, BWP, pp. 300–301. In 1872 Byron Weston computed that half of his fuel costs were for steam other than that used in the steam engine. Weston's records also indicate that, although declining freight rates accounted for part of the decline in coal costs, the price of a ton of coal also fell during the years after 1875. His calculations are discussed further in Chapter 8.

villages many miles away. Finally, the use of steam power greatly augmented fuel consumption and smoke production at local mills. Some mills burned wood as a fuel until at least 1880, contributing to the rapid deforestation of local hillsides. Each of these developments made the mills' influence more pervasive, but from the perspective of local residents, the huge new buildings with their towering smokestacks became the outstanding symbols of the shifting balance between town and mill.[63]

THE NEW PAPER MILL

The final technological challenge facing owners of mechanized mills was housing the new machines in mills that were sufficiently large, resistant to fire, able to transmit power over longer distances, and equipped to operate day and night, summer and winter. They met the challenge by developing buildings with distinctive spatial arrangements, occupying disproportionately large amounts of land; by introducing fire-resistant construction and fire-fighting technology; by adopting improved shafting; and by installing gaslight and steam heat. These changes clearly altered workers' experience within the mills, a subject to which we will turn in Chapter 9. The following pages focus, rather, on how new building technologies combined to differentiate the paper mill from other buildings in the community, making it dominant rather than harmonious.

The most visible change in Berkshire paper mills was their enlarged proportions. Early paper mills had been domestic in scale, similar to neighboring barns in size. Mechanization entailed larger mills. In 1826, when the Laflins decided to invest their powder mill profits in building the region's first mechanized paper mill, they planned it on a grander scale than any previous local paper-making establishment. The main building stretched a hundred feet along the riverbank, extended fifty feet in width, and had three smaller wings. Not surprisingly, its neighbors looked on it as "a marvel in the lavish use of capital."[64]

The growth of the Old Berkshire Mill in Dalton more nearly typifies the expansion of the antebellum paper mill. Retaining the orig-

---

[63] "Crane Brothers," CMF, 12/12/70; VG, 10/14/58, p. 2; 11/16/65, p. 2; 2/8/72, p. 2; and passim; "Old Home Week Celebration in Tyringham," p. 87; "The (Perry Green) Comstock Paper Mill," p. 11; Byron Weston Miscellaneous Records, BWP, pp. 16–17; L. L. Brown Paper Company Daybook, 1874–76, LLBP; L. L. Brown Paper Company Journal, 1877–80, LLBP; Smith Paper Company Test Records, SP.

[64] Weston, "Paper Making," pp. 5–6.

inal wooden structure built by Zenas Crane in 1801, the Carsons gradually enlarged the mill to accommodate new machines "until it finally presented a curious mongrel appearance of brick, wood, and stone." When it burned in 1872, the Carsons replaced it with a 366-foot building (Figure 7.5), suggesting how greatly mechanization had increased space requirements by the 1860s and 1870s. Crane's Old Stone Mill (Figure 7.6) had a similar history. In fact, mill owners took advantage of most of the twenty-six fires that destroyed paper mills between 1857 and 1885 to erect more commodious, convenient structures. More fortunate firms simply constructed entirely new facilities alongside outdated buildings. For example, the new Hurlbut Paper Mill of 1872 (Figure 7.7) was 373 feet long, built on a vastly different scale than the original Owen & Hurlbut Mill of 1822. And whereas early mills (Figure 2.3) had resembled contemporary domestic architecture, the new Hurlbut mill clearly proclaimed itself an industrial edifice.[65]

Indeed, judging from reports in the local press, the impressive new mills helped articulate a new aesthetic in post–Civil War Berkshire County. Hardly a month passed without the *Valley Gleaner* reporting some visible "improvement" in local paper factories. When the Smith Paper Company replaced its fire-gutted Columbia Mill with a much larger brick-and-stone Columbia Mill in 1866, the editor saluted it as "a *splendid* structure . . . and the enterprise manifested in its construction is highly commendable." Especially praiseworthy was "a *beautiful* brick chimney nearly 100 feet high." A year later the newspaper reported, two artists "have recently been taking a view of the mills of the Hurlbut Paper Co. at South Lee, which our correspondent says is '*magnificent.*'" The following year found the press lauding Harrison Garfield of East Lee for taking down "the unsightly willows west of his Washington Mill" in order to build a handsome addition for a new paper-making machine. Six years later Garfield earned commendation by replacing his old chimney with one having a "more substantial foundation and *pleasanter* outlines." The Smith Paper Company acknowledged the important visual impression conveyed by its buildings when, in 1868, the firm painted names on the various mills. As the *Gleaner* explained, "People passing upon railroad trains like to know the names of *fine looking* manufacturing establishments as they appear before their eyes." Local manufacturers also indicated their concern with the external

---

[65] Wilkes, "Old Berkshire Mill," CMF, pp. 1, 6; Wilkes, "Pioneer Mill," CMF, p. 2; Weston, "Paper Making," p. 12.

Fig. 7.5 Carsons' new Old Berkshire Mill of 1873. Courtesy of the Crane Museum.

Fig. 7.6 Cranes' Old Stone Mill, 1844–69. This photograph, taken in 1868, shows the mill near the end of its gradual construction.
Like this one, many late nineteenth-century mill photographs show a man perched on the roof or atop the chimney. Courtesy of the Crane Museum.

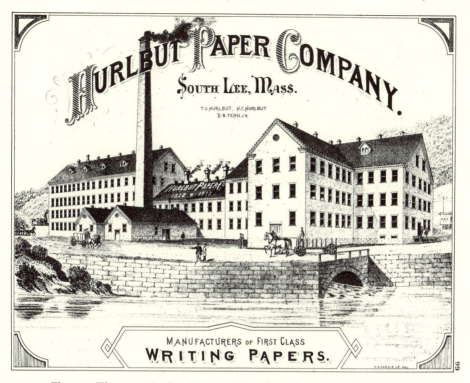

Fig. 7.7 The new Hurlbut Paper Mill of 1872. Symbols of "progress,"
new mills were often represented in advertisements. From Beers,
County Atlas of Berkshire, Massachusetts.

appearance of their mills when they spared "no pains" in "beauti-
fying their grounds" or topped a factory roof with a "gilt vane and
eagle."[66]

New machinery not only made local paper mills differ in size
from surrounding domestic structures, but it also gave paper mills
a form distinct from other large industrial buildings. Paper-making
machines, beaters, and washers all required substantial amounts of
floor space, firm foundations, and easy access to drainage facilities
and water. Thus, paper mills needed disproportionate amounts of
first-floor space and covered relatively large plots of land. The resulting mixture of single and multistory buildings, expressing the
different functions of various sections of the mill, distinguished pa-

[66] *VG*, 2/22/66, p. 2; 5/11/65, p. 2; 7/25/67, p. 2; 7/2/68, p. 2; 7/17/68, p. 2; 1/22/74,
p. 2; 9/19/67, p. 2; 11/13/73, p. 2; and passim. Emphasis mine.

per mills from textile mills, for example, which assumed a uniform, multistory, rectangular block form. After 1860 their increasingly distinctive form ended the conversion of other industrial structures into paper mills, a practice common during the paper mill boom of the 1840s and 1850s.[67]

Figures 7.8 and 7.9 illustrate the distinctive paper mill shape as embodied in one of the smaller frame mills built in East Lee in 1879 and in Crane's Pioneer Mill, built in 1869. In both figures the long low buildings numbered 2 housed the paper-making machines and the lower story of the adjacent buildings numbered 1 held grinding engines. Building number 1 in Figure 7.9 hides an additional single-story wing of beaters.[68]

Paper-making machines required spacious accommodations, but improved transmission technology helped make enlarged mills efficient. The introduction of metal shafting in the 1830s enabled millwrights to begin transmitting power over hundred-foot distances. Power transmission three or four hundred feet awaited the introduction of hollow, lightweight, high-velocity shafting. It became available in the 1870s, at the same time that local paper mills burgeoned beyond the hundred-foot lengths the first machines had helped introduce.[69]

The cost of these substantial new buildings showed up in greatly augmented paper mill capitalization. In the Lee paper industry, despite the fact that manufacturers closed or consolidated a number of older mills, leaving fewer mills in operation, total capitalization climbed from $550,000 in 1855 to $687,397 in 1870, and $896,000 by 1883. Census statistics also reveal the increasing dominance of the industry by fewer, better-endowed firms as capital requirements mounted. Whereas the average Lee firm had $42,308 invested in 1855, by 1870 average investment had more than doubled to $85,925 and by 1883 it had risen another 30 percent to $112,000.[70]

[67] Pierson, "Industrial Architecture," 1:254–57.

[68] Descriptions and floor plans accompany the original illustrations.

[69] Zachariah Allen of Rhode Island was conducting experiments with light, high-velocity shafting in the 1850s. By 1871 he had perfected his system sufficiently to make the information public. Pierson, "Industrial Architecture," 1:135, 247–49; Hunter, *Waterpower*, pp. 450–78.

[70] *Massachusetts Census, 1855*, p. 39; United States Manuscript Census, Lee, Berkshire County, 1870; BSL, *Fourteenth Annual Report*, p. 368.

In addition to mills already mentioned, Weston's Defiance Mill; L. L. Brown's Lower Mill; Smith's Eagle, Housatonic, Union, and Pleasant Valley mills; John Carroll's two New Marlborough mills; May & Rogers's Upper Mill; and Carson & Brown's Dalton mill each was enlarged in the early 1870s. "The Present Day Defiance Mill," "History of the B.W. Co.," p. 4; Wilk, "History of Adams," p. 157; *VG*, 4/6/71,

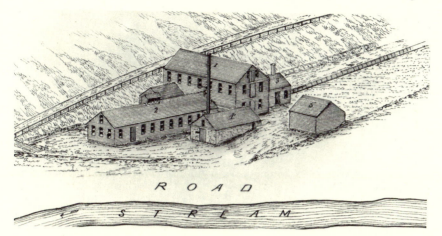

Fig. 7.8 McAlpine Bros. & Co. Mill, East Lee, 1884. The McAlpines
were endowed with paper-making skill, but had limited capital and a
poor location. They bought this mill in 1884 and failed in 1885.
(Barlow & Bancroft Insurance Survey, no. 8257.) Courtesy of
Baker Library, Harvard Business School.

Because the extensive new mills represented substantial investments by their owners, manufacturers made greater efforts to protect them and their contents from fire. Fire insurance companies
gave them added incentive to construct fire-resistant mills by clas-
sifying paper mills as hazardous fire risks and charging them higher
premiums. So did the devastation wrought by at least thirty-four
fires that ravaged Berkshire paper mills between 1820 and 1885,
twenty-six of them after 1857 (Figure 7.10). Extensive local deposits
of clay and limestone abetted efforts to reduce fire hazards by making bricks cheap. Except for marginal mills in towns the railroad
had bypassed (Figure 7.11), only one local mill built after 1830 had
a frame exterior. Indeed, in the 1870s mill owners such as Byron
Weston tore down the shuttered wooden dry lofts above their mills
and built upper stories of brick.[71]

---

p. 2; 6/15/71, p. 2; 7/27/71, p. 2; 10/17/72, p. 2; 7/10/73; p. 2; 10/30/73, p. 2; 11/6/73,
p. 2; 1/1/74, p. 2; and passim. As late as 1862, by contrast, Colt built a new mill one
hundred feet by fifty feet, only slightly larger than the Laflin Mill built thirty-six years
earlier. Snell, "Government Paper Making," CMF, p. 1.

[71] Appendix A; "Early Fire Insurance Policies, 1844–1846," CMF; Pierson, "Industrial Architecture," 1:98–99, 106, 109, 154. Information on material of which
mills were constructed derives primarily from the twenty Barlow and Bancroft Insurance Surveys for the county and reports in the local press. "The Present Day Defiance Mill," BWP, p. 4.

Fig. 7.9 Crane & Co. Pioneer Mill, Dalton, 1889; built to replace the
Old Stone Mill after the 1869 fire. (Barlow & Bancroft Insurance Survey,
no. 9790.) Courtesy of Baker Library, Harvard Business School.

Wood remained far cheaper than iron in America, so that Berkshire mill owners did not build the interiors of their mills with fire-
proof materials as did their British contemporaries. Rather, they
concentrated on retarding a fire's spread through a technique called
slow-burning construction. They replaced the traditional board on
joist floors with heavy, double-thickness floors supported by large
transverse beams. Thicker beams and boards took longer to burn
through, and the elimination of joists decreased the amount of
wood surface exposed and rid mills of hollow firetraps. Enclosed
stairs and trapdoors on elevator shafts reduced a fire's chance of
spreading from floor to floor. All but marginal mills incorporated
these features by the 1860s.[72]

By the 1870s and 1880s, paper mill owners installed fire-fighting
equipment to provide additional protection for their investments.
Most mills had hydrants, hose, and ladders available. A majority
also purchased fire buckets, extinguishers, and a fire pump. The
large Smith Paper Company operated its own fire engine and tested
both engine and alarm whistles regularly. After all, the Smiths
hardly wanted a repetition of the 1865 fire that had called bride-
groom and male guests away from Elizur Smith's wedding recep-
tion.[73]

Fire-fighting equipment protected the expensive machines and
mills, but to protect the mill owners' mounting investments the ma-

[72] Pierson, "Industrial Architecutre," 1:177–80, 187; Wilkes, "Old Berkshire Mill,"
CMF, p. 6. Complete information is limited to the twenty mills surveyed by Barlow
and Bancroft.

[73] Again, complete information is limited to that provided by Barlow and Bancroft.
Smith Paper Company Test Records, SP; Weston, "Paper Making," p. 10; VG, passim.

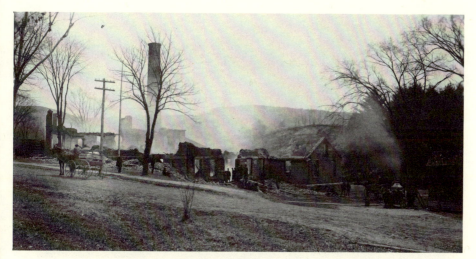

Fig. 7.10 Fire-gutted remains of Colt's 1862 mill. Fires grew
less common, but did not cease. The former Colt Mill, now Crane's
Government Mill, caught fire in 1892. The Pittsfield fire engine (*right*)
arrived too late. Courtesy of the Crane Museum.

chines had to operate as many hours as possible. After mechanization, therefore, mills needed good artificial lighting. Before machine production, only flickering candlelight had brightened work
during the dim morning and evening hours. The advent of machinery first introduced day and night operation in the hard-pressed
beater rooms, where whale oil lamps supplemented candles initially.
Later, after night work spread to the machine room, mills used kerosene lamps and, occasionally, coal oil. All oil lamps represented a
serious fire hazard, however, so as early as 1858 Elizur Smith experimented with a rosin gas system, and by the early 1870s mill owners
such as the Cranes, Carsons, Westons, and Smiths installed Springfield Gas Machines, which produced gasoline vapor and piped it to
gaslights in the mills. The three Adams mills also used gas, theirs
supplied by a municipal gas company.[74]

[74] The principal incentive to adopt round-the-clock operations in the paper industry was that paper-making machines made substantial amounts of broke (unmarket-
able paper) each time they were started and stopped. Fixed costs of the machines may
have been an added incentive, but variable costs associated with the technology were
the critical factor.
  Owen & Hurlbut Blotter, 1822, HP; Owen & Hurlbut Blotter, 1824, HP; David
Carson Daybook, 1828–34, CA, winter 1828–29; Ledger of the Aetna, Housatonic,
and Defiance Mill, BWP; WPA Guide, p. 142; L. L. Brown & Co. Daybook, 1853–54,

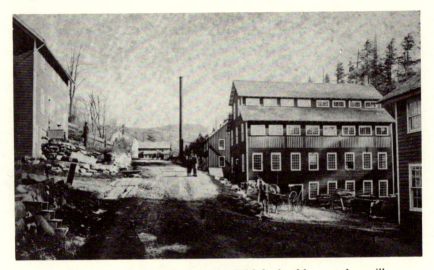

Fig. 7.11 P. C. Baird Mill, East Lee. With luck, older wooden mills
survived in towns bypassed by the railroad. Courtesy of Lee Library.

Finally, technological change abetted year-round operation by
providing more adequate heating. Stoves had heated early Berkshire mills, but they warmed only within a limited radius, inadequate for increasingly large buildings. After mills installed rotary
bleach boilers and machine dryers, steam pipes heated the areas of
the mill through which they passed. In the Cranes' Pioneer Mill, at
least, some steam also heated a small room where the workers could
sit when not otherwise employed. By the 1870s and 1880s, manufacturers provided steam heat throughout the mills, assuring more
rapid evaporation of water from the paper stock as well as more
healthful working conditions. Similar considerations prompted the
installation of patent ventilators in steamy machine rooms by the
1870s.[75]

LLBP; "Paper Making in Monterey, Mass.," p. 5; VG, 12/2/58, p. 2; Wilkes, "Pioneer
Mill," CMF, p. 5; L. L. Brown & Co. Journal, 1867–71, LLBP; Snell, "Government
Paper Making," CMF, p. 1; "Machinery, Engineering, and Chemistry, 1866–1871,"
CMF, 5/19/71; Correspondence to Byron Weston, 1871, BWP, 3/22/71; Barlow and
Bancroft, "Insurance Surveys."

[75] "1820s," HP; Owen & Hurlbut Blotter, 1822, HP, 8/28/22; Ledger of the Aetna,
Housatonic, and Defiance Mill, BWP, 12/15/46; "Philo Brownson and Edwin Brown-
son," interview typescript, CMF, p. 2; Barlow and Bancroft, "Insurance Surveys";
VG, 1/2/73, p. 2.

BETWEEN 1857 and 1885, then, the problems machines had introduced motivated mill owners to adopt a number of new technologies. Within the mills mounting capitalization led manufacturers to introduce fire-resistant construction, fire-fighting equipment, and improved heating and lighting systems. Outside the mills the consequences of mechanization were equally apparent. Huge new mills attracted larger crowds of workers. Local wood helped end growing shortages of fiber and power, but at the cost of denuding surrounding hillsides. New chemicals compensated for scarce fiber and sizing, but local streams and rivers carried large quantities that had been dumped as waste. Finally, Berkshire paper mills no longer stood inconspicuously among local shops and houses all in the shadow of the church. They stretched out massive brick wings and their chimneys rose higher than the tallest steeple, casting shadows across the Berkshire landscape.

In sum, mechanization began a process of technological change that affected the world outside the paper mill as well as the activities within its walls. Fortunately for local citizens, paper makers' continuing need for pure spring water and their continuing preference for waterpower kept the environment more pristine and the mills more dispersed than in many other industrial centers. The growing mills created bustling towns, not teeming cities.

Nonetheless, industrial technology influenced all local citizens, for it was the most striking aspect of their surroundings. Gradually, it revised their aesthetic sensibilities and permeated their vocabulary. For example, whereas George Platner's 1855 eulogist had employed traditional biblical rhetoric, describing Platner as the Lord's steward, a man with a calling, and one who invested in accordance with the parable of the talents; in 1889 Elizur Smith's clergyman instinctively chose a technological metaphor to capture the deceased Smith's virtues. He intoned:

> I was accustomed to compare him *in my own thoughts* to an engine hidden in the heart of some great manufactory, which, while furnishing motive power to the whole establishment, setting in motion hundreds of clashing looms and thousands of whirring spindles, makes its own movements in almost perfect silence.

The image was certainly appropriate. In the years after 1857, mill owners, like their machines, became increasingly powerful.[76]

[76] *In Memoriam, Hon. Elizur Smith*, p. 4. Emphasis mine.

CHAPTER 8

MEN OF SUBSTANCE, ORDER,
AND POWER: OWNERS OF
MECHANIZED PAPER MILLS,
1858–1885

John Ambrose Decker, who bought one of Harrison Garfield's paper mills in 1882, was a paper manufacturer cast in Zenas Crane's mold. Born in Ancram, New York, he had acquired only a common school education when he started working at the local paper mill, an establishment owned by George Platner and Platner's brother. There Decker learned all phases of paper making from superintendent George W. Linn, a skilled paper maker who had previously worked at Platner & Smith's Tyringham mill and who later superintended one of their Lee mills and ultimately became a successful East Lee mill owner. Decker continued his training in Lee and eventually spent fifteen years superintending for the Smiths; in 1882 credit reporters noted that he was "thoroughly acquainted with paper making." All the while Decker, like Zenas Crane, saved his wages, expecting one day to buy a paper mill. His investment in local real estate totaled $20,000 by 1882. This encouraged the credit reporter, who pronounced Decker "energetic, of good character & habits . . . [and] strictly attentive" to business. He predicted that Decker "will undoubtedly be an economical careful manager." Had Decker been entering the paper business in 1801, as had Zenas Crane, his success would have been highly probable. In the less predictable 1830s and 1850s, when Elizur Smith and George Linn got their starts, Decker's prospects would have compared favorably with theirs, for he had strong ties to other paper makers and, after 1884, a partner, former hardware merchant Thomas Sabin, who could "take care of the financial branch of the business."[1]

In 1882, however, Dun's credit reporter did not predict Decker's success, and in 1885 Dun relayed news of his failure. John Decker's misfortune was that he celebrated his twenty-first birthday only in 1857. After that year mill owners operated in a business and tech-

---

[1] *SF* 5 (February 1932):2, 7; Hyde, *History of Lee*, p. 292; R. G. Dun & Co. Ledgers, 4:713.

nological climate irrevocably altered by mechanization. Although paper-making skill and ties to other mill owners remained important, they conferred less of an advantage as machines became standardized, mills larger, and managerial decisions more complicated. Because friends and technical skills were Decker's only substantial assets, his failure could be anticipated.[2]

This chapter documents in general terms what Decker discovered through personal experience. By the 1860s and 1870s, mechanization and its technological consequences had transformed the rapidly growing, rapidly changing, highly volatile paper industry that existed between 1827 and 1857 into an increasingly mature, predictable, capital-intensive business. Whereas uncertain technological and economic conditions had given the edge to the man who could call on others for advice and assistance, the more stable, more developed postwar industry favored the man who was self-sufficient—endowed with ample resources, organizational skill, and informal managerial training. Between 1858 and 1885 such men increasingly dominated the mechanized paper industry and, through their economic power and organizational ability, the paper mill towns.

Predictable Successes: The Emergence of a Mill-Owning Establishment

As depicted earlier, between 1827 and 1857 the mechanizing paper industry's immense opportunities attracted a diverse group of investors, while the industry's enormous risks rendered every man's success uncertain, whatever his assets or associates. For mill owners, the outstanding consequence of mechanization and its technological aftermath was that success or failure grew increasingly predictable, increasingly dependent on previously acquired wealth and skill. Men without substantial assets and specialized preparation for paper mill management could no longer entertain legitimate hopes of succeeding. Diminished opportunity became evident in 1857 as the panic and ensuing depression drove out marginal producers and chastened those who remained. Wartime prosperity offered a brief respite, but after 1865 rapidly mounting capital requirements; concentration of production in fewer, larger mills located near railroads; and new costs attributable to resource scarcity each restricted entry and reinforced the advantages held by men who had survived the depression and, later, by their heirs. Between 1866 and 1885,

[2] R. G. Dun & Co. Ledgers, 4:713.

then, the conditions of a technologically mature industry consistently favored the established mill owners.

Mill owners who entered the paper industry before 1857 and managed to survive the ensuing depression brought substantial technical and economic assets to the postwar paper industry, assets that conferred enormous advantages (see Table 8.1). Of the 146 men and women who owned Berkshire paper mills between 1866 and 1885, twenty-nine first acquired mills before 1857. Only one retained ownership too brief a time to be considered successful. Nor does the remarkable success rate of established mill owners (97 percent) simply reflect the fact that anyone who owned a mill continuously from 1857 through 1866 automatically qualifies as a success. Considering only the years after 1865, nineteen owned mills longer than ten years, twelve remaining in business for the entire twenty-year period. Furthermore, of the nine who survived fewer than five years, two sold to buy mills outside the county, one retired, and two died of old age. Even if we reclassify the four others as failures, men who entered the industry before 1857 and weathered the difficult years between 1857 and 1865 achieved an impressive 83 percent success rate. In fact, simple longevity figures understate established mill owners' predominance. As the industry consolidated after 1865, established men most often gained control of several mills. Taking account of multiple ownerships, established paper manufacturers averaged 28.75 mill-owning years after 1865.[3]

TABLE 8.1
MILL ACQUISITION AND SUCCESS, 1866–85

	Successes	Failures	% Successful
Invested before 1857	28	1	97
Inherited mill	20	5	80
New entrants	26	66	28

Lambda$_b$ = .55; level of statistical significance, .001 (Chi square)

NOTE: See Appendices A, B, and C. Categories are mutually exclusive. Those individuals inheriting mills before 1857 are classed as pre-1857 investors.

[3] See Appendix A. Average mill-owning years results from totaling all of the years men owned each of their mills and dividing by number of mill owners. Only mill-owning years after 1865 have been counted.

As discussed in Chapter 5, there is no totally satisfactory definition of success. The ten-year survival criterion is used here for much the same reasons as outlined in

Inheriting a mill gave a paper maker almost as promising a start. In addition to five mill owners who inherited mills before 1857, twenty-five men and women had shares of mills given them by living kin or attained ownership when relatives died. These heirs successfully stayed in business 80 percent of the time. Again, Table 8.1 understates their dominance between 1866 and 1885. Summing the years heirs owned each of their mills, these individuals averaged 36.88 years of ownership.[4]

Inheritance conferred such advantages that by 1885 men and women whose fathers, fathers-in-law, or uncles had previously owned Berkshire paper mills controlled all of the county's principal paper-making establishments. Zenas Crane's sons and grandsons owned three Dalton mills and a fourth in Pittsfield. Sons and grandsons of David Carson owned another Dalton mill. At South Lee Thomas Hurlbut's sons operated his mills, and in Housatonic the paper mill belonged to Charles Owen's daughter-in-law and her second husband. The county's other large mills had passed to nephews of childless uncles. Thanks to his uncles' aid, L. L. Brown held most of the stock in Adams' two paper mills. Byron Weston held sole title to two Dalton mills, having gradually paid back his original silent partner, uncle Franklin Weston. In Lee and Lenox Elizur Smith's nephews DeWitt and Wellington had assumed active management of the numerous Smith mills.[5]

After 1865, then, knowing how and when an owner acquired a mill made it relatively easy to predict his success or failure (Lambda$_b$ = .55). Established paper manufacturers and heirs succeeded more than three times (3.18) as frequently as did new entrants. They dominated the industry because they commanded two important assets for an era characterized by increasingly standardized machines and new technologies that permitted greatly enlarged operations: capital and experience. And in contrast to the era of

---

Chapter 5, and to ensure comparability of data between the two eras. Use of mill owners' entire career spans makes certain that all individuals are equally at risk, which would not be the case if only years after 1866 were considered. Excluded from this analysis are nine individuals who both entered and left the industry between 1858 and 1865.

Unless specified, here and elsewhere in this chapter, averages are means.

[4] See Appendices. Figures are for the twenty-five post-1857 inheritors.

[5] See Appendices. L. L. Brown and Byron Weston have not been considered heirs in earlier calculations because they and their uncles entered the industry simultaneously. Clyde and Sally Griffen note a similar concentration of inherited capital in the most substantial firms in nineteenth-century Poughkeepsie, New York. "Family and Business in a Small City," pp. 323–24.

mechanization, when only paper-making skill conferred much of an advantage, financial resources, commercial experience, and paper mill training all proved important to success after 1865. Mill owners lacking any one of these assets were more likely to fail than had been the case between 1827 and 1857. Moreover, after 1865 capital and commercial expertise became the leading prerequisites for success, whereas paper-making experience conferred only a modest advantage.[6]

Increased costs of constructing, operating, and equipping a mechanized paper mill made adequate financing a significant determinant of a mill owner's success. Dun's Berkshire correspondents identified insufficient capital as a factor in the majority of local paper mill failures they reported and cited it as the sole reason for failure in 40 percent of the cases. Statistical evidence confirms credit reporters' assessments. Knowing a paper manufacturer's initial assets enhances our ability to guess his fate after 1865 (Lambda$_b$ = .23). By contrast, during the era of mechanization an investor's initial economic resources had little to do with his success or failure (Lambda$_b$ = .00). Adequate initial capital helps especially to explain the success of mill owners' heirs, who tapped family capital accumulated over earlier decades. Mill owners whose families assured them financial backing had nearly twice (1.85 times) the probability of success as those who started with little capital.[7]

[6] Calculation is based on data in Table 8.1. Comparison of data in Table 8.2 with data in Table 5.1 shows the greater association of these three attributes with success after 1865.

Although eleven women were part owners of Berkshire paper mills after 1865, all acquired their interest through prior investments in the industry by male relatives and none played an active role in management, in part because the sexual division of labor (see Chapter 10) precluded their training as skilled paper makers. Because this was the case, I will generally refer to "men" who owned mills and employ masculine pronouns in the discussion that follows, although data for the few women have been included. A partial exception to the generalization that female mill owners were inactive was Sarah Chittendon Owen Cone. She had inherited her share of the Owen Paper Company from Edward H. Owen, her first husband. Later she married H. D. Cone, who was active in managing the mill and already had invested a small amount. At the death of Charles M. Owen, Mrs. Cone's father-in-law, the Cones came to own the mill jointly. When Cone persisted, after five years, in building his huge and architecturally pretentious new mill, despite depleted corporate funds, Dun reporters noted that Mrs. Cone was a good businesswoman, actively enough involved in company affairs that "it had recently been intimated that she was becoming a little tired of the manner in which building operations were being conducted." Two months later work on the new mill had ceased. R. G. Dun & Co. Ledgers, 5:646.

[7] Dun credit reports began after 1835, but remained relatively infrequent for a number of years, so that most of these reports originated after 1857. In all, Dun re-

TABLE 8.2
ASSETS, ASSOCIATES, AND SUCCESS, 1866–85

Attribute	Successful with Attribute	Successful without Attribute	Lambda_b	Level of Statistical Significance (Chi square)
Financial resources	63%	40%	.23	.10
Commercially trained partners	60	24	.28	.001
Paper mill trained partners	55	36	.10	.10

Of course, established mill owners did not need substantial initial investments because they had entered the industry while capital requirements remained modest. They gradually built up the financial resources needed after 1865. Moreover, those who weathered the depression and operated throughout the Civil War sometimes reaped huge profits. For example, Dun reporters estimated in 1866 that Elizur Smith had made $100,000 in each of the last three years, a phenomenal 100 percent return on nominal capitalization and 25 percent return on assets. If we consider the substantial resources Smith and others brought to paper making by 1866 (Table 8.3), we find financial assets clearly the best predictor of a man's success (Lambda_b = .45). Postwar data also depict men with access to family money, a group dominated numerically by heirs, succeeding more than three times (3.09) more often than did new entrants with limited financial assets.[8]

---

porters identified causes for failure for twenty-three firms. Nine failures were attributed solely to insufficient capital; ten were traced to a variety of other principal causes, including panics, fires, bad luck, and poor judgment; and four were reported caused by inadequate financing and one or more other factors. On the history of Dun and the usefulness of the reports see James H. Madison, "The Evolution of Commercial Credit Reporting Agencies in Nineteenth Century America," *BHR* 48 (Summer 1974): 164–86, and "The Credit Reports of R. G. Dun & Co. as Historical Sources," *Historical Methods Newsletter* 8 (September 1975):128–31.

R. G. Dun & Co. Ledgers, 3:75, 83, 120–21, 144, 150, 240–41, 288; 4:361, 389, 504, 518, 570, 713; 5:167, 244, 295, 325; 6:370, 509, 523, 551.

Here and in the following paragraphs, the discussion of data on mill owners and success refers to information presented in Tables 5.1 and 8.2. The data, its sources, and its liabilities are treated more fully in Appendix B.

[8] R. G. Dun & Co. Ledgers, 3:272. Categories in Table 8.3 are mutually exclusive.

TABLE 8.3
ASSETS AFTER 1865 AND SUCCESS

	Successes	Failures	% Successful
Mill ownership	28	1	97
Family money	23	11	68
Personal savings	13	19	45
Little or nothing	8	29	22
Insufficient information	2	12	—

Lambda$_b$ = .45; level of statistical significance, .001 (Chi square)

Smith's case suggests as well that survival through the difficult years between 1857 and 1865 conferred less tangible financial advantages. Smith used some of his wartime profits to repay creditors who had lost money through the 1857 failure of Platner & Smith. No legal obligation bound him to do so, but his demonstration of financial responsibility established his reputation as credit-worthy, an asset that abetted Smith's recurrent innovation after 1865.[9]

Experience also helped assure established men's success. Men who bought mills before 1857 had the opportunity to learn paper-making technology, accounting, and paper marketing during a relatively forgiving period. Mistakes did not jeopardize huge investments and high profits concealed many inadequacies. Men entering the industry between 1866 and 1885 had much more at risk and, because the industry had expanded, much lower average returns. In 1867 Byron Weston reported, "Many of the mills . . . are not making legal interest [6 percent] on capital." During the same year Weston's books showed a loss because his mill shut down for three months while undergoing a complete overhaul, a necessity confronting most mills of the era. Later, from 1874 through 1880, L. L. Brown paid dividends of 14 percent a year, but passed up dividends entirely for the next five years, except for 1883, when the firm paid only 5 percent. Massachusetts labor statisticians' figures suggest that low profits were general in the 1880s. In 1883 they reported that Lee mills averaged only 3 percent net profit on capital invested. Under these circumstances, new entrants could not afford to guess

---

In the few cases in which an individual began with access to family money, but had also acquired substantial personal savings before buying a paper mill, I have assigned the individual to the Family Money category, in keeping with my interest in the resources originally underwriting a man's career.

[9] R. G. Dun & Co. Ledgers, 5:52.

wrong. They needed to master paper mill management before acquiring a mill.[10]

Men who inherited mills had precisely this advantage: they had learned and practiced paper mill management in advance. Like their fathers before them, the sons of David Carson, Zenas Crane, and Thomas Hurlbut had worked in the mills, as had the nephews of Josiah Weston and Elizur Smith. Despite the increased importance of formal education, Zenas Crane, Jr., grandson of the industry's founder, began attending school in the summer and tending paper machinery in the winter at the age of eleven. At nineteen he had mastered the mill routine and he went on the road to learn salesmanship.[11]

Mill owners who groomed successors were conscious that experience in all phases of the industry had become essential. Writing to his fourteen-year-old son, Philip, Byron Weston explained that when Philip left private school for the summer, he would start his education for paper manufacturing.

> You must learn something of the mill this summer & not wait till you get so large you won't like to go in and work. You can learn paper making in a few months what would take you years after you get older. You must know the business as a foundation for life. . . .

The younger generation of Cranes, he informed Philip, "learned the whole business before they were of age and can manage anything from Rag Room to office work and do it well, and keep their business going right up to date and are not at the mercy of a foreman or Book Keeper." Familiar with the larger scale and more rapid pace of mechanized mills, Weston explained that paper mill owners needed advance preparation for decision making because, "a man at that business must keep a good many things going all at once and see every thing at a glance and be quick at it—" He concluded, "You must learn the business thorough for you are liable to have it all to attend to before you know it."[12]

[10] Byron Weston Letter Book, 1867–68, BWP, 1/31/68, 3/6/68; L. L. Brown Paper Company Minutes of Stockholders and Directors' Meetings, 1873–1922, LLBP, passim; BSL, *Fourteenth Annual Report*, pp. 368–69. By comparison, the county's other leading industry, woolen cloth manufacture, fared much better. Labor statisticians' data show Pittsfield woolen mills returning a net profit of 16 percent on capital. Additional comparative profit data is presented in Chapter 9.

[11] Child, *Gazeteer*, part 1, p. 129; R. G. Dun & Co. Ledgers, 3:33; Winthrop M. Crane III, interview, Crane & Co. office, Dalton, Mass., July 18, 1975; File 521, CMF, 12/19/51; "Bay State Mill," CMF, p. 9.

[12] Cited in Wheelwright, "Paper Making Since 1863," BWP, p. 63.

Byron Weston's counsel mentioned two bodies of knowledge. "You must," he wrote, "know about the business and paper making." His more frequent references to business suggest that, in contrast to the handmade and mechanizing periods, after 1865 knowledge of accounting and marketing had assumed greater importance than technical expertise. Quantitative evidence confirms this impression. Between 1866 and 1885 mill owners who had commercial training or commercially skilled partners succeeded two and a half times as frequently as those without. By comparison, access to paper-making experience gave men only half again (1.54 times) more probability of success. In other words, a man's commercial expertise made his success far more predictable (Lambda$_b$ = .28) than did his familiarity with paper machines and mill tasks (Lambda$_b$ = .10).[13]

Several contemporaneous trends precipitated this shift in the relative advantage conferred by the two bodies of knowledge. As we shall see, new paper-making technologies prompted manufacturers to employ increasingly sophisticated accounting and marketing techniques. Taking full advantage of new fibers and steam power sometimes depended on mill owners inventing new quantitative or promotional methods, an easier task when mill owners thoroughly understood the logic of conventional commercial activities. Simultaneously, increasingly standardized machines routinized both technical decisions and operating procedures. Moreover, whereas the rapidly growing industry of the 1827–57 period had strained the capacity of existing mills to supply trained paper makers, after 1865 fewer mills drew on the enlarged group of men trained by an expanded paper industry. Berkshire partnerships reflected these demographic trends. Between 1827 and 1857 only two-thirds (67 percent) of all mill owners managed to find mill-trained partners, but between 1866 and 1885 nearly five-sixths (83 percent) did so. If most paper manufacturers sought partners with paper-making skill, they obviously considered mill training important. It had simply grown too common to confer much of an advantage.[14]

In fact, less than one-eighth (12 percent) of the men who succeeded lacked both mill training and mill-trained partners. Thus, although paper-making skill no longer sufficed for success, it remained necessary. After mechanization, local correspondents of R. G. Dun & Co. repeatedly emphasized that they considered paper mill training essential. For example, in 1857 one credit reporter ex-

[13] See Appendix C.   [14] See Appendix C.

pressed doubts about P. C. Baird's ultimate success, despite Baird's commercial experience and ample financial backing supplied by his wealthy, landowning father. He noted, "The greatest obstacle to his success is that he has no practical knowledge of his business." Even in an established concern such as the L. L. Brown Paper Company, skill in paper making ranked high in credit reporters' estimation. When part-owner James Osborne, Brown's superintendent for thirty years, resigned as part of an economy measure and T. A. Mole, part owner and former company bookkeeper, became active manager, Dun's agent concluded, "New manager not a practical paper maker—not judicious change." Similarly, when Dun's correspondent learned that Thomas Bradley contemplated withdrawing from Mill River's Berkshire Paper Company partnership, he predicted, "if he does don't think it will run very long for he is the only paper maker."[15]

Indeed, although mere paper makers such as John Ambrose Decker did not succeed as principal owners, paper-making skill alone still enabled a few men to acquire limited equity in Berkshire mills. L. L. Brown had given mill superintendent James Osborne shares in what was essentially a family concern because he acknowledged Osborne's crucial contribution to Brown's success. Probably reasoning that a man with a working interest would exert himself more fully, other mill proprietors also offered shares as inducements to skilled paper workers. For example, when several of Adams' leading dry goods merchants and textile manufacturers formed the Adams Paper Company, they included as a partner Henry Putnam, a man of "modest means," because Putnam was a skilled paper maker. When new investors superseded the founders, Putnam remained as the essential "practical man," to use the phrase of credit reporters.[16]

The Adams Paper Company exercised good judgment in recruiting and retaining Putnam. Paper making remained sufficiently distinctive that, of the nineteen men whose previous manufacturing experience had come in other industries, only seven succeeded. That they failed one and a third times (1.34) more frequently than did other mill owners suggests that their prior experience often constituted a liability. The investment decisions of men who entered paper making from other industries confirm that they frequently

[15] R. G. Dun & Co. Ledgers, 3:139; 6:386; 5:244; and passim.
[16] L. L. Brown Paper Company Stock Book, 1873–1920, LLBP, 7/1/73; L. L. Brown Paper Company Minutes, LLBP, 6/7/73, 1/16/82; R. G. Dun & Co. Ledgers, 3:328; 4:427.

brought unrealistic expectations with them. For example, George C. Walter and Edwin L. Booth converted their New Marlborough shoe lace factory to paper making in 1881. By that date such small mills located far from the nearest railroad already had difficulty competing and the partners compounded the difficulty by expecting to compensate for limited capital by doing most of the work themselves. They failed in 1882. Similarly, Henry C. Carson, Hinsdale fork manufacturer, underestimated both the capital and the commercial risks paper making entailed. Heavily mortgaged from the outset, Carson failed within eight months, in part because he accepted commercial paper that he could not get discounted at local banks.[17]

By contrast, the county's more substantial textile manufacturers were prepared to understand the importance of adequate capital, but their behavior indicates that both operating difficulties and profit levels surprised them. Textile manufacturers Amasa Richardson and Stowell Dean and their two partners evidently had very strong and very diverse beliefs about how to run the Adams Paper Company. Five years after they organized the company, credit reports read: "Mill stopped & partners are quarreling. Are not likely to resume business under this style." The prediction proved correct. Six new partners took over the following year, including cotton manufacturers Charles T. and William C. Plunkett. Their success as cotton mill owners did not help them make paper profitably and the corporation survived ten years only because W. C. Plunkett lent it large sums, and for the final five years the company rented two floors of its mill to cotton warp manufacturers. Ultimately, Plunkett converted the whole mill to cotton production.[18]

The distinctiveness of paper manufacture reinforced the advantages of the mill-owning establishment, those who had inherited mills and those who had owned mills prior to 1858. Because these men had mastered paper making, they could oversee their mills, an activity the *Valley Gleaner* pronounced "a very important matter, if one wishes to become a successful manufacturer." Owners of smaller mills generally acted as their own superintendents, as did some owners of large mills, such as H. D. Cone, who regularly put in an eleven-hour day. Even the leading members of the papermaking establishment owed much of their success to overseeing paper production. For example, Zenas Marshal Crane, who became an owner in 1842, brought his office work down to the mill even after

[17] R. G. Dun & Co. Ledgers, Konkapot Paper Co. entries; 4:361; 5:142.
[18] R. G. Dun & Co. Ledgers, 4:427; 5:175, 338, 364.

the office had moved to a separate building. From time to time he would also

> bring his dinner, and eat, while Ophelia Young would read the local news to him. There were seven sorters. After eating he would dig down in the baskets and look through the sheets, and if he found a clear sheet, he would lay it on the block near her table and ask if she thought he was "going to pay his good money for them to waste paper."

His son Zenas, Jr., followed his example. He visited his finishing room daily when not away on sales trips. Zenas's brother Winthrop Murray invested even more energy in supervising production. After he took over management of Crane & Co., he drove his buggy to each of the three mills every day. Arriving at a mill, he visited every department and looked over paper orders in process; then he was off to his next stop. Paper worker Thomas Bolton recalled: "His horse would be on a gallop all the way. He was always in a hurry." Similarly, workman Alfred Hoxie remembered W. M. Crane as "a very energetic man. Of course he was new and green at the business. He made us fellows step around. . . ."[19]

In many ways, the ubiquitous Winthrop Murray Crane epitomizes the men who dominated paper making after 1865. Like his grandfather Zenas, he had always lived near paper mills and spent many years working in them; but unlike Zenas, he had always expected to own substantial mills and manage them successfully. His substantial initial capital also contrasted sharply with that of his grandfather or even his father. In addition, Winthrop Murray Crane spent far more time on the road and in the office than had his predecessors. Whereas Zenas Crane had been able to concentrate on making good paper, his grandson spent long hours counting costs and captivating customers.

Captivating Customers and Counting Costs

While Alfred Hoxie remembered Winthrop Murray Crane for making the "fellows" step lively at the mills, office worker Henry Hosburgh recalled him as the man who dictated ninety-six letters

[19] *VG*, 1/22/72; Robert F. Bailley, "Rising Paper Company," (undergraduate paper SUNY-Cortland, in Housatonic Library, Great Barrington, Mass.), p. 4; "David Barnard," interview typescript, CMF, p. 1; "Philo Brownson and Edwin Brownson," interview typescript, CMF, p. 2; "Miss Alice Lyman," interview typescript, CMF, p. 2; "Charles Groesbeck," interview typescript, CMF, p. 3; "Thomas J. Bolton," interview typescript, CMF, pp. 3, 8; "Alfred Hoxie," interview typescript, CMF, p. 5.

one long evening. Of course, Hosburgh cited that evening because it was unusual, but Crane's generally heavy load of correspondence was not atypical of contemporary paper manufacturers. As early as 1847 mill owner Josiah Weston advised his schoolboy nephew, Byron, to "attend to your English grammar" as preparation for mill ownership. Later, after Weston returned from distinguished service in the Civil War and purchased a mill, he made ample use of that training. Byron Weston Company records include numerous thick volumes of his letters copied onto damp tissue with a copy press. They provide eloquent testimony that letter writing was the tool late nineteenth-century mill owners commonly employed to recruit buyers and bargain for better raw material and machine prices. After mechanization, however, successful mill owners such as Weston faced tighter, more sophisticated paper markets and they were offered a bewildering variety of machines, fibers, and fuels. In response, they supplemented their correspondence with new advertising techniques and backed it up with careful cost analyses.[20]

Byron Weston's business letters provide sustained documentation that marketing required more attention and greater creativity after 1865. Following the organization of the Writing Paper Maker's Association in 1861, collective output restrictions helped reduce what manufacturers perceived as the "glut" of paper that had depressed paper prices beginning in 1857, but all grades of paper remained far more plentiful than in earlier years. Moreover, in the fine paper business, firms with established reputations offered stiff competition for new entrants such as Weston. Winning customers required direct, forceful arguments. Writing to one paper merchant, Weston exhibited the persuasiveness that later earned him political office:

> Many parties are dissatisfied with L. L. Brown and Jessup & Laflin paper and with them my papers do not want much urging and I think you could without much trouble (merely your opinion) sell my paper to the malcontents at lest. In some smaller markets my papers are used in preference to any others.

He warned another, "Don't be superstitious and think but one man can make paper for he will surely die some day and then you must get from others." He also offered discounts as inducements, requesting that they be kept *strictly confidential.*"[21]

[20] "Henry Hosburgh," interview typescript, CMF, p. 12; "Byron Weston—Early Life and Family," BWP, 9/47, 9/20/47, 11/6/47.

[21] "Writing Paper Maker's Association," CMF, passim; Weeks, *History of Paper Man-*

After getting his paper adopted, Weston used regular correspondence to clarify orders and to keep dealers in line. On one invoice he noted, "I am informed that you have sold my paper at
7 1/2% from list. Please bear in mind that I request all paper dealers
in your city not to sell less than 5%." Facing a buyers' market, Weston resourcefully portrayed himself as bargaining from strength.
He informed a first-time customer, "If you are my regular customer
you will get paper when you want it as promptly as it can be got up,
but if you get of me when others don't care to make it I may not be
so prompt." Another letter notified a Boston firm that Weston had
withdrawn their exclusive local distribution rights, but that he
would reinstate their right if given evidence that they were "push-
ing" his papers.[22]

Although Berkshire mill owners did most marketing from their
desks, they took increasing advantage of rapidly improving transportation to visit paper markets and use face-to-face persuasion to
recruit customers. Byron Weston, for example, missed few chances
to promote his wares. Entering a new bank, he approached the
bookkeeper and asked him what kind of paper he used.

> When the clerk replied he did not know, Weston told him to
> look at the water mark. It proved to be "Weston's Linen
> Ledger." "I made that paper," Weston is reported to have said,
> "it is the best ledger paper made, and don't you forget it."

More important, mill owners called regularly on established customers, promoting personal loyalty and facilitating communication.
Henry Hosburgh recalled Winthrop Murray Crane's itinerary:

> He would go to Washington for two days, then come back and
> then go to New York, and then come home and go to Boston,
> but he would always come back for two days a week and take
> care of the accumulated mail. When he got that cleaned up, he
> would be ready to start right out again.

Similarly, the *Valley Gleaner* kept local citizens posted on Lee paper
manufacturers' frequent comings and goings, especially to New

---

ufacturing, pp. 285–86; Byron Weston Letter Book, 1867–68, BWP, 7/13/68; Byron
Weston Letter Book, 1868–69, BWP, 2/6/69, 6/7/69; Byron Weston Letter Book,
1873-74, BWP, 11/7/73. Zenas Crane, Jr., for example, gave a variety of discounts: a
standard one, one for cash in thirty days, and one for larger orders. Sometimes these
totaled as much as 25 percent off list. Zenas Crane, Jr., Journal, 1879–81, CA.
[22] Byron Weston Letter Book, 1874–75, BWP, 9/7/74; Byron Weston Letter Book,
1867–68, BWP, 4/10/68; Brown & Weston Letter Book, 1864–65, BWP, 7/26/65.

York; Julia Weston's diary noted regular sales trips by her husband and other Dalton paper makers; and L. L. Brown's ledgers recorded recurrent travel expenditures by Adams mill owners, including occasional trips "west," meaning to Cincinnati and Chicago.[23]

Until the 1860s written and oral communication met virtually all of the mill owners' promotional needs, because wholesale markets remained relatively small and concentrated in the Northeast. To win and retain retail customers, manufacturers relied on their wholesalers and on distinctive printed wrappers that differentiated their products (see Figures 2.3 and 5.2). By the 1860s and 1870s, product identification had grown important enough to warrant copyrighting wrappers and registering distinctive paper names as trademarks. Except for wrappers, however, mills confined their formal advertising to listings in city directories.[24]

As a result of mechanization, population growth, and improved transportation, by the late 1860s Berkshire paper makers sold their paper through many more wholesalers who were dispersed throughout the nation. The records of Crane & Co., L. L. Brown, and the various owners of Dalton's Defiance Mill all show that after the Civil War a national paper market gradually supplanted the regional markets of the antebellum era. Berkshire mill owners especially expanded the proportion of their business west of New York State and south of New York City. Recognizing that scattered wholesalers and manufacturers had difficulty exchanging information informally, in 1872 Howard Lockwood founded the *Paper Trade Journal*, providing mill owners with a vehicle for reaching more numerous and distant potential customers. Byron Weston ran a price list in Lockwood's journal the following year. Once inaugurated, paper trade journalism proliferated. By the 1880s several individuals published specialized stationers' periodicals and Berkshire mill owners found themselves spending growing amounts of money on advertising. L. L. Brown, for example, recorded nearly $3,000 a year in advertising expenditures by 1885.[25]

[23] Wheelwright, "Papermaking Since 1863," BWP, pp. 35–36; "Henry Hosburgh," interview typescript, CMF, p. 13; *VG*, passim; Katharine Weston Crane, "Excerpts from the 1865–1897 Diaries of My Grandmother Julia Mitchell Weston," typescript lent to the author by Mrs. Crane, Dalton, Mass.; LLBP, passim.

[24] On increasing use of the telegraph to supplement written and oral communication see McGaw, "Sources and Impact," pp. 174–75; ibid., p. 252, illustrates wrapper. Brown & Weston and Byron Weston Letter Books, BWP, 1/2/65, 3/7/67, and passim; "Patents, 1867–1886," CMF.

[25] McGaw, "Sources and Impact," pp. 171–72, graphs the changing geographic dis-

Berkshire paper manufacturers' early trade journal advertisements show considerable diversity, suggesting that mill owners devoted time and personal ingenuity to devising them. By supplying local manufacturers with a national voice, trade journalism also encouraged them in supplementary promotional ventures. Byron Weston developed printed sample sheets of ledger paper and included in his journal advertisement the line "SEND FOR SAMPLE SHEET, ERASE AND REWRITE FOUR TIMES ON SAME SPOT." Zenas Crane, Jr., who introduced tinted stationery, began making and distributing sample books. Mill owners also prepared exhibits for the era's numerous expositions, assured of ample trade journal coverage should they win prizes. By 1876, for example, Byron Weston had collected awards from the Massachusetts Charitable Mechanics Association, the American Institute, the Cincinnati Industrial Exposition, the Franklin Institute, and the Paris Exposition. He listed his prizes in his advertisements, helping him establish his paper's reputation quickly to compensate for his late entry into ledger paper making.[26]

The great American Centennial Exposition stirred especially intense promotional efforts. Workers recalled that H. D. Cone took the event so seriously, he practically lived in the mill while they made the display paper. He ordered the mill thoroughly cleaned and had the beaters furnished entirely with linen shirt cuttings, first having had rag sorters remove all seam pieces. The resulting product permitted a convincing demonstration of his paper's strength. With a photographer standing by, Cone had the mill's 275-pound trimmer man stand in the middle of a large sheet while four fellow workmen raised him by lifting the corners. Likewise, the Cranes took care to have their elaborate 1876 exhibits photographed.[27]

In 1881 L. L. Brown, who had spent nearly $700 on his Centennial exhibit, undertook the period's most novel and costly advertising venture. He revived the practice of hand paper making in the United States. Because mechanization had made the American craft

---

tribution of these firms' sales. Weeks, *History of Paper Manufacturing*, p. 298; Byron Weston Letter Book, 1873–74, BWP, 10/7/73; L. L. Brown Paper Company Journal, 1884–85, LLBP. Between August 1884 and July 1885 Brown debited $2,816.91 to his advertising account.

[26] McGaw, "Sources and Impact," pp. 252–55 offers a selection of contemporary advertisements. "Byron Weston Mill Owner," BWP, 5/15/75; Byron Weston Company advertisement, *Paper World* 1 (July 1880):28; Zenas Crane, Jr., Journal, 1879–81, CA; Wheelwright, "Papermaking Since 1863," BWP, p. 34.

[27] "H. D. Cone," *SF* 3 (February 1930): 5; Photograph Collection, Crane Museum.

extinct, he had to import equipment and recruit the Normans, a family of skilled paper makers, from England. Although an extensive trade in the handmade paper followed, that branch of Brown's business was probably never self-supporting. Instead, knowing the publicity he would receive in the trade press, Brown evidently conceived of it as a way to improve ledger paper sales by lending all his products the aura of hand-crafted excellence. He reinforced the image by showing customers how the Normans made paper either at his mill, at expositions, or in photographs such as the one reproduced in Figure 8.1.[28]

Without more sophisticated accounting procedures, however, the new and creative promotional activities would have been wasted. The most extensive markets and the most loyal customers will not earn profits for mill owners who sell below cost, as many learned they had been doing after 1857. As described in Chapter 7, when Addison Laflin in 1862 identified mill owners' disastrous pricing policies, he proposed cost accounting as the logical remedy. Chapter 7 focused on accounting procedures mill owners developed to determine rag costs. This was only one of the period's accounting innovations. Owners of mechanized mills discovered that they needed to associate costs with particular production processes, to determine the relative expense of alternative fuels and power sources, and to control for inefficient use of increasingly diverse raw materials. Berkshire paper manufacturers solved these problems by calculating an array of actual (historic) costs and by experimenting with standard costing.

By 1857, Addison Laflin observed, mechanization had created an urgent need for paper makers to assign costs to particular stages of paper manufacturing. Production cost information became important primarily because, as described in Chapter 4, the paper-making machine was far more efficient than the many new machines devised to finish paper. Consequently, mechanization lowered paper-making costs more than finishing costs. Because smaller papers required as much finishing as large sheets, traditional price ratios no longer bore much relationship to the relative production costs of various sized papers. In addition, as Laflin recognized, mills could sell paper as "book paper, hanging paper, tea and shoe paper, and even wrapping paper" without any finishing so that, as mechaniza-

[28] L. L. Brown Paper Company Journal, 1874–76, LLBP, 6/76; "Hand Made Paper," *SF* 4 (July 1930):7–8; "Old Home Week, Tyringham," p. 89; Britton, *Paper Merchandising*, p. 47.

Fig. 8.1 The Norman family making paper by hand, L. L. Brown Mill, Adams. Imported, along with their equipment, from England, the Normans are shown at work as vatman (*left foreground*), coucher (*center foreground*), and layman (*right background*). A traditional screw press full of paper appears on the right and a large wooden stuff chest appears in the left background. Departures from early American hand paper-making equipment include the stone vat (*center*) and the cart and rail for carrying paper and felts from coucher to layman. Courtesy of the Adams Historical Society.

tion changed the relative cost of finishing, men specializing in cheap writing paper "would have made more money if their finishing rooms had never been built."[29]

Based on this observation, Laflin introduced the notion of process costing to the national Writing Paper Maker's Association, a group dominated numerically by Berkshire mill owners. Subsequently, a report in the *Valley Gleaner* carried his message to any Lee manufacturer unable to attend. Aware that he had to overcome longstanding assumptions about the very nature of paper making, Laflin outlined the underlying principle of process costing so clearly that he is worth quoting at length.

> To ascertain definitely the cost of writing papers . . . it is necessary to consider the manufacture as consisting of two distinct departments. 1st, Converting the rags into the flat dry sheet in which condition it is delivered to the finishing room. 2d, Converting the flat dry sheet into the forms for use. These two de-

[29] Laflin, "Address," CMF, p. 16.

partments are not dependent upon each other or necessarily connected with each other. Each is a perfect manufacture without the other, and each could be carried on equally well without the other. Each should likewise be self supporting, and not dependent for profit upon the other. In most kinds of manufactures, the corresponding processes, if they were ever united, have long since been separated. Thus it is not common to attach a machine shop to a pig iron furnace, a shoe shop to a tannery, or a clothing factory to a woolen mill. Although it is common to connect together in writing paper mills the manufacture of the dry sheet and the subsequent processes, each department is really as independent as in the cases referred to.[30]

Having shown the mill owners that their mills were "really two mills," Laflin supplied them with actual cost calculations to guide pricing policy. His figures derived from "several successful establishments . . . working quite as carefully as any of us can expect to do" and they summarized accounts kept over periods ranging from several weeks to five years. Laflin's analysis identified two distinct aspects of finishing costs, each making small papers disproportionately expensive. The first was "loss in quantity of paper from the dry sheet to the finished paper," including trimmer shavings and "broken" paper damaged in calenders and other machines. Laflin charged, "This great loss has generally been entirely underestimated if not overlooked altogether." Careful cost calculations found it averaged "one-sixth part on all papers, weighing 5 lb. per ream or less, and one-eighth part on papers weighing from 5 to 10 lbs., one-tenth part on papers weighing from 10 to 18 lbs., and something less upon the heavier ledger papers." The expenses of processing constituted the second part of finishing room costs. Here Laflin's sources found, "The cost for labor in finishing writing paper under 18 lbs. per ream is for each and every ream, however small, 11 cents for labor done in the finishing room, foreman not included." Properly apportioned, he maintained, other costs, including superintendence, wrappers, packing cases, transportation, and the "proportion of clerk hire, office expenses, loss of interest, incidental expenses and personal services of owners or agents . . . chargeable to the finishing department" did not vary between reams weighing eighteen pounds or less. They totaled nine cents.[31]

Estimating that "the value of the shavings . . . cover the rent or in-

---

[30] *VG*, 1/16/61, p. 2; Laflin, "Address," CMF, p. 13.
[31] Laflin, "Address," CMF, pp. 13–15.

terest upon the cost, insurance, taxes, light, heat, ink, oil, repairs, and depreciation," Laflin formulated a new rule for pricing machine-made paper: "Ascertain the actual weight of dry paper before finishing, and fix the price per lb. upon this weight, and then add twenty-five cents per ream for finishing. This done, no trouble need be apprehended about our business."[32]

Although Laflin also supplied association members with a detailed table of costs for various paper weights and sizes, he offered little information on ledger paper costing. Several years later Byron Weston conducted his own analysis, calculating costs peculiar to finishing ledger paper. Because the expense of ruling varied little with size, Weston found it cost him four and three-quarters cents per pound to finish five-pound note paper, whereas large cap paper cost only one and one-half cents per pound to finish. Weston also learned that he spent six times as much on wrappers for note paper as for the same weight of cap.[33]

Abetted by wartime scarcities and spurred by wartime inflation, once manufacturers derived accurate cost figures, they successfully raised average writing paper prices from thirteen cents to forty cents a pound. Simultaneously, printing paper makers raised prices from eight cents to twenty-two cents a pound, suggesting that mill owners had also underestimated the cost of making unfinished paper. Thereafter, fluctuating wage and rag costs and rapidly improving paper-making machines continually altered paper-making expenses. To keep their businesses profitable, mill owners Byron Weston and Elizur Smith frequently recalculated wage and fiber costs between 1866 and 1885.[34]

During the same period, paper makers applied cost accounting to fuel and power expenses associated with new steam technologies. By the mid-1860s manufacturers using steam-heated dryers found wood an increasingly expensive fuel and wanted to know the relative costs of using the several grades of coal offered locally. As manufacturers installed steam engines, they also needed to estimate cost differences between running on water power exclusively and generating part of their power with steam.

[32] Ibid., pp. 15, 17.

[33] Ibid., p. 16; Byron Weston Miscellaneous Records, BWP, p. 19.

[34] Weeks, *History of Paper Manufacturing*, p. 286; Byron Weston Miscellaneous Records, BWP, passim. Smith also took Laflin's advice and calculated costs separately for different mills. Laflin maintained that most firms failed to do this and, thus, often obscured the unprofitability of one of their establishments. Smith Paper Company Test Records, SP, passim.

Byron Weston's records provide the earliest surviving evidence of fuel cost calculation. He computed fuel costs per pound of paper annually beginning in 1865. As compared to labor costs, which consistently declined, he found that fuel costs fluctuated erratically, a problem he attacked through further quantitative analysis. He compiled annual series of coal costs per ton and coal freight charges per ton, isolating for study two aspects of fuel costs he could not control. Another calculation separated the cost of steam heat, which mills incurred whenever they operated, from the cost of steam power, which mills used only when water ran low. Weston needed this information to estimate whether he could profitably complete orders received during low-water periods. A final series of figures compared the expense of wood and coal, allowing Weston to conclude that the greater labor required to get wood from the yard into the mill had made wood the more costly fuel.[35]

Fuel and power costing, process costing, and raw material costing all exemplify historic costing, cost determination based on past performance. Because makers of writing paper were able to set prices through their manufacturers' association, accurate knowledge of actual costs could ensure profitable operation. Newsprint manufacturers such as Elizur Smith and John Carroll found themselves in a very different situation. Their market remained competitive and depended on keeping prices low. In addition, the use of non-rag fiber and chemical fillers introduced so many and such complex possible stock combinations that printing paper manufacturers needed more sophisticated costing techniques. Elizur Smith responded by introducing standard costing, a singularly impressive accomplishment.

The notion of standard costing is one of the most important innovations in the modern history of accounting. Rather than judging industrial performance by comparing present costs with records of previous costs, standard costing measures worker efficiency or raw material waste against an ideal, but obtainable, performance carefully established under test conditions. Thus, standard costing is more an engineering concept than an accounting one. Historians of accounting have generally credited its emergence to the Scientific Management movement of the early twentieth century, a lineage that associates it with attempts to discipline machine shop labor and control wage expenditures.[36]

[35] Byron Weston Miscellaneous Records, BWP.

[36] Without more scholarship on nineteenth-century accounting it is not possible to assess how singular or innovative Smith's technique was. Because the available schol-

Smith applied this kind of accounting procedure to alternative paper fiber combinations as early as the 1870s. By that time Smith used various combinations of cheap rags, hemp, jute, and wood pulp, generally mixing three different fibers and often four. He varied the relative proportions to produce different grades of paper. By adding varying amounts of clay, starch, and other chemicals, Smith further complicated pulp formulae. The resulting range of possible raw material costs made informal assessment impossible and greatly increased the difficulty of calculating historic costs. In any case, Smith could not use actual costs to set prices because of his market. Instead, assessing and controlling operating efficiency had become essential to profitable paper manufacture.[37]

Smith Paper Company management solved the novel problem of judging efficient use of many different stock combinations by applying standard costing to raw materials. A volume of "test records" compiled by Smith in the 1870s and 1880s documents the new procedures. Unlike calculations preserved by other mills, this record does not simply compute the historic cost of producing a pound of paper. Rather, it catalogues the results of a series of discrete tests conducted to establish how much paper the firm could anticipate from different combinations and quantities of stock. Subsequent calculations adjusted these standard costs for actual stock price levels. The company factored out variation among facilities by conducting tests at each of its four mills. In the same book, Smith included annual figures summarizing actual raw material costs at each company mill, showing that test results served as a check on efficiency as well as a guide to profitability. Later, he applied the same procedures to test various grades of coal, both when using steam heat in processing and when using steam power in operating various company facilities, including the machine shop. Smith's very early use of rudimentary standard costing procedures offers the most striking confirmation that paper mill owners needed considerable commercial skill to cope with the technological and economic changes that followed mechanization.[38]

---

arship makes his use of standard costing look extremely early and unprecedented, I have called it impressive. David Solomons, "The Historical Development of Costing," in idem, *Studies in Costing* (London, 1952), pp. 36–42; Ellis Mast Sowell, *The Evolution of the Theories and Techniques of Standard Costs* (University, Ala., 1973), pp. 148–219 and passim; Marc Jay Epstein, "The Effect of Scientific Management on the Development of the Standard Cost System" (Ph.D. diss., University of Texas, 1944), passim.

[37] Smith Paper Company Test Records, SP.   [38] Ibid.

At first glance, paper makers' many accounting innovations make it difficult to understand their failure to calculate and allocate fixed costs or overhead, such as depreciation on their huge new mills and elaborate paper-making machines. For example, in comparison to his other careful computations, Addison Laflin's overhead estimate was distinctly arbitrary. Byron Weston's and Elizur Smith's cost calculations simply ignored depreciation. But when one considers their situation, mill owners' disinterest in the problem of overhead becomes understandable. Overhead costs are not relevant to the routine management decisions for which cost accounting developed, only to decisions about whether or not to stay in business. In other words, to determine whether or not a paper order was worth accepting, Berkshire manufacturers only needed to know whether the revenue it guaranteed would exceed the variable costs of making the paper. As long as they owned their mills, they bore their fixed costs whether they made paper or not. Given the long years they and their families had invested in the industry, late nineteenth-century Berkshire mill owners were clearly committed to paper making and to continued reinvestment. They could ignore the problem of overhead costs.[39]

Between 1866 and 1885, then, successful mill owners demonstrated the advantages conferred by their long careers as paper makers or their careful preparation in family mills. Faced with larger, tighter markets, they could call upon their experience in written and oral negotiation to develop effective new promotional and bargaining strategies. Simultaneously, they could use their training in the mill and with company books to create new accounting procedures that helped them set prices and control costs. Both their marketing and their accounting techniques reflect mill owners' highly developed analytic skills—skills that, combined with their economic influence and social prominence, made them increasingly powerful in the mill towns.

BROTHERSHIP AND PATERNALISM IN
THE MILL TOWNS

Just as mechanized paper mills increasingly dominated the mill town landscapes, mechanized mills' owners came to exert dispro-

[39] Laflin, "Address," CMF, p. 15; Byron Weston Miscellaneous Records, BWP; Smith Paper Company Test Records, SP; R. S. Edwards, "The Rationale of Cost Accounting," in Solomons, *Studies in Costing*, p. 101; David Solomons, "Cost Accounting and the Use of Space and Equipment," in idem, *Studies in Costing*, pp. 277–91. For a

portionate influence among local residents. Emblematically, whereas in 1800 the relatively homogeneous congregation had gathered communally to erect the town church, after the 1857 fire the Lee Congregational Church established a formal building committee and delegated authority to leading laymen: three paper manufacturers, a textile and machinery manufacturer, and a fifth member, closely tied to the local elite after nearly twenty years of conducting a private school. The resulting edifice (Figure 8.2) embodied the mill owners' aesthetic preferences, its ornate Victorian interior contrasting sharply with the bare simplicity of the previous sanctuary. Similarly, although church leaders such as Elizur Smith and Harrison Garfield were evidently deeply religious, as laymen and paper manufacturers their assumption of religious leadership, beginning in the 1830s, altered the tone of local church creeds, governance, and services. Increasingly, church statements and practices embodied mill owners' preferences for order, discipline, and temperance, a morality well suited to businessmen's demanding work schedules.[40]

---

fuller discussion of manufacturers' "failure to depreciate" see McGaw, "Accounting for Innovation."

[40] *VG,* 4/2/57, p. 2; Hyde, *History of Lee,* pp. 13–14, 286.

It is impossible to judge the piety of another person, much less persons who lived a century ago. Obituaries and funeral orations customarily praised deceased mill owners for their deep religiosity, but that might be expected, given the occasion. On the other hand, I find no evidence that paper manufacturers were hypocrites, manipulating the church and the religious for purposes of social control. Mill owners have left little personal correspondence and what survives may not be representative, but it is worth quoting one letter at length to indicate why I have assumed that mill owners were deeply religious and that they promoted their version of piety because it provided them with invaluable emotional sustenance. The letter was written by Zenas Marshal Crane to his sister shortly after the death of Crane's first wife, Caroline Laflin. It suggests not only Crane's profound religious conviction, but also the private evangelical role played by mill owners' wives. The letter is dated January 23, 1849, and Crane writes: "She wasted gradually, but surely, by the hand of *Consumption,* and like a beautiful light that once guided my boyish ambition & also my more mature energies, it gradually burnt to its socket & then after flickering & fading— anon brightening up, to allure us with fond temporary hope, it at last quietly went out at almost the midnight hour—Her departure tho' marked strongly with the characteristics that make the 'King of Terrors' so hideous, was still happy & cheerful—It was mark'd strongly with such feelings & enthusiasm, as often become so much the follower of Christ in the dying hour—Her Saviour was her constant theme & she spent her last 20 hours in urging his beautiful precepts upon her friends as her strength permitted—Her parting with her children was calm & serene, even to smiling on her part, . . . Some hours before her death she sang the hymn, 'Our days are as the grass / or like the morning flower / When blasting winds sweep o'er the field / It withers in a hour.' She sang this with uncommon distinctness & strength—She told

Fig. 8.2 The Reverend Nahum Gale in the Lee Congregational Church pulpit. Both the ornate interior and Gale's "executive faculty" reflected mill owners' preferences. Courtesy of Lee Library.

In the church and in the era's proliferating voluntary associations, which mill owners often organized and led, manufacturers formed bonds of brotherhood that reinforced their shared middle-class values and their conviction that all local citizens would benefit from adopting their morality. Originally, because it was the most influential community social organization, leadership within the church conferred special power and prestige upon mill owners. Thus, we need to look first at the changing religious order of the antebellum period. Then we can examine how, after 1857, the

Mr. Sears [their clergyman], as she did all that she was confident that her Redeemer lived—She died with my arm beneath her—gasped out the last breath of life—Oh God—I can never—never forget that hour—We all in strength & could not help her! . . . It seems as if every day added to my solitude—But I have children & friends to labor & care for & I hope I may have my energies & reason & also above all my consciousness of dependence on God, preserved to me & the latter more than ever . . . I can't write more now—Good bye—God bless your afflicted brother[.]"

brotherhood of manufacturers exercised religious, social, political, and economic leadership to promote shared values, particularly among mill workers.

Whatever the revivalists' intentions, the evangelical initiatives begun in the Second Great Awakening ultimately helped usher in modern industrial society by articulating and reinforcing new middle-class values. In addition, new religious preoccupations, such as temperance and Sabbatarianism, enabled the emerging middle class to substitute more formal, remote discipline for the family governance that had characterized stable agricultural communities and manufacturing villages of the preindustrial era. Such was the case in Rochester and Utica, New York, at least.[41]

Although Berkshire County, with its long revivalistic tradition, significant manufacturing sector, and more settled population, differed considerably from the better-known "burned-over district" across the New York state line, paper mill town church records document similar developments. As noted earlier, Berkshire mill owners found revival-induced Sabbatarianism and temperance congenial. Both reforms encouraged habits of discipline and order, helping mill-owning converts maintain the heavy reinvestment, long work hours, and close management that were conducive to successful mechanization. Mill owners assumed governance of local churches in the late 1830s and 1840s. Thereafter, they increasingly institutionalized middle-class values—the values they knew their society rewarded. By the 1840s and 1850s local churches had come to emphasize personal morality rather than Calvinist orthodoxy.

In both Dalton and Lee, the end of the orthodox clergy's long reign followed closely the onset of rapid technological change in the paper industry. Expressing concern over waning local faith in the

[41] Johnson, *Shopkeeper's Millennium*; Ryan, *Cradle of the Middle Class*.

The ensuing discussion focuses on mill owners' activities in the churches and emphasizes uniformities in their approaches to religious institutions. At the same time, profound personal faith could result in different assessments of appropriate business ethics. For example, in private correspondence with the Cranes, Lee paper dealer Horace Taylor subjected Elizur Smith to scathing ridicule because, despite his prominence in local revivals, Smith's determination to salvage Platner & Smith's credit meant that he was not very prompt in paying his employees in the late 1850s and early 1860s. Describing Platner & Smith as "a very pious concern having taken a large amount of stock in revivals and the work of Divine Grace . . . ," Taylor reported: "One of Platner & Smith's men was seen to have 2.50 in money yesterday. he will be tried for theft—if found innocent he will be put on exebition [sic] as a great curiosity." Taylor added that the mill's superintendent had recently been converted and had become "a great stickler for Christ & poor pay for their help." "Horace Taylor," CMF, 3/14/60, 4/6/60, and passim.

necessity and sufficiency of divine grace, Alvan Hyde died in Lee in December 1833, nearly sixty-six years of age. Almost simultaneously, in early 1834, Dalton's Ebenezer Jennings resigned rather than countenance what he deemed religious error. Hyde's and Jennings's successors never approached these aged clergymen's dominance of local religious and secular life, as their comparatively brief tenure suggests. Six pastors served the Lee church in the twenty years after Hyde's death, and four occupied Jennings's pulpit in twenty years.[42]

During the same years Dalton's detailed church records show that lay leaders, including local mill owners, greatly enhanced their influence within the church. Formerly, egalitarian congregational polity had permitted any church member to come directly before the church and point an accusing finger at backsliders. In 1835, however, church members began to bureaucratize governance when they decided

> to choose a Standing Committee whose duty it shall be to take a general supervision of the discipline of the church. . . . And whereas from the want of *prudence or judgment* on the part of church members *improper subjects* are sometimes brought before the church, or proper subjects are *presented in a manner . . . irregular and improper* by which [the] church is divided & religion brought into disrepute, therefore—Resolved—That every subject of discipline and every complaint shall be presented to this Committee whose duty it shall be to *make out the documents in due form*, to see that the steps of gospel labour have been taken . . . & that *everything proper has been done* to remove the reproach & reclaim the offender before the subject shall be presented to the church . . . by said committee.

Although they agreed that "the Pastor, whenever one is settled, shall be ex-officio chairman of this Committee," four "brethren" composed it, a group that usually included at least one manufacturer alongside prominent landholders and local shopkeepers. Another lay committee, led by Zenas Crane beginning in 1838, examined candidates for church membership. Additional evidence of the new church leaders' preference for order, regularity, and discipline is supplied by an 1838 decision "to establish uniformity in public worship." Abandoning the prerogative of behaving as the spirit moved,

---

[42] Cooke Collection, Dalton Church Records, BA, pp. 53–54, and passim; Hyde, *History of Lee*, pp. 215–19.

Dalton Congregationalists agreed "to sit with their heads bowed during prayer and stand up facing the Choir during singing."[43]

Mill workers converted during the earlier revivals continued to worship alongside the mill owners and additional paper mill employees joined the church from time to time, but church records provide little evidence that they shared equally in church governance. Rather, the evidence implies that middle-class leaders were especially concerned with governing workers. Within a month and a half of its establishment, the committee on discipline introduced the first charge of intemperance ever brought before the church. They made paper worker Ephraim S. Tucker confess his "sin" and promise "to abstain from strong drink." In subsequent years, intemperance became one of the most commonly cited offenses and all but two of those named between 1835 and 1850 worked or had worked in local paper mills. The committee also accused workers of other offenses, including staying away from Sunday worship, "profane swearing, and other unchristian conduct." By contrast, no mill owner was charged with any offense. Moreover, the language of workers' confessions sometimes suggests that they had transgressed the values of mill owners as much as God's law. For example, Stephen A. Pelton, an employee of both Platner & Smith and Crane and a habitual drunkard who was finally excommunicated in 1845, confessed in 1838 that "he had been guilty of the sin of intemperance and brought reproach upon the cause of religion and *offended the brethren*."[44]

A similar emphasis on right behavior characterized the new church covenant of 1843. In 1841 the church delegated the task of writing a new creed to a committee composed of the pastor, Zenas Crane, and Granville D. Weston, a textile manufacturer, brother of two paper manufacturers, and brother-in-law of Henry Marsh, Crane's earlier retail partner and, briefly, David Carson's mill partner. In marked contrast to previous Calvinist professions of faith, the new covenant required all church members to state, "We believe the moral law to be the great standard of duty & that believers though delivered from the curse of it are bound to yield obedience to it & any deficiency in conforming to it is sin" and that "God will

[43] Emphasis mine. Cooke Collection, Dalton Church Records, BA, pp. 54–55, 60.

[44] Emphasis mine. Ibid., pp. 57, 59, 60, 84, and passim; Zenas Crane Time Book, 1809–36, CA; Crane & Co. Ledger, 1844–49, CA; Crane & Co. Journal, 1840–, CA; Ledger of the Aetna, Housatonic, and Defiance Mill, 1844–45. Because employment records are fragmentary, this can only be an understatement of the overrepresentation of mill workers among those cited by the committee on discipline.

judge the world by Jesus Christ & render to every man *according to his deed*." It also extracted the specific promise that members would "by precept & example . . . promote the interest of vital piety in the world to maintain characters of *sobriety*, purity, justice *temperance* and godliness." Simultaneously, the shift from the traditional phraseology, "You believe," to "We believe" emphasized the brothership of men with shared values instead of individuals interacting directly with an inscrutable God.[45]

Unfortunately, other paper mill town church records for the 1830s and subsequent decades have not survived. Lee's centennial historian, however, had access both to church records and to contemporaries' recollections, and he documented a parallel process in the Lee Congregational Church. During Hyde's successor's tenure,

> The strong Calvinistic expressions of the old creed of the church, seemed to some to require modification and the 11th article in which the grace of God, . . . was described originally "as a free, unpromised, sovereign gift," was, to meet their wishes, amended by the omission of the epithet "unpromised."

Emphasis on right behavior evidently replaced the older emphasis on predestination and faith, for between 1836 and 1839 letters penned by Carolyn Laflin of Lee, an ardent believer, to her fiancé, Zenas Marshal Crane, report the Lee church actively promoting both temperance and Sabbatarianism.[46]

Starting in 1857 the *Valley Gleaner* provides ample evidence that Lee's many paper manufacturers assumed leadership roles in local protestant churches. Before that time definite documentation exists only for a few leading mill owners. But the centennial historian's descriptions of why Hyde's successors had such short tenure suggests that, as in Dalton, congregational decision makers wanted their clergymen to exemplify self-discipline and manage church affairs in a businesslike fashion. The Reverend Mr. Smith, who lasted less than five years, "was an original thinker and close observer of men and things, but *not a systematic student*." In addition, "he often neglected preparation for the Sabbath till Saturday evening." His successor, the Reverend Mr. Clarke, remained only two years and "did not incline to stay long enough to *harvest the fruit of his labors*." By contrast,

---

[45] Emphasis mine. Cooke Collection, Dalton Church Records, BA, pp. 74, 77–78; Donald M. Weston, *Weston, 1065–1951* (Pittsfield, Mass., 1951), p. 26. Another lay leader, church clerk Abel Whitney, later replaced Weston on the committee.

[46] Hyde, *History of Lee*, p. 217; File 479, CMF.

Nahum Gale, who served more than twenty-three years after arriving in 1853, was "naturally vigorous" and "had the rare *executive faculty* of making the most of himself and of all by whom he was surrounded." Moreover, "his preaching was *logical rather than emotional*."[47]

The mill towns also felt manufacturers' influence through a growing variety of voluntary associations. This was especially the case for paper mill owners because, as long as success in the industry required close supervision of both mill and office, almost all paper manufacturers resided locally. In fact, Byron Weston, who lived within sight of his mills, typified Berkshire paper mill owners. The 1876 county atlas map of Dalton shows all but two contemporary mill owners living within easy walking distance of their mills. Former and future Crane and Carson family residences exhibit similar proximity. Even the Pittsfield mill, which the Cranes purchased in 1879, lay just beyond the Dalton town line, adjacent to the Cranes' residences. Figure 8.3 depicts the same residential pattern for East Lee mill owners. North and west of East Lee, Elizur, DeWitt, and Wellington Smith lived on or within sight of Lee's Main Street, which ran past several of their mills, and the Hurlbut family resided across the highway from its South Lee mills.[48]

For the county as a whole, the vast majority of Berkshire paper mill proprietors lived in the same town as their mills and nearly all of the rest lived in adjoining towns, as did H. D. Cone, who commuted daily by train from Stockbridge to Housatonic. Absentee ownership remained virtually unheard of even in 1885, the exceptions generally being creditors who took title to mills after failures. A few others simply invested to aid relatives who actively managed the firm and resided locally, such as William H. Allen of Boston, part owner of the local mill managed by his partner and brother, Joseph B. Allen of Lee. William W. Carson spoke for most local paper makers when, after moving to Newburgh, New York, he refused election to Carson & Brown's Board of Directors because

> It has been a rule with me to decline any position of the kind unless I could give the personal attention that the position of

[47] *VG*, passim; Hyde, *History of Lee*, pp. 219–20. Emphasis mine.

[48] Maps of Dalton and East Lee from F. W. Beers, *County Atlas of Berkshire Massachusetts* (New York, 1876). Charles O. Brown still lived next to the Weston mill in which he had been a partner. The location of the residence of Thomas G. Carson is not clear. "Crane Family Houses," CMF; interview with Winthrop M. Crane III; Hyde, *History of Lee*, passim.

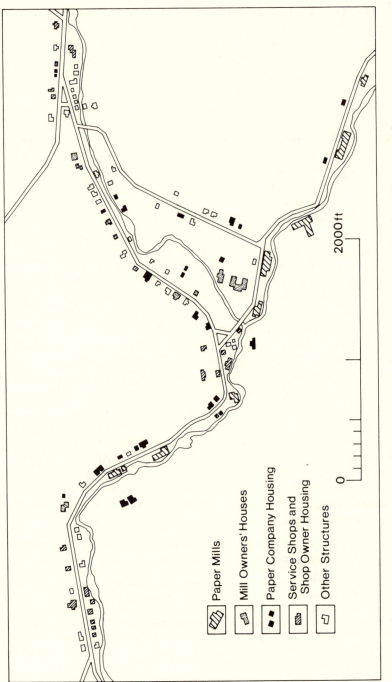

Paper Mills

Mill Owners' Houses

Paper Company Housing

Service Shops and
Shop Owner Housing

Other Structures

2000 ft

0

Fig. 8.3 Map of East Lee in 1876. Adapted from Beers, *County Atlas of Berkshire, Massachusetts.*

trust calls for. This I cannot do on account of the distance from home. I therefore give this notice of my resignation.[49]

Locally resident paper manufacturers joined with their brother mill owners and other Berkshire citizens to form a variety of voluntary associations. Leadership in these institutions helped confirm the mill owners' social importance and gave businessmen additional chances to practice organizational skills. Equally important, during the national economy's formative years acceptable business character and habits were disseminated and selected through emerging formal communications networks, much as were business and technical innovations. Thus, local voluntary associations were functionally analogous to local improvements in transportation and communication. Linked to an extensive system of similar institutions throughout the Northeast, local lodges, lyceums, reform associations, and agricultural societies reinforced ties among like-minded men and created regional and national networks of trust by defining and certifying what R. G. Dun's credit reporters summarily termed "good character and habits." By the 1850s the litany of adjectives reiterated in positive credit evaluations—*temperate, regular, steady, honest, hard working*—shows widespread agreement about what constituted acceptable business character.[50]

As was the case with their religious leadership, paper manufacturers' associational activities also promoted middle-class values in the mill towns during and after mechanization. Relying primarily upon newspaper reports and local histories, which generally identify only officers, it is nonetheless possible to recapture a sense of the range of mill owners' activities, especially afer 1857. In addition to holding church offices, particularly positions on boards of trustees, a number of local paper mill owners promoted their moral convictions through local and county Bible societies, the YMCA, and Ma-

[49] Of the 157 mill owners whose residences are known, 125 lived in the same town as their mills, 17 lived in other Berkshire towns, and 15 lived in New York and Connecticut. See Appendix B. Carson & Brown Clerk's Record, 1867–90, CA, p. 170.

Local ownership appears to have been generally typical of paper making. In Holyoke the textile mills were owned by nonresidents, "But in paper making nativism prevailed. The paper making men of Holyoke were no shadowy persons without local associations." Green, *Holyoke*, pp. 82, 87, 91, 92, 176. See also, Glaab and Larson, *Factories in the Valley*, passim.

[50] Don C. Doyle, "The Social Functions of Voluntary Associations in a Nineteenth-Century American Town," *Social Science History* 1 (Spring 1977):333–55, provides a helpful discussion of the several local functions of these institutions. Pred, *Urban Growth*, pp. 277–83, and the R. G. Dun & Co. Ledgers indicate and document their regional functions for mill owners.

sonic lodges. In particular, mill owners took an interest in local agencies disseminating middle-class morality among the working people. They organized, led, and supported financially Sabbath schools, public schools, and a local commercial college; local and regional libraries and reading rooms; public lecture series; and temperance organizations, especially Good Templars lodges. According to Berkshire Manufacturers' Association president Thomas F. Plunkett, they viewed such activities "as a means of promoting the mutual interests of employer and employed."[51]

The associational career of W. C. Plunkett, Adams textile and, later, paper manufacturer, shows how one individual combined such activities to promote his values locally and consolidate his reputation nationally. A member of the Adams Congregational Church since 1840, in the 1850s Plunkett became president of the Berkshire Bible Society and superintendent of the Congregational Sunday school, entertaining the scholars annually at his home and donating 175 books to the Sunday school library by 1868. Trained as a teacher and active in local politics, he regularly advocated good schools and good schoolhouses. After retired paper manufacturer Walter Laflin led in founding the Berkshire County Temperance Convention in 1859, the organization elected Plunkett president in 1860. Later that year he addressed the Adams children's temperance auxiliary—the Greylock Band of Hope—and in 1861 assumed leadership of local citizens opposing liquor licenses. In 1869 he presided over a temperance meeting of five hundred local citizens, and two years later he crowned his efforts when, as moderator of the Adams town meeting, he proved instrumental in outlawing local liquor sales. By the late 1870s, then, Dun's reporters could recommend him not only as "wealthy" and "good for all legitimate obligations," but also as "among our best men for moral worth and integrity."[52]

<hr/>

[51] *VG*, 3/3/58, p. 2. Because the *Valley Gleaner* was the only newspaper published in a major paper-making center, I have relied on a close reading of its local news during its first twenty years of publication. Because it regularly picked up news items from other local newspapers and reported news gleaned orally from other towns, its pages include considerable information on mill owners in all county towns. Additional information comes from a more cursory scanning of Pittsfield, Adams, and Great Barrington newspapers; biographical and organizational information in local histories; and brief biographies in Child, *Gazeteer*, part 1. Of successful paper manufacturers after 1866, information on church-related activities is available for 49 percent; information on voluntary association membership or leadership is available for 44 percent.

[52] *VG*, passim; Child, *Gazeteer*, part 1, p. 100; R. G. Dun & Co. Ledgers, 5:175.

Fig. 8.4 Wellington Smith and his trotters, Fleet and Commissioner.
Well-bred trotters speeded travel between the many Smith mills and
distinguished the successful Smith from less affluent local citizens.
Courtesy of Lee Library.

Simultaneously, mill owners banded together with other local
citizens in organizations designed to "elevate the tone" of local
mill towns. In Lee, for example, they established the Lee Pleasure
Park, where they raced their trotters (Figure 8.4); the Lee Monthly
Club, where they discussed literature; the Lee Philharmonic Society, where they made music; and the Grand Army of the Republic,
where they promoted patriotism. Mill owners living in Stockbridge
joined in founding the local Union League and helped lead the Laurel Hill Association, the first American village-improvement association, an institution common in late nineteenth-century American
towns. Paper manufacturers played an even more prominent role in
the similar Fern Cliff Association in Lee. Frequent newspaper accounts of Lee mill owners placing new mansard roofs atop their old
houses (Figure 8.5), setting fountains and statues on recently land-

Fig. 8.5 Wellington Smith house, Lee. Mill owners added mansard
roofs, towers, porches, statuary, and picket fences to create homes suited to
their taste and growing affluence. Courtesy of Lee Library.

scaped lawns, or simply repainting in new hues their abodes, their
workers' houses, and surrounding fences suggest that these improvement associations fostered a new residential aesthetic, as pervasive in the mill towns as the new mill architecture was dominant.
Supplementing individually financed improvements, mill owners
figured prominently on town committees to pave roads, place lamps
along major thoroughfares, lay out and improve parks, erect obe-
lisks to the Union dead, and replace old town halls with more modern structures, such as the substantial mansard-roofed Memorial
Hall in Lee.[53]

A final group of voluntary associations in which paper manufacturers figured prominently were agricultural societies. For example, the Lee press reported mill owners leading and actively partic-
ipating in six local and two county societies. Initially, mill owners
probably enhanced their social standing by joining such associations, because leading local farmers and the pioneering Berkshire
Agricultural Society were well established before paper making became an important local economic activity. Most manufacturers
maintained farms to feed and house the mills' teams, so they had a
legitimate basis for participation.[54]

[53] See n. 51.   [54] *VG*, passim.

Later, several mill owners conducted large experimental farms, and judging from reports of society deliberations, their participation in agricultural societies helped them cement ties with the county's significant agricultural population and assert cultural hegemony for business principles. Even in 1850 agriculture employed nearly half of the men in the mill town of Dalton, and as late as 1875, 32 percent of the county's citizens reported working in agriculture, not much less than the 39 percent giving manufacturing and mechanical pursuits as their occupations. Within this context, the agricultural activities of leading mill owners provided them with more than a satisfying hobby. Their speeches at farmers' clubs, reported regularly in the local press, stressed the community of interest between local agriculture and local industry and portrayed mill owners as natural leaders of both. For example, in 1872 Elizur Smith served as president of the group organizing milk sales in New York; addressed the Lee Farmers Club, pointing out similarities between paper manufacturing and farming in the relationship of capital to labor; and led off the club's discussion of marketing, arguing that farmers could rely on local industry and its employees for customers. The following year, mill owner and longtime agricultural society leader Harrison Garfield also stressed the cooperative relationship of manufacturers and agriculturalists, and, like Smith, left little doubt whose values should predominate. "By using their business habits in farming," he pointed out, "manufacturers set a good example for their neighbors."[55]

Whether convinced of the general usefulness of business habits, influenced by the identification of mill owners with religious and moral causes, or impressed by the obvious economic success of established paper manufacturers, local citizens ratified mill owners' claim to local leadership, repeatedly electing them to local and state political office. For example, in the twenty years between 1857 and 1876, paper manufacturers served on Lee's governing Board of Selectmen in all but seven years, and in four of those years closely allied paper machine manufacturers were elected. During the same twenty years the district including Lee sent four Lee paper manufacturers to the state house of representatives, one to the state senate, and one to the Board of County Commissioners. Many additional paper mill owners served in a host of local offices ranging from fire warden to constable to town meeting moderator. For the

---

[55] The figures for 1850 are derived from the United States manuscript census schedules for Dalton. Massachusetts Bureau of Statistics of Labor, *The Census of Massachusetts, 1875*, volume 2, *Manufactures, the Fisheries and Commerce* (Boston, 1888), pp. 7–18, 76; *VG*, passim.

county as a whole, incomplete records show that at least 44 percent of successful paper manufacturers held some political office, most holding several. Two, Byron Weston and William C. Plunkett, eventually served as lieutenant governor. Although Berkshire's egalitarian political tradition meant that "if one of [these prosperous manufacturers] assumed too much in town meeting he was as likely to be called down as any other man," the recurrent choice of mill owners for political office suggests that their economic power and active role in local voluntary associations had established their legitimacy as community leaders and garnered widespread support for their social values. Further confirmation comes from the 1872 decision of voters in nine of the thirteen paper mill towns—including all of the major paper-making centers—to outlaw beer.[56]

While mill owners multiplied their individual power through fraternal ties formed in churches and voluntary associations, they exerted their greatest and most direct influence through their paternalistic relationship with their employees. The relationship derived from the family governance mill owners had exercised over hand paper workers. As mechanization increased the size of mill work forces and the relative affluence of mill owners, direct, informal surveillance became both less possible and less attractive. Mill owners gradually substituted more formal mechanisms to govern workers' behavior.

The new system emerged slowly. As early as the 1840s mill work forces had grown too large to live with the owners or owners' rela-

---

[56] Hyde, *History of Lee*, pp. 341–42; Appendix B; Washington Gladden, *Recollections* (Boston, 1909), p. 161; *VG*, 5/23/72, p. 2; Daniel Pidgeon, *Old-World Questions and New-World Answers* (London, 1884), p. 108. The four paper towns that failed to outlaw beer included Monterey, a rural community in which the small paper mill would soon cease to operate, and three towns in which the paper mill played a minor role in the local economy—Becket, Pittsfield, and Great Barrington. Indeed, the mills in Becket and Pittsfield were located on town lines and were more closely tied to Middlefield and Dalton. The Great Barrington (Housatonic) paper mill was set at some distance from any population center, and the mill owner enforced temperance strictly within the confines of the mill village.

Of course, money also helped make Berkshire paper manufacturers a force in politics. For example, Byron Weston and Wellington Smith solicited $100 from each of Berkshire's leading Republicans to defray 1879 campaign expenses. L. L. Brown alone contributed $500 to the Republican campaign of 1884. Like these men, most local paper mill proprietors in the postwar era were Republicans. "Byron Weston—Political," BWP, 10/13/79; L. L. Brown Paper Company Journal, 1877–80, LLBP, 11/78, 10/79; L. L. Brown Paper Company Daybook, 1881–85, LLBP, 11/84; Appendix B. Political activity also helped manufacturers secure government orders when their party was in power. See, for example, File 660, CMF, 2/18/59, and "First Government Contract," CMF.

tives and formal apprenticeship was generally on the decline, but traditions of family governance persisted and shaped early industrial paternalism. For example, well into the 1850s parents occasionally sent young sons to Berkshire manufacturers for several years' paper mill training. Writing to the Cranes in 1845, Oliver Steele clearly expected traditional family supervision for the son he destined for paper making. His letter requested that they

> do by him as well as . . . by other boys of same age and capabilities, and . . . exercise a sort of parental care over him that may induce him to become a useful and desireable member of your community. . . . I would like to have Mrs. Crane see that he preserves his best suit for Sunday purposes and that some exertion be made to have him attend your Sunday School. . . .

Later, after young Steele had proven recalcitrant, his uncle wrote, "If you think corporal punishment would have a proper effect you have my full permission to apply the same."[57]

Two letters written to the Cranes in 1849 show some community members holding mill owners personally responsible for workers' behavior long after the onset of mechanization. One correspondent wrote from Lee:

> Misters Crane,
>
> One of my neighbors, a married woman, called on me this morning with a request that I would write to you. It seems that her husband has been intimate with a family that you have at work in your mill and her wish is that they may be removed in hopes that he may do better. I do not know the family . . . but if half that is said of them is true thay [sic] are not fit to live in civilized society. Their name is Parker . . . a mother and two daughters. Of the mother I have heard nothing, but the daughters, if I am not mistaken, are as great strumpets as walk the earth.

Another contemporary epistle called the Cranes' attention to the needs of the family of their employee, David Kites:

> Gentlemen,
>
> I take the liberty to write to you and ask you to give Mrs. Kites some advice in regard to leaving her husband and removing herself and family out of his reach. Elizabeth has written me the whole particulars about his last carousal, commitment, etc. I have been to see her brothers who are ready and willing to take

[57] "James Brewer Crane," CMF, 5/6/45, 10/14/45.

her and take care of her and her family. Can't she leave him in
some way either by swearing the peace against him, or have a
guardian appointed over the children so that he can have no
control over them. As you well know he is unfit to take care of
them and little do you or any one know the trouble that he
makes them or the abuse they receive from him. If you can give
them any advice I wish you would. Also, if he has any idea of
following them try to stop him as it will be useless for him ever
to attempt to get her to live with him again.[58]

Nonetheless, the very fact that third parties were pointing out
workers' derelictions to mill owners suggests that work forces in
mechanized mills had outgrown traditional institutions of social
control. Gradually, paper manufacturers developed alternatives.
Probably the most important was a system of employment designed
to weed out undesirable workers and keep good employees on the
job. Basically the system depended on letters of reference, which
mill owners supplied their former employees. Workers writing to
request employment generally offered to provide such letters.
When a worker applied for a position and lacked references, mill
owners wrote to former employers and inquired , "Is he a steady reliable man and *strictly* temperate . . . ?" Because mill owners had developed strong mutual ties, they expected and received candid re-
plies. When asked about one worker Byron Weston responded:

> . . . I can recommend him to be a *first class Engineer* for first class
> paper and a honest man. In short, he is all right I think as a En-
> gineer. There is but few men that is all right in every respect.
> Every man, as the saying is, has his failings. Mr. Fuller some-
> times drinks to [sic] much. After all he loses but *little* time in the
> course of a year.

Although generally mill owners preferred temperate workers, Weston's letter suggests that their dependence on workers' skills necessitated compromises. The Cranes, for instance, hired a habitual
drunkard, but required him to sign the pledge as a condition of employment.[59]

Paper manufacturers also cooperated to discourage good workers from changing jobs. They maintained an unwritten agreement
not to hire another mill's help without permission. Charles O.

[58] "Labor," CMF, 10/29/49; "Lindley Murray Crane and the Mill at Ballston Spa,"
CMF, 2/5/49.

[59] "Miscellaneous Historical Items," CMF, 7/13/65; "Letters to Byron Weston,"
BWP, 11/27/67; "Labor," CMF, 7/29/72.

Brown revealed how the agreement functioned when he wrote to the Cranes in 1867:

> Our Mr. Weston understood the Watkins girls were out of work and sent word for them to come and see us. Miss Watkins or Mrs. Jackly came yesterday—but said she was working for you. The writer told her we could not talk with our neighbor's help—but would see you and if she were going to leave you, we would see her or write. . . .
>
> Be assured we have no intention of inviting *your* help to come and talk with us and in no case would we hire one till we had seen you and known it was satisfactory.

Claims on workers even extended to some former employees who had been allowed to work for another mill owner. Byron Weston replied to a note from Carson & Brown that listed several of his workers, "I think the people *you* mention that *you claim* who work here is all right and we allways [sic] consider that they are yours." When another manufacturer violated the code, however, mill owners felt free to ignore it. Weston informed one worker, "I don't like to hire hands from other mill owners—but your company at Holyoke . . . try to get my hands and I suppose it could not be considered wrong if I should hire you. . . ."[60]

As a system of reciprocal obligations, paternalism conferred benefits on workers as well as on owners. Once they discovered skilled, reliable employees, paper manufacturers made every effort to guarantee them continuous employment, both because they felt concern for the workers and their families and because they wanted to have a competent work force on hand during busy seasons. When water ran low Byron Weston noted, "In order to have hands to work when we have water, we have to give them 'full time' to keep them." Similarly, after Zenas Crane, Jr. & Bro.'s mill burned, the company arranged for its help to work for Carson and Brown, preventing unemployment. Later, an elderly worker recalled, "Carson and Brown wanted some of the employees to stay with them, but Mr. Crane wanted to have all the old hands back. . . ."[61]

[60] Byron Weston Letter Book, 1867, BWP, 4/7/67, 4/23/67; Zenas Crane Time Book, 1809–36, CA, 12/8/24, 3/7/25; Byron Weston Letter Book, 1874–75, BWP, 12/11/74; Brown & Weston Letter Book, 1865–66, BWP, 8/30/65, 2/10/66; Byron Weston Letter Book, 1873–74, BWP, 6/26/74; Brown & Weston Letter Book, 1864–65, BWP, 12/14/64; Brown & Weston and Byron Weston Letter Book, 1866–67, BWP, 7/2/66; Carter, *Cyrus Field*, p. 76.

[61] Brown & Weston and Byron Weston Letter Book, 1866–67, BWP, 8/18/66; Brown & Weston Letter Book, 1865–66, BWP, 9/22/65; "Miss Alice Lyman," inter-

Faced with expanded work forces, mill owners erected company housing, another measure designed to attract and retain desirable employees and disseminate middle-class values among them. After mechanization began, growing work forces quickly exhausted the local housing supply. For example, in Tyringham, where only two small paper mills operated, at least half the local farm households boarded mill workers, some housing as many as twenty. Anticipating difficulty boarding the larger numbers of workers a mechanized mill might eventually employ, the Laflins erected a boardinghouse capable of accommodating eighty persons at the same time as they built the county's first mechanized mill. Other mill owners followed suit.[62]

Housing for families proved especially important in attracting and retaining skilled male employees. In 1867, for example, one Lee paper worker applied to Byron Weston for a job because "I cannot get me a house & do not wish to walk so far as now. . . ." Another prospective worker was described as "at work for the Co. at the Valley Mill [in Lenox] but they have no house for him and he does not want to stay unless he can have his family with him." Several years later the *Valley Gleaner* generalized: "There is an urgent and increasing demand for more dwelling houses in this town. Good mechanics are leaving town and other families are deterred from coming here in consequence of the scarcity of even comfortable tenements."[63]

While company housing helped mill owners attract and retain competent workers, it also promoted mill owners' behavioral standards in the community. Paper manufacturers could specify in contracts with boardinghouse keepers, "You are to keep an orderly house, having no dances or liquor about. . . ." In general, however, mill owners preferred to avoid such congregations of unmarried individuals. Instead, they encouraged most workers to reside in families by erecting single-family or double houses almost exclusively (Figures 8.6 and 8.7). That mill owners usually housed workers in small dwellings similar to their own houses, rather than constructing cheaper rows of connected tenements, underscores their commitment to disseminating their values locally. Such structures pro-

---

view typescript, CMF, p. 4. We lack data on employment policies in the county's smallest and least successful mills. Given their periodic failures, their employees were probably most vulnerable to unemployment, although their work forces were generally quite small and their owners frequently performed some of the skilled work. For a discussion of unemployment and job turnover from workers' perspectives see Chapters 9 and 10.

[62] "Paper Making in Tyringham, Mass.," p. 1; Carter, *Cyrus Field*, p. 49.

[63] Letters to Byron Weston, 1867, BWP, 3/12/67, 10/3/67; VG, 4/25/72, p. 2.

vided workers' families with middle-class standards of privacy and multiplied local examples of mill owners' architectural tastes.[64]

Likewise, mill owners supported workers' institutions that paralleled their own. In addition to their personal church offerings, paper manufacturers contributed as employers to churches attended by their workers. The South Lee Manufacturing Company committed funds both to repairing the local Methodist church and the "Donation Visit" to support its pastor. Indeed, mill owners considered religious activity sufficiently supportive of industry that L. L. Brown debited to "Manufacturing" the company's contributions to the Congregational church and minister's salary in Cummington, where the company operated a mill. In the same spirit, the board of directors of the Carson & Brown Paper Company voted in 1874 "to give in the name of the corporation and convey by deed to the Rt. Rev. P. T. O'Reilly, D.D. the two first lots from Main Street on east side Curtis Avenue, on which to build a Catholic Church and parsonage," thus promoting religion among Irish members of the local work force.[65]

Mill owners throughout the county also financed various wholesome alternatives to the saloon as a leisure-time resort. In 1883 Zenas Crane, Jr., and his brother built a library for employees (Figure 8.8), contributing five hundred volumes as well as magazine subscriptions. They purchased fifty new volumes for the collection each year. Dalton and Adams paper mill proprietors supported company baseball teams, with L. L. Brown's bookkeeper again charging the item to the manufacturing account. Paper manufacturers in Lee, Dalton, and Adams all contributed money to bands (Figure 8.9). The Adams musicians were denominated the "French band," reflecting the large number of French Canadians in Brown's

[64] Byron Weston Letter Book, 1873–74, BWP, 12/8/73; "An Example to Manufacturers," *SA* 25 (October 21, 1871):263; Rent Book, "Miscellaneous Historical Items," CMF. There are exceptions to this generalization, including dwelling units constructed by the L. L. Brown Paper Company in two brick wings attached to their upper mill. More common were two-family residences, similar in architecture to owners' houses, but sharing a party wall. The character of worker housing and owner housing has been ascertained by comparing structures still standing with maps in Beers, *County Atlas of Berkshire*. Winthrop M. Crane III and Betty Dennis, Librarian, Lee Library Association, have assisted me with their knowledge of the history of local residential structures. In addition, numerous photographs in the Crane Museum Files and the Lee Library Association Historical Collection provide contemporary evidence. For a fuller discussion and illustrations of the relatively unpretentious dwellings of mill owners see McGaw, "Sources and Impact," pp. 295–98.

[65] *VG*, 1/29/63; L. L. Brown & Co. Journal, 1867–71, LLBP, 2/71; L. L. Brown Paper Company Journal, 1874–77, LLBP, 5/74; L. L. Brown Paper Company Daybook, 1881–85, LLBP, 12/82; Carson & Brown Clerk's Record, CA, 6/12/74.

Fig. 8.6 Bill Foley, his family, and their company house. Foley,
a paper mill steam engineer, resided in half of a double house,
as did many Dalton paper workers. Courtesy of the Crane Museum.

Fig. 8.7 Dalton worker housing. Two-family houses line Wilson Avenue.
The street bears the name of Zenas Crane's longtime vatman and early
machine tender. Courtesy of the Crane Museum.

Fig. 8.8 Bay State Mill and Library. In this advertisement, Zenas Crane, Jr. & Bro. proudly show potential customers the library they built for mill workers. Courtesy of the Crane Museum.

work force. Brown's books also listed contributions to a "French Fair."[66]

Although increasingly powerful mill owners cooperated formally and informally to promote their values in the mill towns, as long as the manufacturers resided locally, paternalism remained an institution of men, not laws. Mill owners varied considerably in the rigor with which they espoused common standards, such as temperance. H. D. Cone of Housatonic, for example, was a genuine eccentric. He believed in temperance absolutely and fired immediately and irrevocably anyone caught imbibing. To guard his workers from the pernicious influence of "grog shops" and of local cotton mill workers, who he believed encouraged his employees to drink, Cone bought up all the land within several miles of his mill on both sides of the river. Near the mill he built homes for all employees, varying "in size and elegance according to the business responsibility of the occupant" and a boardinghouse for unmarried women "conducted un-

---

[66] Child, *Gazeteer*, part 1, p. 129; Hyde, *History of Lee*, pp. 334–35; "Alfred Hoxie," interview typescript, CMF, p. 8; L. L. Brown Paper Company Journal, 1874–77, LLBP, 9/76; L. L. Brown Paper Company Daybook, 1881–85, LLBP, 8/81, 6/83, 11/83, 8/84. Lee mill owners tended to found common community institutions jointly, rather than organizing individual mill clubs or libraries.

Fig. 8.9 Cranesville Band in the 1880s. Several paper companies supported workers' bands. Courtesy of the Crane Museum.

der the careful superintendence of a matron." The company also built a school for workers' children, a church (Methodist, although Cone was a Congregationalist), and a library. He expected workers not to stray from this refined and genteel community. They dared not venture into the main village of Housatonic until Cone had departed on the eight o'clock train.[67]

[67] "An Example to Manufacturers," p. 263; "Henry D. Cone," p. 5. On the other hand, even this unusual case of benevolent despotism provided workers with consid-

By contrast, Dalton manufacturers adopted a more flexible approach to drink, perhaps because, unlike Cone, they had prepared for ownership by working among their employees. For example, Zenas Crane, Jr., knew when any of his employees got drunk and immediately fired them. Several days later, having allowed them time for sober reflection, he called them in, gave them a lecture on temperance, and rehired them, providing them with some money to make up for lost pay. His concern for the welfare of the worker's family precluded rigidly enforced rules. Byron Weston pursued a similar course, modifying general principles to suit particular circumstances. While his men braved the cold April water trying to fix the paper-making machine, Weston made eggnog for them. In fact, he apparently joined them, for his wife's diary reported the next day that he was suffering the ill effects of "too much tasting."[68]

WHEN contrasted with social relations in the years before mechanization, however, the occasional shared eggnog, the egalitarian rhetoric of town meeting, and the neighborly proximity and general similarity of owners' and workers' residences appear less remarkable than the widening gulf between established mill owners and their workers. Because mechanized mills required much greater capitalization and more highly developed accounting, advertising, and managerial skills, paper mill workers could no longer expect to become mill owners. Rather, they found themselves, like other local citizens, living in communities whose physical and social environment the mill-owning establishment had shaped. Moreover, they increasingly worked for men bred to mill ownership, not to mill work. Given their divergent perspective on mechanization, appreciating the consequences of machine production requires that we consider the workers' experiences with and responses to declining social mobility, paternalistic institutions, and an altered work experience.

---

erable benefits, so that the *Scientific American* cited Cone as "an example to manufacturers." Despite the restrictions, it should be noted that Cone's workers had clean, newly constructed, well-maintained buildings in which to live and work. The *Scientific American* reporter found that the women's boardinghouse "looks more like a boarding school for young ladies than a place in which women live who work hard to earn their daily bread." Rents were very cheap. The library housed five hundred varied volumes as well as an assortment of periodicals and had a librarian on duty at company expense from 11:00 A.M. until 9:00 P.M. In addition, Cone paid good wages and supplemented them by selling the produce of his large farm at extremely low prices.

[68] William G. O'Connell, retired Crane & Co. employee, interview at Crane & Co. office, July 21, 1975; Crane, "Julia Weston's Diaries," p. 13.

CHAPTER 9

MACHINES AND THE
WORKING CLASSES:
MALE PAPER MILL EMPLOYEES,
1827–1885

No group experienced paper mill mechanization as intimately as did the workers, because no group spent so much time with the new machines. And yet, of the manifold social developments accompanying machine production, none are more difficult to establish and interpret than those affecting paper industry employees. Our image of most of these men and women must be conjured up from the bloodless statistical remains preserved by federal and state census takers. Fragmentary company records afford a glimpse of a much smaller number entering and leaving the work force, collecting their wages, or making purchases at the company store. An even smaller group has left us a few of their words: letters applying for paper mill work and recollections of life in the 1870s and 1880s evoked by interviews and requests for correspondence in the 1920s and 1930s.[1]

Relying on such limited historical evidence, which expresses workers' concerns and preferences obliquely, I have sought answers to three basic questions: Who were the paper workers? How did mechanization affect their work and their economic and social circumstances? How did employees influence or respond to technological change and its social concomitants? Two themes recur. First, male workers' backgrounds, circumstances, and actions gradually came to distinguish them from the middle-class mill owners. Because such distinctions had been foreign to the earlier hand paper industry in which male workers had often been mill owners-in-training, one theme is the emergence of an identifiable working class. At the same time, however, workers grew increasingly diverse in origin, prior experience, and behavior, making the term "work-

[1] Although these are my principal sources of information, they are not the only important ones. Others include the county gazeteer and atlas, newspapers, and local histories. Each of these sources supplies more information about owners than about workers. The last two also exhibit greater sympathy for the owners' point of view.

ing classes" a more apt description. Because workers grew more heterogeneous while only gradually becoming differentiated from the mill owners, my second theme is that workers achieved little sense of class solidarity before 1885.

The growing diversity of the paper mill work force reflected the addition of men who performed a host of new full-time occupations. However, in discussing the conditions of work and the workers' responses, I devote most attention to employees directly engaged in fabricating paper or supervising its manufacture, because their roles best permit comparison with earlier hand paper makers. Furthermore, because the characteristics of the workers, the effects of mechanization on work, and the workers' responses differed substantially between male and female employees, this chapter confines its attention largely to male workers. Chapter 10 considers the contrasting fate of the industry's female workers.

Who Were the Workers?

As we have seen, mechanized paper mills grew larger, more numerous, and more specialized, and mill owners' concerns came to encompass problems such as repairing machines, marketing, constructing factories, accounting, and disciplining workers, as well as making paper. Each of these developments helped alter the character of the work force. The number of men working in the Berkshire paper industry, the number laboring in each mill, and the proportion of adult males employed each increased. Simultaneously, workers brought more varied, specialized prior training and more diverse ethnic backgrounds to the mills. Together these changes made the workers less like the owners and less likely to become owners.

A number of elements of continuity balanced these fundamental changes in the worker's character and prospects. Paper mill work forces grew less rapidly than did numbers employed in such other major local industries as textiles. Their relatively small numbers permitted paper workers to continue interacting directly with mill owners and to reside near their employers in similar households. Like their counterparts prior to 1827, men engaged in mechanized paper manufacture still needed considerable skill, which they had to acquire through mill experience. Moreover, although mill ownership ceased being a realistic goal for workers, skillful men could advance to the intermediate positions of superintendent and foreman, roles that grew more common as paper firms expanded.

Several thousand men worked in the Berkshire paper industry between 1827 and 1885. Of necessity I have relied primarily on statistical summaries to identify who comprised the work force and how its composition changed over time. By itself, however, such an approach cannot answer the question "Who were the workers?" It automatically excludes from consideration salient but nonquantifiable characteristics. One of these—workers' pride—deserves special notice at the outset, because it pervades workers' correspondence and memoirs and should influence the interpretation we place on the quantitative evidence that follows. It was expressed most directly by Alfred Hoxie in 1930 as he recalled his fellow employees in the 1880s:

> The old paper makers took a lot of pride in their work. If a man was a machine tender, he thought of course he was the big fellow in the paper business. Best paid job, and most skilled man. The loft man—[I] was a loft man. He took pride in that. They had learned their trade, and it was a matter of pride to them.[2]

Hoxie's recollection might be suspect as filtered through the haze of memory, but the same message reverberates in contemporary workers' correspondence. Writing from Bridgeport, Connecticut, in 1849, Charles Barnes informed the Cranes:

> I thank you for the offer which you have made me, but I must now decline accepting it, and as you have another person engaged to fill the place designed for me, I trust it will not be much of a disappointment to you that I refuse to accept.
>
> As to the other situation you mention, at Ballstown Springs [Ballston Spa] I would say that I consider it no compliment to be tendered such a one, under J.G. [the mill's sometimes drunken superintendent], a being with more tongue than conscience. It would be beneath the dignity of any man with a mind sensitive to attempted injuries, and that too without the least provocation.

Thirty years later, despite diminished prospects for advancement, A. M. Martin's letter from Holyoke sounds the same note of pride:

> Mr. S. R. Wagg informs me that you are in want of a first class machine tender and I having a good experience of 14 years on machine I think I could suit you in every respect. I do not get drunk and neglect my work and can say that I neither chew to-

---

[2] "Alfred Hoxie," interview typescript, CMF, p. 4.

bacco or drink rum. I am now to work for the Crocker Mfg. Co. Have been for the last year. One thing I will say two is that in changing orders I do not change as most machine tenders do at random or guess work but use figures to [do] it and there by know just what my machine is making per hour and also being very corect to weight in changing and starting on difrent orders. Can furnish you any amount of the best recomends in the hand. Should you feel like giving me a trial pleas state wages and if steady work etc. My object in changing is to better my self[.]

Writing from the same town two years later, Edward Breck expressed the same sentiment more succinctly: "This sheet I write on was made by my self." Keeping the existence of such vital emotions in mind, let us now examine the bare statistical bones of the work force.[3]

Both the increasing diversity of workers and the growing dissimilarity of workers and owners reflected a fundamental feature of the work force: its burgeoning numbers. As mechanization proceeded, the Berkshire paper industry employed many more workers, more workers per mill, and larger percentages of male workers (Table 9.1). In the long run, these trends reduced each worker's prospects of ownership. On the other hand, during periods when employment grew rapidly, they enhanced workers' bargaining power and encouraged recruitment of new groups. Thus, in order to understand most other changes in the work force, we need first to establish the timing, causes, and dimensions of each kind of numeric increase.

Overall growth came early and suddenly. Once reduced pa-

[3] "Employment, 1844–1865," CMF, 3/29/49; "Employment, 1879–1886," CMF, 6/12/79, 2/20/81. The letters quoted here and elsewhere in this chapter are part of a collection of about two hundred written to Byron Weston and the Cranes. Most were authored by men seeking jobs, although a few were penned on their behalf by their wives or by mill owners, superintendents, or co-workers acquainted with them. The letters span the years 1844 to 1886. The Crane collection is probably relatively complete, although many workers applying from Dalton and other nearby towns must have approached the Cranes in person, leaving no written record. Census data and pay roster signatures indicate that illiteracy was rare among paper workers, so most applying from a distance probably could write. Crane and Weston were not employers of last resort and I make no claim that these letters and workers were typical, only that they offer a glimpse of workers that is missing in other sources. Here and elsewhere I have given a verbatim transcription of workers' words. Errors in spelling, punctuation, and grammar occur so frequently in most that I have abstained from using sic.

TABLE 9.1
EMPLOYMENT, BERKSHIRE COUNTY PAPER INDUSTRY, 1832–85

Year	Total Workers	Men	Women	% Male	% Female	Workers per Mill
1832	292	116	176	40	60	22.5
1837	299	114	185	38	62	19.9
1845	421	109[a]	149[a]	42[a]	58[a]	21.0
1850	504[a]	221[a]	283[a]	44[a]	56[a]	
1855	1080	228[a]	505[a]	31[a]	69[a]	30.9
1860	1503	516	987	34	66	57.8
1865	1452	576	876	40	60	42.7
1870	1408					54.2
1875	1428	638	790	45	55	
1880	1403	733	670	52	48	66.8
1885	1272	595	677	47	53	

SOURCE: Data from *McLane Report,* part 1, pp. 144–45, 156–57; *Massachusetts Census of Manufactures, 1837; Massachusetts Manufacturing Census, 1845,* pp. 212–40; United States Manuscript Census, 1850, Products of Industry; *Massachusetts Census of Manufactures, 1855,* pp. 20–63 passim; *United States Census of Manufactures, 1860; Massachusetts Industrial Census, 1865,* pp. 23–73 passim; *United States Census of Manufactures, 1870,* p. 674; *Massachusetts Manufacturing Census, 1875; United States Census of Manufactures, 1880; Massachusetts Population Census, 1885.* Except as indicated, see Berkshire County and paper industry sections. These documents vary in reliability, making minor fluctuations in numbers relatively meaningless, but they are sufficiently complete to capture general trends.

NOTE: The letter [a] indicates data available for Lee paper mills only. For purposes of comparison, total workers in Lee in 1832, 1845, and 1855, respectively, were 250, 258, and 733. In 1832 male workers in Lee numbered 100 and female workers, 150.

per-making costs permitted mills to proliferate, the number of Berkshire paper workers rose dramatically. Most of the increase occurred between 1840 and 1860, when paper industry workers multiplied about five times, more than fifteen times as rapidly as the county's population. Thereafter, machines became more automated; the depression following 1857 forced smaller, marginal mills to close their doors; and wartime labor shortages further curtailed employment. Consequently, the number of county paper workers declined slightly, stabilized, and then fell nearly 10 percent during the depression of the early 1880s.[4]

At the same time, mills that survived periodic depression and new mills constructed after mechanization were much larger and aver-

[4] Child, *Gazeteer,* part 1, p. 420. Both before and after this decade, county population grew more rapidly than the number of paper workers.

aged more employees. Growth in employment per mill occurred later than overall growth in employment. Initially, machines simply enabled each mill to produce more paper with the same complement of workers, and average employment hovered around twenty, as it had in the 1820s. But after 1845 larger mills employing faster, wider, more fully automated machines produced more and more paper. They hired additional workers to prepare raw materials, finish the paper, and perform repair work, teaming, and clerical tasks. The average mill's work force grew by half in the prosperous decade between 1845 and 1855, then more than doubled over the next quarter century.

On the other hand, we need to place this growth in perspective. Cotton and woolen textile mills, the county's other large factories, expanded much more rapidly and attained much greater average size. Berkshire woolen firms quadrupled average employment be-

Fig. 9.1 Workers at Harrison Garfield's Forest Mill, 1872. Work forces grew, but remained small as compared to other local industries.
Courtesy of Lee Library.

tween 1837 and 1860, while local cotton manufacturers nearly quadrupled their work forces between 1837 and 1880. Even in 1880 paper mills, with an average of 67 employees, offered a greater chance for workers and owners to communicate directly than did cotton mills, averaging 137 employees, or woolen mills, with 147.[5]

Finally, technological change and industrial expansion fostered a relative rise in male employment, the last of the numeric changes to occur. At first men and women shared the growing number of jobs, although women experienced slightly greater gains. After 1860, however, the number of positions for women declined more rapidly than did employment generally, whereas men's tasks continued to multiply. By 1880 women, who had once held two-thirds of paper mill jobs, found themselves in the minority, a loss offset only slightly when male employment plummetted nearly 20 percent in the depression of the 1880s.

Unlike the local textile industry, in which immigration and mechanization persistently reduced women's relative employment between 1837 and 1885, belated technological and economic responses to the adoption of paper-making machines account for men's later and more modest relative gains in the paper industry. As noted earlier, mechanization lowered paper-making costs more than finishing costs, placing firms manufacturing writing paper at a disadvantage. As such firms failed or converted to printing paper manufacture, they eliminated disproportionate numbers of women's finishing jobs. Somewhat later, the adoption of non-rag fiber reduced local employment for female rag room attendants. Improved rag processing and finishing technology also developed relatively late, so that women experienced most technological unemployment after 1860. Finally, most of the new work created by expanded firm size came at jobs traditionally reserved for men: supervisory positions, office tasks, skilled craftswork, and heavy manual labor.[6]

The addition of these new men's positions helped make paper workers more diverse as well as more numerous. Our best picture of the new array of masculine occupations comes from the county directory of 1885, summarized in Table 9.2. Unlike manuscript census schedules, which listed either job title or mill, precluding the possibility of linking many new occupations to the paper industry, the directory allowed men to specify their employment more fully.

[5] See notes with Table 9.1.

[6] See notes with Table 9.1. The percentage of women employed in Berkshire cotton mills fell from 69.3 in 1837 to 55.7 in 1860 and 47.2 in 1885. Comparable figures for woolens are 46.3, 38.0, and 33.9.

TABLE 9.2
OCCUPATIONS OF MALE PAPER MILL EMPLOYEES, 1885

Directory Listing	Number Listed	% of Total	% of Total Specifying Jobs
Unspecified (employee of . . . , works in . . .)	269	51.3	
Skilled paper worker (job specified)	88	16.8	34.5
Paper maker	30	5.7	11.8
Supervisor	35	6.7	13.7
Skilled trades (trade specified)	29	5.5	11.4
Steam engineer	17	3.2	6.7
Clerical	9	1.7	3.5
Laborer	30	5.7	11.8
Teamster	12	2.3	4.7
Night watchman	5	1.0	2.0

NOTE: Child, *Gazeteer*, passim. Owners and their sons, frequently listing themselves as "paper maker," have been excluded. Where an individual listed both occupation and employer, occupation has been tabulated. Unfortunately, this is the earliest directory to be published.

At the same time, it listed 524 male paper workers, as compared to 595 enumerated in the census, making it sufficiently complete to be useful.

As revealed in the directory, by 1885 men entered paper mill employment with a variety of skills. Interestingly, the majority of workers chose to identify who they worked for rather than what they did, a point to which I shall return later. Less skilled paper workers and laborers probably comprised much of this group. Of those who specified occupation, the most obvious contrast with Zenas Crane's or the Laflins' employees is the large proportion—40 percent—not engaged in paper fabrication. Whereas hand paper mills and small mechanized mills had employed casual labor or contracted for construction, ditch digging and pipe laying, teaming, or machine repair; large, mechanized firms had sufficient work to employ full-time outdoor laborers, teamsters, carpenters, machinists, millwrights, and blacksmiths. Together with steam engineers, pipe fitters, wood choppers, and coal shovelers, who helped meet enlarged mills' power requirements, and night watchmen, who protected mill owners' more substantial investments, these men differed from skilled paper workers, "paper makers," and supervisors chiefly in that their employment opportunities and experiences encompassed a wider universe than the paper industry. Thus, although many of them, especially unskilled laborers, commanded lower wages than did skilled paper workers, they were less vulnerable during paper industry depressions.[7]

This was also the case for some of the clerks and salesmen enumerated as clerical workers and for the much larger number of bookkeepers and clerks who do not appear in Table 9.2 because they evidently listed their profession but not their place of employment. Of the small group of prospective bookkeepers who have left letters of application, for example, one had worked for a cotton manufacturer, one for a grain-and-feed dealer, another served as a high school principal, and an unemployed bookkeeper was engaged in farming. On the other hand, nineteenth-century office work often required close familiarity with a particular business and it still served as a route to management, so that a number of those who applied for bookkeeping jobs cited previous paper industry experience, including mill ownership. For example, in 1854 Edward M. Bridgeman's former paper industry partner recommended him as having eight years experience, writing "a plain and handsome hand," being "strictly moral & industrious & . . . as fully competent to take charge of any set of books as any other man, besides having been so long in the same style of business as your own." Similarly, prospective salesmen sometimes mentioned previous employment with paper merchants. Whatever their prior experience, longtime office workers differed from other employees in working most closely with their employers; by 1885 the county's leading mill owners spent most of their time in the office.[8]

[7] Even if all those who failed to specify their occupations were paper makers, 20 percent of the industry's employees worked at tasks other than making paper. The actual percentage must have been considerably higher because laborers were probably most likely simply to list their employers, judging from the small number of them listed in the directory generally. Moreover, all paper workers listed in the directory are identifiable, whereas skilled craftsmen, laborers, clerical workers, and others who merely listed their occupations cannot be linked to the paper industry. This probably especially influences figures for skilled craftsmen and clerical workers.

Those able to find employment both in paper making and in other industries or firms had additional security. Business consumed most nineteenth-century paper, so that paper industry depressions generally lagged behind those in the rest of the economy.

[8] "Employment, 1844–1865," CMF, 5/17/54 (two letters), 5/18/54 (two letters), 5/23/54; File 334, CMF, 3/14/81; "Employment, 1866–1878," CMF, 11/20/75; "Employment, 1879–1886," CMF, 5/20/85.

Mill owners also visited the mill, yard, engine room, and machine shop, however, maintaining familiarity with all of the skills their diversified work force possessed. Their increasingly generalized knowledge contrasted sharply with their workmen's growing specialization. The divergence was especially noteworthy between owners and skilled paper workers, those workmen with whom owners had once held much in common. As Table 9.2 indicates, by 1885 most paper workmen no longer designated themselves "paper maker," the traditional term signifying training and expertise in all phases of paper manufacture. Only a small group of retirees used the term in preference to any other. Instead, over four-fifths (80.4 percent) of those specifying paper-making occupations identified themselves as possessing more specialized skills and knowledge. Paper workmen listed themselves as "machine tender," "back tender," "engineer," "finisher," "assistant finisher," "foreman of the drying room," "superintendent of the rag room," and so forth.[9]

Workers' letters convey the same sense of specialization. Almost all asked for a specific job and those mentioning two positions usually indicated a preference. When enumerating their qualifications, workers listed their experience at a particular task far more often than any other trait. Some were even more specific, such as William P. Phair, writing in 1852, who had "attended Cylinder Machines on course paper"; James Lovell, who heard of a machine-tending position in 1870 and explained, "I have not been used to Cylinder Machines, but thinking it might be for the Fordrinier I concluded to write you"; or Walter R. Brooks, applying in 1872, who noted his expertise at bank note paper making. Those few who claimed the broad experience of "a paper maker by trade" or "a regular bred paper maker" were atypical, such as Mr. Grady, an old man when he sought work in 1847, and Peter Sulivan, a newly arrived Englishman writing in 1881. More common were unemployed individuals who noted their special skills, but expressed willingness to perform other tasks. For example, Joseph Carroll wrote in 1871: "I am used to engines & finishing, but am not particular to making myself generally useful in the line of papermaking. I am just from England and am desirous of obtaining a situation as soon as possible."[10]

Carroll, a foreign-trained paper worker seeking employment in the Berkshires, typified a growing number of the industry's employees as mechanization proceeded. Ethnicity, like specialization, had come to differentiate paper workers from one another and from

[9] Child, *Gazeteer*, passim.

[10] "Employment, 1844–1865," CMF, 12/6/52, 12/22/47; File 331, CMF, 11/21/70, 3/1/71; File 332, CMF, 3/26/72; "Employment, 1879–1886," CMF, 11/21/81.

mill owners. Although the hand paper industry had employed some skilled immigrants, especially Englishmen and Scots, their numbers had remained small. For example, the 1820 census of Dalton found only six unnaturalized foreigners, four of whom may have worked in manufacturing.[11]

Skilled Scottish and English paper workers continued to be represented among Berkshire workers, comprising nearly 10 percent of male paper mill employees in 1870, almost 8 percent in 1880, and more than 6 percent in 1885. More important in swelling the ranks of the foreign born were Irish and French Canadian immigrants, who first appeared in Dalton time books in the 1820s and 1830s. Judging from Table 9.3, their numbers rose dramatically in the 1840s, when rapid growth in the Berkshire paper industry coincided with adverse conditions at home to encourage Irish paper makers, especially, to emigrate. By 1870 nearly one-third (31.9 percent) of Berkshire paper workers had been born in Ireland and almost a tenth (8.9 percent) hailed from Canada. Moreover, by 1870 many of the immigrants' offspring had entered the work force, lending it further diversity. As Table 9.4 indicates, ethnic composition also differentiated the work forces of leading Berkshire papermaking centers. Adams, in northern Berkshire, drew more French Canadians, while Lee, closer to the port of New York and famed as a paper-making town, attracted men trained in the Irish paper industry.[12]

TABLE 9.3
NATIVITY OF MALE PAPER WORKERS, 1850–85

Date	% Native Born	% Foreign Born	% Native Born of Foreign Parents
1850	58	42	
1860	47	53	
1870	45	54	13
1880	65	36	27
1885	64	36	

SOURCE: See n. 12.

[11] United States Manuscript Population Census, Dalton, 1820. Two of the foreigners lived in households engaged exclusively in agriculture.

[12] Time book evidence depends on ethnically identifiable surnames. See McGaw, "Sources and Impact," pp. 351–52.

Figures for ethnicity and nativity in 1850, 1860, 1870, and 1880 have been calcu-

TABLE 9.4
NATIVITY OF MALE PAPER WORKERS BY TOWN, 1880

Nativity	Lee	Dalton	Adams	New Marlborough	Great Barrington and Stockbridge
Massachusetts	105 (49%)	85 (63%)	39 (34%)	15 (37%)	17 (52%)
Other U.S.	33 (15)	10 (7)	14 (12)	3 (7)	4 (12)
Ireland	58 (27)	19 (14)	12 (11)	18 (44)	3 (9)
Canada	6 (3)	6 (4)	43 (38)	1 (3)	0 (0)
Britain	7 (3)	12 (9)	5 (4)	3 (7)	8 (24)
Continental Europe	5 (2)	3 (2)	1 (1)	1 (3)	1 (3)
TOTAL	214	135	114	41	33

SOURCE: See n. 12.

NOTE: Figures for Lee include three Tyringham paper makers; those for Dalton include fifteen Pittsfield paper makers who worked near the town line; and those for Adams include one man who lived in North Adams.

While the rapid growth and general prosperity of the paper in-dustry in the 1840s and 1850s assured immigrants employment, the sudden influx of foreigners created divisions within the community of paper makers. The newcomers spoke, acted, and worshipped differently, and they were clearly seen primarily as members of a foreign group and only secondarily as individuals. Supervisors and timekeepers at the mills recorded payments to or work done by "Irishman," or "Little Frenchman" and "Big Frenchman." In con-trast to their practice with Anglo-Saxon names, they treated immi-grant names carelessly, alternating between Ryan and Rian, Calla-han and Callaghan, and Bridget and Bridgid for the same individual. French names came in for even more cavalier treatment. Duprey became alternately Dupey, Dupay, Dupery, Durpey, and Duper, and Charbonneau varied between Shebeenho, Sharbeenho, Cherbeenho, Cerbenho, and Cerbeenho. Simultaneously, the *Valley Gleaner* regaled its readers with humorous anecdotes featuring drunken Paddys and Bridgets, and mill owner L. M. Crane con-cluded a letter to his brothers, " 'If you don't get this letter write me & inform me of its non-arival' Irishman's Postscript."[13]

Suspicious of Irish intemperance, some mill owners initially dis-criminated in hiring, despite the paper-making skills many Irish-men brought with them. In 1852, for example, T. G. Carson wrote to Byron Weston in Lee, "Do you know of a single man that is a good

---

lated from the federal manuscript population census schedules for these years. For the three earlier censuses, only the county's four leading paper-making towns—Lee, Dalton, Adams, and New Marlborough—have been included. Manuscript census material is missing for Lee in 1860, thus, if anything, the 1860 figures understate the influx of foreign born. The 1850 returns for Adams indicate that enumerators made their visit before the town's first mill began operating. Figures for 1885 are from the published returns of the Massachusetts Population Census. Figures for Scots and Englishmen in 1870 do not include New Marlborough, whose returns distinguished only between native and foreign born. Although the proportion of British workers declined, their number increased slightly.

Figures in Table 9.4 derive from a computer-assisted analysis of all paper workers listed in the 1880 federal manuscript census schedules for Berkshire County. In that year local numbers and percentages of native-born workers of foreign parentage were: Lee, 48 (22 percent); Dalton, 33 (24 percent); Adams, 18 (16 percent); New Marlborough, 15 (37 percent); and Great Barrington/Stockbridge, 7 (21 percent). One additional reason for concentration of French Canadians in Adams was the availability of a French Catholic church in North Adams and a French chapel in Ad-ams, beginning in the 1870s. Wilk, "History of Adams," pp. 212–14.

[13] L. L. Brown & Co. Journal, 1856–57, LLBP; L. L. Brown & Co. Time Book, 1850–61, LLBP; L. L. Brown & Co. Time Book, 1861–65, LLBP; Crane & Co. Time Book, 1863–76, CA; *VG*, passim; File 452, CMF, 11/22/52. The dearth of such anec-dotes in the post–Civil War *Gleaner* stands in marked contrast.

Engineer and a Yankee?" Similarly, in 1865 a Crane & Co. correspondent in neighboring Hinsdale recommended two local residents as "good, respectable Yankee girls." In the wake of the Civil
War, however, the established patriotism of the Irish as well as the
organization of a Father Matthew Temperance Society by the Lee
parish priest promoted general acceptance of skilled Irish paper
workers. According to local resident W.E.B. DuBois, Berkshire citizens made distinctions between the skilled, "better class of Irish"
and the inferior class, who worked in the textile industry and lived
in squalor. Mill owners' contributions to ethnic organizations and
Roman Catholic churches, discussed earlier, provide added evidence of the immigrants' growing acceptance.[14]

While the work force became more diverse ethnically after mechanization, it remained racially homogeneous. Blacks made up more
than 7 percent of the population of some Berkshire towns in the
1840s and were more common in Pittsfield than in Boston or
Springfield throughout most of the nineteenth century, but discrimination made them rarities in county paper mills. Those few
who did find employment, such as an unnamed "Black Man" listed
in Owen & Hurlbut's 1825 records; John F. Wilson, alternately referred to as "Freeman Wilson" and "Negro Wilson" in Crane's
books for 1836; and several members of the Hoose family, who
signed Crane's pay rosters in the late 1860s, were probably outdoor
laborers or teamsters rather than mill hands. "Pomp" Hoose, for example, worked as Z. M. Crane's coachman. From 1850 through
1880, years during which the size and ethnic composition of mill
work forces changed dramatically, federal censuses listed only two
black paper mill employees.[15]

Mechanization also left the age, household status, and residence

[14] "Byron Weston—Early Life and Family," BWP, 6/21/52; "Employment, 1844–
1865," 12/14/65; VG, passim; Donald B. Cole, *Immigrant City: Lawrence, Massachusetts,
1845–1921* (Chapel Hill, 1963), pp. 26–67 passim; W.E.B. DuBois, *The Autobiography
of W.E.B. DuBois: A Soliloquy on Viewing My Life from the Last Decade of Its First Century*
(New York, 1968), p. 82. Anecdotal evidence offers some confirmation for the distinctions DuBois was taught. Irish paper workers brought with them the skills, including mechanical skills, learned in Irish paper mills, whereas Irish textile workers
were often unskilled.

[15] Textile mills were even more discriminatory. Despite their much larger work
forces, no black textile workers appeared in the four federal manuscript censuses.
Steve Turner, "Berkshire Blacks: The Struggle for Equality Began Two Centuries
Ago," *Berkshire Eagle*, August 28, 1976, p. 18; Owen & Hurlbut Blotter, 1825, HP, 8/
17/25; Zenas Crane Journal, 1829–41, CA, 8/20/36, 10/7/36; "Crane & Co. Signatures of Employees," CMF; "David Barnard," interview typescript, CMF, p. 2.

patterns of workers relatively unchanged. As shown in Table 9.5, young adults held most men's jobs, as they had in the hand paper industry. Over half of the work force consistently fell between the ages of sixteen and thirty-five, and over three-quarters between sixteen and forty-five. Rapid growth in employment prior to 1860 probably accounts for the somewhat greater youthfulness of the work force in that year, while the sudden contraction in jobs in the early 1880s is reflected in the slightly larger proportion of older men in 1885. In every year, however, most male employees, like their employers, were old enough to be relatively independent. Most (60 percent in 1880) headed their own households.[16]

Although employment information about boys is suspect because parents had reason to hide their illegal employment from census takers, the small number of very young workers probably reflects accurately the diminished importance of apprenticeship after mechanization. By eliminating tasks such as those performed by the layboy, machines reduced the amount of productive labor that someone without strength or skill could perform in a paper mill. At the same time, workers destined for increasingly specialized careers had less need to acquire familiarity with all paper-making tasks. Thus, after mechanization, time books listed few boys other than the owners' sons, who received the traditional general mill training for management. The Cranes' correspondence indicates that they also occasionally accepted friends' sons for management training through mill experience. When contrasted with Zenas Crane's employees, then, the male work force had become more homogeneous in age and household status, more like the owners.[17]

Also like their employers, the vast majority of male workers continued to reside in male-headed households comprised of nuclear family members. The 1880 census offers the earliest detailed portrait of these households. At that time male paper mill employees lived in 422 Berkshire households, averaging 5.5 members each. A man, usually the mill worker himself, headed nine out of ten. Virtually all male paper workers (87.8 percent) resided with their wives

[16] See n. 12 on federal census data. Figures for 1885 from the published Massachusetts Population Census grouped workers by age, but are included for rough comparison.

[17] "Employment, 1844–1865," CMF, 12/22/47, 11/14/48, and passim. When John Mulchaey began working for the Smith Paper Company in 1867 he was eleven, but his biography indicates that by that date he was considered unusually young. He also became a machine tender at the unusually young age of eighteen. "John E. Mulchaey," SF 1 (November 1927):5–6. Holyoke mills, beginning after mechanization, employed few boys from the start. Green, *Holyoke*, p. 101.

TABLE 9.5
Age Distribution of Male Paper Workers, 1850–85

Year		Under 16	16–20	21–25	26–30	31–35	36–40	41–45	46–50	Over 50
1850	Number	1	15	21	15	16	15	7	13	10
	Cumulative %	1	14	33	46	60	73	80	91	100
1860	Number	0	14	22	25	11	12	5	8	9
	Cumulative %	0	13	34	58	68	79	84	92	100
1870	Number	20	58	47	54	44	41	30	24	47
	Cumulative %	5	21	34	49	61	72	81	87	100
1880	Number	11	92	98	82	58	58	47	48	62
	Cumulative %	2	19	36	51	61	72	80	89	100

Year		14–19	20–29	30–39	40–49	Over 50
1885	Number	72	176	148	102	97
	Cumulative%	12	42	67	83	100

SOURCE: See notes 12 and 16.

and children or their parents, while less than a tenth (8.1 percent) boarded. Likewise, few (11.6 percent) male paper workers' families took in boarders, and the majority of those who did housed a single boarder, usually (57.4 percent of the time) another paper worker. In fact, mill owners were more likely than their male employees to have unrelated persons living in their households, because they generally employed and boarded a domestic servant.[18]

Among both owners and workers, however, primary housekeeping responsibility devolved upon wives. Most male paper workers (63.9 percent) were married, and they and their families evidently preferred to limit wives' and mothers' work to housekeeping, as did the middle-class households of the owners. A substantial percentage (81.0) achieved that goal, while most of the rest (17.0 percent) had their wives or mothers working near them in the paper mills. The few sons living in female-headed households also kept most of their mothers (58.7 percent) at home, while the remainder (41.3 percent) worked with fellow family members in the paper industry.[19]

More than half a century after the onset of mechanization, owners and workers apparently still had much in common. But when the characteristics of paper workers after 1840 are contrasted with the shared career expectations, training, skill, and ethnic and religious heritages of workers and owners in the 1820s, it becomes evident that machine production and the industrial expansion it abetted had helped create two increasingly distinct groups. The best way to assess the social and economic significance of these emergent class differences is to return to the mills and examine the altered experiences, risks, and rewards of working there.

MACHINES AND WORK

As described in Chapter 4, inventors and developers of new machines most successfully replicated the manual skills of male employees: vatmen, couchers, layboys, loftmen, sizers, and some finishers, such as rulers. Thus, we might expect that, for men at least, mechanization altered paper mill work adversely. In some respects it did. Accelerating the trends that had originated in the hardpressed hand mills of the 1820s, the adoption of new and improved machines subjected workmen to a more hectic pace, longer hours, and periodic unemployment. Moreover, unlike earlier paper mak-

[18] Figures derive from the United States Manuscript Census for all Berkshire mill towns, computer-assisted analysis.
[19] Ibid.

ers, machine tenders and many of their fellow male employees risked being killed or maimed. Added to the workers' increased specialization and diminished prospects of social mobility, these changes further differentiated the work experience of worker and owner, in this case clearly to the detriment of the worker.

Yet we should not exaggerate the degradation of paper mill work in the wake of mechanization. As noted above, the men who tended paper mill machinery were highly skilled, proud, and often greatly in demand. During prosperous times especially, they capitalized on these attributes to bargain for steady work, more healthful conditions, higher wages, and promotion to supervisory positions. Also, most had only infrequent supervision, so that they could exercise some measure of control over their work. In addition, we should recall that employers had substantial incentives to eliminate or minimize the principal sources of unemployment: low water, equipment failure, fire, and depressed paper markets. And owners spent enough time in the mills to be aware of the hardships associated with long hours, dangerous machines, and unhealthful workplaces, so they generally improved conditions as they found themselves more economically secure. Of course, economic circumstances fluctuated with the business cycle and differed among firms, and so did working conditions.

The worker's situation also varied with his position, so that to visualize men's experience of mechanization, we must first look at the tasks they came to perform. Although machines most often assumed men's traditional paper-making tasks, they did not alter the terms of the sexual division of labor that had prevailed in the unmechanized industry. The new or modified work that men performed around machines bore fundamental similarities to the hand operations the machines superseded. Men continued to hold positions requiring long training, strength, or initiative, and jobs conferring prestige or authority. Mechanization multiplied workers' output, changed their specific duties, and transformed their working conditions, but it did not free mill owners from their dependence on workmen's skills and judgment.

The role of the machine tender, successor to the vatman, best illustrates this point. As earlier quotations from machine tenders' letters have suggested, these men epitomized the proud workmen of the mechanized paper industry because of the complex skills their job required. The machine tender had to know how to adjust his machine to make different weights and grades of paper and to maintain uniform speed throughout all sections of the complicated

Fig. 9.2 Machine tender, backtender, and Fourdrinier machine. The wet end of the machine appears on the right; a dandy roll awaits use in the left foreground. (This and subsequent mill interior photographs were taken between 1892 and 1913, after electric lights had been installed. The paper-making machinery shown is representative of what workers encountered in the 1880s; much of it dates from at least that era.) Courtesy of the Crane Museum.

mechanism, tasks that required particular skill on early machines, which often ran directly off the waterwheel and had their speeds adjusted by dipping canvas in rosin and wrapping it around cone pulleys to increase their diameter. In addition, the machine tender had to anticipate and counteract lateral slippage of wires and felts, and had to spot and replace worn wires and felts before they left visible marks on the paper. When the continuous sheet broke, he had to spot the problem immediately and manually thread the sheet through press and dryer cylinders. He had mastered these and other skills during a stint of three or four years as a backtender, a position in which he had assisted the machine tender at his work, and assumed responsibility for cleaning and filling the machine room's lamps, oiling the machinery, picking up refuse paper and trimmings and returning them to the beater room, and carrying stacks of paper from the layboy to the finishing room.[20]

[20] Green, *Holyoke*, pp. 100, 207; Byron Weston Letter Book, 1867–68, BWP, 4/14/

Fig. 9.3 Machine tender and backtender at the Fourdrinier's dry end.
Courtesy of the Crane Museum.

Machine tending also required strength, especially in the early years, when wires and felts were made endless and their installation involved removing and reassembling all of the rolls on the machine. Later, wires and felts were stitched together after installation, but lifting heavy brass wires, dandy rolls, and other machine parts needing replacement still required more upper-body strength than most women could have mustered. Working with almost no supervision, machine tenders also had to possess considerable initiative. All of these qualities made the machine tender the most likely candidate for superintendent and, in the years before 1857, mill owner. These chances for advancement further enhanced the prestige of the position.[21]

As this partial list of his tasks suggests, the machine tender's work was far less repetitious than the vatman's, but he lacked his predecessor's freedom to pause when his shoulders ached or to quicken

---

68; "Early Machines," *SF* 1 (November 1927):5–6; "John Mulchaey," pp. 5–6; "Philo Brownson and Edwin Brownson," interview typescript, CMF, p. 3; "Henry Hosburgh," interview typescript, CMF, p. 1.

[21] "Early Machines," p. 5; Green, *Holyoke*, pp. 100, 207; *VG*, passim; Winthrop M. Crane III, interview.

his pace so as to leave work early. Machines repaid mill owners' investments only when machine tenders minimized "down time" and, when in operation, only constant monitoring ensured the continuous formation of uniform sheets of paper. Later machines required less human intervention, but they also ran much faster, placing a different kind of pressure on the man charged with identifying and compensating for any problem.

Like the machine tender, the engineer was a proud, skillful man. In fact, engineers and machine tenders specified their occupations with equal frequency in the county directory and, together, they account for more than three-quarters of those skilled paper workers listing particular job titles. Unlike the machine tender, whose job mechanization created, the engineer did not experience radical change in his work after 1827. His job had always involved regulating a mechanism and, in some respects, became less difficult as engine builders made the Hollander easier to adjust. On the other hand, how hard to set the roll against the bed plate and how long to beat the stock for a particular kind of paper remained matters of judgment, learned only by working alongside a skilled engineer. The introduction of new fibers and new chemical additives multiplied the knowledge to be mastered. Since beating determined the paper's quality more than any other stage in processing, specialization for more exacting markets further heightened the engineer's responsibilities. At the same time, the advent of paper-making machines and their continuous improvement required more and more pulp, giving the engineer more and larger beaters to supervise and greatly increasing the mill owner's costs if the beaters failed to deliver timely supplies of pulp.[22]

The mills' other principal male employees had charge of the partially mechanized rag room and finishing room. For them, the adoption of the paper-making machine brought increased supervisory responsibilities, several new machines to master, and, ultimately, insistent pressure to keep pace with the machine room. Most of the workers these men supervised were women, whose numbers burgeoned to keep pace with the paper-making machine. In addition to supplying female sorters and cutters with rags and making certain that they performed their work carefully and expeditiously, the rag room boss either loaded, unloaded, and operated dusters and bleach boilers, or, as mills grew larger, supervised unskilled men

[22] Child, *Gazeteer*, part 1, passim; Green, *Holyoke*, p. 1; "Employment, 1866–1878," CMF, 3/26/72. In those few mills where Jordan refiners were installed, they also became the engineer's responsibility.

Fig. 9.4 Engineer attending a mechanized mill's numerous beaters.
Courtesy of the Crane Museum.

charged with this heavy, dirty work. Many rag room bosses also practiced size making, a traditional skilled craft that grew more exacting as output rose and hides became more expensive.[23]

The boss finisher acquired a similar variety of responsibilities. Women tended most of the new finishing machines, but their male supervisor performed the skilled tasks of rearranging ruling machine pens to replicate various ledger book formats and of adjusting calender rolls to handle products ranging from heavy board to light tissue. Maintenance and some repairs also occupied his time. Added to these new technical responsibilities, superintending greater numbers of women, many of whom worked only briefly, and scheduling

[23] "John Mulchaey," p. 5; "Miss Alice Lyman," interview typescript, CMF, p. 1; "David Barnard," interview typescript, CMF, p. 7; "Rewey & Evans Glendale Paper Mill," *SF* 3 (February 1930):11; L. L. Brown & Co. Daybook, 1853–54, LLBP; Crane & Co. Time Book, 1863–76, CA; Bryon Weston Letter Book, 1867–68, BWP, 4/16/68, 6/29/68; "Alfred Hoxie," interview typescript, CMF, p. 3. George Mason, Crane & Co.'s rag room boss in 1881 made both animal and rosin size.

Fig. 9.5 Duster room, rag room boss, and duster operators. Unskilled men performed this heavy, dirty work. Courtesy of the Crane Museum.

work so as to keep the various machines fully employed must have been especially taxing. As in the rag room, less skilled male assistants performed tasks requiring more upper-body strength than the average woman possessed, including trimming, wrapping, packing, and loading heavy reams of paper. In a busy mill such work was evidently quite strenuous, for Byron Weston replied to one job applicant, J. H. Phillips: "My impressions of you are that you are not heavy enough to earn the wages you want at that work. Is it not too much heavy work for you?"[24]

The loftman found his tasks least affected by mechanization, and fewer mills required his services after machine builders developed mechanical dryers for unsized and, later, sized paper. In fine paper mills, however, his duties increased as loft space expanded and loft workers multiplied to handle the paper-making machine's in-

[24] Zenas Crane Journal, 1829–41, CA; Crane & Co. Ledger, 1844–49, CA; "Employment, 1866–1878," CMF, 2/14/72, 11/12/72; "Charles H. Groesbeck," interview typescript, CMF, pp. 2, 5, 9–10; Brown & Weston Letter Book, 1864–65, BWP, 5/6/65, 3/22/65; Brown & Weston Letter Book, 1863–64, BWP, 6/9/64; Letters to Byron Weston, 1867, BWP.

Fig. 9.6 Male finisher operating a plater. The woman behind him is preparing paper for plating. Courtesy of the Crane Museum.

creased output. Pressed, like the rag room and finishing room bosses, to keep pace with the machine, the loftman's work, like theirs, continued to require skill, supervisory ability, and, in most cases, strength, for either he or his male assistants had to carry barrels of wet paper up to the loft and bring stacks of dry paper down. Some mills eventually installed elevators, but they still depended on muscular men to operate hand windlasses.[25]

Of all the skilled positions held by men in mechanized paper mills, that of superintendent best symbolizes the mixture of continuity and change that was the legacy of machine production. In the wake of mechanization, the increased size of mills, the growing number of mills per firm, and the greater variety of nonmanufacturing problems preoccupying mill owners led more and more firms to hire superintendents, although owners oversaw some

[25] "Philo Brownson and Edwin Brownson," interview typescript, CMF, p. 2; "Alfred Hoxie," interview typescript, CMF, p. 10; Brown & Weston and Byron Weston Letter Book, 1866–67, BWP, 6/23/66, 3/20/67.

county mills, especially small ones. By contrast, owners had superintended virtually all unmechanized mills. The increasing commonness of hired superintendents further widened the distance between most workmen and their employers.

At the same time, the role of superintendent provided a measure
of continuity with the skilled paper-making tradition, because it
opened avenues of advancement to men "*thoroughly* conversant with
every department of the business," to use the words of one prospective superintendent. In addition to possessing the hand paper maker's general knowledge, superintendents had to be able to tailor output to orders so as to keep the mill's expensive machinery operating
as continuously as possible. Employers also relied on superintendents to survey machinery at other mills and at machine shops, to recommend purchases, and to assess the character and ability of job applicants. Most important, they had to motivate the mill's various
employees, for as Lindley Murray Crane discovered, an unpopular
superintendent could be worse than none at all. In 1847, after losing his superintendent, he reported to his brothers:

> I am going to be on hand at my mill myself & can get along just
> as well & a little better without him. The hands never liked him
> & now he has gone every one seems to take an interest in mak-
> ing the mill go better without him.[26]

These capsule portraits of paper-making tasks offer little evidence that mechanization altered the basic character of work in the
industry. Machines did not replace workers, reduce their level of
skill, or subdivide their tasks. Rather, as intended, mechanization
multiplied the output of the limited number of skilled workmen.
Eventually, by reducing paper's cost and abetting its more general
use, mechanization also multiplied jobs for skilled paper workers,
jobs filled by men trained while performing less skilled tasks such as
backtender, engineer's assistant, duster or bleach boiler attendant,
and trimmer man. Of the new, non-paper-making positions added
by enlarged mills, skilled occupations such as bookkeeper, carpenter, steam engineer, and machinist employed about as many men as
did unskilled jobs such as ditch digger, teamster, and night watch-
man.

Although mechanization did not entail any profound redefini-
tion of paper mill tasks, it did transform the conditions of work. As

[26] "Employment, 1844–1865," CMF, 6/26/57 and passim; "Machinery, Engineering, and Chemistry, 1854–1865," CMF, 10/10/65; File 329, CMF, 8/11/59; File 326,
CMF, 8/6/45; File 445, CMF, 9/25/47; Winthrop M. Crane III, interview; *VG*, passim.

noted above, whether or not they tended paper-making machines, all workmen experienced unprecedented pressure to keep the mill's expensive machinery fully employed. The result was a more hectic, less flexible work pace, the most pervasive and permanent deleterious effect of mechanization. Less common and shorter-lived indications that machine production affected paper mill work adversely were longer work days, periodic unemployment, and more dangerous and unpleasant surroundings. Skilled male workers experienced most of this deterioration in working conditions.

Extremely long work hours were confined almost exclusively to early mechanized mills and to the machine room and engine room. Nonetheless, the situation of machine tenders and engineers warrants particular attention because their experience represents the fate of skilled craftsmen as the paper industry mechanized. When mills first installed machines, the men who operated them learned only through months of experience how to keep them operating more or less continuously. Each time the machine started up or shut down it produced broke, or refuse paper, so that initially machine tenders and their assistants often put in long hours merely to produce as much paper as the vatman had made. By the 1840s and early 1850s improvements in the machines and experience in operating them had reduced down time, but at least some machine tenders and engineers labored fifteen, sixteen, or even eighteen hours a day as mill owners sought to meet demand for paper or to ensure sufficient pulp before they could afford investments in additional or enlarged beaters. In an era of rapidly evolving machines, long machine-tending hours also served as temporary expedients, substituting labor for new machines or improved parts. For example, in 1850 Lindley Murray Crane notified his brothers:

> I hope you will not forget to forward the Cylinder[.] We can save on Machine tender's time at least 3 dollars pr week. & to it is to much to ask of one man to stay in that Machine room from 13 to 18 hours pr day & tend to the Machine.[27]

By the 1860s installation of larger, more complete machines had multiplied the operating costs attributable to broke produced in daily start-ups and shutdowns, an expense that increasingly cost-conscious mill owners were prepared to recognize. They instituted round-the-clock operation of the industry's principal machines, di-

[27] "T. G. & W. W. Carson, 1845–1855," CMF, 2/45; File 448, CMF, 6/23/50; File 463, CMF, 6/50.

viding machine hands and beater hands into two twelve-hour shifts known as tours. Hands on "tower work," as it was pronounced, worked from noon to midnight or from midnight to noon. Because most workers preferred not to work night tour, most mills rotated shifts. Men worked days one week and nights the next. This schedule had become standard by the 1870s, when paper manufacturers reported to the Massachusetts Bureau of Statistics of Labor that paper mill technology made the ten-hour day inconceivable. They explained:

A large part of our machinery is run twenty-four hours each day, and operated by men working twelve hours. . . . It would not be practicable to run this part of our works less than twenty-four hours. . . . We do not see how the hours of labor in our manufacture could be fixed by law to the advantage of employer or employee.

Night work might be curtailed temporarily during periods of slack demand, but the "double tower" and seventy-two-hour week generally persisted until 1900.[28]

Most men, however, were not subjected to this exhausting new schedule. Differences in hours reflected the diversity of men's tasks in mechanized mills. As Chapter 10 will discuss, women worked shorter hours so that men who worked with or supervised women in the rag room, finishing room, and dry loft put in a sixty-hour week by the 1860s. In some mills daily hours in these departments fell to nine between November and May, responding to changes in the number of daylight hours, much as all workers' hours had done in the preindustrial era. Such "natural" schedules almost certainly prevailed for teamsters, ditch diggers, and other outdoor workers. Still others attained an eight-hour day as early as the 1860s because they performed carpentry or millwright's tasks; in shops filled with sawdust and wood shavings, artificial lighting constituted an unacceptable fire hazard.[29]

---

[28] Three eight-hour shifts replaced the double tower at the turn of the century. "Employment, 1866–1878," CMF, 12/2/72; File 621, CMF, 8/8/65; *Tenth Annual Report of the Bureau of Statistics of Labor* (Boston, 1879), p. 153; Commission on the Hours of Labor, 1865, 1866, First Commission (1865) Correspondence and Questionnaires, November 1–15, 1865, MA, Box 1, File 9, and Box 2, File 14; File 458, CMF, 5/3/75; "Philo Brownson and Edwin Brownson," interview typescript, CMF, p. 1; "Alfred Hoxie," interview typescript, CMF, p. 1; "Henry Hosburgh," interview typescript, CMF, p. 2; "David Barnard," interview typescript, CMF, p. 8.

[29] Commission on Hours, Second Commission Correspondence and Hearings, October–November, 1866, MA, Box 3, File 26, 10/3/66; Box 2, File 14, 10/3/66; First

The holidays that provided respite from mill labor also changed in the course of the nineteenth century, reflecting both the new religious diversity of the work force and the increasing secularization of New England society. At Zenas Crane's hand paper mill only traditional Congregationalist religious holidays had been observed, including Sundays; Fast Day, a Thursday in early April; and Thanksgiving, a Thursday in late November or early December. In 1824 some workers were also excused for muster. Beginning in 1826 most of the employees did not have to work on the Fourth of July, a holiday that evoked growing enthusiasm. By 1841 the custom of celebrating July fifth when the fourth fell on a Sunday had been established, and in the 1850s some male workers at L. L. Brown's mills began extending their celebration to the fifth whether the fourth fell on a Sunday or not. In the mid-1860s mills began shutting down for Christmas in deference to the numerous Roman Catholic workers, who, unlike the New England Congregationalists, celebrated the day. After 1881 Decoration Day, honoring the Union dead, joined the list of mill holidays.[30]

As new holidays achieved popularity, observance of traditional religious holidays waned. As early as the 1850s L. L. Brown's mills no longer shut down for Fast Day. One Dalton worker's reminiscences tie this change to the passing of a generation of mill owners. He recalled, "I remember one time—I think it was Fast Day—he [Zenas Marshal Crane] shut the mills down and Zene [his son, Zenas Crane, Jr.] was running his. He sent word to Zene to shut the mill down and to go up to church." The worker, clearly a man of the new generation, concluded, "Nice old man, but queer." In 1882 the secularized mill schedule at Zenas Crane, Jr.'s Bay State Mill listed only the Fourth of July and Decoration Day as holidays.[31]

Commission Records, MA, Box 1, File 9, 11/8/65; "Thomas J. Bolton," interview typescript, CMF, p. 2; "Miss Alice Lyman," interview typescript, CMF, p. 4; "Alfred Hoxie," interview typescript, CMF, pp. 2–3; "Charles H. Groesbeck," interview typescript, CMF, p. 4; Crane & Co. Time Book, 1863–76, CA; L. L. Brown & Co. Daybook, 1853–54, LLBP; *Tenth Annual Report of the BSL*, p. 153; *Fourteenth Annual Report of the BSL*, pp. 217–18; *Census of Massachusetts, 1885*, 2:1134–35; Brown & Weston Letter Book, 1864–65, BWP, 1/14/64; Jones, *Jones Story*, p. 5.

[30] Zenas Crane and Crane & Co. Time Books, CA; L. L. Brown & Co. Time Book, 1850–61, LLBP; Vera Shlakman, *Economic History of a Factory Town: A Study of Chicopee, Massachusetts* (Northampton, Mass., 1915), p. 97; Michael Maher, Machine Tender's Book, CMF.

[31] Chastened by the early years of the Civil War, L. L. Brown's workers observed Fast Day in 1863. L. L. Brown & Co. Time Book, 1850–61, LLBP; "Charles H. Groesbeck," interview typescript, CMF, p. 7; Michael Maher, Machine Tender's Book, CMF.

Assuming that most mills recognized five holidays, in 1885 Massachusetts census officials estimated 308 possible workdays per year. In practice, few men worked so many days in any given year, either before or after mechanization. As discussed in Chapter 7, some unemployment resulted from seasonal waterpower shortages, a problem present in hand paper mills, initially aggravated by mechanization, and eventually mitigated by the adoption of auxiliary steam power. Even in the late 1870s, however, mill owners explained to state labor statisticians that "the reason the whole number of days run each year . . . does not average over two hundred and ninety-two is from the fact that many mills through the State are closed some weeks each year from want of water, and some are stopped eight to ten days by too much water in the spring. . . ." On the other hand, as noted in Chapter 8, mill owners could not afford to lose their most skilled workers, so that many male employees were guaranteed work despite low or high water.[32]

Mechanization entailed additional unemployment when mills shut down to repair existing machines or install new ones, although, again, skilled male workers experienced less technological unemployment because they assisted in repairs and start-ups. For example, in May 1835 all but one or two men continued working at Crane's mill, while nearly all of the women stayed home, and the timekeeper noted, "Repairing cylinder and machine room." A similar employment pattern resulted in October when an "Iron Shaft Broke." Likewise, almost no women worked for one and a half months in August and September 1841, but most men were listed in the time book next to the annotation "Repairing mill.—putting in new main wheel and belts to engine."[33]

After the mid-1850s the unemployment experienced by most male paper workers was less directly attributable to mechanization and less predictable than waterpower fluctuations or machine repairs. It resulted from the industry's increasing vulnerability to regional and national business cycles. The demand that had spawned mechanization kept employment levels high in the early 1850s. For example, in 1853 and 1854 men at L. L. Brown's mill averaged 313 and 306 days of work. The same was true during the Civil War, when skilled paper workers became so scarce that Elizur Smith paid a commutation fee rather than lose his superintendent. In 1864 a Lee correspondent seeking a machine tender for the Cranes re-

[32] *Census of Massachusetts, 1885*, 2:1180; *Tenth Annual Report of the BSL*, p. 153.

[33] Zenas Crane Time Book, 1809–36, CA, 5/35, 10/35; Zenas Crane Time Book, 1836–48, CA, 8/41, 9/41.

ported, "Smith will pay them any Price rather than have them leave." But in the late 1850s and early 1870s business crises resulting in paper mill failures and slowdowns especially curtailed employment in the industry's marginal enterprises, the mills of East Lee, New Marlborough, and Tyringham. As Table 9.6 reveals, even at a successful mill steady employment was rare in the early 1870s. The average male paper worker lost one or two months time each year. By 1885 renewed prosperity allowed most surviving Massachusetts paper mills to operate 307 days a year, although workers' experiences varied with the success of individual enterprises. For the state's paper industry as a whole "net actual time worked" averaged only 293 days and individual mills ranged between 313 and 52 days of operation.[34]

Mechanization had a more direct impact on the atmosphere and safety of the workplace, especially affecting the industry's most skilled workers. In the early years, the odor of lard oil, the principal lubricant, and the smoke of kerosene or coal oil lanterns fouled the air over the long hours that unventilated machine rooms operated. Water evaporated from the paper on the machine and dryers and condensed on the cooler walls and ceilings. Some mills lined ma-

TABLE 9.6
AVERAGE NUMBER OF DAYS PER YEAR OF EMPLOYMENT FOR
MEN AT THE CRANES' MILL, 1864–75

Year	Days Worked	Year	Days Worked
1864	277	1870	301
1865	259	1871	240
1866	283	1872	225
1867	298	1873	247
1868	300	1874	267
1869	272	1875	259

NOTE: Crane & Co. Time Book, 1863–76, CA. The total number of male workers listed each month has been divided into the total number of days worked each month. The twelve monthly totals have been added to arrive at yearly totals. Since some men left or arrived during a month, this method of calculation slightly overstates the extent of unemployment.

[34] *Census of Massachusetts, 1885*, 2:1180; L. L. Brown & Co. Daybook, 1853–54, LLBP; Crane & Co. Time Book, 1863–76, CA; "Robert McAlpine," *SF* 3 (September 1929):1; "The Civil War and the Post War Period, 1860–1877," CMF, 3/22/64. Judging from Zenas Crane's earliest time book, employment was also unpredictable in early hand mills, probably reflecting the limited market and rag supply, as well as waterpower fluctuations.

chine room ceilings with heated coils to reduce condensation, but others remained so damp that one worker seeking employment with Z. M. Crane explained, "My object in leaving this place is on acount of the Room in which I work, it is verry wet and is ingering my health." After quoting his wages he concluded, "you see my wages is good—But money will not purches health." Engineers also endured wet working conditions, while rag room workers breathed in air filled with dust and lint from dusters and rag cutters.[35]

In later years improved ventilation, heating, hoods over the machines, better lubricants, and gas lighting alleviated these problems. Mill owners also improved the cleanliness of their establishments. For example, in 1871 a *Scientific American* reporter found H. D. Cone's Housatonic mill so clean that he thought of "carefully removing all dust from his shoes before entering." Similarly, in their 1879 renovation of the Colt mill, Z. M. and J. B. Crane invested in improved sanitation by installing urinals, water closets, and copper-bottomed basins.[36]

By contrast, nothing could be done to still the deafening noise that Fourdriniers and more numerous beaters brought to the mills' machine rooms and engine rooms. The many moving parts of paper-making machines forced machine tenders to shout when they needed to be heard over the continuous clash of metal against metal, a sharp contrast to the quiet conversation and easy jests the vat room had permitted. Louder talk had prevailed in early beater rooms, as engineers seeking diversion raised their voices over the rumble of the rag engine, but as mills added more and larger engines, the thunder of the beaters reduced engine room conversation to a minimum. Also, while the rising tumult of their surroundings effectively isolated skilled male employees from life outside the mill's walls, machines incorporated more tasks and became more automated, making men's work more solitary.[37]

The noise, isolation, dust, odor, and dampness of mechanized mills impaired workers' health and affected the quality of their working lives gradually and undramatically, attracting little con-

[35] "Early Machines," p. 5; "Employment, 1844–1865," CMF, 4/3/49. The lint in the rag room air was substantially less than in contemporary cotton mills. Rag cutting machines intensified the problem and confined its impact to male workers. Protective masks were not introduced until OSHA (Occupational Safety and Health Act) regulations mandated them. Ralph Kendall, Superintendent of Bay State Mill, interview and tour.

[36] "An Example to Manufacturers," p. 263; "The Colt Mill, 1879," CMF; "Early Machines," p. 6.

[37] Tours of Pioneer, Bay State, and Wahconah mills; visit to Hurlbut Mill.

temporary comment. By contrast, the dangers of the new machines were highly visible. Any reader of the local press learned repeatedly of their destructiveness of workers' lives and limbs. For example, in its first fifteen years (1857–71) the *Valley Gleaner* of Lee reported fifty-four paper workers injured on the job, eight of them fatally. Because men performed most mechanized work, almost all accident victims (87 percent) and all but one of those killed were men. Over two-thirds of these accidents were directly attributable to machine production, while the remainder involved construction workers and teamsters, whose work increased as mechanized mills grew and prospered.[38]

Workers had to exercise particular care around the flying shafts and belts that transmitted power throughout the mechanized portions of the mill. The majority of fatalities and the second largest number of injuries occurred when the transmission system caught men's clothing or arms and they were drawn in and crushed, or thrown across the room. Accidents involving paper-making machines, rag cutters, and machine shop tools caused fewer fatalities, but affected more workers, most of whom lost fingers, hands, or arms. Boiler explosions and escaping steam injured the rest. In the worst instances, high-pressure steam scalded workers, in one case fatally, while the force of explosions and flying debris cut and bruised others, including one man who was blown out a window by the blast of an exploding bleach boiler. By the 1870s and 1880s machine makers advertised safety features on cutters and trimmers, and experience with steam boilers made explosions uncommon, but the mill's principal machine and its transmission system remained hazardous. In sum, mechanization had transformed paper making from a relatively safe craft to a relatively dangerous industry.[39]

Against this background of increasingly demanding work, longer hours, and dangerous, unhealthful working conditions, there can be no objective standard for assessing the adequacy of workers' compensation. Moreover, given that rapidly changing technology forced owners to reinvest their earnings in mills that frequently failed and changed ownership, comparing workers' and owners' shares in the financial rewards of increased productivity involves too many arbitrary judgments to produce meaningful figures for the era of rapid mechanization. Certainly by the 1880s most of the surviving mills' owners lived in much greater affluence than their

[38] *VG*, passim.

[39] *VG*, passim; Universal Paper Cutter advertisement, "Machinery, Engineering, and Chemistry, 1879–1886," CMF.

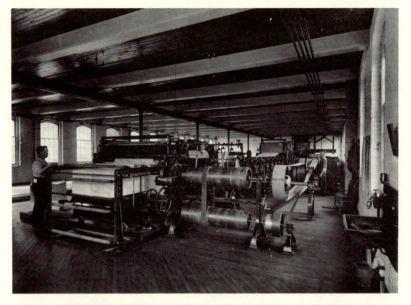

Fig. 9.7 Back side of a Fourdrinier machine, a dangerous place to work.
The backtender had the job of moving about among these belts and shafts.
Courtesy of the Crane Museum.

male employees, but their success was exceptional and their accumulation of wealth had been gradual.

Annual wage and profit figures suggest that Berkshire paper mill employees fared comparatively well. Lee data for 1883 show owners reaping a net profit of $50 per worker or 3 percent on capital invested, a very low rate of return when compared with other Massachusetts paper mills or with Berkshire County's other leading industry, woolen textile manufacture. Holyoke paper mills returned profits of $161 per employee or 12 percent on capital. In the same year North Adams and Pittsfield woolen mills earned net profits of $537 and $188 per worker or 65 percent and 16 percent on capital invested. At the same time, average yearly earnings of $395 by Lee paper workers exceeded earnings of $318 by Holyoke paper workers and wages of $315 and $321 to North Adams and Pittsfield woolen workers both in absolute terms and as a percentage of their mills' profits.[40]

It is more difficult to say how well industrial paper workers fared financially in comparison to hand paper workers because most

[40] *Fourteenth Annual Report of the BSL*, passim.

available figures give averages, which obscure increasingly diverse wages paid an increasingly diverse work force. The uneven and unpredictable impact of unemployment also makes weekly and daily wage figures deceptive. For most workers, however, a higher standard of living accompanied the advent of machine production and was retained despite wartime inflation and subsequent deflation.

Incomplete data from a number of company store account books indicate that during the early years of mechanization weekly and yearly wages for men generally rose, while prices remained constant or fell. About the time machines were introduced, McLane's inquiries found that the average male paper worker in Berkshire County received about $5.50 a week, just as he had in Zenas Crane's original mill. Wages differed little among male workers. Almost all earned $0.90 a day, a few received $1.00, and one took home $1.68. By the mid-1830s median weekly wages had reached $6.00. Although hard times in the mid-1840s and late 1850s reduced wages briefly, average earnings in these decades usually fluctuated between $6.00 and $7.00. By the 1850s, however, paper mill employees had grown so diverse that wages varied considerably. Some men received less than $3.00 a week, while others earned as much as $15.00.[41]

For the 1860s and 1870s Table 9.7, which takes account of differential pay rates, reveals that skilled paper workers and skilled craftsmen who worked in paper mills continued to fare well economically despite wartime inflation. Figures are for the Massachusetts industry as a whole, but the same report found wages in Lee, the Berkshire town most dominated by the paper industry, increased 63 percent between 1860 and 1878, so that, if anything, skilled workers in Lee probably experienced greater gains. Even after inflation, these wage increases remained substantial. During the same period labor statisticians found that groceries in Lee "advanced 12.8 per cent, provisions 21.4 per cent, boots and shoes 13 per cent, and the price of board 18.9 per cent. Fuel is 9 per cent lower, and dry goods 8 per cent. Rents remain unchanged." They calculated an average increase of 5.8 percent on all expenses in Lee and a 5 percent increase in Adams. Living in small towns within a rural county evidently moderated the growth of workers' expenses. Primarily because of

[41] *McLane Report*, part 1, pp. 144–45; Zenas Crane Daybook, 1819–24, CA; Zenas Crane Journal, 1829–41, CA; Crane & Co. Journal, 1840–, CA; Crane & Co. Ledger, 1844–49, CA; Ledger of the Aetna, Housatonic, and Defiance Mill, 1839–47, BWP; Carson & Brown Ledger, 1849–53, CA; L. L. Brown & Co. Time Book, 1850–61, LLBP; L. L. Brown & Co. Time Book, 1861–65, LLBP; L. L. Brown & Co. Daybook, 1853–54, LLBP.

TABLE 9.7
WEEKLY WAGES OF MASSACHUSETTS PAPER WORKMEN, 1860–78

Job	1860 Wages	1872 Wages	1878 Wages	% Increase
Foreman	$16.63	$16.00	$26.49	59
Millwright	9.86	16.00	15.21	54
Paper-machine tender	10.00	16.00	15.25	53
Mechanic	9.75		13.20	35
Finisher	7.70	11.33	10.20	34
Rag-engine tender	7.90	14.67	10.41	32
Engineer/fireman	6.64	10.52	8.77	32
Finisher's helper	5.80		7.27	25
Cutter	6.90	8.89	7.95	15
Bleacher	6.70	8.89	7.56	13
Men on stock	5.88	9.33	6.57	12
Laborers	5.50	8.33	6.55	19

SOURCE: *Tenth Annual Report of the Bureau of Statistics of Labor* (Boston, 1879), p. 74.

greater increases in board and rent, workers in Pittsfield, the county's only city, saw average expenses increase 18 percent. Even this inflation appears modest when compared with eastern Massachusetts. For example, prices in Lawrence rose 27 percent and in Lynn, 32 percent.[42]

During the same years workers came to exercise considerably more control over their earnings. In contrast to preindustrial practice, which had continued into the period of mechanization, workers no longer received wages at unpredictable intervals, but could anticipate regular paydays. Their legal rights to wages owed by bankrupt proprietors also increased. Somewhat earlier, cash payments superseded daybook credits, for company stores disappeared once towns grew large enough to support independent retailers. After mid-century workers in all but the smallest mill towns could choose among a number of establishments. Abetted by these devel-

---

[42] *Tenth Annual Report of the BSL*, passim. A number of workers further reduced their cash expenses by maintaining gardens, keeping livestock, hunting, and fishing. DuBois recalled that in Great Barrington in the 1870s "some food like local fruit was almost common property; vegetables like potatoes and navy beans and cabbage were grown in small home gardens; corned beef and chickens fetched low prices and eggs could often be raised at home; 'greens' and rhubarb grew in the back yard and in the Fall canning and preserving cost only the sugar." DuBois, *Autobiography*, p. 79. It is worth noting that in the 1870s Great Barrington was more urbanized than any of the paper mill villages.

opments, a growing number of workmen saved enough to purchase real estate.[43]

For most skilled Berkshire paper industry employees, then, industrialization fulfilled the main promise of its contemporary promoters: their wages commanded a greater abundance of material goods. At the same time, however, mechanization altered adversely the conditions of work, subjecting all men to a more hectic pace and many to greater danger and less pleasant surroundings. Some also labored longer hours on rotating schedules or found themselves periodically unemployed.

Yet these developments, both positive and negative, changed male employees' circumstances, not their fundamental situation. Paper workers escaped the degrading effects of mechanization in some industries: machines neither subdivided their tasks nor reduced the skill, judgment, and initiative their jobs entailed. Although paper mill workers who chose to remain in the Berkshires could no longer become successful mill owners, they could advance to more skilled positions, including mill superintendent, a job that promised much higher wages, conferred substantial prestige, and involved making many of the decisions that had belonged to preindustrial mill owners. In sum, the proud men who labored in mechanized mills retained many of the attributes and attitudes of the craftsmen they superseded. More than their changed circumstances and prospects, this shaped their responses to mechanization and its social consequences.

WORKERS AND MECHANIZATION

Much of the history of the workers' response to mechanization lies beyond the scholar's ability to reconstruct. For the Berkshire paper industry, extant sources supply little evidence of what men thought or felt about working with machines or about living in industrial mill towns. What we have, instead, is some evidence of how men who labored in Berkshire paper mills acted while machines were installed and after the process was complete. Analysis of such evidence cannot supply definitive answers to labor historians' principal questions: Did workers develop class consciousness or a distinct culture during the Industrial Revolution? Why were organization and collective protest comparatively uncommon among American workers? And how did workers square diminished social mobility with contemporary assertions that America was a land of opportunity?

[43] *VG*, 8/20/57, 4/15/58, and passim.

In addition, the information available is fragmentary, difficult to interpret, and biased. Surviving letters by workers were written to obtain jobs or ask advice, composed to elicit a favorable response from potential or former employers. And they were penned by atypical workers, those who lived too far from the mill owners to make inquiries orally. Time books supply evidence of turnover rates and absenteeism, but rarely indicate whether workers quit or were fired; whether they stayed away by choice or lost a day's pay because work was curtailed. Newspapers offer some accounts of how workers spent their leisure time, but they reported more about formal than informal social activities and more about officers than members. Finally, collections of workers' memoirs, biographies of paper workers, anecdotes of early mill life, and other lore of the paper industry were compiled by a company museum in the 1930s and by *Superior Facts*, a publication of a paper makers' chemical corporation in the 1920s, and they generally feature longtime paper workers, successful individuals, or entertaining eccentrics.

Nonetheless, within the context of what we know about workers, owners, and mechanized paper mill work, this limited data does suggest tentative answers to labor historians' questions. And the answers are probably more representative of contemporary American employees than are the alienation and protest depicted in studies of some urban laborers, Lowell-system textile workers, shoemakers, and metal workers; cases featuring relatively large congregations of workers, sharp differentiation of management from labor, or marked changes in skill and job control. By contrast, paper workers typified the situation of most American workers: they were members of small work forces, knew their employers as fellow men, experienced some mobility, and retained considerable skill. Under these circumstances, paper workers' actions indicate that mechanization and its concomitants did not evoke consciousness of themselves as a class. Rather, machine production reinforced much of the preindustrial craftsman's sense of common interest with his employer. Workers' diversity and their sense of shared manhood and equality with their employers made them opt for personalized negotiation rather than collective protest. Moreover, their notion of manliness precluded protest against dangerous working conditions, the most obvious adverse effect of mechanization on work. At the same time, workers' relatively small numbers and considerable skill meant that individualized bargaining remained both possible and effective. Finally, workers' growing diversity and occasional mobility gave them disparate definitions of the promise of American life and enabled most to maintain a sense of opportunity as their prospects for local mill ownership gradually diminished.[44]

The absence of evident class consciousness is not surprising given the limited and gradual change in the relative status and comparative activities of workers and owners. Unlike industries in which factories superseded self-employed craftsmen or household manufacture, paper making had always taken place in mills that some men owned and in which others collected wages. Mechanization did not alter this situation; instead, emergent distinctions in the tasks and prospects of employer and employed constituted changes in degree rather than in kind. For example, owners came to spend more time in the office and on the road, but they still learned paper making in the mills and maintained familiarity with the workers and their work. Similarly, before the Civil War some workers still advanced to ownership and owners frequently failed and became employees. After the war workers continued to become owners, although those who bought Berkshire mills failed or held small working interests, and the numbers and ultimate fates of those who bought mills outside the county are difficult to ascertain. Moreover, mechanized paper making entailed long hours for owners as well as workers and subjected both entrepreneurs and employees to the uncertainties of a boom-and-bust economy.

Simultaneously, the introduction of machines forged new bonds between worker and owner as they shared responsibility for mechanization. Workers built, installed, operated, and repaired machines, usually supervised by other employees. In the process workers helped shape the equipment, organization, and operating methods of mechanized mills. For example, in the early 1850s skilled employees J. D. Gibbons and T. T. Chapin authored many of the letters relaying technical information from L. M. Crane's Saratoga and Ballston Spa mills to his brothers in Dalton. The correspondence documents especially the continuous expertise workmen

[44] Important examples of workers whose situation and behavior differed from Berkshire paper workers are David Montgomery, *Workers' Control in America* (Cambridge, 1979); Thomas Dublin, *Women at Work: The Transformation of Work and Community in Lowell, Massachusetts, 1826–1860* (New York, 1979); Alan Dawley, *Class and Community: The Industrial Revolution in Lynn* (Cambridge, Mass., 1976); Paul Faler, *Mechanics and Manufacturers in the Early Industrial Revolution: Lynn, Massachusetts, 1780–1860* (Albany, 1981); Daniel J. Walkowitz, *Worker City, Company Town: Iron and Cotton-Worker Protest in Troy and Cohoes, New York, 1855–1884* (Urbana, 1978). For a different interpretation of a case characterized by virtually no organized protest and high turnover rates reflecting substantial geographic mobility, see Prude, *The Coming of Industrial Order*.

contributed to developing procedures for processing stock and adding new chemicals. Mechanical invention occurred more sporadically, but between July 1857 and October 1858 the *Valley Gleaner* reported four improvements made by Platner & Smith's workmen: a "letter copying press of a large and unique pattern, which . . . reflects great credit upon the maker . . . an apprentice . . . named William Jenne"; "a new and simple apparatus for handling paper for trimming," which increased output by one-third and cost only half as much as a conventional press; Robert McAlpine's "very simple and excellent device for raising and lowering the pens" on the ruling machine; and a mechanism for grinding the paper-making machine's seven-foot cutter knives "so that any number of knives may be ground exactly alike, thus saving very much, both of labor and the wear of knives," "invented and built by those ingenious mechanics, Messrs. A. and W. Palmer." Workers also abetted and shaped mechanization when training additional workers, sometimes acting as mentors to future mill owners. For example, Byron Weston acknowledged that when Saugerties paper worker James McDonald taught him how to beat stock, he "laid the basis . . . which has enabled [me] to be a manufacturer of the finest grade of paper made in this country." Workers who moved from mill to mill, as many increasingly did, helped disseminate and standardize the new technology, exerting an influence that complemented mill owners' visits and correspondence.[45]

The shared experience and goals of mechanized mills' workers and owners made those character traits that credit reporters encouraged in owners and owners promoted in workers equally attractive to many of the industry's skilled workmen. Temperance, steadiness, reliability, and hard work became essential to the safe and effective performance of most skilled tasks around machines, as well as to earning promotion or advancing to ownership. Men who prided themselves on their work understandably cultivated these

[45] Files 448 and 449, CMF; *VG,* 7/30/57, p. 2; 6/10/58, p. 2; 10/14/58, p. 2; 3/18/58, p. 2; and passim; McDonald obituary, BWP. See also Chapter 5.

Of the four improvements noticed by the *Gleaner* in 1857 and 1858, apparently only one, the device for handling paper, was patented. The patent was issued to A. Palmer. McAlpine's device was probably not patentable, for he did patent his later invention of a felt cleanser. The patent was issued jointly to McAlpine and fellow workman George Dunn in 1874. *General Index to Patents, 1790–1873,* p. 1005; *General Index to the Official Gazette* 5 (1874):410. Patent office records offer no evidence that Lee mill owners patented improvements devised by their workers, but the numerous patents issued to H. D. Cone suggest that the situation may have been different for Housatonic workmen.

virtues. Given the interdependence of mechanized tasks, many workers also preferred temperate and reliable colleagues.

Because machines made paper mill work dangerous, workers who were drunk or hung over increased their chances of injury and jeopardized the safety of their fellow workers. They might also mistreat their subordinates. Even the romanticized lore of the paper industry conveys this message. It depicts the humorous escapades of "Nosey" Hill, a peripatetic and often drunken machine tender who apparently existed in the 1880s, but who had taken on larger-than-life proportions by the 1920s and 1930s, when accounts of his activities were collected. While Nosey escapes the consequences of his actions by moving on, in each of the tales a fellow worker suffers: the backtender has to work harder to compensate for Nosey's derelictions, he is physically abused by Nosey when things go awry, or he is left to clean up the mess.[46]

Thus, workers had a direct interest in promoting temperance and a number espoused it actively. One of the earliest was a highly skilled paper maker named Cole, who came to Lee in the 1820s. Fifty years later the *Valley Gleaner* reported, "It is said that to him more than any other one man are paper manufacturers indebted for many excellent improvements in paper machinery." In the early 1830s, however, Cole left paper making to open a temperance hotel with town financial support. Later he returned to the mills, perfected a method of washing felts on the machine, and retired only after paralysis in old age made continued work impossible. Like Lee workers who patronized Cole's establishment, Dalton company store customers shifted from alcohol to coffee and tea, beverages more conducive to alert workmanship. These stimulants increased from less than 3 percent to nearly 12 percent of purchases between 1819 and 1850, while depressants, principally patent medicines by 1850, fell from nearly 11 percent to 1.5 percent. Revivalism probably abetted self-interest in encouraging the shift.[47]

Later, temperance societies increasingly elicited workers' support. The Lodge of Good Templars, which mill owners had helped

[46] *SF*, passim.

[47] *VG*, 3/28/72, p. 2; Crane Daybooks, CA. Daybooks are not necessarily a complete account of the beverages workers purchased or consumed, and owners' efforts, discussed in the preceding chapter, account in part for the decline in alcohol purchases. Nonetheless, the increase in the purchase of stimulants is dramatic and could not have come about simply because owners altered the items they vended. My unit of measurement, number of purchases, is a rough one, but prices and quantities were not consistently assigned to items purchased, precluding the use of more precise units. On other purchases see McGaw, "Sources and Impact," pp. 335–36.

organize, listed paper worker Robert McAlpine and his wife among its 1867 officers. The Lee lodge disbanded in 1869 after St. Mary's Roman Catholic Church organized a local temperance society, numbering one hundred adult male members at the outset and doubling in size within three months. Its size suggests heavy participation by the town's numerous Irish paper workers, who promised to abstain from gambling as well as drinking and paid one dollar annually plus a small monthly tax to support a library and fund for mutual aid. An earlier Hibernian Benevolent Society evidently served similar purposes for, in addition to covering the occasional expense of a worker's funeral and collecting money for the family, its 1861 Saint Patrick's Day celebration inspired the *Valley Gleaner* to comment, "If our adopted citizens will always conduct themselves with the good order and decorum of the members of this society we may well be proud of them."[48]

Nonetheless, it is quite clear that many male paper workers drank occasionally and that some drank habitually and excessively. It is impossible to tell whether drunkards grew more common during mechanization or whether they were simply more likely to evoke comment from contemporary reformers and mill owners who had come to identify drunkenness as a problem. Whatever its frequency, the evidence that survives makes it hard to view recurrent drunkenness as a manifestation of working-class culture. The occasional individual who engaged in regular, heavy drinking suffered greatly and caused great suffering. The case of James Lowell, Jr., conveys a vivid sense of the toll alcohol abuse took on some workers' mental and emotional health. A forty-year-old paper worker, husband, and father, Lowell attempted suicide by cutting his own throat with a razor after several days spent "indulging in dissipation . . . and while under the influence of liquor." Lowell was rescued, but as his self-inflicted wound was being stitched his drunken father repeatedly called out from the next room asking, "Why he didn't cut his head entirely off, so that no one would try to save him?"[49]

As noted earlier, other habitual drunkards threatened family members and co-workers. An incident recalled by David Barnard, who began working for Zenas Crane, Jr., in 1880, indicates that drunken workmen compounded the dangers of the mechanized workplace.

[48] *VG*, 1/31/67, p. 2; 1/28/69, p. 2; 2/11/69, p. 2; 4/15/69, p. 2; 6/24/69, p. 2; 3/21/61, p. 2.

[49] *VG*, 12/19/61, p. 2 and passim; see also the anecdotal evidence in Chapter 8.

One rainy night, after they had recently put in a new boiler, [Barnard] heard the boiler blowing off. Jim Davin was standing on the running board with a scoop shovel over his shoulder, and swore that he would split any one in two who came nearer. Finally, after some discussion, he was tripped up. They found the fires out—filled with wood. Davin would not go home, but Zac Cady went to the boarding house below the Government Mill, and got Richard Goodhind, the superintendent, who threw Davin out of the door. Every rivet under the fire box was loose. In the meantime Davin ran around behind him and was groping around to turn the cold water into the red hot boilers. He was finally buried in a heap of dust and about smothered.[50]

Frequent excessive drinking was not typical. More representative were workers who experienced what one local newspaper diagnosed as July fifth symptoms: tiredness, headaches, large eyes, sore feet and heads, and poor appetites so that "paper mills, factories, shops are but half manned." The editor's prescription, adding more holidays so as to reduce the intensity of celebrations, implies that such overindulgence occurred infrequently. Time books spanning the years before, during, and after mechanization confirm this impression, for they offer no evidence that absenteeism was higher on Mondays or Saturdays.[51]

Nor is it possible to conclude that workers were more prone than owners to occasional overindulgence. Owners usually imbibed privately so that their drinking was less likely to evoke comment. An English traveler who visited with Z. M. Crane summarized the mores that shaped observed drinking behavior.

I suppose there is scarcely a family in all New England where wine or beer is habitually taken, either with or between meals. Men are half ashamed to drink and women think themselves disgraced by it. But wine is kept in the house, as we found, even in sober Dalton, where it was quite funny to see our kind host, seeking private occasions to gratify my English tastes without indecorum.

Dependence on favorable credit reports also gave owners an economic incentive to avoid public evidence of drinking. John Carroll, for example, achieved a "good reputation" because he got "fu-

50 "David Barnard," interview typescript, CMF, p. 7.
51 *VG*, 7/6/65, p. 2 and passim; Crane and L. L. Brown Time Books.

riously drunk" only when away from New Marlborough and his mills.[52]

It is also hard to distinguish workers by their social activities, primarily because mill towns remained too small to support many specialized organizations. As with temperance and benevolent societies mentioned earlier, religion or ethnicity served as the basis for organizing some groups in which paper workers must have predominated, but most local social organizations attracted members from both emergent classes. Worker James Toole and owner W. M. Crane played on the same baseball team, just as worker Adam Thompson and owner Zenas Crane had gone to singing school together. Fire companies enlisted both owners and workers. Employees, like employers, had fought in the war and joined the Grand Army of the Republic. Lee and Dalton paper worker Charles Groesbeck served as a G.A.R. officer and helped lead the local Masonic lodge. Workers' talents also enriched cultural activities. Robert McAlpine, for example, directed the Lee Congregational Church choir and attended the Lee Literary Club, where he read his essay on papermaking history to an audience that included mill owners. Lectures, laughing gas exhibitions, agricultural fairs, parades, public school examinations, and protestant church socials must have attracted men from both groups. Both also frequented summer vacation resorts. As with the owners, the *Valley Gleaner* reported workers visiting northern New England, upstate New York, and the New England seacoast. For example, Daniel Pultz, Smith's machine shop superintendent, accompanied the Methodist church pastor "on a pleasure trip and recreation among the fashionable watering places" and spent a few days with others blue fishing from a chartered boat.[53]

Common activities reinforced the most fundamental bond between worker and owner: shared masculinity. In accord with the relatively clear, distinct, and rigid notions of masculine and feminine behavior that emerged in nineteenth-century America, workers viewed themselves first and foremost as men and, thus, as the mill owners' equals, an attitude that made personal negotiation more appropriate than collective bargaining. The refrain of a poem quoted in a twentieth-century publication devoted to early papermaking history and lore expresses this attitude succinctly: "Business

[52] Pidgeon, *Old-World Questions*, p. 110; R. G. Dun & Co. Ledgers, 3:162.

[53] Zenas Crane Journal, 1829–41, CA; James A. Toole to W. M. Crane III, CMF; *VG*, passim; "Notes on the History of Lee," LLHR; "David Barnard," interview typescript, CMF, p. 1.

is business, but men are men." Similarly, workers' memoirs humor-
ously recount mill owners' foibles and the pranks workers and owners played on one another, emphasizing that owners were fellow
men, not remote or superior beings.[54]

The egalitarian implications of shared manliness were underscored during the years of paper industry mechanization by Jacksonian rhetoric and the achievement of manhood suffrage. That
some contemporary workers achieved ownership, while some owners reverted to the status of employee conveyed the same message.
By the 1860s, 1870s, and 1880s, widely shared masculine experience on Civil War battlefields had reinforced this sense of shared
manhood and had helped certify Irish workmen as equals.[55]

Workers' sense of manliness helps account for the absence of protest against the new dangers of the workplace. One suggestive an-
ecdote comes from the lore of the paper industry and involves
Nosey Hill.

> It used to be said that one would never be a good machine
> tender until his fingers had been nipped in the calenders. How-
> ever true this may be, "Nosey" had little sympathy for his back-
> tenders when they were nipped in this manner. When asked
> whether he had ever been nipped, "Nosey" promptly an-
> swered. "Sure, but I never made a fuss about it. Why I had my
> arm drawn into a calender up to the elbow once, but I just took
> it calmly and when the rolls started jumping I jerked my arm
> out and went along about my business."

As usual, Nosey embodies common experience in exaggerated
form. The tale's message—that injury forms an inevitable part of
learning, which real men bear with fortitude—simply expresses
contemporary notions of manhood, notions that were reiterated

---

[54] *SF* 4 (October 1930):7; interview typescripts, CMF.

[55] Several decades of serious scholarship devoted to the history of women have
made clear that we do not have a history of men, that we know little about how norms
of masculine behavior changed or shaped men's experiences. Such scholarship
would be especially helpful in explaining the nineteenth-century work experience
because available scholarship makes clear that in that era work was defined as a masculine behavior. Scholarship in labor history has generally assumed the central role
of work in men's lives, but, as women's history has shown, nineteenth-century rhetoric was not necessarily nineteenth-century reality. Daniel T. Rodgers, *The Work Ethic
in Industrial America, 1850–1920* (Chicago, 1978), pp. 182–209 and passim. Research
in progress by David F. Noble promises to offer insight into the relationship between
masculinity, technology, and work. See Noble, *Forces of Production: A Social History of
Industrial Automation* (New York, 1984), p. xiv.

and glorified locally in commemorations of Civil War battlefield
bravery. At the same time, the dangers men encountered outside
the mills must have minimized their sense that paper mill dangers
were unusual or avoidable. Horses injured far more local citizens
than did paper machinery, and local newspapers reported frequent
railroad and steamship accidents, including the death of thirty-six-
year-old paper worker John Quirk, killed after he boarded the
wrong train and fell between cars while searching for the conduc-
tor.[56]

Equality based on shared masculinity also helps explain the absence of evidence that Berkshire paper workers acted collectively as
adversaries of the mill owners, in contrast to reported organization
or spontaneous and sporadic group protest in county industries employing larger numbers of less skilled workers. The skill and small
size of the paper mill's male work force apparently enabled workers
to keep protest individualized, to express grievances man to man. A
few extant letters depict such interactions, although most took place
face to face and left no record. Writing to the Cranes in 1857, the
father of one of their workers lodged the following protest: "my
Boy says that you have paid three Dollars of his wages out to Charles
Whitcom[.] if you pay eny mony out for me with out my orders You
will pay it again if i can make you[.] you have no rite to pay out my
mony without my orders[.]" In a similar tone, James Wells casti-
gated Marshal Crane in 1865 as not having "acted manley by me"
when employing him in a different mill and at different hours than
they had originally negotiated.[57]

Because owners varied in their personalities, the outcome of individualized protest depended on the man being approached; thus,
workers probably exercised most control over their circumstances
when they decided to apply to a particular man. Many workers indicated the importance they placed on their choice of employer
when they listed who they worked for, rather than their occupation,
in the county directory. Job application letters emphasize preference for a particular mill owner, some stating their reasoning explicitly. An 1848 applicant to the Cranes explained, "I think I
should choose to work for you—we know each other—and I wish (as
ever) to be employed where I can feel interested enough to *fancy* the
business is my own." Another paper maker used Civil War experience to identify the man he preferred. He wrote to Byron Weston:

[56] " 'Nosey' Hill's Plastic Arm," *SF* 4 (October 1930):7; *VG*, 7/11/72, p. 2 and passim.

[57] "Employment, 1844–1865," CMF, 5/31/57, 2/14/65.

I presume you will not remember me. I frequently saw you when the 49th Reg. was formed. I then lived in Mill River and had many intimate friends in your company whose description of your character and ways led me to think I should like to engage with you.[58]

The experience of satisfied employees guided other workers. For example, when L. P. Williams came seeking work as the Cranes' rag room superintendent, he acted on the advice of his earlier employer, C. S. Lambdin, a former Crane employee who had established his own paper mill at Beaver Meadow, Alabama. Although a few applicants, especially office workers, referred to newspaper advertisements, far more merely mentioned that they had heard of a job opening, suggesting that informal networks of paper workers directed most men to particular employers. As with the owners, workers' access to information was increased by the concentration of paper mills in Berkshire County and by the employment of many workers' relatives in paper mills. Charles Groesbeck moved from Lee to Dalton after a machinist serving mills in both towns recommended Crane as a "pretty good firm to work for." And Henry J. Dean notified the Cranes: "I was informed by my Brother Wm. Dean that you would soon be wanting to Engage the Second Machine tender. I wish to apply for the situation."[59]

Having obtained work with a desirable employer, workers formed bonds of personal loyalty. During the Civil War W. H. Blake turned down an excellent job offer from the Cranes because "Mr. Swain's help has most all left him, and he is in such a hurry that it would not be right to leave him under such circumstances." Some years later H. D. Cone's employees lent him money and went without wages when he found himself in difficult economic straits. Like the individualization of protest, workers' decisions to confer favors suggest their sense of equality. An incident reported in the *Valley Gleaner* dramatizes their positive assertion of equality albeit within the limitations imposed by differences in wealth and power. On the

[58] "Salesmen, Crane & Co., 1845–1857," CMF, 4/2/48; letters to Byron Weston, 1867, BWP, 4/29/67.

[59] "Employment, 1866–1878," CMF, 4/11/68, 10/17/72, and passim; "Charles H. Groesbeck," interview typescript, CMF, p. 1. The percentage of workers at one mill who shared a surname with at least one other co-worker was 53 percent before mechanization (1820–34), 64 percent during mechanization (1834–48), and 57 percent after mechanization (1863–76). Anecdotal evidence suggests that this rough measure of kinship does not overstate the commonness of workers with family members in paper making. McGaw, "Sources and Impact," pp. 355–58.

last Saturday in 1864, each hand working for Elizur Smith "lugged a fat goose home on his shoulder," representing about $500 expended by Smith. About a month later Smith's male employees responded by presenting him with a forty-five-piece tea service valued at nearly $500. Female employees contributed an additional $100 in presents and Smith, in turn, entertained his workers at an oyster supper, complete with music for dancing. Although the paternalism of the industry is apparent in Smith's behavior, the reciprocity implied by male workers' roughly equal expenditure is also clear.[60]

As superintendents assumed routine management responsibilities in many mills, their personalities also influenced workers' assessments of desirable situations. In 1868 John Wolfinger, Thomas Ray, George Dunn, and other workers at Smith's Columbia Mill addressed their superintendent, Frank Hollister:

> We the operatives of the above mill herewith present you with the following articles, viz.: one set of harness, also one lap robe, fly-sheet and whip, which you will please accept as a token of our respect and esteem, and as an acknowledgement of the uprightness and impartiality which in the discharge of your numerous duties you have ever manifested toward us.

Hollister replied:

> Please accept my sincere thanks for your very valuable presents. I esteem them highly for their practical worth, but *more especially* as an indication of your kind feelings towards me. Hoping that we may continue to pull true together in the same *harness*, with the *robe* of forebearance lined with good will for our mutual comfort, and the *sheet* of charity to keep off the flies of envy and discontent, and that we may need no *whip* to urge us forward but that of desire to please our employers; and finally wishing you one and all a full measure of health, wealth, and happiness. I remain
>
>   Your Friend

Hollister had received a $200 gold watch from the Smith Paper Co. the previous year, but in this instance, as in the many reported cases of workers' gifts to departing superintendents, employees symbolized their ability also to reward a superintendent who worked alongside them and treated them equitably. As noted earlier, workers

---

[60] "Employment, 1844–1865," CMF, 2/24/64; "Henry D. Cone," p. 5; *VG*, 1865.

were as capable of punishing a superintendent through diminished effort at their tasks.[61]

With mill productivity depending greatly on workers' efforts, their capacity to quit gave them their most effective bargaining chip, especially during the years of mechanization, when skilled paper makers were in short supply. After mechanization some men remained in a position to punish employers by withdrawing their skills. For example, in 1872 engineer Walter R. Brooks promised to bring to the Cranes the Hudson Paper Company's booming bank note business because "the mode of preparing and using the stock and chemicals is unknown to this Co., nor do I propose to give them the information as this is part of my trade." Job turnover rates suggest that large numbers of workers used this individualized strategy to improve their circumstances or protest unsatisfactory conditions. Crane & Co. time books show average tenure of twenty-three and a half months for male workers in an unmechanized mill (1821–34) falling to less than thirteen months during the years of rapid mechanization and rapid industrial growth (1834–48). As the industry consolidated after mechanization (1863–76) workmen may have had fewer chances to move locally, but they still averaged only sixteen months on the job.[62]

As discussed earlier, some of this turnover was occasioned by owners and by conditions over which neither workers nor owners had control, but newspapers, letters, and memoirs depict many workers moving on by choice. In addition to increasing the demand for paper workers, the growing number of paper mills in Berkshire County made changing jobs relatively easy. By 1848, for example, workers at the Cranes' mill had a choice of five mills within walking distance. Names of Crane workmen show up even in the fragmentary records preserved for other contemporary Dalton paper companies, suggesting that many moved without uprooting their families or disrupting social ties. The attraction of nearby mills is also revealed by contrast with L. L. Brown & Co. time book data showing workmen averaging nearly twenty months on the job between 1850 and 1865. During half this period Adams had only one paper mill, and for the remainder both mills were owned by L. L. Brown, so

[61] *VG*, 5/21/68, p. 2; 1/3/67, p. 2 and passim.

[62] "Employment, 1866–1878," CMF, 3/26/72; Crane Time Books, CA. The total number of months each worker was employed during each period has been used in computing average (mean) length of time worked, even if the worker's time was scattered throughout the period in single-month spans.

that workers' greater persistence on the job probably reflects their more limited alternatives.[63]

Geography also made travel and communication easier between Dalton and southern Berkshire paper-making centers than between Adams and other county paper mill towns. Lee applicants figured especially prominently among those writing to Byron Weston and the Cranes. Likewise, the *Valley Gleaner* frequently noticed with regret the movement of "enterprising young men" from Lee paper mills to mills in other southern Berkshire towns. After the Civil War, the emerging Holyoke paper industry evidently compensated for more modest Berkshire paper industry growth and helped keep turnover rates high. The *Valley Gleaner* especially lamented the lure of Holyoke, reporting the loss within a single month of four local workers to the Connecticut River valley industry.[64]

Although the *Gleaner* emphasized the improved circumstances of those who moved on—higher pay, better housing, supervisory positions, shares in the company—high levels of turnover actually resulted from workers pursuing varied options and encountering diverse outcomes, choices and circumstances as disparate as the workers themselves. Not all workers wanted to move; some who left to advance themselves were disappointed and returned; and some were lured away by noneconomic rewards. Such diversity makes generalization hazardous but suggests that most workers spent little time bemoaning their diminished prospects for Berkshire paper mill ownership. Rather, they retained their optimism because they inhabited a world in which other places promised to be better, or at least significantly different; in which hiring was informal enough

[63] Ledger of the Aetna, Housatonic, and Defiance Mill, 1839–47, BWP; "T. G. & W. W. Carson, 1844–1845," CMF; Carson & Brown Ledger, 1849–53, CA; L. L. Brown & Co. Time Book, 1850–61, LLBP; L. L. Brown & Co. Time Book, 1861–65, LLBP.

Because the L. L. Brown data covers an additional year's time, intermittent workers may have been able to average slightly more time, but hardly enough to account for the considerable differences in longevity between Dalton and Adams mill workers. In addition to having fewer nearby paper mills, access to French Canadian institutions (see n. 12 and also Chapter 8) in Adams probably discouraged some of L. L. Brown's workers from moving to other mill towns. Higher rates of persistence among L. L. Brown's workers also suggest that, unlike French Canadians in textile mill communities such as Whitinsville and Manchester, French Canadians in Adams did not have an exceptionally high turnover because of the ease with which they could return to Quebec. Navin, *Whitin Machine*, p. 161; Tamara K. Hareven, "Family Time and Industrial Time: Family and Work in a Planned Corporation Town, 1900–1924," *JUH* 1 (May 1975):373.

[64] *VG*, 3/18/69, p. 2; 4/8/69, p. 2 and passim.

and skill sufficiently general that men could envision alternative careers, even after working in a paper mill for some years; in which the increasing stability of the local industry and simple beauty of the Berkshire landscape offered opportunities for security and contentment. In sum, we cannot measure nineteenth-century workers' achievements simply through quantitative social mobility estimates without showing much less imagination than they displayed.[65]

Quantitative evidence does indicate that job security appealed to a growing number of workers. At Crane's mill the most persistent 10 percent of the work force accounted for increasing percentages of total employee work time. They put in 44 percent of total months worked between 1820 and 1834; 48 percent between 1834 and 1848; and 53 percent from 1863 to 1876. The mill's employment grew over the same years, so that these figures reflect increasing numbers of steady workmen as well as longer average tenure by those who chose to stay. These men are easy for the historian to lose sight of amidst the far larger number who came and went, but from their contemporaries' perspective their regular presence in the mills and mill towns must have made them seem most representative. Their considerable experience probably meant that they performed even larger percentages of the mill's work and earned most of the promotions and pay increases. Of course, successfully becoming a long-term employee depended on choosing a successful employer, another way in which workers' informal networks paid off.[66]

Judging from letters of job applicants, workers' sense of particular places as desirable homes complemented the rewards of steady employment and helped keep men on the job. Despite mill towns' growth, Berkshire County remained a distinctively beautiful place, and workers could not have been immune to the nearby scenery, which excited the imaginations of contemporary residents Nathaniel Hawthorne, Herman Melville, and Edith Wharton. Unlike literary men and women, workers expressed preferences for particular places cryptically, but many letters treated location as an important consideration. R. J. Woods wrote from East Lee: "I want to get me a Home somewhere that I can have steady employment but not here. Dalton is on the railroad. I rather like the place." Charles Symons applied from Washington, D.C., explaining, "i wish to get a more

[65] Howard P. Chudacoff, "Mobility Studies at a Crossroads," *Reviews in American History* 2 (June 1974):185 and passim; Clyde and Sally Griffen, *Natives and Newcomers: The Ordering of Opportunity in Nineteenth-Century Poughkeepsie* (Cambridge, Mass., 1978), pp. 32–49.

[66] Crane Time Books, CA. See n. 62.

Settled Place for my family than this is." Other men mentioned job offers in Pennsylvania and Delaware, but wanted to stay in New England rather than "move my family such a distance."[67]

Families were not only cumbersome to move, but also forged ties in the mill towns that could be hard to break. Given the identification of women with home, family, and church in nineteenth-century American culture, many workers probably had wives who discouraged mobility. Writing from Lancaster, a woman who signed herself Chloe appealed to Byron Weston to reemploy her husband because

> I am home sick and want to go back to Dalton, this may seem foolish to you, but the ways of the people are so different here, and everything seems so strange to me that I cannot feel at home. I have endeavored to over come it, but as I was never away from home and friends before, had no idea how I should feel.

She especially missed "the dear old Church." Similarly, James Pecoy wrote from Cleveland that he had "left Mr. Weston's mill last spring my health was so poor. I thought it would be better for me out west. I have been tough & well. I like it well here but my family wants to go back."[68]

By contrast, at least a few men continued the preindustrial paper makers' practice of tramping, wandering from mill to mill, working briefly, and then moving on. For example, George Irwin, appropriately nicknamed "Legs," worked for the Smith Paper Company but must have arrived with no intention of remaining. His career had begun in Steubenville, Ohio, and carried him through thirty-two jobs in thirteen states. He also returned to several mills at widely separated intervals. That workers writing to the Cranes in the 1870s referred to the "disagreeable practice of tramping" or preferred to "write for a chance than to tramp and spend my money" indicates that tramping remained an option, but one whose liabilities had become apparent to those not infected with wanderlust. Like Nosey Hill, some men may have moved frequently to evade responsibility for their actions or debts, rather than in search of greener pastures. For example, clever deception paved the exit of "a man employed in Smith Paper Company's Housatonic Mill [who] on Tuesday night

[67] "Employment, 1879–1886," CMF, 10/23/85, 5/21/85; "Employment, 1844–1865," CMF, 12/5/53, 12/21/63.

[68] Letters to Byron Weston, 1871, BWP, 1/28/71; "Employment, 1879–1886," CMF, 7/22/79. With Congregational churches rare outside New England, missing "the dear old church" may have been a common experience.

. . . excused himself from labor for the next day, and at night being called upon to see if he was ready to resume work, said he was 'troubled with piles, and couldn't go.' Thursday morning developed the fact that he had been *piling* his household goods and with his family he had decamped."[69]

For workers interested in travel, Berkshire's ties with American centers of international trade offered a few exotic paper-making jobs. In 1867 Boston paper merchants Hooper, Lewis & Co. requested Crane & Co.'s help in finding a "man who is practically acquainted with making such collar paper as you make . . . to go to France and show them how to make it for our Company in Paris." Several years later Lee paper worker Thomas Bottomly received transportation, a liberal salary, and the promise of part ownership in exchange for building and superintending a paper mill in Japan, where abundant bamboo and cheap labor encouraged several New York investors to anticipate large profits.[70]

More common were workers who headed west in search of opportunity, perhaps heeding the advice of Horace Greeley, who delivered lectures on "Self-made Men" and the American West in Lee, Great Barrington, North Adams, and Pittsfield. For some of these men, remote, newly settled communities appeared promising sites for new paper mills, offering protected markets similar to the Berkshire market Zenas Crane had initially tapped. Thus, as early as 1840 Oliver Morris Butler left his job in South Lee for Saint Charles, Illinois, where he became one of that state's pioneer paper makers. During the same decade L. M. Crane commented that workers were leaving for Wisconsin, soon to become an important paper-making region, and former Crane operative C. S. Lambdin reported news of his Wheeling paper mill. Closer to home, Pennsylvania and New York provided some workers with chances at ownership. After the Civil War, workmen willing to take risks in exchange for the independence of proprietorship sought opportunity farther afield. C. S. Lambdin moved to Alabama and Lee paper worker John W. Bliss, after gaining experience as a Colbrook, Connecticut, mill owner, proceeded west to New York, Indiana, Ohio, Nebraska, Kansas, and Michigan.[71]

[69] "George 'legs' Irwin," *SF* 4 (March 1930):8; "Employment, 1866–1878," CMF, 7/13/77, 9/30/75. The sense of nostalgia permeating the Nosey Hill tales suggests that the practice of tramping became increasingly rare in the late nineteenth century.

[70] File 331, CMF, 7/24/67; *VG*, 2/27/73, p. 2.

[71] *VG*, 11/29/60, p. 2; 12/20/60, p. 2; "Pioneer Paper Manufacturers of Illinois," *SF* 5 (April 1932):1; File 446, CMF, 6/9/48; File 327, CMF, 11/9/49, 9/18/52; "Charles Smith West," p. 9; "John W. Bliss," *SF* 4 (February 1931):8.

Equally peripatetic were members of the O'Neil family, who carried paper making to the West Coast. Four O'Neil brothers worked in various local mills, including the family's marginal Monterey establishment, which failed in 1866. Thereafter, Frank O'Neil surveyed railroad routes in New York, labored as a carpenter and store clerk in Lee, and worked as a builder in North Adams, putting aside money that enabled him to lease a Middleburg, New York, mill with his brothers Edward and John. Failing there, Frank returned to Lee, where he earned enough as a rag merchant to finance a trip to California. Initial jobs laying and repairing telegraph lines and building windmill frames allowed him to save enough money to build a modest paper mill. Brother Edward came west to join him, and together they ran one of the state's first paper mills at Soquel, where they made cheap paper by purchasing straw from local wheat growers. Later, when fruit cultivation supplanted wheat farming, the brothers followed the grainfields north to Lebanon, Oregon, and established another early West Coast mill.[72]

Like Frank O'Neil, many Berkshire paper workers did not consider paper mill employment their only career option. Garry Van Bergan used his paper mill experience and Berkshire connections to become a rag dealer, and Cyrus W. Field parlayed similar assets into a spectacular career as a New York paper merchant. Nor were paper workmen limited to closely related occupations. After eight years working for Zenas Crane, twenty-year-old William Renne learned salesmanship vending neck stocks in Pittsfield, then turned to the lucrative field of patent medicine, growing rich on "Renne's Pain-Killing Magic Oil," which he distributed throughout the nation. By contrast, John Carty found himself "destitute of funds" in 1856 and applied to the sons of his former employer for work, but could report that his years as a seaman had taken him "to several parts of the world since I saw you."[73]

Finally, farming remained a viable alternative for male paper workers who, unlike urban laborers, earned enough to afford the costs of farm making and lived in communities where they could acquire agricultural experience. Most workers had gardens and a few were more heavily engaged in agriculture, including Elisha Van

[72] "The Autobiography of Frank O'Neil," SF 2 (September 1928):9–10; "The O'Neils," p. 8; "Employment, 1844–1865," CMF, 10/3/50; "Employment, 1866–1878," CMF, 2/3/77.

[73] Byron Weston Letter Book, 1867–68, BWP, 4/2/68; Carter, Cyrus Field; Child, Gazeteer, part 1, p. 85; File 332, CMF, 2/27/73; "Employment, 1844–1865," CMF, 3/20/56.

Bergan, an extensive dealer in "fancy stock," and John Verran, who harvested forty bushels of potatoes and more than enough apples to supply his family for a year. The shift to full-time farming evidently disagreed with machine tender Ezekiel Smith, for he resold the Lee farm he and his father-in-law had purchased and returned to the mills tending P. C. Baird's new machine. A Mr. Merryman found farming more to his taste. He disappeared from mill records, and former co-worker C. S. Lambdin reported, "he & Family are all in good Health[,] have 190 Acres good Ohio River Bottom Land & all well pleased." For others, paper-making skills afforded insurance against the risks of agriculture. Thus, in 1877 Mrs. P. S. Dusenberg wrote to the Cranes and explained:

> I don't know as you remember us. Mr. Dusenburg work for you 10 years a go. we have been west where the Grasshoppers are so bad we can't live there such hard times. he wants to know if you will give him work in the mill. I come east 2 months ago. I work in you Brother's mill. it would be a great favor if you would give us work.[74]

ALL TOLD, the costs and benefits of mechanization to workers were numerous and incommensurable. There is no objective way to calculate whether they finally profited or lost. By 1885 paper workers clearly had less power and wealth than successful mill owners and ran more risk of injury, while working longer and more intensely than had their predecessors. They had also become more specialized and less likely to become independent proprietors. But each skilled paper-making employee had experienced promotion from a less remunerative and responsible job and a number could expect to become superintendents. While working with machines they had retained, and probably enhanced, their pride in, skill at, and control over their work. Most could supply their families with more material comforts than could their predecessors and, if they chose, more security.

Given the workers' increasingly diverse ethnicity, religious beliefs, skills, and backgrounds, during the years of mechanization each must have struck the balance of his experiences with the paper industry rather differently. A few could recall earlier American paper making and compare their work to it, but the many newcom-

---

[74] DuBois, *Autobiography*, p. 79; "George C. Maynard," interview typescript, CMF, p. 3; *VG*, 10/29/57, p. 2; 10/16/73, p. 2; 1/22/74, p. 2; File 317, CMF, 7/13/48; "Employment, 1866–1878," CMF, 9/22/77.

ers—immigrants, farmers' sons, and men trained in trades not confined to paper mills—brought to the industry new and various standards of comparison. The emotive content of their assessments must have been even more personalized. Publicly the workmen expressed little discontent. Insofar as public culture molded private reflection, optimism and a sense of personal responsibility were encouraged by political rhetoric emphasizing progress and individualism, evangelical sermons and reform tracts stressing private morality as the key to individual and social salvation, and sex role stereotypes attributing activity to men and passivity to women. But whether in private workers chose to credit or blame their own decisions, their families, the mill owners, or the nation's economic system for their self-estimated success or failure was ultimately a matter of temperament.

I am inclined to believe that, favored by growing numbers and greater local longevity, workers who valued security and pride in a job well done came to exert far greater influence in Berkshire mill towns than those who valued power or affluence. Their expertise with machines, preference for sobriety, and rough sense of equality with the owners left them with few regrets over industrialization and few grievances that they could not express openly. For those anxious to risk seeking greater independence or adventure, the mill doors swung both ways and opened on a variety of paths. Such was not the case for their female co-workers. Their tale remains to be told.

CHAPTER 10

"MERE COGS TO THE WHEELS": FEMALE PAPER WORKERS AND THE "SEPARATE SPHERE," 1827–1885

In late January 1851, Herman Melville drove his sleigh from his Pittsfield farmhouse to the Old Red Mill in neighboring Dalton. He returned home with a load of paper and with vivid mental images of paper-making machinery and female paper workers. Using these materials, he constructed a tale depicting the impoverished, unnatural lives of contemporary men and women who inhabited separate sexual spheres. Entitled "The Paradise of Bachelors and the Tartarus of Maids," the story especially evokes the deprivation and exploitation of women in industrializing America. Most important for our purposes, Melville's imagery portrays the restrictive feminine sphere as inextricably linked to mechanization. Surveying female paper workers and paper machinery, the tale's narrator immediately concludes, "Machinery—that vaunted slave of humanity— here stood menially served by human beings. . . . The girls did not so much seem accessory wheels to the general machinery as mere cogs to the wheels."[1]

[1] Jay Leyda, *The Melville Log: A Documentary Life of Herman Melville, 1819–1891* (New York, 1951), p. 403; Melville, "Tartarus," p. 221 and passim. Melville's deliberate alteration of what he must have observed underscores the impression that he sought to emphasize woman's role in industrialization and to equate paper mill women's work with women's employment generally. Although his description of the paper mill and its machinery is essentially accurate, he excluded all male paper workers and their jobs. He also clearly based his description of his narrator's route to the mill on the road connecting Adams with North Adams, a textile manufacturing center, rather than on the road he took from Pittsfield to Dalton. (Compare Melville, "Tartarus," pp. 215–17, with Washington Gladden, *From the Hub to the Hudson with Sketches of Nature, History and Industry in Northwestern Massachusetts* (Greenfield, Mass., 1870), pp. 135–36.) Combined with the deliberate implication that paper mill women, like textile mill women, were machine tenders, the author's choice of setting implies that he meant his tale to convey a critique of the treatment of the period's well-known female textile mill employees as well as of the more general exploitation of women in industrializing America. As usual, Melville has a number of other themes at work in

My investigation of female paper workers and their work finds Melville's portrait essentially accurate. The women who labored in Berkshire paper mills *were* confined to a separate sphere; they acted within and reacted to a system of beliefs that made their work and lives increasingly different from men's. Mechanization both fostered the conviction that women had unique and limited roles and was abetted by that conviction. One of Melville's phrases, "mere cogs to the wheels," is a particularly apt metaphor for woman's role in industrialization. Like cogs, women's tasks when viewed in isolation appear insignificant, little changed despite the rapid mechanization of paper making. But viewing women as separate was and is deceptive. Attached to the wheel of mechanization, these feminine cogs enabled the wheel to function as it could not otherwise have done.

Melville, too, perceived the "separate sphere" as deceptive social myth. Having previously noted the wrinkled faces of some female workers, the narrator questions the proprietor's reference to "our girls": "Why is it, sir, that in most factories, female operatives, of whatever age, are indiscriminately called girls, never women?" By scrutinizing paper mill women, I find similar anomalies, women whose existence contemporary rhetoric denied. Paper mills employed many married women, widows, and separated or deserted wives. Such women contributed disproportionately to the mechanization of the paper industry, because they brought their skills to paper making as their best available option. Their history illustrates the dilemmas many female employees experienced in an era that taught its women to expect homebound lives but forced many to seek employment.[2]

---

the same tale. See Marvin Fischer, "Melville's 'Tartarus': The Deflowering of New England," *AQ* (Spring 1971):79–100; Leon Howard, *Herman Melville: A Biography* (Berkeley, 1967), p. 218.

[2] Melville, "Tartarus," p. 228. Briefly stated, the doctrine of separate spheres involved sharpened distinctions between appropriate male behavior and appropriate female behavior, distinctions that were linked to assumptions about men's and women's essential character and to sex-appropriate spheres of activity. It specified that woman's place was in the home and man's place was at work. Women belonged at home because they were naturally emotional, passive, and moral, whereas men were inherently insensitive, aggressive, and inclined to pursue self-interest and, thus, destined for the world of work. Activities that went on inside the home were not deemed work because they were performed out of love rather than for money and because they were simply extensions of woman's role as mother. In sum, "working woman" became a self-contradictory phrase. The only acceptable feminine activities derived from woman's natural roles as wife and mother, so that housework, teaching, nursing, and other permissible women's activities were considered acts of love and nurture, rather than vital economic contributions. Theologians, physicians, and scien-

The beliefs about and characteristics of women, women's work, and "woman's place" that figure prominently in the following pages were not unique to Berkshire County or to paper mills, but were common throughout industrializing America. Like Melville, therefore, I focus on female paper mill workers, but I consider them significant as dramatic exemplars of nineteenth-century woman's status and function. To establish the larger significance of their story, I necessarily allude to women at home and in other industries. Likewise, the roles of women in paper mills both reinforced and were reinforced by the similar roles of women laboring elsewhere, so that some discussion of women outside paper mills is essential to explaining woman's place in paper making.

In each section of this chapter, then, I consider female paper workers in some detail and consider briefly the general situation of their female contemporaries. I first survey the jobs women held in industrializing paper mills and find them significant in their broad similarity to the tasks assigned most nineteenth-century American women. I next consider how paper mill women's work contributed to mechanization and to the nineteenth century's heightened sense of woman's distinctiveness, contributions abetted by the social fiction that woman's place was in the home. Finally, I examine the discrepancy between the general belief that women belonged at home and the reality that many women, including wives and mothers, labored in paper mills, disclosing the high price some American women paid to reconcile social fiction with social fact.

"MERE COGS"

Turning our attention from male to female paper workers, we seem to enter another world, a world cut off from the dynamic arena where male workers and owners wrestled with the problems and opportunities of mechanization. In 1885 most women working in paper factories performed tasks identical to those of women in preindustrial paper mills, and the few who tended machines did

tists buttressed these sharp role distinctions by attributing them to God and nature.

The literature on the doctrine of separate spheres is substantial and growing. The best general discussion of early nineteenth-century developments is Nancy F. Cott, *The Bonds of Womanhood: "Woman's Sphere" in New England, 1780–1835* (New Haven, 1977). Two "classic" statements are Barbara Welter, "The Cult of True Womanhood: 1820–1860," in *Dimity Convictions: The American Woman in the Nineteenth Century* (Athens, Ohio, 1976), pp. 21–41; and Gerda Lerner, "The Lady and the Mill Girl: Changes in the Status of Women in the Age of Jackson," in Jean E. Friedman and William G. Shade, eds., *Our American Sisters: Women in American Life and Thought* (Boston, 1976), pp. 120–32.

essentially similar work, seated alongside the mill's smallest and least efficient mechanisms. Women continued to earn far less than men and encountered few of the novel risks and arduous conditions associated with men's mechanized work. For most, apparently, labor outside the home continued to be a transitory stage, peripheral to the domestic and maternal vocations that earned them social approbation. All told, outward appearances imply that earlier notions of women's work exerted such profound influence as to preclude technological change making any significant difference where female paper workers were concerned.

As in preindustrial paper mills, most women could be found laboring in the predominantly female rag rooms and finishing rooms of mechanized mills. The largest number still worked at rag processing, where they either sorted rags by color, fabric, and condition or cut them to open seams, remove fasteners and damaged portions, and reduce the rags to small, uniform squares. Mechanization altered only the number of workers and the distribution of rag room work. The development of more standardized rag grades reduced the relative demand for sorters, especially in fine paper mills. Simultaneously, mechanized mills' greatly augmented fiber consumption made more work for cutters, an increase offset only belatedly and partially by the use of mechanical rag cutters and non-rag fiber.[3]

For most of the nineteenth century, rag rooms remained technologically primitive. Rag sorting involved manual manipulation and visual discrimination, just as it had in Zenas Crane's mill. Rag cutters employed the same simple hand tools as women had used in Berkshire's original mill. Melville has left us a graphic account of these women's tools and tasks. In the rag room there "stood rows of girls. Before each was vertically thrust up a long, glittering scythe. . . . The curve of the scythe, and its having no snath to it, made it look exactly like a sword. To and fro, across the sharp edge, the girls forever dragged long strips of rags, washed white, picked from baskets at one side; thus ripping asunder every seam, and converting the tatters almost into lint. . . . [Occasionally] the girls, dropping their rags, plied each a whetstone up and down the swordblade."[4]

[3] Green, *Holyoke*, p. 101; L. L. Brown & Co. Time Book, 1850–61, LLBP; L. L. Brown & Co. Time Book, 1861–65, LLBP; Crane & Co. Time Book, 1863–76, CA; "Employment" Files, CMF. Relevant technological developments are discussed in Chapter 7.

[4] Melville, "Tartarus," pp. 222–24. Chapter 2 discusses preindustrial rag room work.

Fig. 10.1 Female rag cutters and rag sorters. Equipped with the same technology Melville had described years earlier, women cut rags, protecting their hair, but not their lungs, from the lint. Note the male rag room boss (*center*). Courtesy of the Crane Museum.

Nor did mechanization alter the pace of women's rag room work. Because mill owners depended on women's care in sorting and cutting rags for their paper's quality, they did not press for greater individual output. The women worked under a modified piece-rate system in which they cut or sorted a specified number of pounds to earn a day's pay and received added compensation for "over work." Expected productivity depended on the quality of the rags and did not increase with mechanization. In 1833, for example, Zenas Crane listed the quantities of rags to be dressed as follows:

50 lbs.	No. [1] Rags
55 lbs.	fine foreins [sic]
85 lbs.	No. 2 & L[ight] Blues
130 lbs.	Course [sic] prints
140 lbs.	Deep Blues & Blacks

Forty years later at Crane & Co.'s fine paper mill, where women worked exclusively with fine white rags, rag cutters had a sixty-

pound standard, but received a day's credit for thirty-four to sev-
enty-one pounds. Moreover, when the women encountered unusual difficulties the superintendent noted in the time book,
"Threads very bad to dress," and gave the "girls" credit for smaller
amounts. Sorters put less labor into each pound and routinely
scanned the work of about eight cutters.[5]

Likewise, most finishing room women performed manual labor
requiring considerable care and received a day's wages for producing the same output as had women in preindustrial mills. As discussed in Chapter 8, after 1860 finishing rooms especially characterized fine paper mills. Because fine paper mills promised their
customers perfect paper, sorting occupied the largest number of female finishers. Although mechanization multiplied the amount of
paper to be scanned, the process of looking over both sides of each
sheet could not be hastened. Like the rag room, then, the finishing
room simply hired more female paper sorters. As in the rag room,
expected productivity varied with the product's quality. Crane &
Co. required sorters to survey about the same number of reams in
1870 as in 1833, varying from four or five reams of large, meticu-
lously sorted bank note paper to more than twenty reams of smaller
letter paper, which warranted only cursory scanning.[6]

Tedious but unhurried manual labor also engaged most other
finishing room women. Female workers continued to count paper
by hand, a task unchanged by mechanization save for there being
more paper to count and more women busily counting it. As with
other feminine tasks, quantitative standards derived from qualitative concerns. At Crane & Co.'s Government Mill, which made currency, bond, and bank note paper, counts had to be precise and verified by a second counter. There, an average pair of female counters
turned out forty thousand sheets per day. Counts of letter and
ledger paper could be less accurate and need not be verified, so that
each worker had sole responsibility for somewhat more paper. Finishing room women also folded paper by hand, using wooden
blocks as guides. Like other traditional feminine tasks, the work required dexterity and care, but not long training.[7]

[5] L. L. Brown & Co. Daybook, 1853–54, LLBP; Zenas Crane Time Book, 1809–36,
CA, 8/1/33; Crane & Co. Time Book, 1863–76, CA, 1/70–10/72; "Alfred Hoxie," interview typescript, CMF, p. 2.

[6] Zenas Crane Time Book, 1809–36, CA, 8/1/33; Crane & Co. Time Book, 1863–
76, CA, endsheet.

[7] Snell, "Government Paper Making," CMF, p. 5; Brown & Weston Letter Book,
1864–65, BWP, passim; "Thomas J. Bolton," interview typescript, CMF, p. 4; "Miss
Alice Lyman," interview typescript," CMF, p. 1.

Fig. 10.2 Female paper sorters. Seated near the windows for the best light, most female finishers scanned sheet after sheet of paper. Courtesy of the Crane Museum.

The same attributes characterized the few new jobs women performed around machines. As noted earlier, men adjusted and maintained finishing room machines. Women simply sat alongside the mechanisms, feeding in paper or withdrawing the finished product. Most of these women—those tending platers, calenders, and ruling machines—worked in pairs, one woman placing paper in the machine and the other removing it. Perhaps, as Melville described, they obtained "some small variety to the monotony" by occasionally changing places. Smaller stamping and envelope machines required only one attendant, each generally working beside similarly employed women. Apparently, as mechanization created new jobs, owners simply assigned women to those that resembled traditional women's work: those that were monotonous and interruptible, requiring neither long training nor initiative.[8]

The few short-lived jobs women performed in the machine room

<hr />

[8] Brown & Weston Letter Book, 1865–66, BWP; Brown & Weston Letter Book, 1863–64, BWP; Byron Weston Letter Book, 1867, BWP; "Charles H. Groesbeck," interview typescript, CMF, p. 5; "Miss Alice Lyman," interview typescript, CMF, p. 1; Melville, "Tartarus," p. 221. See also Chapters 2 and 9.

Fig. 10.3 Calender "girls" and calenders. Feeding paper into and removing it from calenders required some skill, but male finishers were on hand to adjust the machines. Courtesy of the Crane Museum.

conform to the same pattern. Before mechanical layboys were perfected, women tended the cutter end of the machine, removing and stacking the sheets by hand. Such work must have appeared perfectly appropriate to women who had performed and continued to perform the same tasks in dry lofts. As long as loft drying persisted, women continued the traditional, repetitive work of hanging sheets to dry and jogging dry stacks to even the edges.[9]

The relative uniformity of women's paper mill jobs is confirmed by their letters of application. They were much less likely than men to request a particular job or to cite their prior experience. Reflecting the limited training required, a few mentioned their lack of paper mill experience, in sharp contrast to male applicants. Owners' letters offering women employment also depict women's tasks as interchangeable. Byron Weston, for example, offered Mary and

[9] Crane & Co. Time Book, 1863–76, CA, 10/66–12/66; L. L. Brown & Co. Time Book, 1850–61, LLBP; L. L. Brown & Co. Time Book, 1861–65, LLBP; Zenas Crane Journal, 1840–, CA; "Automatic Layboy, 1849–1858," CMF; "John E. Mulchaey," p. 5; "Paper Making in Monterey, Mass.," p. 2; "Thomas J. Bolton," interview typescript, CMF, p. 4; Brown & Weston Letter Book, 1864–65, BWP; "Miss Alice Lyman," interview typescript, CMF, p. 1.

Sarah Hall work on the calender and the ruling machine, but noted, "We think we can keep you busy at the work we name but want to feel at liberty to ask you to change to other work when we have not enough of the kind you work at generally." Similarly, he told Lydia Smith, "We will give you a good chance, either at finishing & stamping, on the calender or ruling machine. We want you as an extra hand & to do anything in the finishing room. . . ."[10]

Profound continuity despite mechanization also characterized female paper workers' wages, hours, and working conditions. Women continued to earn substantially less than their male co-workers and to lack the unskilled man's expectation of acquiring skills that commanded considerably higher incomes. When compared to Table 9.7, Table 10.1 reveals both women's lower wages and the relatively uniform incomes associated with their relatively uniform jobs. Statewide data collected in 1885 make the same point. They show 70 percent of paper mill women earning less than $6 a week, whereas only 5 percent of male paper workers earned so little. The majority of men earned $6 to $10 a week, but almost as many, 43 percent, earned more than $10. By contrast, only 1 percent of the women earned more than $10, probably by far exceeding standard piecework requirements.[11]

At the same time, because women's work was not tied to the pace of the machine, women's hours, unlike men's did not increase, come to require shift or night work, or lose their earlier flexibility. Most women routinely accomplished one and a half times the required

TABLE 10.1
WEEKLY WAGES OF MASSACHUSETTS PAPER MILL WOMEN, 1860–78

Job	1860 Wages	1872 Wages	1878 Wages	% Increase
Finisher	$3.92	$6.93	$5.27	34
Cutter	3.40	5.33	5.00	47
Rag sorter	3.27	4.00	4.53	39

SOURCE: *Tenth Annual Report of the Bureau of Statistics of Labor* (Boston, 1879), p. 74.

[10] "Employment" Files, CMF; Brown & Weston Letter Book, 1865–66, BWP, 11/1/65, 2/16/66.

[11] *Massachusetts Census of Manufactures, 1885*, 2:1113–25.

The addition of new male paper mill occupations makes comparison of long-term changes in the relative wages of men and women difficult. If women's wages are compared with those of machine tenders and beater engineers, jobs most analogous to preindustrial male paper workers' jobs, women's wages remained about one-half to one-third of men's, as in the preindustrial era.

day's work so that some came to work fewer than the traditional eleven hours even in the early years of mechanization, when female workers were greatly in demand. Most Berkshire paper mill women obtained a ten-hour day long before an 1874 Massachusetts legislative decree mandated a ten-hour limit for female employees. In fact, state commissioners studying the problem in 1865 found that women at the Hurlbut Paper Company worked only nine hours. Thereafter, Saturday work gradually declined to a half day. By 1885 one-quarter of the state's paper mills assured all female workers less than ten hours daily. Some women further curtailed their work hours by taking advantage of the piecework system. In the 1880s married women left Crane's mill two hours early.[12]

Likewise, women's working conditions remained much like those of preindustrial workers. Separated from the mill's heavy machinery, they worked in comparative quiet, permitting conversation to relieve the tedium of their work. Moreover, unlike men's increasingly solitary jobs, all women worked in groups, in pairs, or alongside other women, so that conversation remained possible. Their separate workrooms kept women away from most new workplace hazards. Men suffered nearly seven times the reported injuries and all but one of the fatalities. And of the few accidents involving women, nearly half occurred when women ventured out of their workrooms and came too close to revolving shafts.[13]

This is not to say that women's work entailed no risks, only that the dangers changed little with mechanization and either remained invisible to contemporaries or were deemed too trivial to report. As Melville observed, "The [rag room] air swam with fine, poisonous particles, which from all sides darted, subtilely, as motes in sunbeams, into the lungs." In addition to risking respiratory disease, at least two women apparently contracted smallpox from infected rags before mills began providing vaccination. Rag room women, especially newcomers, must have cut their hands; paper cuts were certainly ubiquitous among finishing room workers; and long-time paper sorters sometimes snapped tendons after years of rotating their wrists through the same motion. Mechanization increased the num-

---

[12] "Thomas J. Bolton," interview typescript, CMF, p. 2; "Miss Alice Lyman," interview typescript, CMF, p. 4; Green, *Holyoke*, p. 199; "Alfred Hoxie," interview typescript, CMF, pp. 2–3; "Charles H. Groesbeck," interview typescript, CMF, p. 4; L. L. Brown & Co. Daybook, 1853–54, LLBP; Crane & Co. Time Book, 1863–76, CA; First Commission on Hours, MA, Box 1, File 9; *Tenth Annual Report of the BSL*, p. 153; *Massachusetts Census of Manufactures, 1885*, 2:1134–35.

[13] *VG*, 1857–71, passim.

ber of women at risk, but may have decreased the percentage seriously affected because women, like men, worked shorter average stints in mechanized mills.[14]

As in preindustrial mills, women's tenure in mechanized mills was briefer than men's suggesting that women continued to give employment a secondary place in their lives. Census takers in 1880 compiled substantial evidence that women worked temporarily, before marriage, and near home. The preponderant female worker was young, single, and lived under parental supervision. Girls under the age of twenty-one made up 41 percent of the mills' female work force, 64 percent of the women remained unmarried, and 46 percent lived with one or both parents. Time book data during the years of mechanization substantiate the impression that most women viewed their work as temporary. At Crane's mill single women averaged less than a year's employment between 1834 and 1848, and only slightly over a year between 1863 and 1876. Single females put in slightly longer average stints at L. L. Brown's mill, but there, too, they were the mill's least persistent workers.[15]

These characteristics of paper mill women and their work typify the vast majority of nineteenth-century women, whose history is "a tale of continuity despite superficial change." For virtually all wage-earning women, "sex-segregated labor markets, the assumption that female workers are transient, and the persistence of lower pay for women encouraged the conceputalization of 'women's work' according to preexisting sex-role stereotypes and permitted the continued employment of women in less mechanized or industrialized occupations. . . . Even when machines or the emergence of new industries created apparently novel jobs, employers consistently assigned women to jobs that were relatively monotonous and did not

[14] Melville, "Tartarus," pp. 222–23; *VG*, 8/24/65, p. 2; Frank J. Kelly to author, July 1977; File 335, CMF, 1/24/82; File 374, CMF, 4/1/82; "Alfred Hoxie," interview typescript, CMF, p. 9; Irving Hughes, tour of Bay State Mill, Dalton, Mass., October 13, 1976.

[15] Data derive from the 1880 Federal Manuscript Census and company time books. See Table 10.2 and 10.10 for fuller information.

Amidst these apparent continuities, one gradual change in the female work force was the withdrawal of members of the emerging middle class. By mid-century, in accord with the doctrine of separate spheres, mill owners' wives and daughters no longer worked in paper mills, a contrast with the practices of the preindustrial era. Weston ("Paper Making," p. 9) mentions that in the early years of the Benton and Garfield partnership (the mid-1830s), both men's wives worked in the mill to help out, but Weston's own wife mentions the mill in her diary only as a place where she took the children to be weighed. McGaw, "Sources and Impact," p. 350, offers evidence that by the 1880s mill work was a last resort for middle-class women.

call for rapt attention, were interruptible and easily resumed, and were not visibly hazardous," jobs like those of preindustrial women. Moreover, the characteristics of female employees' tasks made their work essentially the same as that of the majority of nineteenth-century women: wives and mothers performing housework. In fact, the largest groups of female employees labored as domestic servants and needlewomen, performing tasks identical to those of unpaid wives and mothers.[16]

The striking absence of mechanization from homes and most other feminized workplaces underscores the uniformity of women's work throughout industrializing America. That women usually performed unmechanized work encouraged demeaning generalizations in the mechanically innovative nineteenth century. Contrasting apparent continuities in women's manual labor with dramatic changes in men's mechanized jobs, contemporaries readily concluded that God or nature had assigned women their work and that society could not or should not alter it. Such assertions minimized the novel functions of women's traditional tasks in their new technological context, obscuring women's contributions to mechanization. Placing women in technological history requires that we set their work in the context of technological innovation.

"Cogs to the Wheels"

Paper mills provide a valuable perspective on the role of women's work in a mechanizing society because rag rooms and finishing rooms were visibly connected to the sites of men's technologically innovative work, unlike contemporary homes, laundresses' kitchens, seamstresses' garrets, and most other feminized work locales. Contrasts between men's and women's work in paper mills reveal why women retained their traditional tasks and how those tasks contributed to mechanization. Whereas machines took over craftsmen's skilled occupations in paper mills, women's apparently simpler jobs proved difficult or impossible to mechanize. Yet women's unmechanized work compensated for and abetted mechanization; it assured machine-made paper a market by maintaining its quality. As a result, mechanizing mills grew increasingly dependent on their female employees. Moreover, by remaining relatively unspecialized, female workers gave mill owners considerable flexibility in their employment, a valuable asset as the employment of specialized male

[16] Judith A. McGaw, "Women and the History of American Technology: Review Essay," *Signs* 7 (Summer 1982):804–5 and passim.

workers and expensive paper-making machines reduced flexibility elsewhere in the mills.

Nonetheless, woman's traditional, quality-oriented, unspecialized work earned diminished recognition as Americans came to value progress, quantitative increases in productivity, and specialized skills. The sharpened contrasts between men's and women's paper mill work strengthened traditional assumptions that women lacked skill and did not deserve high wages, beliefs reinforced by women's analogous activities in homes and other feminized work sites. As men grew less experienced in comparable work, employers and supervisors readily accepted that women's skills and financial needs were inferior to men's and greatly benefited from their society's elaboration of those beliefs. Judging from paper mills, then, it appears no coincidence that the doctrine of separate spheres emerged to minimize women's skills and economic importance at the very time that mechanization actually made their work more critical. The obvious serviceability in paper mills of new beliefs about women helps identify women's substantial contributions to industrial mechanization through their labor in the more separate feminine sphere: the home.

Women continued to perform their traditional preindustrial tasks in mechanized paper mills primarily because, as discussed in Chapters 4 and 6, machine builders did not and probably could not devise commercially viable mechanical alternatives. In particular, the sorting of rags and the inspection of finished paper entailed visual discrimination not replicable by machines and only partially superseded in twentieth-century mills by electronic scanning devices. Similarly, although machines were devised to reduce rags to relatively uniform pieces, mechanical rag cutters could not open seams, remove fasteners, or eliminate damaged portions, tasks for which female rag cutters relied on their eyes as well as their hands.[17]

Women's work around finishing room machines underscores the limitations of nineteenth-century mechanization. Although machines successfully imitated the manual labor of ruling or stamping, the precise placement of sheet after sheet of paper, a task involving hand-eye coordination, evidently eluded consistent mechanical replication. Judging from the substantial costs attributable to paper broken or damaged by finishing room machines, the capacity to handle dry paper without wrinkling or tearing some sheets also proved difficult to build into machines. This accounts for women's

[17] The technological and economic limits to innovation in rag cutting and other feminine paper mill activities mentioned below are discussed in Chapters 4, 6, and 7.

retention to remove paper from machines, feed it into calenders, fold it manually, and even its edges after stacking it. Likewise, while it is possible to conceive of mechanical paper counters, it is hard to imagine a machine operating much more rapidly than hand counters but not damaging sheets so as to require further sorting. Only modern electronic technology has produced such an efficient mechanism, suggesting that the hand-eye coordination character- izing the female paper counter's work had no acceptable mechanical analog.[18]

Evidently, then, mechanizing women's work either proved im- possible or remained difficult to accomplish without producing an inferior product. The belated and uneven adoption of technologies that eliminated some women's work—rag cutters, machine dryers for sized paper, and non-rag fiber—reflected similar reluctance to produce paper of markedly lower quality, especially in fine paper mills. As noted in Chapter 6, innovations that adversely affected the product's quality were largely confined to mills manufacturing pa- per for new markets, such as the mass-circulation dailies whose re- liance on cheap paper made them willing to accept paper that fell farther and farther below traditional standards.

Women's irreplaceable contribution to product quality increased female workers' importance to mechanizing paper mills, an impor- tance reflected in increased female employment. As noted earlier, employers recognized the association of women's work with quality when they maintained traditional piecework requirements for women, in marked contrast to the pressure for greater output that accompanied the mechanization of men's work. The resulting growth in number and percentage of employed women appears in Table 9.1. In fact, these figures understate female paper processors' growing prominence, because all women worked at making paper, whereas growing proportions of male workers held non-paper- making jobs. In addition, the women who worked in mechanized paper mills had come to work year-round so that each processed more paper annually than had the seasonal employees of preindus- trial paper mills. Women's diminished statistical prominence after 1865 reflected some mill owners' decisions to specialize in inferior products.[19]

Recalling the market that underwrote paper mill mechanization makes clear the critical role of female workers. Paper mills mecha- nized to supply the New York market, which offered mill owners opportunities to sell larger quantities of finer paper, principally

[18] See n. 17 and also Chapter 8.   [19] See Chapter 3.

ledger, letter, bond, and bank note paper required by New York businessmen. Thus, mechanization initially proved successful only because it was accomplished without apparent product deterioration. Female employees, who kept the quality of raw materials high, applied finishes that enhanced quality, and removed inferior sheets before shipment, assumed principal responsibility for maintaining traditional standards. After mechanization, the prolonged search for an acceptable alternative fiber shows that even after reduced paper prices created new markets, markets associated with mass journalism and dime novels, customers still maintained standards below which paper manufacturers could not risk falling. Thus, even mills that came to produce cheap wood-pulp-based printing paper employed some women to prepare the rags that kept the paper's quality acceptable and to give the final product a cursory scanning.[20]

In helping to establish and maintain the quality of machine-made goods, paper mill women performed an essential function, one shared by women in other mechanizing industries. Without these women's labors, mechanization might well have been delayed or prolonged by more limited markets for the machines' augmented output. This is not to dispute the general contention that Americans mechanized more readily than the English because Americans more readily accepted inferior machine-made commodities. It is certainly conceivable that, given paper mills' reliance on business markets, maintaining traditional standards figured more prominently in the paper industry than in industries producing consumer goods. But quality is relative, not absolute. Like late nineteenth-century newsprint mills, all industries encountered some market-imposed standards of acceptable product quality and these standards probably declined only gradually as mechanization progressively opened new markets by lowering prices. The role of paper mill women, therefore, suggests that nineteenth-century female industrial employees, although disproportionately concentrated in unmechanized finishing and inspection jobs, made a substantial contribution to mechanization, and one that has been minimized by simply comparing the American emphasis on price and quantity to the British concern with quality. By performing unimpressive manual operations, women successfully enforced standards and applied finishing touches that maintained and created markets for the products of mechanized industry.[21]

Women also helped mill owners adjust output to the unpredicta-

---

[20] See Chapters 3, 5, and 7.

[21] McGaw, "Women and the History of American Technology," p. 808; Nathan Ro-

Fig. 10.4 Work force at the Cranes' Bay State Mill, 1885. Women, whose work maintained product quality, continued to predominate in fine paper mills' work forces. Courtesy of the Crane Museum.

ble fluctuations of nineteenth-century markets, for demand was fickle as well as selective. Publishers and paper wholesalers could not usually predict customer response to new commodities such as specialized periodicals, books by American authors, or tinted stationery. In filling rush orders, coping with the business cycle, and tailoring production to meet varying demand for various products, mill owners could rely on the willingness and ability of their female workers to alter their tasks and modify their work schedules. Initially, flexible female workers especially helped unspecialized mills balance out finishing work that varied with the product. Later,

senberg, *Technology and American Economic Growth* (White Plains, N.Y., 1972), pp. 43–51; Cochran, *Frontiers of Change*, p. 12.

Like other aspects of woman's role in industrialization, the increasingly feminized role of consumer has received very little attention from historians of technology. See Judith A. McGaw, " 'Woman's Place' in the Industrial Revolution: Some Thoughts on the 'Separate Sphere' and Technological Change" (paper presented in the Humanities Seminar Series, West Virginia University, 2/2/84).

women's flexibility continued to be an asset because it compensated in part for the specialization and inflexible schedules of men and machines.[22]

As noted above, employers sought women who would "work at anything in the finishing room" so as to keep them fully employed when demand flagged for the products of one specialized machine. Unlike men, women were expected to move back and forth between various tasks no matter how long they had been employed. For example, Alice Lyman, who worked in the rag room, in the loft, and at various finishing tasks before settling into calender work, reported that she "sorted at times when there wasn't enough calender work" throughout her more than fifty-three years in Dalton paper mills. Finishers also varied considerably in the overtime credits they earned, suggesting that opportunities for increased income varied from task to task as demand dictated. Rag room women had less reason to change tasks, but their average "over work" fluctuated erratically from month to month, indicating that many responded to unpredictable demand by modifying their hours. Variation among workers in overtime shows that, when available, extra work was optional. Some women evidently valued overtime opportunities and considered them when selecting employment, for Byron Weston took care to tell Lydia Smith, "We will pay you $5.00 pr. week; and at present there is all the over work any of the girls want."[23]

As new technology came to require periodic shutdowns for repairs and maintenance, employers could also more readily reduce female than male employment, thus helping to lower the costs associated with unpredictable technology. When mills stopped for repairs, female workers were simply told to stay home, sometimes for weeks at a time, whereas male employees continued to work and receive wages. Routine maintenance also curtailed women's employment. For example, rag room women at L. L. Brown's mill lost two days in May 1858 while other workers were "Washing up for Spring."[24]

Mill owners' flexibility in their employment of women reflected the comparative ease with which women learned paper mill work

[22] Mary Kelley, *Private Woman, Public Stage*, pp. 3–27; Mott, *American Journalism*; Mott, *History of Magazines*; see also Chapter 6.

[23] Brown & Weston Letter Book, 1864–65, BWP, 6/12/65; "Miss Alice Lyman," interview typescript, CMF, p. 1; L. L. Brown Daybook, 1853–54, LLBP; Crane and L. L. Brown Time Books; Brown & Weston Letter Book, 1865–66, BWP, 2/16/66.

[24] Zenas Crane Time Book, 1809–36, CA, 5/35, 10/35; Zenas Crane Time Book, 1836–48, CA, 8/41, 9/41; L. L. Brown Time Book, 1850–61, LLBP, 5/58, 11/60.

and transferred their skills from one mill to another. Employers revealed their expectation that almost any woman could do the work by issuing frequent general newspaper advertisements for female workers, whereas they relied almost exclusively on informal informational networks to select appropriately skilled men. The rag room work and paper sorting that engaged most female laborers was also the work most quickly mastered. Of the seventy women's jobs advertised in the *Valley Gleaner* from 1860 through 1874, fifty-six fell into these categories, and none of these advertisements cited skill or experience as a requirement. A few finishing room tasks involved somewhat more training, thus a few advertisements and workers' letters of application mentioned experience. But women mastered even these jobs with relative ease, allowing mill owners to make do with inexperienced women. For example, calender work took the longest to learn, but when Crane & Co. sought an experienced woman, Ballston Spa mill superintendent Fred Thompson found that the only skilled woman available was a widow who anticipated child-care problems if she moved to Dalton. Rather than offer the widow special inducements to come, as owners often did for male workers, Thompson suggested, "There is lots of Yankee girls about here—but none at liberty that understands the Callenders but it would not take very long to learn on Collar Paper—so I think perhaps it would be better to send you a girl than the widow."[25]

Women also adjusted quickly to differences between mills, whereas even highly skilled men needed time to acquire familiarity with the idiosyncrasies of individual paper-making machines and rag engines. As a result, mill owners could meet short-term demand for female workers through arrangements with fellow manufacturers. Crane family correspondence frequently mentions "girls" sent from Dalton to the New York state mills operated by Crane and Laflin family members, or women brought to Dalton from New York state. Similarly, Byron Weston inquired of May & Rogers: "Can you send us a good girl finisher & one paper sorter for 2 or 3 weeks? Three of our girls are out, sick, & the work is getting very much behind." Evidently the practice was common, for Weston promised, "If you can send only the finisher & will do it we will try & reciprocate." He sent similar requests to Carson Brothers, Platner & Smith, and the Union Paper Company. Such work, at employers' convenience, contributed to single women's brief average tenure, especially during the early years of mechanization, when mill owners coped with very unpredictable markets. For example, Weston was "very

[25] *VG*, 1860–74, passim; "Employment" Files, CMF; File 330, CMF, 3/8/66.

much obliged for the favor" when Sarah Hall filled in for three days on his ruling machine. She had evidently come some distance, for Weston supplied temporary boardinghouse accommodations.[26]

The ease with which large numbers of women learned paper-making tasks, exchanged one task for another, and adjusted to different mills helped confirm the impression conveyed by emergent differences between men's and women's work: that women's work was unskilled, natural, and God-given. From the mill owners' perspective the work was justly designated "unskilled" because it required little mill training and no formal education. Yet the evidence that machines could not replicate women's work and that mill owners benefited from the relatively low wages such work commanded should caution us not to accept at face value mill owners' assessments of their female employees' skills. Comparison of women's "unskilled" paper mill work with women's domestic labor indicates that housework, a new nineteenth-century feminine occupation, ensured all women substantial training in useful manufacturing skills and served to minimize the value of those skills.

As we have seen, female paper workers, like most female employees, performed tasks that required care and attentiveness, despite the monotony of the work. Had their attention lapsed frequently, they would not have fulfilled their function: maintaining quality. Yet the work itself had so little inherent interest that constant alertness must have been difficult to maintain. Indeed, the only apparent stimulation women experienced on the job came from their simultaneous conversation with other women. It seems likely, then, that conversation not only made the work bearable, but also contributed to alert workmanship. One twentieth-century superintendent acknowledged as much when he concluded from an attempt to employ male paper sorters that men could not do the job because they could not work fast enough while talking.[27]

There is little evidence that the ability to talk while performing monotonous work resides in a sex-linked gene, but there is abundant evidence that women, especially nineteenth-century women, acquired the ability through their socially prescribed preparation for housework. The availability of cheap commercial goods had modified domestic labor so that only women performed household work and they each spent more time doing repetitive tasks that required precise movements or visual discrimination, including sew-

[26] Files 330, 448, 496, CMF; Brown & Weston Letter Book, 1864–65, BWP, 6/5/65, 6/9/65, 6/10/65 (two letters), 6/12/65, 7/4/65.

[27] Ralph Kendall, interview and tour of Bay State Mill, July 17, 1975.

ing, cleaning, and laundering. Housewives also devoted increased attention to child care and meal preparation, particularly baking, work that required only intermittent physical intervention and was performed while simultaneously carrying on the monotonous tasks that took up most time. Thus, as girls and women mastered housework, they learned to keep their eyes and hands on their work while keeping their minds on the angel food cake in the oven or on the children playing nearby. Women likewise acquired the ability to listen to children and servants and to issue advice, instructions, or reprimands without interrupting the progress of their needles or dust rags. In sum, housework trained virtually all women in the skills paper mills required, making potential workers plentiful.[28]

The relative maturity of the paper mill work force supports this interpretation. Young girls, those least likely to have mastered housework, were comparatively rare in paper mills. Girls younger than sixteen comprised nearly 20 percent of female textile mill employees, but only 10 percent of female paper mill employees. This meant that in Berkshire County girls with limited housekeeping experience were hired to tend textile mill machinery more than four times more often than they were hired to do unmechanized paper mill work. Furthermore, of the few young girls who did work in paper mills, many had maternal supervision, much as they would have in their housekeeping apprenticeships. More than one-third worked with their mothers. At least one girl, Addie M. Beale, had learned from experience that paper mill work required maturity. Applying to the Cranes in 1878, she explained, "I would like very much to get a place in the Finishen room as I have worked there before and as I am older than I was then perhaps I could do better than I did then."[29]

[28] Ruth Schwartz Cowan, *More Work for Mother: The Ironies of Household Technology from the Open Hearth to the Microwave* (New York, 1983), pp. 16–68. McGaw, "Women and the History of American Technology," pp. 813–19, discusses other scholarship that supports these generalizations.

There is, of course, some evidence that females' earlier maturation results in biologically based superiority in verbal skills. At the same time, however, mothers clearly verbalize more frequently to female than to male infants long before sex differences in verbal behavior manifest themselves, making the separation of biological and social factors difficult. In any case, neither biological predisposition nor early socialization would account fully for the skills women brought to the workplace. For an introduction to some of these issues, see Ashton Barfield, "Biological Influences on Sex Differences in Behavior," and Vivien Steward, "Social Influences on Sex Differences in Behavior," in Michael S. Teitelbaum, ed., *Sex Differences: Social and Biological Perspectives* (Garden City, N.Y., 1976), pp. 62–121, 138–74; Nancy M. Henley, "Psychology and Gender: Review Essay," *Signs* 11 (Autumn 1985):106–11.

[29] For data on workers' ages and on mothers working with daughters see Tables

While women were taking on housework, changes in men's work made housekeeping skills less likely to receive recognition or reward. Most obviously, men increasingly earned wages or profits for their labors, while housewives theoretically labored for love, a form of remuneration that discouraged women from realistically assessing their skills or bargaining for better pay. At the same time, men's labor drew them from the home, so that men had less reason to understand and appreciate women's skills. Men no longer experienced the demands of simultaneously working and supervising their sons. Their long hours in the workplace decreased their awareness of their daughters' gradual mastery of domestic labor and of the skills their wives brought to the household. And their growing involvement with mechanization and quantitative increases in productivity no doubt gave them less sensitivity to the qualitative improvements in home life attributable to women's work.[30]

As industrialization proceeded, then, the doctrine of separate spheres proved serviceable and received confirmation. The delegation of housework to women prepared most women to do the tasks industry asked of them, made feminine skills so common that increased industrial demand did not create scarcities, and left both men and women ill-prepared to value working women's skills. Simultaneously, increased industrial demand for traditional women's work kept most employed at tasks so similar to domestic activities that women's jobs reinforced the belief in woman's distinctive natural abilities. This left only one potentially troublesome social question: Why were women in factories if their place was in the home?

"INDISCRIMINATELY CALLED GIRLS"

Most nineteenth-century Americans had ample reason to believe and act on the belief that "woman's place is in the home." Mill owners profited from the training homes supplied and could justify low wages and periodic unemployment for women by presuming that they all had homes in which they belonged, homes supported by men. Male workers, who now spent long hours in separate workplaces, could not perform household duties and had great incentive to support wives who kept house, made most household purchases, and supervised the children. As documented in the previous chap-

---

10.2 and 10.9. Seven mothers each supervised two young daughters. On family decisions and work opportunities that shaped young women's employment see McGaw, " 'A Good Place to Work,' " pp. 227–48; File 333, CMF, 1/7/78.

[30] Cowan, *More Work for Mother*, pp. 16-68.

ter, most male paper workers exercised this option. Meanwhile, the vast majority of nineteenth-century women chose to marry, and when compared to the jobs open to most women, they must have found housework the most varied and interesting career available. At the same time, the majority of employed women labored in domestic settings at domestic tasks, generally left their jobs upon marriage, and probably valued their homes more and tolerated housework more readily after their tedious work experiences.[31]

The characteristics and experiences of most female factory workers also confirmed the precedence of the home in women's lives. The largest group of Berkshire County's female paper workers entered employment when old enough to have acquired domestic skills, but young enough to expect marriage to terminate the brief period they spent contributing to family income and supplying themselves with finery. The numerous female employees of local woolen and cotton mills were even more likely to be young, single, and living at home. Observing the typical female factory employee, contemporaries readily labeled them "mill girls," a phrase that succinctly reconciled woman's appearance in industry with the conviction that her place was in the home by characterizing all mill women as young, unmarried, temporary employees.[32]

While not manifestly at variance with what most people observed or experienced, the phrase "mill girl" was, as Melville recognized, an indiscriminate one. It denied the existence of women whom we know to have worked in paper mills, women such as the Ballston Spa widow, whose maternal responsibilities precluded her taking a job she preferred, and women such as Alice Lyman, who never married and worked in paper mills most of her life. These women were casualties of the doctrine of separate spheres. They labored because men could not or would not support them, but earned wages predicated on the assumption of paternal or husbandly support. Their histories deserve particular attention because they document potential risks all women incurred.

[31] McGaw, "Women and the History of American Technology," p. 816; Kelley, *Private Woman, Public Stage*, p. 34; Leslie Woodcock Tentler, *Wage-Earning Women: Industrial Work and Family Life in the United States, 1900–1930* (New York, 1979), passim.

[32] Lerner, "The Lady and the Mill Girl," suggests the pervasiveness of this stereotype among feminists as well as among other nineteenth-century Americans. Most evidence on how workers spent their wages comes from the antebellum era, when owners maintained company stores. Computer-assisted analysis of purchases recorded in Crane daybooks indicates that single female employees often retained a substantial portion of their earnings. For examples of their purchases of finery, see McGaw, "Sources and Impact," pp. 335–36.

In Berkshire County women forced to labor at girls' wages chose paper mill work disproportionately. Thus, the study of female paper workers reveals many of those who had most reason to doubt that woman had her place in the home and shows how they accommodated themselves to the social order by entering paper mills, how paper mills helped allay potentially troublesome social questions. By providing such women with relatively safe, flexibly scheduled, socially acceptable work, paper mill owners served the women by giving them a measure of choice, served society by hiding the misfits among the mill girls, and served themselves by obtaining reliable long-term employees.

In contrast to local textile mill employees, substantial minorities of paper mill women had found that they could not remain in the home or expect men to support them (see Table 10.2). By 1880, although the largest number of female paper workers lived at home with one or both parents, the majority did not. Female household heads comprised 12 percent of the work force, wives of household heads 18 percent, women residing with nonrelatives made up 16 percent, and those living with extended family members, 8 percent. While the majority remained single, more than one-third had married. Over two-fifths had passed the age of twenty-five, hardly girls whatever their household or marital status.[33]

Nor could local citizens dismiss these anomalous women as

[33] Here and elsewhere my comparison of paper mill women with textile mill women reflects the fact that cotton, woolen, and paper mills employed the vast majority of Berkshire County's female nondomestic workers. The only other significant employer was the shoe and boot industry, which hired only 210 women, according to the 1880 census of manufactures. This much smaller group of women was concentrated in four factories and in the northern part of the county, so the industry was neither a major local employer of women nor a viable choice for most central and southern Berkshire women.

My discussion of paper mill women, textile mill women, and their households is based on data derived from a computer-assisted analysis of the 1880 Federal Manuscript Population Schedules for Berkshire County. I included all households sending any workers into paper mills and all households sending female workers into textile mills. I also analyzed households including female teachers. For a discussion that gives more attention to single female employees, see McGaw, " 'A Good Place to Work,' " pp. 227–48.

I selected the 1880 census as the most complete in its documentation of household members' characteristics. Less thorough analysis of paper workers and their households listed in earlier federal manuscript population censuses and of paper workers treated in published Massachusetts census reports suggests that 1880 data are broadly representative of paper workers for the period from 1850 through 1885. For some evidence from the 1870 federal manuscript census see McGaw, "Technological Change and Women's Work," pp. 90–92.

TABLE 10.2
HOUSEHOLD STATUS, MARITAL STATUS, AGE, AND
PARENTAGE OF PAPER, COTTON, AND WOOLEN
MILL WOMEN, BERKSHIRE COUNTY, 1880

	Paper Mill	Cotton Mill	Woolen Mill
Number	829	1,222	751
Female household head or wife of household head	30%	8%	10%
Daughter at home	46	76	71
Resides outside nuclear family	24	17	19
Single	64	86	85
Married	24	10	11
Widowed or divorced	12	3	3
Under 16	10	22	17
16–20	29	39	40
21–25	17	20	19
26–40	23	15	18
Over 40	19	4	4
Native parentage	26	13	7
Foreign parentage	70	81	86
Mixed parentage	4	5	7

NOTE: All figures have been rounded so that totals for each of the four sets of characteristics may equal more or less than 100 percent. Missing data have been deleted prior to calculations. Relationship to household head data are missing for one cotton worker, marital status data for one paper worker, and parentage data for one paper worker, one woolen worker, and five cotton workers. For Lambda$_b$ values see Table 10.6. For each set of characteristics, differences between paper workers and cotton workers, and between paper workers and woolen workers, are significant at the .001 level (Chi square).

temporary exceptions, immigrant women not yet Americanized. Female paper workers more frequently came from native households than did textile mill women. Moreover, female paper workers of Irish parentage conformed most closely to the mill girl stereotype. Working women with native-born parents more often were widows (15 percent) or boarded with nonrelatives (27 percent), whereas only 38 percent lived at home with their parents. French Canadian women also departed from the norm; nearly half had been married.[34]

[34] Four hundred thirty-one female paper workers were of Irish parentage and ninety-four were of French Canadian parentage. Of the French Canadians, 47.8 percent were listed as married, widowed, or divorced. Most of these French Canadian

Married, widowed, or separated female employees especially suffered from social assumptions that made women exclusively responsible for housekeeping and child care, and set low wages for women. Thus, few simply opted to work outside the home. Rather, they found themselves in the work force primarily because of risks inherent in the doctrine of separate spheres. Like most nineteenth-century women, their ability to remain at home had depended on their husbands' longevity, faithfulness, and employment, factors over which they had little control. As Table 10.3 indicates, most wives and former wives sought employment because their husbands had not conformed to the stereotype of the reliable breadwinner. More than one-quarter of the wives lived with men who had no jobs or men who earned low wages as common laborers. Among female heads of households, more than three-quarters were widows and more than one-fifth had been deserted or had chosen to separate.[35]

Voluntary separation probably occurred rarely and only after severe abuse, for it imposed special burdens. Mrs. L. B. Chaffee implied as much when she wrote asking for a job so as to be able to support her child. Evidently her husband had abused others besides herself for she "had herd the reson why you did not hire me was on account of Mr. Chaffee" and explained, "that nead not make any diffrence to you fore we are to diffrence Peopel now." She appealed to the Cranes a second time because she lived in rural Windsor, which offered little work for women, and she preferred Dalton "where my Brother is fore he alwas stands by me and wants me to come there to live if I can." Less fortunate in family support, but probably more typical in her situation, was Mrs. Eroosbeck, for whom a female neighbor requested work. It remains unclear whether the husband of this "very worthy meathodist woman" had died or deserted her, but it is clear that she found herself destitute and with two children to support. Left without financial resources, she had survived only because "the neighbors have helped her thus far."[36]

---

women were wives of household heads (28.7 percent) or lived with extended family members. Relatively few (9.6 percent) headed their own households. Further discussion of ethnic differences in local women's employment appears in McGaw, " 'A Good Place to Work,' " pp. 240–41 and passim.

[35] Husbands heading households have been considered common laborers if they listed themselves in the census as "laborer" or "farm laborer."

[36] "Employment, 1878–1886," CMF, 3/15/86; "Employment, 1848–1865," CMF, 11/16/65. See Chapter 8 for further evidence that women did not readily separate from their husbands, even after prolonged abuse.

Hereinafter, I generally refer to the married, widowed, and separated as "wives and widows." Although, properly speaking, separated and deserted women were still

TABLE 10.3

INCENTIVES TO EMPLOYMENT AMONG WIVES AND
FEMALE HOUSEHOLD HEADS, 1880

	Wives	Female Household Heads
Number	*150*	*89*
Husband absent, unemployed, or common laborer	25.3%	100%
No children	22.7	15.7
5 or more children at home	19.3	16.8
Co-resident dependent relative	13.3	11.2
Child over 15 at home or unemployed	3.3	9.0
Child over 15 in school	5.3	5.6

NOTE: Because my interest here is in household responsibilities prompting work or affecting work, I have included in the category Wives only those married women who resided in households headed by their husbands (18 percent of the female paper mill work force). Nineteen other married women workers headed households from which their husbands were absent. They have been included in the Female House-hold Heads category. Most of the remaining married women lived in households headed by their fathers or fathers-in-law and a few boarded, thus most were young women working to earn enough to establish their own households. For similar rea-sons I have excluded from the data on female heads of household the nine female household heads who were single. One female heading a household had no marital status attributed to her, but was old enough to have been married and to have had children who had left home. She has been included in my calculations. Except where noted, the same groups of women appear in all of the following tables.

Motherhood, another part of women's lives over which they had limited control, also structured the work decisions of most married or formerly married women. Motherhood provided the strongest rationale for women remaining in the home and made working out-side the home more difficult so that women felt freest to enter the mills when they had no children or after all their children had left home. Wives, who averaged thirty-seven years of age, as compared to forty-seven for female household heads, more frequently la-bored prior to motherhood, helping to furnish new households and expecting to retire when they began having children. A few never

---

wives, their situation generally resembled that of the widows with whom they are grouped as female household heads. In 1850 some deserted wives indicated their sense of kinship with those whose husbands had died by listing themselves as "Cali-fornia widow," a reference to the departure of some men to seek their fortune in the gold rush.

conceived or lost their first child. In a society where women were valued and valued themselves as mothers, depression could afflict the childless woman or grieving mother and neighbors or relatives sometimes "thought [it] best for her to go to work in the mill . . . in order to occupy her mind." A few abandoned wives may also have been deserted by their children or had them taken away. Such was probably the case for Mrs. Ellen Kneiderhoff, better known by her maiden name, Ellen Dorcey, a forty-five-year-old woman who lived alone and worked in the Smith Paper Company's Housatonic Mill. Dorcey could easily have been deemed an unfit mother after she grew "addicted to the use of liquor," an addiction that caused her solitary death when her lamp set fire to the bed on which she had evidently passed out.[37]

For the women who bore them, children might prove a mixed blessing and motherhood sometimes meant that woman's place was in the mill. A number gave birth to more children than their husbands could support, an incentive to employment confirmed by the substantial percentage of employed wives who had five or more children in the household. Women with five or more children but no husbands simply felt compelled to enter the work force. In such households the only mothers who remained at home and sent their children to work in paper mills were those with at least two children over eighteen. Moreover, a woman's brood did not always mature and leave the nest. A few mothers labored to support unemployed adult sons or grown daughters who remained idle. Mothers also chose to work rather than remove their children, especially their sons, from school and send them to work. Although daughters reaped some of the benefits conferred by working mothers, they also often labored to help their brothers. Thus, when compared to textile mill women's households, households including one or more female paper workers kept many more sons and slightly more daughters in school. Female paper workers enabled nearly half (49.2 percent) of the sons in their households to attend school, while

[37] On the possibilities and problems of nineteenth-century family limitation, see Linda Gordon, *Woman's Body, Woman's Right* (New York, 1977), pp. 47–115. *VG*, 2/13/62, p. 2; 9/24/68, p. 2. The case of the woman sent to the mill to occupy her grieving mind involved a textile worker, the choice having been determined by her husband's occupation. The solution failed; she committed suicide.

As was the case for mill owners, social expectations encouraged female workers to be more secretive drinkers than male workers, but company store account books and occasional newspaper items suggest that neither occasional drinking nor alcohol abuse was confined to men. As is still the case, drunken wives such as Dorcey were probably more likely to be abandoned than were drunken husbands.

only one-seventh (14.3 percent) entered paper mills. By contrast, families of female woolen and cotton mill workers sent more sons into the textile mills (41.1 percent and 43.1 percent) than into the schools (38.5 percent and 39.4 percent). Similar but less pronounced differences existed between daughters in the various mill households. Given the demanding work women did and the low wages they commanded, it is particularly impressive that a number of wives and widows kept children over fifteen in school.[38]

The comparison with textile mill families suggests that many wives and widows took up the burden of paper mill work voluntarily, as did women who assumed financial responsibility for aged relatives, especially mothers and mothers-in-law. As society's principal caretakers, women also went to the mills to provide for grandchildren, who arrived in the arms of widowed or deserted daughters or had been left by daughters who had died. That many hard-pressed female household heads opted for such responsibilities provides eloquent testimony that women often labored in mills because they placed home and family first.[39]

To a large extent, then, wives' and widows' employment followed from their acceptance of nineteenth-century notions of woman's place. They had vowed to marry "for better or for worse" and had stayed with men who failed to provide adequately or had assumed the financial burdens left behind by departed husbands. They took their roles as mothers seriously and labored to provide their offspring with the necessities and some of the amenities of life. Such

[38] Although the categories in Table 10.3 are not mutually exclusive, wives of laborers and of unemployed men rarely had five or more children at home. Differences between paper and woolen mill households and between paper and cotton mill households in proportions of sons at school and at work are statistically significant at the .001 level (Chi square). Differences in the fate of daughters in the various households are significant at the .05 level.

[39] Dependent relatives taken in were quite a varied group. I refer specifically to aged mothers and mothers-in-law and to grandchildren related through daughters because they were most common. One other apparent pattern was women's special concern for female relatives. Almost all co-resident dependent relatives other than parents and grandchildren were female, including sisters, nieces, cousins, and aunts, as well as daughters. As with women's employment, this pattern reflects the special dilemmas posed for some women by the doctrine of separate spheres. It also reflects women's ability to recognize and respond emotionally and economically to other women's needs, a pattern captured in Carroll Smith-Rosenberg's classic article "The Female World of Love and Ritual: Relationships Between Women in Nineteenth-Century America," *Signs* 1 (Autumn 1975):1–30; and in Suzanne Lebsock, *The Free Women of Petersburg: Status and Culture in a Southern Town, 1784–1860* (New York, 1984), especially pp. 112–45.

women were unlikely to take the demands of child care and housework lightly, although the demands were often inconsistent with mill work.

Whether they chose to labor or were forced to work, almost all paper mill women who headed households or had married household heads bore the double burden imposed by the nineteenth-century delegation of housework to married women. Only one such household listed a domestic servant among its members, and only a few included female boarders who kept house or remained unemployed and might have kept house. A somewhat greater number left female family members at home, but more than four-fifths of working wives and widows had no one to perform housework while they labored in the paper mills (see Table 10.4). Even the small minority favored with someone who might complete domestic tasks probably shouldered most housework themselves; over half of their potential helpers remained younger than sixteen or had passed sixty. For example, in the Lee household headed by widowed paper worker Margret Keenan, ninety-five-year-old Sarah Sullivan listed herself as keeping house for her daughter Margret, her working grandson and his employed wife, two granddaughters who attended school, an infant great-grandson, and her grandson's hired man—a heavy load had she been half the age. Similarly, Emily Jarvis

TABLE 10.4
AVAILABILITY OF HOUSEKEEPING HELP TO WIVES AND
FEMALE HOUSEHOLD HEADS WORKING IN PAPER MILLS

	Wives	Female Household Heads
Number	150	98
Household member aged 10 or older listed as keeping house	10.7%	4.1%
Co-resident woman aged 10 or older with no occupation	9.3	10.2
No evident houseworker except employed woman	80.8	85.7

NOTE: In addition, one household included a seventy-three-year-old woman who boarded with the family and listed her occupation as "washer woman." Two other households had seven- and eight-year-old daughters who had not attended school within the year and evidently remained at home. Figures here include the nine single female household heads because they also had responsibility for housework.

labored with her husband, Charles, in an Adams paper mill, leaving her eleven-year-old daughter, Mary, to keep house; but she also left her infant and four-year-old sons with Mary, so Emily certainly faced plenty of work when she came home.[40]

Like Margret Keenan and Emily Jarvis, the vast majority of employed wives and widows had at least one child living with them, and they bore ultimate social responsibility for child care. Working wives, because they were younger, tended to have more young children. Nearly 90 percent of those with children had at least one younger than ten. Almost three-fifths of mothers who headed households also had at least one child under ten. As shown in Table 10.5, local schools provided the most common child-care solution for both groups of women. Like Margret Keenan and Emily Jarvis, smaller numbers left preschool children with adult relatives or adolescent daughters, most of them quite elderly or very young. For women who had learned to place motherhood first, all such compromises must have been emotionally taxing, and some proved devastating. For example, Mrs. William Groscher helped support her five-member household by working with her husband in an East

TABLE 10.5
CHILD CARE STRATEGIES OF WIVES AND FEMALE
HOUSEHOLD HEADS WORKING IN PAPER MILLS

	Wives	*Female Household Heads*
Number with co-resident children	*116*	75
Youngest child in school	38.8%	37.3%
Adult female at home with preschoolers	9.5	6.7
Child over 10 at home with young children	10.3	6.7
Preschool children home alone	30.2	8.0
All children over 10	11.2	41.3

NOTE: See Table 10.9 for information on adolescent daughters.

[40] Only 8.1 percent of wives and female household heads had potential helpers at home between the ages of sixteen and fifty-nine. Information on the Keenan and Jarvis households comes from the 1880 federal manuscript census schedules.

Lee paper mill. Each morning she bid goodbye to her only child, "a bright little girl, named Ida, two years and eight months old," expecting the child's grandmother and young aunt to supervise her. In the spring of 1873 Ida wandered outside, attended only by neighborhood children at play. She fell into a swollen stream and drowned. Her parents were called from the mill "to find their home stripped of its idol, and desolate." Nearly one-third of working wives and mothers evidently adopted more demanding and risky child-care strategies. Having no one to stay home with preschool children, they either deposited their children with a neighbor before going to the mill or left them unattended, perhaps living close enough to the mill that they could occasionally run home.[41]

Women with family and housekeeping responsibilities demonstrated a consistent preference for paper mill work. Table 10.6 summarizes the statistical evidence that women in charge of households, older women, and married or widowed women concentrated disproportionately in paper mills, that they did not end up there by chance. Their greater age and less dependent status placed most in a position to choose their employer; few had to defer to parents or husbands. Female household heads clearly exercised most choice,

TABLE 10.6
HOUSEHOLD STATUS, MARITAL STATUS, AND AGE
AS PREDICTORS OF BERKSHIRE
WOMEN'S INDUSTRIAL OCCUPATIONS

Lambda$_b$ with Independent Variable as:	Paper Workers vs. Cotton Workers	Paper Workers vs. Woolen Workers
Relationship to household head	.19	.20
Marital status	.15	.14
Age	.18	.14

NOTE: See Table 10.2 for numbers, percentages, and levels of statistical significance. Lambda$_b$, as noted earlier, measures our ability to predict the dependent from the independent variable on a scale from 0 to 1. In calculating Lambda$_b$, the independent variable Relationship to Household Head was broken into the categories Wife or Female Household Head, Daughter at Home, and other. Marital Status was broken into three categories: Single, Married, and Widowed or Divorced. Age was broken into eight categories: Under 16, 16–20, 21–25, 26–30, 31–35, 36–40, 41–45, and Over 45.

[41] VG, 5/15/73, p. 2.

but even wives had considerable latitude. As compared to wives working in cotton and woolen mills, who often labored in the same industry as their husbands (67.2 percent and 52.7 percent, respectively), only a minority of paper mill wives had husbands working with them (36.7 percent), so men's work decisions rarely dictated their choice of job. Nor did location limit these women's work choices. Women's letters of application show that many rural women willingly moved to obtain paper mill work and that wives sometimes determined their husbands' locational preferences. For those unable to move, almost all Berkshire towns offering factory work also supplied women with a choice among industries.[42]

The principal constraints on these women's work choices were those they had internalized, constraints that followed from their acceptance of "woman's place." Although all wives and widows entered paper mills out of economic necessity, they had not chosen the most lucrative work. Rather, they opted for paper mill jobs because the work was most compatible with domestic responsibilities. The concerns that prompted their work and made work away from home more difficult also determined their work choices.

Given the relatively low wages paid all female employees, financial considerations were usually less influential in women's work choices than in men's, but income data indicate that potential earnings played no part in wives' and widows' work choices. As com-

TABLE 10.7
AVERAGE ANNUAL WAGES OF BERKSHIRE COUNTY COTTON,
WOOLEN, AND PAPER MILL WOMEN, 1875

	Paper Mill	Cotton Mill	Woolen Mill
Number of women's wages reported	790	1133	1049
Mean wages all women	$238.13	$294.19	$272.52
Mean wages pieceworkers	$252.10	$337.15	$273.44
Proportion on piecework	29.4%	45.7%	55.0%
Proportion married	34.4%	8.7%	11.9%

NOTE: *Massachusetts Manufacturing Census, 1875.* As discussed above, female paper workers generally labored on a modified piecework basis, whereby they could earn additional "over work" pay. Evidently most were classified as day workers in the census, because they earned a standard wage if their day's output fell within an easily obtainable range.

[42] My argument here is presented more fully in McGaw, " 'A Good Place to Work,' " pp. 230–42.

pared to textile mills, paper mills offered lower annual incomes and fewer opportunities for higher piecework incomes (see Table 10.7). Indeed, Table 10.8 shows that women with the greatest household financial responsibilities concentrated in occupations promising the lowest average earnings. Even within paper mills they selected the least remunerative work: paper sorting and rag preparation. The consistent association of higher household living costs with lower annual incomes indicates that acceptance of "woman's place" created yet another double-bind for working wives and widows: the greater their family financial responsibilities, the more their household duties curtailed their ability to earn money. What we know about paper and textile mill women heading households supports the incomplete evidence on cost of living. Female textile workers heading households were twice as likely to be single, suggesting much lower living costs. And female paper workers must have had higher living costs; they headed households of five children about four times more often.[43]

TABLE 10.8
AVERAGE ANNUAL INCOME VS. COST OF LIVING,
BERKSHIRE PAPER, COTTON, AND WOOLEN MILL
WOMEN HEADING HOUSEHOLDS, 1875

	All Paper Workers	Rag Room Workers	Paper Sorters	Cotton Workers	Woolen Workers
Number reporting income	119	37	24	74	25
Average annual income	$181.46	$138.19	$163.25	$232.74	$228.92
Number reporting cost of living	74	27	12	32	14
Average annual family living costs	$231.23	$252.89	$235.08	$200.47	$168.64
Cost of living as percentage of income	127%	183%	155%	86%	74%

NOTE: *Seventh Annual Report of the Bureau of Statistics of Labor* (Boston, 1876), pp. 116–18. Data derive from individual schedules submitted to household heads who were asked to state the "Cost of supporting your family (or yourself) for the year ending May 1, 1875" (p. viii). The shortfall among paper workers between wages and living costs was evidently made up by the work of other household members (see Table 10.9). Comparison with Table 10.7 shows female household heads earning lower incomes in all industries. In the textile mills this probably reflected less regular employment and less access to better-paying jobs.

[43] According to the 1880 manuscript census, 9 percent of female paper workers

While less remunerative than textile mill work, paper mill work attracted wives and female household heads because it best suited women with children and homes to care for. Paper mill jobs offered two great advantages: flexible hours and safety. As noted earlier, most paper mill women had comparatively short hours by contemporary standards, whereas a number of textile mills employed women longer than ten hours even after legislative prohibition. Lacking housekeeping assistance, wives and widows sorely needed the extra weekday and Saturday hours that paper mills assured all female employees. By choosing to process rags or sort paper, occupations that permitted the adept worker to leave early, a woman could further shorten her hours. Women with unsupervised infants and preschool children must have willingly accepted the lower pay in order to leave work early. At least some mothers also left the rag rooms and finishing rooms several hours early so as to supervise children returning from school, a substantial boon for those with all children between the ages of five and ten, about one-seventh of working wives and widows.[44]

In addition, paper mills accommodated women whose family responsibilities occasioned periodic work interruptions. For example, Elizabeth Wharfield began working at the Cranes' mill in 1846, shortly after her daughter's birth, but left work for several months in 1848. Perhaps she lost her babysitter or her sick toddler required special motherly care. The following year Charlotte Tifeny, who had left work to be with her brother, informed the Cranes, "I would like to come back." She evidently expected reemployment for she wrote in late September and told the Cranes, "I would like an anser beefore cattle show."[45]

---

heading households were single, whereas 18 percent of female textile workers heading households were single. Among those who had married, 16 percent of paper workers headed households with five or more children, but only 4 percent of textile workers did so. On the relationship between potential income and household work decisions affecting female paper workers, see also McGaw, " 'A Good Place to Work.' "

[44] According to the *Massachusetts Manufacturing Census, 1885*, 2:1131–37, women and minors worked more than ten hours in 8 percent of woolen mills and 8 percent of cotton mills, but in no paper mills. Women worked less than ten hours in 25 percent of paper mills, but in only 1 percent of woolen mills and 1 percent of cotton mills. Of wives in paper mills, 14.7 percent of those with children had all of them in school and under the age of ten. For female household heads the percentage was 13.3.

[45] N.E.H.G.S., *Vital Records of Dalton*, p. 45; Zenas Crane Time Book, 1836–48, CA, 11/46–12/48; "Employment, 1844–1865," CMF, 9/28/49.

Married women especially availed themselves of the opportunity to leave the mills and return. Between 1863 and 1876 nearly half of the Cranes' married female employees left work for at least a month, averaging five months away before returning. Over the same period, only one-fifth of the unmarried women interrupted their employment. Recurrent work interruptions also occurred most frequently among married women. At the Cranes' mill between 1863 and 1876, married women took two or more sustained work breaks over three times more often than did single women. L. L. Brown's time book showed a similar pattern. And timekeepers' records missed additional married women who left one mill and returned to work for a different employer. For example, Mrs. Hutchens of Cheshire had worked as a paper sorter, probably for L. L. Brown, but applied to the Cranes in 1864 when she wanted renewed employment after spending "some months in taking care of a sick friend."[46]

Paper-making technology permitted women's flexible schedules. Women's shorter hours reflected the technical feasibility of ending women's workdays without shutting down the machines. Likewise, women's ability to leave and return periodically rested on the greater awareness of individual needs that a less labor-intensive industry permitted. As noted in the previous chapter, in 1880 paper mills averaged 67 workers, about half of them women. By contrast, cotton mills employed an average of 137, about half female, and woolen mills averaged 147, about two-fifths female. Merely in planning, then, paper mills had an easier time accommodating married women's special needs.[47]

The size, technology, and paternalism of paper mills assured female paper workers greater safety, something particularly precious

[46] Data on work interruptions derives from Crane and L. L. Brown time books so that "married women" have been identified by the time book designation "Mrs." Thus, widows are included. I defined a worker as interrupting her work if she disappeared from the time book for at least one calendar month but returned subsequently. Only whole months have been used in computing average length of interruption. This method minimized the risk of counting layoffs as work interruptions. "Employment, 1844–1865," CA, 1/11/64.

[47] *U.S. Census of Manufactures, 1880*, p. 255, shows females over fifteen making up 56.4 percent of the cotton mill work force and 37 percent of the woolen mill work force. Sex was not given for the 476 children working in cotton mills and the 385 children working in woolen mills, thus these percentages understate the proportion of women and girls. For paper mills 47.7 percent of the work force was composed of women over the age of fifteen. No children were enumerated. *Tenth Annual Report of the BSL* shows paper mills relatively more capital intensive than textile mills.

to women who were homemakers and mothers as well as workers. Unlike textile women, who tended machinery and risked injury and disability, paper mill women rarely lost time from household work because of job-related injuries. Paper makers' need for pure water set mill enclaves apart from the most congested sections of towns, giving women the added safety of knowing most of those they met on the street and most with whom they worked. For victims of drunken husbands or fathers, mill owners' ability to discourage drinking in these small villages may have been another important consideration.[48]

Paper mill women, especially rag processors and paper sorters, also enjoyed the protection of working in groups, discouraging unwelcome attentions from foremen. Mothers evidently took advantage of the collective organization of work to supervise and protect working daughters, easing their transition into the work force. As shown in Table 10.9, married and widowed paper workers often brought daughters to work with them. Youthful daughters especially evoked maternal concern, motivating their mothers to work. One-half to three-quarters of these mothers worked with adolescent daughters exclusively. By contrast, nearly two-thirds of female household heads sending daughters to paper mills without motherly oversight sent only daughters older than twenty. Mrs. Amy Fuller's application letter to the Cranes conveys the same sense of

TABLE 10.9

MATERNAL RESPONSIBILITY ON THE JOB: MOTHERS AND DAUGHTERS WORKING IN PAPER MILLS, 1880

	Wives	Female Household Heads
Number with co-employed daughters	42	36
One employed daughter under sixteen	35.7%	19.4%
All employed daughters under twenty	78.6%	52.8%

NOTE: Data from 1880 manuscript census schedules. The overwhelming majority of women with co-employed children had daughters working with them. An additional 2.7 percent of wives and 9.0 percent of female household heads had co-employed sons only.

[48] Beers, *County Atlas of Berkshire*; Chapter 8.

motherly concern. She wrote from Sheffield, a town thirty miles distant from Dalton, after identifying the Cranes' mill as "a good place to work" for herself and her daughters. She also specified her plans for each of her girls: "one I would like to have work in saul [finishing room] and one in the rag room with myself."[49]

In providing work suited to wives and widows with domestic responsibilities, enabling them to keep their families from destitution, paper mills helped minimize public awareness that the role prescribed for all nineteenth-century women entailed substantial hardship for a sizable minority. Mill owners also benefited; they found married or widowed women more reliable than most employees. In the years after mechanization, married women became the mills' most permanent employees (see Table 10.10). As compared to male and single female employees, their total time on the job declined least during the chaotic early years of mechanization. Thereafter, they alone achieved levels of persistence reminiscent of preindus-

TABLE 10.10
TOTAL EMPLOYMENT TENURE IN MONTHS FOR MALE,
SINGLE FEMALE, AND MARRIED FEMALE
PAPER MILL EMPLOYEES, 1821–76

	Male	Single Female	Married Female
Mean tenure at Crane Mill, 1821–34	24	19	21
Mean tenure at Crane Mill, 1834–48	13	10	15
Mean tenure at L. L. Brown Mill, 1850–65	20	18	24
Mean tenure at Crane Mill, 1863–76	16	14	19

NOTE: Longevity figures derive from Crane and L. L. Brown time books and include all months worked, but not work interruptions. As noted earlier, especially between 1834 and 1848, down time interrupted women's employment in particular. During the same years, single women sometimes interrupted their employment to work briefly for another employer. My method of calculation, counting a worker as employed if he or she worked for any portion of a month, minimizes the impact of both sorts of short-term unemployment at mill owners' behest.

[49] Data on female-headed households sending daughters into the mills derives from 1880 manuscript census schedules. Of those sending daughters to the mills, 64.7 percent sent only daughters aged twenty or older. File 326, CMF, 11/25/48.

trial levels. Dependent on women to maintain paper quality, makers
of fine paper such as the Cranes and L. L. Brown had ample incentive to welcome and accommodate working wives and widows.
Thus, even in its casualties, the doctrine of separate spheres suited
the needs of an industrializing society.

Married female paper workers were not unique in their contribution to industrialization, but they dramatize the contributions
and dilemmas of employed wives and widows because such women
congregated in Berkshire County paper mills. Elsewhere, many employed wives and widows served industry through household manufacturing, making their labors and hardships less visible. Such
women sewed shoes in eastern New England homes; made brooms,
hats, and cigars in the Connecticut River valley; manufactured garments and artificial flowers in New York City; and laundered the
heavy washloads of sooty Pittsburgh. Like mothers who worked in
paper mills, these outworkers chose work that paid quite poorly so
as to be able to fulfill family responsibilities.[50]

The virtual absence of such home-based employments in Berkshire County offers the best evidence that paper mill work filled the
same niche in the local industrial ecology. In 1865, for example,
Massachusetts state commissioners studying women's work clearly
expected to find domestic manufacture throughout the state. They
asked "particularly the wages and conditions of that large class of
female laborers, called needle-women." Berkshire respondents dismissed the question as inappropriate. One simply noted, "no needle
women," while another offered the Boston commission a fuller
sense of Berkshire's distinctive economy, writing, "We may hardly
be said to have women amongst us who depend upon the employment of the needle for support." Berkshire paper mill wives and
widows differed from needlewomen in earning more money and in
spending more time away from home, but their forced contribution
of cheap labor to American industrialization was quite similar.[51]

Thus, Berkshire's married and widowed paper mill employees
exemplify the extraordinary price many women paid to sustain the
useful doctrine of separate spheres. Laboring at the lowest wages,
they helped support poor men, young children, and dependent rel-

---

[50] McGaw, "Women and the History of American Technology," pp. 808–9, 813.

[51] First Commission on Hours, MA, Box 1, File 9, 11/8/65, 10/23/65. Fuller information was provided in the *Massachusetts Manufacturing Census, 1875*, 2:825–28.
Fifty-one Berkshire women were furnished with work at home, twenty-six by the
clothing industry and twenty-three by whip manufacturers. No other Massachusetts
county reported such modest totals. The state total was 30,916 women.

atives through seasons of economic distress, while simultaneously managing to keep house and rear children. Although only a minority of women faced these hardships at any given moment, almost all nineteenth-century women potentially shared them and many must have encountered them at some stage in their lives. Perhaps that is one reason women especially thronged the churches of industrial America; they sought reassurance that heaven rewarded those whose domestic and industrial labor fed the hungry, clothed the naked, and sheltered those needing a home. Assuredly they received little earthly reward from a society that prattled of ladies and mill girls, preferring to forget that women worked.

MELVILLE chose well when he selected a paper mill to depict the fate of women in nineteenth-century America. The role women played there dramatized the bitter irony of the "separate sphere": the very doctrine that refused to recognize women's work served admirably to supply industrializing America with cheap and essential female labor. By emphasizing "woman's place" at home, Americans prepared all women to perform the manual labor that abetted mechanization, made such work appear "natural" and "unskilled," and provided a rationale for women's low wages. Simultaneously, by employing women at traditional manual tasks, manufacturers managed to cope with their machines' limitations, to minimize the novelty of women's industrial work, and to reinforce the valuable doctrine of separate spheres. Rather than a "mere cog," the flexible and functional role assigned nineteenth-century women seems to me the most ingenious contrivance invented in industrializing America.

While there is no denying that the separate sphere resulted in women's exploitation, I find little evidence that women were its passive victims. Most men, women, and children apparently found ample reason to believe its tenets, and even its casualties were partially accommodated through jobs such as those supplied by paper mills. Nor does the evidence imply a partiarchal conspiracy. Woman's new role was built upon her traditional pursuits, which were gradually reinterpreted through contrast with men's novel mechanical and industrial work. Women helped to construct the role that gave most of them relatively rewarding work most of the time. Men's contribution generally reflected simple ignorance of what went on outside their sphere.

As was true for male workers, I see no objective way to calculate and balance women's costs and benefits during American industrialization. Their principal benefits were clearly emotional, hard to measure and harder for the historian to recapture. In most cases, I believe, society inflicted its principal costs rhetorically. It denied women recognition for their substantial contribution to industrialization, nineteenth-century America's principal accomplishment. Moreover, it accorded least recognition to those making the greatest contribution. Unfortunately, historians have too often mirrored and perpetuated that injustice. This glimpse of Berkshire paper mill women has sought to redress the balance, partly out of respect for some long-dead mill women, but mostly as their legacy to living American women who daily confront the legacy of the separate sphere.

EPILOGUE AND
CONCLUSION

A great deal of water has flowed over Berkshire paper mills dams since 1885—so much, in fact, that a persistent search turns up only a few stones along the stream banks to indicate that paper mills once flanked the Konkapot River in New Marlborough and Hop Brook in Tyringham. In Becket the Union Mill is also crumbling to ruin and in Adams one L. L. Brown mill has been razed and the other stands padlocked. Forests have overgrown many of the old southern Berkshire mill sites and again cover the central Berkshire hillsides where nineteenth-century farmers harvested steam boiler fuel and pulp wood. Most local citizens do not even know that Interlaken was once called Curtisville, much less that the village once led the nation in ground-wood-pulp manufacture.

To one acquainted with the Berkshire paper industry's nineteenth-century history, most twentieth-century developments appear almost as predictable as the slow disintegration of the abandoned dams and the gradual regrowth of the woodland. The use of wood pulp, initiated in the wake of mechanization, has become so pervasive that "rag" now designates a comparatively unusual paper. New technologies, especially chemical pulping methods, have figured prominently in the change. Like the earlier use of paper makers' chemicals, the use of soda, sulfite, and sulfate pulping procedures has served once again to make cheaper raw materials suitable for paper making. As intended, these new technologies have helped increase paper production, a goal and result of paper mill innovation even before mechanization. They have also preserved and expanded markets for cheap paper, an incentive to technological innovation first prominent after mechanization facilitated the industry's expansion. The adverse consequences of using new pulping technologies reflect a similar persistence of earlier patterns of behavior—a long tradition of casually dumping waste into the rivers and exhausting steam and smoke into the air. It is hardly surprising that chemical pulping resulted in serious water and air pollution.

Nor is it surprising that these developments have not been so evident in Berkshire County as in regions favored with abundant timber. The county's assets as a fine paper-making region have permitted the paper industry's local survival, but its inability to supply large quantities of wood pulp, while greatly diminishing the coun-

ty's quantitative contribution to American paper production, has
protected local citizens from much of the environmental havoc
wrought by chemical pulping. Among the county's still important
natural assets is its pure spring water, a resource first recognized by
Zenas Crane, often forgotten during the years of rapid technological change, and rediscovered by the 1880s. Contemporary Berkshire mills recycle most process water, a practice initiated by some
late nineteenth-century mill owners. Following another late nineteenth-century strategy, the local industry has persisted by becoming more and more specialized, by producing such items as fine
technical papers, customized papers for new industries, currency
paper, and elegant stationery.

The Berkshire paper industry survives today in the comparatively large post–Civil War mills of Lee, South Lee, Dalton, and
Housatonic, mills built to house and protect the larger machines developed incrementally during and after the years of mechanization.
In the century since 1885, paper machinery firms have continued to
build larger, faster, more fully automated, and more expensive
Fourdriniers, and a few new Berkshire mills have been erected. Increasing machine and mill prices, new costs of acquiring timber-
lands and pulp digesters, and the growth of the national market,
which took shape in the late nineteenth century, have promoted the
emergence of large-scale national paper corporations, accentuating
trends toward increasing scale and capital intensity that were initiated when Berkshire mills began serving the New York market. One
result is that most Berkshire mills have absentee corporate owners
today. Kimberly-Clark operates the Smith family mills and the
Mead Corporation runs the Hurlbut family enterprise. Corporate
ownership also reflects the inherent weakness of nineteenth-century family capitalism: the difficulty of assuring the next generation's interest and competence in paper mill management and the
likelihood over time that some mill owners will leave no heirs. It is
not remarkable, then, that the Smith, Hurlbut, Brown, Owen, and
Weston families have disappeared from the ranks of local mill proprietors. It is more surprising to find that the Cranes remain, still
training their sons in paper making and marketing.

The survival of Crane & Co. and of Berkshire's other fine paper
mills reflects the substantial skills that Berkshire paper workers still
bring to the task of making paper. In Dalton, recognition of owners'
and workers' continuing interdependence has inspired such twentieth-century developments as widespread home ownership, including ownership of former company housing; profit sharing; and
a system of financial rewards for suggested improvements. It has

also perpetuated the nineteenth-century tradition of personalized interaction, symbolized by the use of first names. In part because their corporate owners have had less interest in keeping Berkshire mills open, Lee paper workers have fared less well. They have also come to depend on formal organization for negotiation with their remote employers. In all of the mills, machine rooms and beater rooms remain noisy and damp, although light, heat, and ventilation have continued to improve. Paper-making machines remain dangerous and occasionally fatal to workers, although electrification has eliminated the belts and shafts that made nineteenth-century mill work especially hazardous. As in the late nineteenth century, some mobility still occurs: backtenders become machine tenders, workmen become superintendents, and workers' sons pursue careers outside the mills. Most dramatically, Benjamin Sullivan, grandson of a nineteenth-century machine tender, Michael Maher, became Crane & Co. president in the 1970s.

The 1970s also saw a woman become a backtender in one of the Lee mills, presaging the possibility of Berkshire County finally having a female machine tender. But, in general, the sexual division of labor has been the hardiest of the preindustrial traditions perpetuated and reinforced during the era of mechanization. Rag rooms gradually disappeared as mills used more wood pulp, mill owners purchased more fiber from textile mills, and clothing and bedding came to incorporate more and more synthetic fiber. But women still sort paper and engage in labor-intensive finishing operations, including the hand-bordering of note paper in Crane's stationery division. As elsewhere in American business, women have also taken their places in the mills' expanding clerical work force, performing such labor-intensive operations as typing, filing, and switchboard operating.

To say that the changes that have come to twentieth-century Berkshire paper making appear unsurprising in light of the industry's nineteenth-century history is to say that the Industrial Revolution marked a great technological and social watershed. Mechanization and the social developments it reflected and fostered helped fundamentally to shape our assumptions about manufacturing, class relations, gender roles, and the uses of technology. As I argued at the outset, then, the story of how and why nineteenth-century Americans adopted and used machines so as to create a new social order is a tale for our times.

WHY AND HOW did Americans adopt machines so readily and what social consequences did mechanization entail or promote? This study has suggested a number of answers, answers that seem to me broadly representative of industrializing America. Like Berkshire County, the nation in 1800 supplied an extraordinary array of natural advantages, ranging from the rapidly flowing rivers and pure water that proved crucial to Berkshire County's development as a paper-making region to the mineral, forest, and agricultural riches that contributed to paper industry development and provided the raw materials processed by most nineteenth-century American industry. As in Berkshire County, the nation's population was relatively homogeneous economically and shared a Calvinist heritage that accorded respect to the craftsman who had learned technical skills, saved his wages, and became a proprietor. Likewise, most of the nation experienced the revivalism that swept through Berkshire towns, promoting disciplined, intensified work by employer and employee; encouraging continued reinvestment; contributing to increased faith in human ability to change; and laying a foundation on which middle-class businessmen constructed networks of trust and exchange. Finally, much of the Northeast shared with Berkshire County its growing access through improved transportation to a major commercial center, enabling rural entrepreneurs to take fuller advantage of natural resources and waterpower, if only they could find an alternative to reliance upon the few skilled craftsmen, whose long training precluded their rapid multiplication. In sum, early nineteenth-century Americans were uncommonly well prepared to adopt machines.

As in Berkshire County, mechanization expressed social preferences and human aptitudes; the American Industrial Revolution was more a social than a technical event. The rapid diffusion of new machines followed prior attempts to expand production and reflected continuing opportunities to sell increased output so long as it did not differ substantially from goods fabricated by earlier methods. Judging from Berkshire County, acquiring the ability to build and replicate machines was not a significant constraint on American industrialization. Given the complexity of the Fourdrinier paper-making machine in particular, paper industry experience suggests that machine-building skill was widespread, not confined to the armories and textile machine shops whose history we know best.

At the mills, mechanization reflected experience with traditional manufacturing technique. New machines embodied craftsmen's motions and mill owners adopted them because they produced something roughly analogous to what particular craftsmen produced. After assessing new technology by applying to machine-made products standards initially derived from the craft tradition, mill owners either purchased machines or relied on their ability to recruit cheap female labor to perform hand operations that maintained product quality. New standards for acceptable paper and for acceptable paper mill technology emerged gradually as incremental changes in machines permitted greater output and opened new markets for cheap paper. Throughout the era of mechanization, then, mill owners' success depended on their knowledge of product and process.

Successful mechanization also required continuous acquisition of new knowledge so that mill owners managed most effectively when they creatively employed family associations, ties to former mentors and co-workers, and links to fellow mill owners forged through churches and other voluntary associations. Using these networks they were able to learn about new machines, choose wisely among them, develop new and improved operating procedures, and minimize the risks associated with burgeoning working capital requirements and long-distance marketing. As in the Berkshire paper industry, high rates of failure characterized the numerous small manufacturing establishments where most American mechanization occurred. This, too, abetted mechanization, for new entrants could readily acquire the old firm's modest fixed assets and, if aided by family and friends, stood to profit by the mistakes of their predecessors and contemporaries. At the same time, the proliferation of cheap paper increased the quantity and timeliness of business and technical information available to all manufacturers.

Cheaper and more abundant paper was the intended result of mechanization, but it was only one of many subsequent developments. The case of Berkshire paper making suggests that the most direct unintended consequences of mechanization were technological. Like manufacturers elsewhere, Berkshire mill owners played an important role in promoting local railroad development and in harnessing local waterpower more fully. Confronted by newly apparent resource scarcities that hampered their attempts to operate continuously and restricted their growing ability to produce paper, mill owners also offered a receptive market for new technologies developed elsewhere: turbines and steam engines, rosin sizing and other chemical processes, non-rag fiber, and fire-resistant mill construction. Use of these new technologies promoted increases in scale and concentration, reinforcing the economic advantages held out by larger, faster new machines. Enlarged mills concentrated in towns served by railroads multiplied the influence of mills and mill owners in local communities.

Although abetted by technological change, most of the social "consequences of mechanization" reflected human social initiatives and cultural values. Mill owners shaped and enhanced their growing influence by cooperating formally and informally to promote industrial development, embody their cultural values in local institutions and civic improvements, and foster desirable behavior among the workers. They also assured continued solvency by adopting traditional mercantile accounting, devising cost accounting procedures, and employing new marketing techniques. Lower profit margins in the expanded paper industry made these business innovations especially important. Combined with the greater scale of operations, lower profits and new business practices made successful ownership less and less likely for men without long personal or family experience in paper mill management. These developments also meant that, like manufacturers throughout the nation, late nineteenth-century Berkshire mill owners required more substantial capital for successful operation.

In the wake of mechanization, male paper workers not only had less chance of becoming local mill proprietors, but also ran more risk of injury and labored longer and more intensely than had hand paper workers, patterns characteristic of industrial labor throughout the nation. Social choice shaped these outcomes as well. Machines made continuous operation advantageous, but they did not determine the division of work into twelve-hour shifts; traditional dawn-to-dusk work schedules, religious belief in the value of work, and prolonged work hours in mills wrestling with new machine technology helped make twelve-hour shifts more conceivable than eight-hour ones. Similarly, intensified work began, not with mechanization, but with the decision to produce for the New York market; and tolerance of workplace hazards reflected shared norms of masculinity, enunciated by Jacksonian democratic rhetoric and underscored by Civil War experience. Notwithstanding the new rigors and dangers, male paper workers were neither passive victims nor class-conscious protesters. They retained their pride in, skill at, and control over their work, assets they used to achieve a higher standard of living and more continuous employment, but not to obtain improved working conditions. Mill workers also grew more diverse and more numerous as mechanization allowed the industry to expand, although not so numerous as to preclude the personalized bargaining their skill and potential geographic mobility made possible and their diversity and sense of manliness encouraged.

New norms of femininity, which emphasized that woman's place was in the home, combined with mechanization simultaneously to encourage and denigrate the traditional work that women continued to perform in paper mills. Women's manual tasks appeared less skilled and less productive when contrasted with men's increasingly mechanized work, while the social fiction that men supported all women permitted their continued low pay. Women's paper mill work was also sufficiently similar to nineteenth-century housework to make recruitment of able female workers comparatively easy and to support the conviction that women held those jobs for which nature and God had destined them. As elsewhere in American society, then, women's unmechanized work made essential contributions to the mechanization of paper making, while contemporary beliefs combined with the character of the work to minimize its importance.

HAVING surveyed an industry characterized by rapid mechanization and employing a remarkable array of complex new technologies, I find little support for the paralyzing technological determinism so pervasive both in contemporary and in nineteenth-century American rhetoric. Machines certainly opened many new doors to nineteenth-century Americans, but the choices among doors and the decisions to enter were primarily social ones. Indeed, without simultaneous social innovation, mechanization would not have become the rapid, pervasive, and economically successful enterprise that Americans made of it. Nor did Americans forego social choice by adopting machines, although mechanization made some technical and economic options increasingly attractive and others less and less rewarding. Equally important, during the early years of mechanization mill owners, workmen, and women earned success, stable employment, and social approbation by adopting new behaviors. As a result, subsequent generations of mill owners, workmen, and women often accepted these behaviors as appropriate, although intervening economic and technological developments increasingly meant that the social and economic benefits of "good" behavior were less and less equally distributed.

If the consequences of these human choices are not what we desire, we need to take stock of our own beliefs and to identify the social expectations and personal assumptions that perpetuate those historic decisions we deem unfortunate. Blaming technology and even living without machines might be much easier, but neither is likely to produce a more humane social order. Machines did not make history. Decisions warped by technological determinism will not free us from its cultural burden.

APPENDIX A
CHRONOLOGY OF BERKSHIRE
COUNTY PAPER MILLS AND
MILL OWNERSHIP,
1801–1885

The following chronology of mills and mill ownership relies on virtually all of the manuscript collections, newspapers and periodicals, government documents, local histories, and industry histories cited in the text and listed in the bibliography. I have generally resolved contradictions by giving preference to local sources and to earlier sources. Some dates remain so uncertain that I have simply listed the event after events that predated it and before events that postdated it, but have not assigned even a rough date.

Mill 1
Old Berkshire Mill, Housatonic River, Dalton

1801   Zenas Crane, Daniel Gilbert, and Henry Wiswell build
1803   Crane and Wiswell buy out Gilbert
1807   Zenas Crane sells to Henry Wiswell
1810   Zenas Crane obtains one-third interest in exchange for an interest in the Old Red Mill
       Wiswell fails; ownership unclear
1812   David Carson, David Campbell, and Daniel Boardman own
1813   Henry Marsh buys out Campbell
1814   David Carson buys out partners
1841   David Carson and Son (Thomas G.) owns
1849   David Carson retires; Carson Bros (Thomas G., William W., and David, Jr.) owns
1852   Thomas G. and William W. Carson own
1858   David Carson dies
1866   Carsons Paper Co. (incorporated; Thomas G. and William W. Carson) owns
1867   Powers & Brown Paper Co. (L. J. Powers & Bro., Charles O. Brown, Thomas Plunkett, G. T. Plunkett, and John D. Carson) owns
1868   Carson & Brown Paper Co. (Thomas G. Carson, John D. Carson, and Charles O. Brown) owns
1872   Burns
1873   Rebuilt; Carsons, Brown & Co. (Thomas G. , William W., and J. D. Carson; Charles O. Brown; John E. Merrill; and T. C. Lewis, with minor interests to Jarvis N. Dunham and David F. B. Carson) owns

1874 Lewis buys out David F. B. Carson
1877 Zenas Crane, Jr., buys an interest
1885 Same ownership

Mill 2
Old Red Mill, Houstonic River, Dalton

1809 Joseph Chamberlin builds; David Carson and Henry Wiswell join as owners
1810 Zenas Crane buys out David Carson and exchanges with Henry Wiswell for an interest in Old Berkshire Mill
1813 Zenas Crane buys out Chamberlin
1816 Zenas Crane sells Martin Chamberlin and William Cole (?) a half interest
1817 Crane buys out Cole
1820 Zenas Crane and Martin Chamberlin own (three-quarters versus one-quarter)
1826 Zenas Crane buys out Chamberlin
1842 Zenas Crane tranfers ownership to his sons (Zenas Marshal and James Brewer)
1845 Zenas Crane dies
1848 Crane & Co. (Zenas Marshal and James Brewer Crane) owns
1870 Burns, not rebuilt

Mill 3
Old Stone Mill, Houstonic River, Dalton

1844 Crane & Co. (Zenas Marshal and James Brewer Crane) builds
1869 Burns; rebuilt as the Pioneer Mill
1879 Winthrop Murray Crane becomes a partner
1885 Same ownership

Mill 4
Defiance Mill, Housatonic River, Dalton

1823 Joseph Chamberlin and David Carson build
1840 Henry Chamberlin buys; Henry and Ezekiel Chamberlin operate (?); enlarged
1844 Platner & Smith (George Platner and Elizur Smith) rent
1850 Ezekiel Chamberlin operates; Henry Chamberlin owns
1851 Ezekiel Chamberlin dies; Henry, Albert S., and Burr Chamberlin operate
1852 Burns; rebuilt by H. Chamberlin & Co. (Albert S. and Burr)
1860 Shut down; Charles O. Brown and Henry A. Hale rent
1863 Franklin Weston buys
1864 Byron Weston and Charles O. Brown buy

1867 Byron Weston buys Brown's share
1871 Addition built
1872 Separate office built
1873, Franklin Weston a silent partner
1885 Same ownership

Mill 5
Centennial Mill, Housatonic River, Dalton

1855 Albert S. Chamberlin builds
1856 Albert S. Chamberlin & Co. (Clark W. Mitchell) owns
1860 Mill shuts down
1861 Fails
1863 Seymour Crane rents
1866 Lease expires; Elisha Mitchell operates
1867 William F. Bartlett and Edwin Moodie buy
1868 Partnership dissolved; William F. Bartlett and William Cutting own
1875 Burns; Byron Weston buys; rebuilds as Centennial Mill
1885 Same ownership

Mill 6
Bay State Mill, Housatonic River, Dalton

1851 Crane & Wilson (Seymour Crane and James Wilson, with Zenas Marshal and James Brewer Crane, as silent partners) convert woolen factory to paper mill
1852 Paper making commences
1856 Crane, Martin, & Co. (George C. Martin replaces James Wilson) owns
1857 Crane, Martin, & Co. fails; mill idle
1858 Crane & Co. (Zenas Marshal and James Brewer Crane) owns; operates and leases mill
1865 Zenas Crane, Jr., rents, then buys
1877 Burns
1878 Rebuilt; Zenas Crane, Jr. & Bro. (Winthrop Murray) owns
1885 Same ownership

Mill 7
Lower or Greylock Mill, Hoosic River, Adams

1849 L. L. Brown & Co. (William and Daniel Jenks) builds
1869 Enlarged
1873 L. L. Brown Paper Company (incorporated; same owners with working interests to employees James Osborne, E. P. Jenks, and Thomas A. Mole)

1879 William and Daniel Jenks dead; J. C. Chalmers, trustee, controls shares
1882 James Osborne leaves
1883 William L. Brown given part ownership
1885 Edmund D. Jenks added to list of owners

Mill 8
Upper or Stone Mill, Hoosic River, Adams

1857 L. L. Brown & Co. (William and Daniel Jenks) buys cotton mill and converts it to paper manufacture
1873 L. L. Brown Paper Company (incorporated; same owners with working interests to employess James Osborne, E. P. Jenks, and Thomas A. Mole)
1879 William and Daniel Jenks dead; J. C. Chalmers, trustee, controls shares
1882 James Osborne leaves
1883 William L. Brown given part ownership
1885 Edmund D. Jenks added to list of owners

Mill 9
Adams Paper Company, Hoosic River, Adams

1867 Adams Paper Company (B. F. Phillips, Daniel Upton, S. E. Dean, A. H. Lamonte, and Henry Putnam) builds
1868 Lamonte and Phillips leave; A. W. Richardson joins
1872 Mill stopped; partners feuding; sold at auction
1873 Adams Paper Company now composed of W. C. and C. T. Plunkett, A. E. and W. A. Taylor, T. T. Hulbert, and W. B. Green
1878 Two floors of mill rented to cotton warp manufacturer
1882 Mill converted to cotton production

Mill 10
Bancroft or Union Mill, Westfield River, Becket

(?)1847 John Mann owns
(?)1850 William West builds more substantial mill
1857 Edwin Bulkley and William C. Dunton own
1859 Bulkley, Dunton & Co. owns; John W. Bliss buys an interest
1861 John W. Bliss sells his interest
(?)1870 Charles Cornelius West buys half interest
Charles Cornelius West sells to John Tracy
1874 Damaged by flood
1880 Jonathan Bulkley enters partnership (Edwin's son)
1885 Same ownership

Mill 11
Second Bancroft or Union Mill,
Westfield River, Becket

1857   Bulkley and Dunton build
1859   Bulkley, Dunton & Co. owns; John W. Bliss buys an interest
1861   John W. Bliss sells his interest
(?)1870   Charles Cornelius West buys half interest
        Charles Cornelius West sells to John Tracy
1874   Damaged by flood
1880   Jonathan Bulkley enters partnership
1885   Same ownership

Mill 12
On Housatonic River, Hinsdale

1872   Henry C. Carson builds; Charles K. Tracey & Bro. backs him
1873   Burns; bankrupt; Charles K. Tracey & Bro. takes over property; not rebuilt

Mill 13
On Housatonic River, Housatonic Village,
Great Barrington

1851   Henry L. Potter builds
1855   Burns before machinery installed
1856   Owen & Hurlbut (Charles M. and Edward H. Owen and Thomas Hurlbut) buys; rebuilt
1862   Owen Paper Co. (incorporated; Charles M. and Edward H. Owen) owns
1864   Edward H. Owen dies; Henry D. Cone buys some shares; Mrs. Chittendon (Edward H. Owen's mother-in-law) owns some shares
1873   Charles M. Owen dies; Sarah Chittendon Owen (Edward H. Owen's widow) inherits
1874   Henry D. Cone marries Sarah Chittendon Owen; new mill construction begins
1878   New mill construction discontinued
1885   Same ownership

Mill 14
Pleasant Valley or Valley Mill, Housatonic River,
Lenox Furnace (Lenoxdale Village), Lenox

1835   Thomas Sedgwick & Co. (Alvin Cone and Joseph Bassett) establishes
1844   George Sabin buys Bassett's share

1849   Cone & Sabin owns
1853   Sabin and George E. Robbins own
1855   Sabin and Samuel Washburn own
1856   Robert Adams joins partnership
1857   Osborne buys Adams's share; Franklin W. Gibbs joins partnership;
        becomes Gibbs & Co.; Benjamin Dean buys Osborne's interest
        Sabin insolvent; Stowell E. Dean buys his share
        Benjamin Dean insolvent; partnership fails; mill idle
1863   Smith Paper Co. (Elizur Smith) rents
1864   Smith Paper Co. (Elizur, DeWitt, and Wellington Smith) owns
1866   Incorporated
1872   Shares given to Smith sisters
1885   Same ownership

Mill 15
On Konkapot River, Mill River Village,
New Marlborough

1836   Warren Wheeler & Co. (John Gibson) builds
1837   Burns; rebuilt by Warren Wheeler & Sons (Warren, Jr., and Uriah
        H.)
1846   Warren, Jr., sells to Sheldon; becomes Wheeler & Co.
1851   Warren Wheeler & Co. (Wheeler, Sheldon, and Babcock) owns
1856   Gibson, Crosby, Robbins & Co. (Noah Gibson, George Crosby,
        George E. Robbins, and Warren Wheeler) owns
1858   Gibson, Crosby, & Robbins owns
1861   Fails; idle
1864   Marlboro Paper Company (George E. Robbins and others) owns; in-
        corporated; Robbins is agent
1872   Marlboro Paper Company (incorporated; George E. Robbins, D. R.
        Williams, Charles M. Owen, J. C. Goodrich, and Thomas O. Hurl-
        but) owns
1874   George E. Robbins owns over half of the Marlboro Paper Company
1875   Fails; reorganized by George E. Robbins
1876   George E. Robbins fails again
1877   H. C. Hulbert & Co. and Daniel Alexander take possession as the
        Brookside Paper Company, Inc.
1879   Closed
1880   Thomas Bradbury joins firm
1881   Daniel Alexander, Joseph H. Sutphin, and Henry C. Hulbert oper-
        ate and own
1882   Fails

Mill 16
On Konkapot River, Mill River Village,
New Marlborough

1840	Beach and Adams build
	Adams and E. C. Brett own
	Paul Face owns
1851	Warren Wheeler & Co. (Wheeler, Sheldon, and Babcock) owns
1856	Gibson, Crosby, Robbins & Co. (Noah Gibson, George Crosby, George E. Robbins, and Warren Wheeler) owns
1858	Gibson, Crosby & Robbins owns
1861	Fails; idle
1864	Marlboro Paper Company (George E. Robbins and others) owns; incorporated; Robbins is agent
1872	Marlboro Paper Company (incorporated; George E. Robbins, D. R. Williams, Charles M. Owen, J. C. Goodrich, and Thomas O. Hurlbut) owns
1874	George E. Robbins owns over half of the Marlboro Paper Company
1875	Fails; reorganized by George E. Robbins
1876	George E. Robbins fails again
1877	H. C. Hulbert & Co. and Daniel Alexander take possession as the Brookside Paper Company, Inc.
1879	Closed
1880	Thomas Bradbury joins firm
1881	Daniel Alexander, Joseph H. Sutphin, and Henry C. Hulbert own and operate
1882	Fails

Mill 17
On Konkapot River, Mill River Village,
New Marlborough

1835	John Carroll builds
1852	John Carroll & Co. (Noah Gibson, John L. Dodge, James Andrews, Ezra Blackman, and Levi L. Smith) owns
	Blackman dies
1862	John Carroll & Co. (Howland & Palser; they received a share for use of a patent they controlled
1866	John Carroll owns
1869	Burns; rebuilt
1873	James Goodwin joins Carroll as John Carroll & Co.
1875	Carroll Paper Co. (John and T. G. Carroll and James Goodwin) owns; incorporated
1876	Fails; John Carroll dies
1877	James Goodwin owns; incorporated

1878   Berkshire Paper Co. (James Goodwin, B. F. Curley, Thomas C. Bradley, and Charles C. Fischer) owns
1879   Berkshire Paper Co. (James Goodwin, B. F. Curley, and L. Olmstead) owns
1881   James Goodwin and Charlotte E. Goodwin own; Charlotte dies
1882   Closed
1844   Property attached

Mill 18
On Konkapot River, Mill River Village,
New Marlborough

1855   James Andrews, George Sheldon, and Chauncey Edwin Adams build
1856   George Sheldon and Chauncey Edwin Adams own
1866   George Sheldon owns
1872   Burns
1873   Fails
1874   John Carroll & Co. (John C. Carroll and James Goodwin) rebuilds
1875   Carroll Paper Co., Inc. (T. G. and John Carroll and James Goodwin) owns
1876   Fails; John Carroll dies
1877   James Goodwin owns; incorporated
1878   Berkshire Paper Co. (James Goodwin, B. F. Curley, Thomas C. Bradley, and Charles C. Fischer) owns
1879   Berkshire Paper Co. (James Goodwin, B. F. Curley, and L. Olmstead) owns
1881   James Goodwin and Charlotte E. Goodwin own; Charlotte dies
1882   Closed
1884   Property attached

Mill 19
On Konkapot River, Mill River Village,
New Marlborough

1881   George C. Walter, Edwin L. Booth, and Edward Blodgett buy shoe lace company mill and convert to paper mill
1882   Mill rented to Berkshire Paper Company; fails

Mill 20
On Konkapot Brook, Monterey

1830   John Manser owns and operates hand paper mill
(?)1854   Discontinued

Mill 21
On Konkapot Brook, Monterey

1846 Frederick D. Ingersoll & Co. (Robert L. McDowell) remodels grist-mill as paper mill
1847 Robert L. McDowell & Co. owns
1857 Suspended payment
1859 Fails; Arnold family owns (Francis, John, Frank, Jr., George, and Thomas Arnold)
1860 Fails
1861 O'Neil family buys (Felix, Lawrence, John, Frank, and Edward O'Neil)
1866 O'Neils bankrupt
1867 John and Lawrence O'Neil own
1870 W. C. Langdon & Co. (his father is the Co.) owns
1874 Fails

Mill 22
On Roaring Brook, Otis

1850 Albert Benton and Daniels build
1852 Burns; rebuilt; Otis Paper Mill Co. owns
1855 Idle
1858 Burns; not rebuilt

Mill 23
Government Mill, Housatonic River, Pittsfield

1847 Benjamin and Alanson Dean convert tannery to paper mill
1848 Wilson, Olcott Osborne, and Gibbs begin buying shares
1849 Incorporated
1850 Wilson, Osborne, and Gibbs own; Osborne and Gibbs buy
1851 Gibbs and Thomas Colt own
1855 Thomas Colt owns
1862 Thomas Colt builds new mill
1873 Fails; James M. Barker take over
1876 Chalmers Bros. & Baxter (Thomas, John, Daniel, Hugh, and Alex K. Chalmers and Robert Baxter) leases
1877 Chalmers Bros. & Baxter buys
1878 Fails
1879 Crane & Co. (Zenas Marshal, James Brewer, and Winthrop Murray Crane) buys
1885 Same ownership

Mill 24
On Clam River, Sandisfield

1852   Daniels and Bidwell convert woolen mill to paper mill; fails; Tanner and Perkins take over
1855   Burns; not rebuilt

Mill 25
On Paper Mill Pond Stream or Taconic Brook, Sheffield

1847   Barton Doten, William and Albert Mansfield, and E. Root convert factory to paper mill
1849   William Mansfield dies
1852   Fails
1854   George B. Curtis rents; fails
1860   Converted to flouring mill

Mill 26
On Housatonic River, Glendale Village, Stockbridge

1850   Frederick Perry builds; Foot and Cole operate
1853   Zadock Rewey leases site and power with option to buy
1854   Agreement renewed; Zadock Rewey, as Glendale Paper Co., builds mill and buys land
1855   Richard Evans and Ebeneezer Wentworth buy half interest
1858   Zadock Rewey dies; James M. Rewey and John Evans own
1862   Purchased by Connecticut firm
1864   Fails; James Hunter buys
1866   Hunter Paper Co. (James, James, Jr., David, Elizabeth, and Jennie Hunter) buys; incorporated
1868   James Hunter & Sons (same partners) owns
1872   George Chaffee and Charles E. and George Callender buy
1885   Same ownership

Mill 27
On Williams River, Williamsville Village, West Stockbridge

1850   Perry Green Comstock converts nail works to paper mill
1866   Burns; rebuilt
1870   Burns; rebuilt
1878   Operating part time
1880   Property attached; Thomas Goodenough leases
1881   Idle; Lawrence O'Neil and Patrick Bossidy prepare to operate
1884   Frank A. Arnold and Lawrence O'Neil own
1885   Same ownership

Mill 28
Turkey Mill, Hop Brook, Tyringham

1828   Milton Ingersoll builds
1833   Jared Ingersoll and George Platner buy
1834   Elizur Smith buys a share
1835   Smith buys out Ingersoll
1855   George Platner dies; widow (Adeline C. Platner) continues in part-
        nership
1857   Fails
1858   Burns; rebuilt
1860   Elizur Smith buys out Adeline C. Platner
1863   Smith Paper Co. (Elizur Smith) owns
1864   DeWitt and Wellington Smith join firm
1866   Incorporated
1869   Watkins, Cassidy & Co. (Samuel Watkins and M. and Ed. Cassidy)
        lease; burns
1870   John and George W. Cannon buy site
1872   Sparks and Casey buy; rebuild
        Fails
1876   Robert Slee buys
1877   Fails

Mill 29
Bay State Mill, Hop Brook, Tyringham

1846   Ezra Heath and Joshua Boss build
1848   S. C. Johnson & Co. (Fargo) buys
1850   Burns
1851   Fails; George W. and John T. West rebuild
1852   J. W. Sweet and John M. Northrop buy
1853   George W. West buys
1866   John Trimble buys
1870   Burns; not rebuilt

Mill 30
On Housatonic River, South Lee Village, Lee

1806   Samuel Church builds
1822   Charles M. Owen and Thomas Hurlbut buy
1849   Edward H. Owen joins firm
1856   South Lee Manufacturing Company (Thomas Hurlbut, and Charles
        M. and Edward H. Owen) owns
1860   Thomas Hurlbut and sons buy as Hurlbut Paper Company, Inc.
1861   Thomas Hurlbut dies; widow, three daughters, and sons, Thomas
        O. and Henry C. Hurlbut, own with Daniel B. Fenn, Jr.
1865   C. H. Plumb buys share

1872 Corporation dissolved; Thomas O. Hurlbut owns one-half, Henry C. Hurlbut owns two-fifths, and Daniel B. Fenn, Jr., owns one-tenth

1875 Dismantled; made into tenement

Mill 31
Phoenix Mill, Housatonic River,
South Lee Village, Lee

1822 Charles M. Owen and Thomas Hurlbut build
1849 Edward H. Owen joins firm
1856 South Lee Manufacturing Company (Thomas Hurlbut and Charles M. and Edward H. Owen) owns
1860 Thomas Hurlbut and sons buy as Hurlbut Paper Co., Inc.
1861 Thomas Hurlbut dies; widow, three dauthers, sons, Thomas O. and Henry C. Hurlbut, own with Daniel B. Fenn, Jr.
1865 C. H. Plumb buys share
1872 Corporation dissolved; Thomas O. Hurlbut owns one-half, Henry C. Hurlbut owns two-fifths, and Daniel B. Fenn, Jr., owns one-tenth
1883 Burns; not rebuilt

Mill 32
On Housatonic River, South Lee Village, Lee

1822 Charles M. Owen and Thomas Hurlbut convert gristmill to paper mill
1849 Edward H. Owen joins firm
1856 South Lee Manufacturing Company (Thomas Hurlbut and Edward H. and Charles M. Owen) owns
1860 Thomas Hurlbut and sons buy as Hurlbut Paper Co., Inc.
1861 Thomas Hurlbut dies, widow, three daughters, sons, Thomas O. and Henry C. Hurlbut, own with Daniel B. Fenn., Jr.
1865 C. H. Plumb joins firm
(?)1868 Discontinued

Mill 33
On Housatonic River, South Lee Village, Lee

1872 Hurlbut Paper Co., (Henry C. and Thomas O. Hurlbut and Daniel B. Fenn, Jr.) builds
1885 Same ownership

Mill 34
Union Mill, Housatonic River, Lee

1808   Samuel Church builds; Joseph and Leonard Church buy
(?)1838   George Platner and Elizur Smith buy and gradually enlarge
1855   George Platner dies; widow (Adeline C. Platner) continues in partnership
1857   Fails
1860   Elizur Smith buys out Adeline C. Platner
1863   Smith Paper Company (Elizur Smith) owns
1864   DeWitt and Wellington Smith join the firm
1866   Incorporated
1872   Share given to Smith sisters
1885   Same ownership

Mill 35
Enterprise or Huddle Mill (later Eagle Mill), Housatonic River, Lee

(?)1820   Luman Church rebuilds carriage shop as paper mill
1832   Starbuck & Co. owns
(?)1838   George Platner and Elizur Smith buy
1855   George Platner dies; widow (Adeline C. Platner) continues in partnership
1857   Fails
1860   Elizur Smith buys out Adeline C. Platner
1863   Smith Paper Company (Elizur Smith) owns
1864   DeWitt and Wellington Smith join the firm
1866   Incorporated
1872   Shares given to Smith sisters
1885   Same ownership

Mill 36
Crow Hollow or Columbia Mill, Housatonic River, Lee

1826   Walter, Winthrop, and Cutler Laflin build
1833   Burns; rebuilt
1836   George H. Phelps and Matthew Field own
1840   Burns; rebuilt
1849   Samuel A. Hulbert begins to purchase an interest
1850   Samuel A. Hulbert and Whyte own
1856   Burns; rebuilt
1860   Fails; run as a cotton mill
1863   Smith Paper Co. (Elizur Smith) buys
1864   DeWitt and Wellington Smith join firm

1865 Burns; rebuilt
1866 Incorporated
1872 Smith sisters given shares
1885 Same ownership

Mill 37
Housatonic Mill, Housatonic River, Lee

1827 Walter, Winthrop, and Cutler Laflin build
1836 Walter Laflin and Joseph M. Boies own
(?)1840 Walter Laflin owns
1850 George Platner and Elizur Smith buy and enlarge
1855 George Platner dies; widow (Adeline C. Platner) continues in partnership
1857 Fails
1858 Burns; rebuilt
1860 Elizur Smith buys out Adeline C. Platner
1863 Smith Paper Co. (Elizur Smith) owns
1864 DeWitt and Wellington Smith join firm
1866 Incorporated
1872 Smith sisters given shares
1885 Same ownership

Mill 38
Castle Mill, Laurel Lake Stream, Lee

(?)1824 Samuel Church and William M. Black build
1825 Zenas Crane and David Carson own
1827 John Nye & Co. buys half interest (Co. may be Isaac Ives)
1830 John Nye, Jr. operates
1832–50 Ball & Bassett buys and operates satinet factory
1850 Platner & Smith buys and operates satinet mill (site may include a separate structure known as the Laurel Mill)
1855 George Platner dies; widow (Adeline C. Platner) continues in partnership
1857 Converted to paper mill; fails
1860 Elizur Smith buys out Adeline C. Platner
1863 Smith Paper Co. (Elizur Smith) owns
1864 DeWitt and Wellington Smith join firm
(?) Becomes feeder mill for the Housatonic Mill

Mill 39
On Lake May Stream, East Lee Village, Lee

(?)1833 Jared Ingersoll owns and operates
1837 S. S. May buys an interest

1839 Burns
1840 E. S. May buys out Ingersoll and mill rebuilt
1851 Benjamin Dean joins the May brothers
1854 Samuel S. Rogers buys out Benjamin Dean
1860 Suspend payment
1877 May and Rogers partnership dissolved; E. S. and S. S. May own
1884 Burns; rebuilt
1885 Same ownership

Mill 40
On Lake May Stream, East Lee Village, Lee

1845 E. S. and S. S. May build
1851 Benjamin Dean joins the Mays
1854 Samuel S. Rogers buys out Dean
1860 Suspend payment
1877 Samuel S. Rogers leaves; E. S. and S. S. May own
1885 Same ownership

Mill 41
Mahaiwe Mill, Lake May Stream,
East Lee Village, Lee

1853 E. S. and S. S. May and Benjamin Dean build
1854 Samuel S. Rogers buys out Benjamin Dean
1860 Suspend payment
1877 Samuel S. Rogers owns
1878 Burns
1879 Rebuilt; James Gilmore manufactures for Samuel S. Rogers; Samuel S. Rogers dies; William May and Phiedam Morin own
1883 Fails
1884 McAlpine Bros. & Co. (Robert, Alex, and Charles H. McAlpine) owns
1885 Fails

Mill 42
Old Forest Mill, Lake May Stream,
East Lee Village, Lee

1819 Luman Church builds; Joseph and Leonard Church operate
     James Whiton & Sons owns
1831 Jared Ingersoll and Caleb Benton own
1835 Caleb Benton and Harrison Garfield own
1852 Burns; rebuilt
1866 Caleb Benton dies
1867 Harrison and Henry Garfield own
1885 Same ownership

Mill 43
Mountain Mill, Lake May Stream,
East Lee Village, Lee

1854 Caleb Benton and Harrison Garfield build
1861 Burns; Benton rebuilds
1866 Caleb Benton dies
1867 J. Frank and Charles C. Benton own as Benton Bros.
1885 Same ownership

Mill 44
Washington Mill, Lake May Stream,
East Lee Village, Lee

1836 Bosworth and Foot build; Joseph B. Allen and Leander Backus buy
1840 Joseph B. Allen begins operation
      Fails
1847 Allen & Co. (Joseph B. and William H. Allen) owns; fails; Platner &
      Porter buys
(?)1849 Luman Phinney & Co. (Joseph Kroh, Caleb Benton, and Harrison
      Garfield) buys
      Caleb Benton and Harrison Garfield own
1866 Caleb Benton dies
1867 Harrison and Henry Garfield own
1882 John A. Decker buys
1883 Burns
1884 Rebuilt; Decker and T. G. Sabin own
1885 Fails

Mill 45
On Greenwater Stream, East Lee Village, Lee

1838 John Baker builds; John Baker and George Wilson own; Ira Van
      Bergan owns(?)
1839 George Platner and Elizur Smith lease
1841 George West owns
1842 Burns; not rebuilt

Mill 46
Greenwater Mill, Greenwater Stream,
East Lee Village, Lee

1843 Samuel D. Sturges and William Costar build
1849 Orton Heath buys
1864 George W. Linn & Co. (P. C. Baird) buys
1869 P. C. Baird buys

1872   Patrick Owen buys; Owen enters partnership with Charles H. Videtto

1875   Closed; fails

Mill 47
National Mill, Lake May Stream,
East Lee Village, Lee

1855   Bradford M. Couch builds; George Linn and Benjamin Dean operate

1859   George W. Linn & Co. (Elizur Smith) owns

1863   George W. Linn & Co. (P. C. Baird) owns

1869   P. C. Baird owns

1885   Same ownership

Mill 48
Upper Forest Mill, Lake May Stream,
East Lee Village, Lee

1846   Caleb Benton and Harrison Garfield build

1855   Chaffee & Baird owns; Caleb Benton and P. C. Baird own

1857   P. C. Baird owns

1861   Burns; not rebuilt

Mill 49
Congress Mill, Lake May Stream,
East Lee Village, Lee

1852   Bradford M. Couch and Werden (Worden?) build

1854   Destroyed by flood; rebuilt

1856   Bradford M. Couch and B. T. Clark own

1857   Bradford M. Couch and B. T. Clark fail

1858   B. T. Clark dies; mill auctioned and T. A. Oman buys B. T. Clark's interest; mill idle, partially used by May and Rogers

1859   Fails; P. C. Baird buys

1885   Same ownership

Mill 50
On Lake May Stream, East Lee Village, Lee

(?)1824   Zenas Crane, Stephen Thatcher, and William Van Bergan operate

1827   Stephen Thatcher owns

1833   Stephen Thatcher and Son (George) owns

1840   Stephen Thatcher and Jared Ingersoll own

1851   Stephen Thatcher owns

1852   Harrison Smith and David S. May buy
1855   Fails; Harrison Smith owns
1856   Fails; Tanner and Perkins own
1863   James Toole and John Bottomly own
1864   John Bottomly owns
1873   Ferry and Wrinkle lease
(?)1874   Burns; not rebuilt

Mill 51
Waverly or New England Mill, Lake May Stream, East Lee Village, Lee

1829   Luman Church builds
1832   Luman Church and Brown operate
(?)1842   Stephen Thatcher and Jared Ingersoll own
1851   Charles Ballard owns
1853   Charles Ballard and Werden own
1855   William P. Hamblin buys Charles Ballard's interest
1856   Prentiss Chaffee and William H. Hamblin own
1863   Prentiss Chaffee and William H. Hamblin partnership dissolved; Prentiss Chaffee owns
1881   John Verran (de Varennes) owns
1885   Same ownership

Mill 52
On Lake May Stream, East Lee Village, Lee

1855   J. M. Northrup and T. P. Eldridge build
1856   Burns; T. P. Eldridge rebuilds with Nichols
1857   Fails(?)
1858   T. P. Eldridge moves to New York; Nichols continues; Tanner and Perkins buy
1864   Sold at auction to State Bank of Elizabeth, N.J.; resold to W. H. Blauvelt & Co. (James and Frederick Gilmore and John Trimble)
1866   John Trimble sells out
1872   Burns
1873   James Gilmore rebuilds
1877   Burns
1878   Fails; Albert C. Sparks and James Gilmore rebuild
1880   James Gilmore, George H. Tanner, and John T. Faxon own
1881   Burns
1882   Rebuilt
1885   Fails

APPENDIX B
MILL OWNERS, SUCCESS,
AND FAILURE:
FURTHER DATA

Data on mill owners derive from virtually all of the paper industry manuscript collections, local histories, paper industry histories, trade publications, newspapers, and genealogies listed in the bibliography. Also, beginning in the 1840s, the records of R. G. Dun & Co. supply increasingly complete information about mill owners' prior experience, assets, and associates. Where discrepancies exist among these sources, I have given preference to those closest in time and place to the mill owners. In general, information grows more abundant over time, so that we have more information about mill owners whose careers began later. As a result of its greater abundance, later information is probably more accurate. It is more detailed and, in many instances, offers corrections or modifications of earlier reports based on incomplete information (especially the case for R. G. Dun and newspaper reports).

In general, as the numbers listed under "insufficient information" make clear, data are more available for successful than for unsuccessful mill owners. In part, this reflects the fact that unsuccessful mill owners were somewhat more likely to live in the Berkshires only briefly, so that local sources offer less information about them. Likewise, those whose business careers were brief commanded less attention from Dun's reporters and in the newspapers. But information is also less available for those men who lacked assets, experience, or skilled associates, because all of the sources were more likely to report that a man had various attributes than to report his lack of them. Thus, the larger number of "failures" for whom there is "insufficient information" probably reflects the greater frequency with which these men lacked various attributes associated with success. If so, the absence of information about some men influences the prevailing patterns in the data relatively little.

Data Summarized in Chapter 5

In the interests of brevity, Table 5.1 offers a statistical summary of the relationship between mill owners' fates and their various attributes, assets, and associates. Tables B.1 through B.4 provide the data from which the statistics in Table 5.1 derive.

TABLE B.1
PAPER MILL EXPERIENCE AND SUCCESS, 1827–57

	Successes	Failures	% Successful
Mill owners with paper mill training	31	9	78
Mill owners without paper mill training	34	34	50
Insufficient information	5	23	—

TABLE B.2
COMMERCIAL EXPERIENCE AND SUCCESS, 1827–57

	Successes	Failures	% Successful
Mill owners with commercial experience	27	15	64
Mill owners without commercial experience	38	27	59
Insufficient information	5	24	—

TABLE B.3
OTHER MANUFACTURING EXPERIENCE AND SUCCESS, 1827–57

	Successes	Failures	% Successful
Mill owners with other manufacturing experience	12	10	55
Mill owners without other manufacturing experience	53	32	62
Insufficient information	5	24	—

The data supplied in the Table B.4 are more detailed than that summarized in Table 5.1. Constructing Table 5.1 required consolidating two categories—men with family backing and men who had accumulated substantial assets on their own—into a single category: those with financial resources. I have generally borrowed the distinction between those with "little or nothing" and those with substantial capital from credit reporters. Where specific property is

TABLE B.4
FINANCIAL RESOURCES AND SUCCESS, 1827–57

	Successes	Failures	% Successful
Little or nothing	22	19	54
Prior capital accumulation	20	14	59
Family backing	18	9	67
Insufficient information	10	24	—

mentioned in the records, I have considered small commercial establishments and personal residences as worth little or nothing, a valuation confirmed by assessments of some of these properties. As noted in the text, those designated as having mill-trained and commercially trained partners include those who themselves possessed the particular attribute.

TABLE B.5
MILL-TRAINED PARTNERS AND SUCCESS, 1827–57

	Successes	Failures	% Successful
Owners with mill-trained partners	52	22	70
Owners without mill-trained partners	15	21	42
Insufficient information	3	23	—

TABLE B.6
COMMERCIALLY TRAINED PARTNERS AND SUCCESS, 1827–57

	Successes	Failures	% Successful
Mill owners with commercially trained partners	51	26	66
Mill owners without commercially trained partners	17	19	47
Insufficient information	2	21	—

TABLE B.7
RELATIVES OWNING PAPER MILLS AND SUCCESS, 1827–57

	Successes	Failures	% Successful
Mill owners with mill-owning relatives	47	21	69
Mill owners without mill-owning relatives	19	23	42
Insufficient information	4	22	—

Data Summarized in Chapter 8

Table 8.2 provides a statistical summary of mill owners' assets, associates, and success. Tables B.8 through B.10 supply the data summarized there. Table B.8 offers more detailed information than that summarized in Table 8.2, because it divides those with financial resources into two groups, those with family backing and those with prior personal capital accumulation. Calculated from these more detailed data, Lambda$_b$ registers .17. Table B.8 also supplements Tables 8.1 and 8.3, which supply information on mill owners' assets after 1865. In supplying information on mill owners' initial assets it is comparable to data summarized in Chapter 5 and presented more fully above. In a few instances, an individual began with family financial resources at his disposal and also accumulated substantial capital on his own before entering the paper industry. I have assigned these individuals to the "family backing" category, because this table's intention is to summarize the assets that originally underwrote a man's career.

TABLE B.8
INITIAL ASSETS AND SUCCESS, 1866–85

	Successes	Failures	% Successful
Access to family money	31	11	74
Substantial personal savings	21	20	51
Little or nothing	19	29	40
Insufficient information	3	12	—

TABLE B.9
COMMERCIALLY TRAINED PARTNERS AND SUCCESS, 1866–85

	Successes	Failures	% Successful
Mill owners with commercially trained partners	65	43	60
Mill owners without commercially trained partners	9	29	24
Insufficient information	0	0	—

Although not summarized in Table 8.2, I offer the data in Table B.11 as background for evidence presented in Chapter 8 and for purposes of comparison with information supplied in Chapter 5. In contrast to Table B.3, "Other Manufacturing Experience and Success," offered as a supplement to Chapter 5, this table offers information on an additional category of men, those with paper manufacturing experience prior to 1866. These were men who had owned a mill either in Berkshire County or elsewhere prior to 1866. At first glance, the very similar success rates of men with paper manufacturing experience and men with no manufacturing experience appear puzzling. Most of the successful men in the latter category were sons of paper mill owners, who entered the business formally only after 1865.

TABLE B.10
MILL-TRAINED PARTNERS AND SUCCESS, 1866–85

	Successes	Failures	% Successful
Mill owners with mill-trained partners	65	54	55
Mill owners without mill-trained partners	9	16	36
Insufficient information	0	2	—

TABLE B.11
MANUFACTURING EXPERIENCE AND SUCCESS, 1866–85

	Successes	Failures	% Successful
Paper manufacturing experience	37	31	54
Other manufacturing experience	7	12	37
No other manufacturing experience	29	26	53
Insufficient information	1	3	—

MILLS, MACHINES, OUTPUT,
AND CAPITAL:
LOCAL DATA

Federal and state government censuses and reports cited in the text provide information on numbers of mills and machines, on mill output, and on capital invested. The principal asset of these documents is their apparent completeness; they report information concerning mills whose records have not survived and mills about which other nineteenth-century sources are quite incomplete. The principal liability of government documents is that they are usually inaccurate (often extremely inaccurate), a problem that becomes apparent when their reports on particular establishments are compared with mill records and other nineteenth-century sources. I have generally preferred accuracy to the deceptive thoroughness of government surveys, so I have relied on local, contemporary sources and the records of regional business institutions in many of my remarks about mills, machines, output, and capital invested. As a supplement to specific citations offered in the text, the following pages offer a brief assessment of this comparatively accurate but incomplete local data.

Data Summarized in Figure 6.1: Numbers of
Paper Mills in Berkshire County,
Massachusetts, 1820–1885

This graph summarizes the data on mill sites presented chronologically in Appendix A. As that appendix makes clear, dates of construction and of ownership changes are occasionally uncertain. In both Appendix A and Figure 6.1, I have chosen to define a mill as a site, because sites remained relatively constant, whereas individual buildings frequently burned or underwent extensive reconstruction, and operating firms changed even more often. In a few cases, sites that were initially independent were eventually consolidated to form a single mill. Such changes occurred gradually, making them difficult to date. Furthermore, reducing the number of mill sites in Figure 6.1 to reflect consolidation would give the impression that county mill capacity declined, whereas consolidation generally enlarged both mills. Thus, I have made no attempt to reflect consolidation in the graph. In constructing Figure 6.1, I have included in my total for each year any mill that operated at some time during that year.

There are a number of discrepancies between sources as to when mills were built, when they were in operation, and when they ceased to operate. Where possible, I have relied on contemporary mill records, which frequently mention mills other than those owned by the firm keeping the record. Other contemporary local records come next in reliability. In particular, I have used the *Valley Gleaner*, published in Lee continuously from 1857 through 1885, to compensate for the relative dearth of southern Berkshire mill records. Contemporary records produced by institutions outside the county, but directly interested in reliable information about local mills, such as credit reporting agencies, insurance surveyors, gazeteer compilers, and map makers, come next in reliability. Their principal liability is a lag between the events they report and the date of reporting. Among primary sources, I have found government census data generally less reliable than any of these sources, especially so before 1860. Published chronologies and local histories, even those authored by contemporaries, all reflect the fallibility of human memory to some extent. I have used them to fill in gaps left by primary sources.

Data Summarized in Figure 6.2: Numbers of
Paper-Making Machines in Berkshire County,
Massachusetts, 1827–1885

The Massachusetts Census of Manufactures for 1875 and for 1885 both enumerated paper-making machines. The 1875 census found twenty-eight machines in Berkshire County and the 1885 census, thirty-one; these are larger numbers than are presented in Figure 6.2, which relies on local records, paper machine builders' records, and insurance records. I have given preference to local and business records because they offer a long-term view of mechanization and because they enable me to distinguish between Fourdrinier and cylinder machines. By contrast, the 1885 census made no such distinction and the 1875 census listed machines as Fourdrinier (two) and "Other Kinds" (twenty-six), figures so much at variance with manuscript records of machine purchases as to suggest that either respondents or enumerators, or both, failed to take the question seriously.

Using manuscript business records still leads to a certain amount of distortion of what must have been the actual numbers, timing, and proportions of different machines. Most obviously, I could find data indicating whether a machine was a Fourdrinier or a cylinder for only twenty-four of the county's fifty-two mills. (I have not used data that simply indicate the presense of a machine.) Other than reducing the total number of machines, especially in the antebellum era, it is difficult to say what effect this limitation has upon the graph. Data on machines in Dalton and Adams mills are most available, a result of the preservation of their records. For the 1840s and 1850s, this may lead to a slight bias in favor of the Fourdrinier. Other mills for which information is available are merely those that happened to be surveyed by Barlow & Bancroft, happened to write to Crane & Co. and describe their machines when ordering layboys, happened to order machines at the Lowell Machine Shop, or happened to reply to Byron Weston's inquiries concerning their machines. It is not clear that these characteristics would generally favor the reporting of one kind of machine over the other.

It is clear, however, that the intermittent nature of the evidence makes precise dating impossible. I have assumed, for example, that a reported machine continued in operation until there is evidence that a new machine was introduced or that the mill ceased to operate, an assumption warranted for mills having fairly complete records. But for many mills, information on the presence of a new machine is not available until some years after its introduction. In particular, the Barlow & Bancroft Insurance Surveys, from which I have drawn much information, took place after 1873. Thus, the rapid increase in the number of Fourdriniers during the 1870s is partially an artifact of my sources. Combined with the fact that I have found evidence only of earliest machine purchases for some mills, the data probably understates the earliness and frequency of Fourdrinier ownership and overstates the persistene of cylinder ownership. Mills for which data are available include numbers 1, 2, 3, 5, 6, 7, 8, 10, 11, 12, 13, 17, 18, 21, 23, 26, 27, 28, 31, 33, 37, 39, 43, and 50.

Local Data on Output and Capital

Data derived from paper company records, other nineteenth-century business records, and a few industry histories are much less satisfactory in supplying a general picture of paper output and mill assets than in documenting the existence of mills and machines. Output data are available for twenty-eight mills, capitalization data for forty-two mills, and asset data for thirty mills. The problem with each of these bodies of data is that information on any given mill is usually available only for a few individual years. Since mills differed substantially in their output and assets, averages of figures that are fortuitously available in any given year result in chronological sequences of data that fluctuate so erratically as to be virtually meaningless. I have therefore assumed that, in the absence of data to the contrary, a mill's output, capitalization, or assets remained constant for ten years. Thereafter, unless further information was available, I dropped the mill from the pool of data. While this precedure results in averages that somewhat understate growth in productivity and capital invested, it also results in data suggesting some change over time, rather than a series of random observations.

In constructing a series of output figures, I also omitted data from eleven mills for which data were available only after 1880. These were among the county's smallest establishments by that date, so inclusion of evidence about them only after 1880 would disproportionately depress figures for those years. As is also true of census data, industry records sometimes report output by reams, sometimes by weight. I have converted data in reams to weight by assuming an average ream to weigh twenty pounds, a reasonable assumption for the early period, when data were most often available only in reams. Tons per day have been converted to tons per year by assuming a 310-day work year. In general these calculations probably deflate somewhat those figures available for the antebellum era.

Data on output are available for some years for mills number 1, 2, 4, 5, 7, 8, 14, 29, 30, 31, 32, 33, 34, 35, 36, 37, and 51. The sample probably tends to overrepresent the larger mills so that average mill production was probably somewhat lower, especially after 1865. Also, production figures often represent a mill's capacity, rather than its actual output, tending to exaggerate the average mill's production, especially in the 1850s and in the decade between 1865 and 1874.

Based on this data, range in annual output is summarized in Table C.1. Readers interested in annual averages, annual ranges in output, and numbers of mills in each year's sample may consult McGaw, "Sources and Impact," pp. 391–93. As may be seen, given the small size of the sample (no more than twelve mills in any given year), data, especially for the early 1840s and early 1860s, are very much influenced by which mills offer information for a particular period. In sum, the data are suggestive, but far from definitive.

The major difficulty in constructing a series of estimates of capital invested is that various reports or records included different items. This was also the case, of course, for government reports, which have the added liability of rarely making clear what they meant by

TABLE C.1
BERKSHIRE COUNTY PAPER MILL OUTPUT IN
TONS PER YEAR, 1820–85

Period	Range in Output	Period	Range in Output
1820–24	15–46	1855–59	30–412
1825–29	15–155	1860–64	65–155
1830–34	15–155	1865–69	73–1433
1835–39	40–155	1870–74	73–1641
1840–44	58–81	1875–79	73–1681
1845–49	30–412	1880–85	155–1962
1850–54	30–412		

capital or assets. I have divided the data available into two categories, capitalization and assets, so as to reduce its diversity somewhat. Capitalization figures include statements of the amount of
capital stock paid in; values assigned to real estate and machinery;
estimates by credit reporters of the value of a firm's real property;
reports of the cost of building and furnishing new mills; and purchase prices of mills. In sum, capitalization generally includes fixed
capital. Asset figures include reports of total assets; the amount for
which mills and their contents were insured; total reported losses in
mill fires; estimated worth of real estate, machinery, and stock for
tax purposes; and total firm worth as estimated by credit reporters.
In sum, assets usually include stock-on-hand, stock-in-process, and
the mill's paper inventory, but usually do not include other components of working capital. In general, the data are increasingly reli-

TABLE C.2
AVERAGE CAPITALIZATION OF BERKSHIRE COUNTY
PAPER MILLS, 1827–85

Period	Range of Annual Averages	Period	Range of Annual Averages
1827–30	$27,500	1856–60	$18,562–30,750
1831–35	13,500–27,500	1861–65	25,038–33,733
1836–40	6,500–13,500	1866–70	32,350–43,229
1841–45	6,500	1871–75	35,561–57,155
1846–50	9,214–27,000	1876–80	52,875–58,845
1851–55	16,526–16,875	1881–85	55,011–72,312

able over time, especially after the 1840s, when Dun's local credit reports began. In addition, small numbers of mills reporting combine with considerable differences in the mills reporting at any given time to render the data on capitalization relatively meaningless before 1850. Readers interested in a year-by-year account of sample size, average capitalization or assets, and annual range of reported values should consult McGaw, "Sources and Impact," pp. 394–400.

TABLE C.3
AVERAGE ASSETS OF BERKSHIRE COUNTY
PAPER MILLS, 1833–85

Period	Range of Annual Averages	Period	Range of Annual Averages
1833–35	$17,000	1861–65	$24,460– 25,500
1836–40	17,000	1866–70	28,167– 42,917
1841–45	17,000–20,000	1871–75	61,417–111,706
1846–50	20,000–22,500	1876–80	97,811–129,384
1851–55	22,500	1881–85	110,963–140,420
1856–60	25,000–27,000		

BIBLIOGRAPHY

ARCHIVES

Berkshire Paper Company Records

L. L. Brown & Co. and L. L. Brown Paper Company

Held by the Adams Historical Society at its headquarters in the Adams Public Library, Adams, Massachusetts, these records include nineteen ledgers, journals, and daybooks covering various years between 1853 and 1885; fifteen other record books of the company, its owners, and affiliated companies for the years between 1849 and 1883; and an envelope containing varied correspondence, orders, accounts, and tax records for the years 1862–63. The Adams Historical Society also owns a collection of photographs that includes a number of items illustrating the mills, mill owners, mill workers, and housing from the late nineteenth century.

Crane & Co. and Its Predecessors

In the company archive at its main office in Dalton, Massachusetts, are twenty-three record books for Crane & Co. and other Dalton paper companies in which members of the Crane or Carson families were involved. These cover various years between 1809 and 1881. In citing items in this collection, I have retained the attributions assigned when the collection was catalogued, although for some of the earlier items overlapping dates suggest that a few of the records are those of David Carson rather than Zenas Crane. The archive also contains the account book of blacksmith David Cogswell for the years 1821–23. Cogswell did considerable business with Zenas Crane. The Crane Museum, housed in a building that was originally the rag room of the Old Stone Mill, Dalton, Massachusetts, holds a number of other archival materials, in addition to its displays of early products and tools. These include extensive files housed in five file cabinets. Most of the material on file dates from the years 1801 through 1885, including a selection of the company's incoming correspondence. The museum also contains an extensive collection of photographs, a rent book beginning in the 1880s, and a machine tender's book kept by Michael Maher at the Bay State Mill in 1882. A bound volume entitled "Dalton Conveyances" contains records of many of the company's nineteenth-century real estate transactions. The museum files also contain manuscript histories of various mills, interviews with eight workers who had been employed at Crane & Co. for at least forty-five years in 1930, and some personal correspondence of the mill owners.

Owen & Hurlbut and the Hurlbut Paper Company

Held by the Mead Corporation, present owner of the Hurlbut Mill, these materials are housed at the company's South Lee, Massachusetts, office. They include a variety of unbound letters, bills, and other papers grouped by decade; other papers of the mills, mill owners, and mill owners' families in an unlabeled folder; and six company record books for various years between 1822 and 1849, two of which have been severely damaged by water. The collection also contains a few photographs.

Smith Paper Company

Held by the present owner of the remaining Smith mills, Kimberly-Clark Corporation, materials are housed at the office of the corporation's Peter J. Schweitzer Division, Columbia Paper Mill, Lee, Massachusetts. They include a Smith Paper Company Record Book, listing important equipment changes, primarily after 1885, and a volume of Smith Paper Company Test Records beginning in 1875. The collection also contains a few photographs.

Byron Weston Company and Its Predecessors

Records of the Byron Weston Company, Brown & Weston, and earlier owners of the Defiance Mill, including Platner & Smith, are housed in the company's Dalton, Massachusetts office. They include nine letter books of company correspondence covering most of the years between 1863 and 1875; ledgers of two earlier firms operating the mill; a volume of various calculations for the years between 1866 and 1955; eight folders containing letters and other unbound material relating primarily to Byron Weston's life; and a fairly complete collection of incoming letters, bills, receipts, and notices for the years 1864, 1867, and 1871. The collection also contains photographs, news clippings, and manuscript histories.

Other Archival Collections

American Philosophical Society, Philadelphia, Pennsylvania

Houses the Coleman Sellers Letter Book for the years 1828 through 1834, which includes correspondence with Berkshire firms.

Berkshire Atheneum, Pittsfield, Massachusetts

The Atheneum's Historical Room holds a typescript of the Dalton Congregational Church Records, which is part of the Rollin H. Cooke Collection of church records. It also holds copies of a number of sermons and pamphlets published locally and the best collection of local histories.

Harvard University. Graduate School of Business Administration, Baker Library, Manuscripts and Archives Division

Records consulted include:

C. A. Barlow and J. M. Bancroft. "Special Insurance Surveys of Manufacturing Risks in the United States."

Dun and Bradstreet Collection. "Early Handwritten Credit Reporting Ledgers of the Mercantile Agency," vols. 3–7.

Saco-Lowell Machine Shops Records. Vol. RA-1, Paper Machinery Memoranda and *Illustrations of Paper Machinery Built by the Lowell Machine Shop, Lowell, Mass.* (1882).

Lee Library, Lee, Massachusetts

The library's historical room contains an extensive collection of nineteenth-century photographs, a number of manuscript histories of local mills and local social organizations, some locally published pamphlets, and some newspaper clippings.

Massachusetts Archives, Boston, Massachusetts

In addition to its collection of statistical compendia published by the state during the nineteenth century, the archives contain the manuscript records of the Massachusetts Commission on Hours and a number of manuscript survey maps of Berkshire towns.

National Archives, Washington, D.C.

Records of the United States Patent Office, including published volumes and a microfilm index to early patent office records.

Stockbridge Library, Stockbridge, Massachusetts

The library's historical room contains a model of the original pulp grinder installed in Curtisville, photographs, manuscript maps, manuscript histories and interviews, and news clippings.

In addition to these collections, local libraries in virtually all of the towns that once had paper mills have among their collections a few relevant historical materials, including photographs, pamphlets, and manuscript histories.

INTERVIEWS AND TOURS

The following individuals granted the author interview or tours:

Mrs. Tracy Ambler, granddaughter of Frederick Wurtzbach. By telephone, Lee, Massachusetts, November 14, 1975.

Stanley P. Benton, retired President, E. D. Jones & Sons Company. At his home, Pittsfield, Massachusetts, July 2, 1975.

Fred G. Crane, Jr., Vice-President for Research and Development, Crane & Co. At his office at the Crane & Co. Laboratory, Dalton, Massachusetts, July 1975.

Winthrop M. Crane III, Vice-President, Crane & Co. At his office in the Crane & Co. office, July 18, 1975.

Irving Hughes, Quality Control Department, Crane & Co. At the Crane & Co. Bay State Mill, October 13, 1976.

Ralph Kendall, Superintendent. At the Crane & Co. Bay State Mill, July 17, 1975.

William G. O'Connell, retired Crane & Co. employee (began working for the firm in 1906). At his office in the Crane & Co. office, July 21, 1975.

Irving Witham, plant engineer. At the Crane & Co. Wahconah Mill, August 19, 1975.

In addition to formal interviews and tours arranged early in my research, I have benefited from a number of subsequent tours of additional local paper mills and from informal conversations with a number of mill employees.

SECONDARY SOURCES

What follows is to some extent a selected bibliography. It lists all of the secondary works cited in the text, with the exception of brief articles published in local newspapers and paper industry publications. Several of these newspapers and industry sources are cited extensively in the text; they include: *Hurlbut's Papermaker Gentleman* (4 vols., January 1933–September 1935), published by the Hurlbut Paper Company; *Superior Facts* (5 vols., 1928–33), published by the Papermakers' Chemical Corporation; and the *Valley Gleaner* (local news read systematically, 1857–85), published in Lee, Massachusetts. Other local newspapers sampled were the *Pittsfield Sun*, the *Berkshire Courier* (Great Barrington, Massachusetts), and the *Adams [North Adams] Transcript*. The bibliography does list a few local histories, genealogies, and paper industry histories not cited in the text. It does not list published works in American history other than those cited in the text. It also does not list government documents cited in the text.

Albion, Robert Greenhalgh. *The Rise of New York Port [1815–1860].* New York, 1939.

"American Industries No. 72: The Manufacture of Writing Paper," *Scientific American* 44 (April 30, 1881):271, 275–76.

American Paper and Pulp Association. *The Dictionary of Paper, Including Pulp, Paperboard, Paper Properties, and Related Papermaking Terms.* New York, 1965.

Archer, Cathaline Alford, Mitchell J. Mulholland et al. *A Bicentennial History of Becket, Berkshire County, Massachusetts.* Pittsfield, Mass., 1965.

The Art of Paper Making: A Guide to the Theory and Practice of the Manufacture of Paper. Being a Compilation from the Best-Known French, German, and American Writers. London, 1876.

Atack, Jeremy, Fred Bateman, and Thomas Weiss. "The Regional Diffusion and Adoption of the Steam Engine in American Manufacturing." *Journal of Economic History* 40 (June 1980):281–308.

Baxter, W. T. "Accounting in Colonial America." In *Studies in the History of Accounting*, edited by A. C. Littleton. Homewood, Ill., 1956.

Beers, F. W. *County Atlas of Berkshire, Massachusetts.* New York, 1876.

Birdsall, Richard D. *Berkshire County: A Cultural History.* New Haven, 1959.

Britton, B. S. *History of Paper Merchandising in New York City.* New York, 1939.

Brown, Judith K. "A Note on the Division of Labor by Sex." *American Anthropologist* 72 (October 1970):1073–78.

Browne, William B. *Genealogy of the Jenks Family of America.* Concord, N.H., 1952.

Bryan, Clark W. *Through the Housatonic Valley to the Hills and Homes of Berkshire.* Great Barrington, Mass., 1882.

Carey, A. Merwyn. *American Firearms Makers.* New York, 1953.

Carter, Samuel III. *Cyrus Field: Man of Two Worlds.* New York, 1968.

A Century of Pioneering in the Paper Industry: 1828–1928. South Windham, Conn., 1928.

Chandler, Alfred D., Jr. *The Visible Hand: The Managerial Revolution in American Business.* Cambridge, Mass., 1977.

Chatfield, Michael. *A History of Accounting Thought.* Huntingdon, N.Y., 1977.

Child, Hamilton, comp. *Gazeteer and Business Directory of Berkshire County, Mass. 1725–1885.* Syracuse, N.Y., 1885.

Chudacoff, Howard P. "Mobility Studies at a Crossroads." *Reviews in American History* 2 (June 1974):180–86.

Clapperton, Robert H. *Modern Paper-making.* Oxford, 1952.

———. *The Paper-making Machine.* Oxford. 1967.

Clark, J. J. and T. L. Crossley. *The Manufacture of Pulp and Paper: A Textbook of Modern Pulp and Paper Mill Practice.* 3 vols. New York, 1923.

Cochran, Thomas C. *Frontiers of Change: Early Industrialism in America.* New York, 1981.

———. "New Views on Industrialization." Paper presented in the Humanities Seminar series, West Virginia University, March 29, 1984.

Cole, Donald B. *Immigrant City: Lawrence, Massachusetts, 1845–1921.* Chapel Hill, 1963.

A Complete Account of the Terrible Disaster at East Lee on Tuesday, April 20th, 1886, with the Impressive Funeral Obsequies, Full Testimony at the Inquest, A List of Contributions for the Relief Fund, Etc., Etc. Lee, Mass., 1886.

Consolati, Florence. *See All the People; or, Life in Lee.* Dalton, Mass., 1978.

Cott, Nancy F. *The Bonds of Womanhood: "Woman's Sphere" in New England, 1780–1835.* New Haven, 1977.

Cowan, Ruth Schwartz. *More Work for Mother: The Ironies of Household Technology from the Open Hearth to the Microwave.* New York, 1983.

Crane Family Record, 1648–1961. Dalton, Mass., 1961.

Danhof, Clarence H. *Change in Agriculture: The Northern United States, 1820–1870.* Cambridge, Mass., 1969.

Daniels, George. "The Big Questions in the History of American Technology." *Technology and Culture* 11 (January 1970):11–16.

Davis, William T., ed. *The New England States: Their Constitutional, Judicial, Educational, Professional, and Industrial History.* 4 vols. Boston, 1897.

Dawley, Alan. *Class and Community: The Industrial Revolution in Lynn.* Cambridge, Mass., 1976.

Deyrup, Felicia Johnson. *Arms Makers of the Connecticut Valley: A Regional Study of the Economic Development of the Small Arms Industry, 1798–1870.* Northampton, 1948.

Dick, William B. *Dick's Encyclopedia of Practical Receipts and Processes.* New York, n.d.

Doyle, Don C. "The Social Functions of Voluntary Associations in the Nineteenth-Century American Town." *Social Science History* 1 (Spring 1977):333–35.

Draheim, Paul H. *Herkimer, New York Sesquicentennial Celebration, 1807–1957.* Herkimer, N.Y., 1957.

Drew, Bernard A., ed. *A Bicentennial History of Dalton, Massachusetts, 1784–1984.* North Adams, Mass., 1984.

Dublin, Thomas. *Women at Work: The Transformation of Work and Community in Lowell, Massachusetts, 1826–1860.* New York, 1979.

DuBois, W.E.B. *The Autobiography of W.E.B. DuBois: A Soliloquy on Viewing My Life from the Last Decade of Its First Century.* New York, 1968.

Edelstein, Sidney M. "Papermaker Joshua Gilpin Introduces the Chemical Approach to Papermaking in the United States." *The Paper Maker* 30 (1961):3–12.

Ellsworth, Lucius F. *Craft to National Industry in the Nineteenth Century: A Case Study of the Transformation of the New York State Tanning Industry.* New York, 1975.

Epstein, Marc Jay. "The Effect of Scientific Management on the Development of the Standard Cost System." Ph.D. diss., University of Texas, 1944.

"An Example to Manufacturers." *Scientific American* 25 (October 21, 1871):263.

Faler, Paul. *Mechanics and Manufacturers in the Early Industrial Revolution: Lynn, Massachusetts, 1780–1860*. Albany, 1981.

Federal Writers' Project of the Works Progress Administration for Massachusetts. *The Berkshire Hills*. New York, 1939.

Fenichel, Allen H. "Growth and Diffusion of Power in Manufacturing, 1838–1919." In *Output, Employment, and Productivity in the United States After 1800*, pp. 443–78. Conference on Research in Income and Wealth, National Bureau of Economic Research. New York, 1966.

Ferguson, Eugene S., ed. *The Early Engineering Reminiscences (1815–40) of George Escol Sellers*. Washington, D.C., 1965.

Field, Aaron W. "Sandisfield: Its Past and Present." In *Collections of the Berkshire Historical and Scientific Society*. Pittsfield, Mass., 1894.

Field, David D. *A History of the County of Berkshire, Massachusetts, In Two Parts. The First Being a General View of the County; The Second, an Account of the Several Towns*. Pittsfield, Mass., 1829.

Fischer, Marvin. "Melville's 'Tartarus': The Deflowering of New England." *American Quarterly* 23 (Spring 1971):79–100.

Fowler, Gail Barbara. "Rhode Island Handloom Weavers and the Effects of Technological Change, 1780–1840." Ph.D. diss., University of Pennsylvania, 1984.

Frisch, Michael H. *Town into City: Springfield, Massachusetts, and the Meaning of Community, 1840–1880*. Cambridge, Mass., 1972.

Gale, the Rev. Nahum. *Remarks at the Funeral of George W. Platner, Esq., at Lee, May 24, 1855*. Pittsfield, Mass., 1855.

Gallman, Robert E. "Human Capital: How Much Did America Owe the Rest of the World?" *American Economic Review* 67 (February 1977):27–35.

Garner, S. Paul. *Evolution of Cost Accounting to 1925*. University, Ala., 1976.

Gibb, George Sweet. *The Saco-Lowell Shops: Textile Machinery Building in New England, 1813–1949*. Cambridge, Mass., 1950.

Glaab, Charles N. and Lawrence H. Larsen. *Factories in the Valley: Neenah-Menasha 1870–1915*. Milwaukee, 1969.

Gladden, Washington. *From the Hub to the Hudson with Sketches of Nature, History and Industry in Northwestern Massachusetts*. Greenfield, Mass., 1870.

———. *Recollections*. Boston, 1909.

Gordon, Linda. *Woman's Body, Woman's Right*. New York, 1977.

Green, Constance McLaughlin. *Holyoke, Mass.: A Case History of the Industrial Revolution in America*. New Haven, 1939.

Griffen, Clyde and Sally. "Family and Business in a Small City: Poughkeepsie, New York, 1850–1880." *Journal of Urban History* 1 (May 1975):316–37.

Griffen, Clyde and Sally. *Natives and Newcomers: The Ordering of Opportunity in Nineteenth-Century Poughkeepsie.* Cambridge, Mass., 1978.

Gutman, Herbert G. "Work, Culture and Society in Industrializing America." *American Historical Review* 78 (June 1973):531–88.

Habakkuk, H. J. *American and British Technology in the Nineteenth Century: The Search for Labour-Saving Inventions.* Cambridge, 1962.

Hancock, H. B. and N. B. Wilkinson. "The Gilpins and Their Endless Papermaking Machine." *Pennsylvania Magazine of History and Biography* 81 (October 1957):391–405.

Harlow, Alvin R. *Steelways of New England.* New York, 1946.

Heaton, Herbert. "The Industrial Immigrant in the United States." In *Proceedings of the American Philosophical Society* 95 (October 1951):519–27.

Henley, Nancy M. "Psychology and Gender: Review Essay." *Signs* 11 (Autumn 1985):101–19.

Henretta, James A. *The Evolution of American Society, 1700–1815: An Interdisciplinary Analysis.* Lexington, Mass., 1973.

Higgins, George B. *A Pastoral Profile or Parsons in the Glen.* Dalton, Mass., 1978.

Hindle, Brooke, ed., *America's Wooden Age.* Tarrytown, N.Y., 1975.

———. *Emulation and Invention.* New York, 1981.

———. *Technology in Early America: Needs and Opportunities for Study.* Chapel Hill, 1966.

Hitz, Elizabeth. "A Technical and Business Revolution: American Woolens to 1832." Ph.D. diss., New York University, 1978.

Holland, Josiah G. *A History of Western Massachusetts.* 2 vols. Springfield, 1855.

Holman, Alfred L. *Laflin Genealogy.* Chicago, 1930.

Hounshell, David A. *From the American System to Mass Production: The Development of Manufacturing Technology in the United States.* Baltimore, 1984.

Howard, Leon. *Herman Melville: A Biography.* Berkeley, 1967.

Hughes, Thomas P. "Emerging Themes in the History of Technology." *Technology and Culture* 20 (October 1979):697–711.

Hulbert, Henry H. *The Hurlbut Genealogy or Record of the Descendents of Thomas Hurlbut.* Albany, 1888.

Humphrey, H. *Old Age: A Discourse Delivered at the Funeral of the Reverend Ebenezer Jennings of Dalton, February 8, 1859.* Pittsfield, Mass., 1859.

Hunter, Dard. *Papermaking: The History and Technique of an Ancient Craft.* New York, 1943.

———. *Papermaking in Pioneer America.* Philadelphia, 1952.

Hunter, Louis C. *Waterpower: A History of Industrial Power in the United States, 1780–1930.* Charlottesville, 1979.

Hyde, Alvan. *Memoir of Rev. Alvan Hyde, D.D. of Lee, Mass.* Boston, 1835.

Hyde, C. M. and Alexander Hyde. *Lee: The Centennial Celebration and Centennial History of the Town of Lee, Mass.* Springfield, 1878.

Jenkins, Reese V. *Images and Enterprise: Technology and the American Photographic Industry, 1829–1925.* Baltimore, 1975.

Jeremy, David. *Transatlantic Industrial Revolution: The Diffusion of Textile Technologies between Britain and America, 1790–1830.* Cambridge, Mass., 1981.

Johnson, Earl H., ed. *Mechanical Pulping Manual.* New York, 1960.

Johnson, Paul E. *A Shopkeeper's Millennium: Society and Revivals in Rochester, N.Y. 1815–1834.* New York, 1978.

Jones, Dwight E. *The Jones Story.* Pittsfield, Mass., 1966.

Kasson, John. *Civilizing the Machine: Technology and Republican Values in America, 1776–1900.* New York, 1976.

Kelley, Mary. *Private Woman, Public Stage: Literary Domesticity in Nineteenth-Century America.* New York, 1984.

Krooss, Herman E. *American Economic Development: The Progress of a Business Civilization.* Englewood Cliffs, N.J., 1966.

Krout, John Allen. *The Origins of Prohibition.* New York, 1925.

Lamb, Robert K. "The Entrepreneur and the Community." In *Men in Business,* edited by William Miller, pp. 91–119. New York, 1952.

Laurie, Bruce. " 'Nothing on Compulsion': Life Styles of Philadelphia Artisans, 1820–1850." *Labor History* 15 (1974):337–66.

Layton, Edwin T. "Scientific Technology, 1845–1900: The Hydraulic Turbine and the Origins of American Industrial Research." *Technology and Culture* 20 (January 1979):67–87.

Lebsock, Suzanne. *The Free Women of Petersburg: Status and Culture in a Southern Town, 1784–1860.* New York, 1984.

Lemon, James T. *The Best Poor Man's Country: A Geographical Study of Early Southeastern Pennsylvania.* New York, 1976.

Lerner, Gerda. "The Lady and the Mill Girl: Changes in the Status of Women in the Age of Jackson." In *Our American Sisters: Women in American Life and Thought,* edited by Jean E. Friedman and William G. Shade, pp. 120–32. Boston, 1976.

Leyda, Jay. *The Melville Log: A Documentary Life of Herman Melville, 1819–1891.* New York, 1951.

Library of Congress. *Papermaking: Art and Craft.* Washington, D.C., 1968.

Lindstrom, Diane. *Economic Development in the Philadelphia Region, 1810–1850.* New York, 1978.

Lozier, John William. "Taunton and Mason: Cotton Machinery and Locomotive Manufacture in Taunton, Massachusetts, 1811–1861." Ph.D. diss., Ohio State University, 1978.

McGaw, Judith A. "Accounting for Innovation: Technological Change and Business Practice in the Berkshire County Paper Industry." *Techology and Culture* 26 (October 1985):703–25.

———. " 'A Good Place to Work.' Industrial Workers and Occupational Choice: The Case of Berkshire Women." *Journal of Interdisciplinary History* 10 (Fall 1979):227–48.

———. "Historians and Women's Work: Insights and Oversights." In *Women and the Workplace: Conference Proceedings,* edited by Valerie Gill Couch, pp. 39–51. Norman, Okla., 1979.

McGaw, Judith A. "The Sources and Impact of Mechanization: The Berkshire Country, Massachusetts, Paper Industry, 1801–1885 as a Case Study." Ph.D. diss., New York University, 1977.

———. "Technological Change and Women's Work: Mechanization in the Berkshire Paper Industry, 1820–1885." In *Dynamos and Virgins Revisited: Women and Technological Change in History*, edited by Martha Moore Trescott, pp. 77–99. Metuchen, N.J., 1979.

———. " 'Woman's Place' in the Industrial Revolution: Some Thoughts on the 'Separate Sphere' and Technological Change." Paper presented in the Humanities Seminar series, West Virginia University, February 2, 1984.

———. "Women and the History of American Technology: Review Essay." *Signs* 7 (Summer 1982):798–828.

McLoughlin, William G. *Revivals, Awakenings, and Reform: An Essay on Religion and Social Change in America, 1607–1977*. Chicago, 1978.

Madison, James H. "The Credit Reports of R. G. Dun & Co. as Historical Sources." *Historical Methods Newsletter* 8 (September 1975):128–31.

———. "The Evolution of Commercial Credit Reporting Agencies in Nineteenth Century America." *Business History Review* 48 (Summer 1974):164–86.

Marx, Leo. *The Machine in the Garden: Technology and the Pastoral Ideal in America*. New York, 1964.

Mathews, Donald G. "The Second Great Awakening as an Organizing Process, 1780–1830: An Hypothesis." *American Quarterly* 21 (Spring 1969):23–43.

Melville, Herman. "The Paradise of Bachelors and the Tartarus of Maids." In *Herman Melville: Selected Tales and Poems*, edited by Richard Chase, pp. 206–29. New York, 1966.

In Memoriam, Hon. Elizur Smith: Funeral Services, Resolutions, Extracts from the Press. Lee, Mass., 1889.

Merrill, Michael. "Cash is Good to Eat: Self-Sufficiency and Exchange in the Rural Economy of the United States." *Radical History Review* 7 (1977):42–71.

Miller, Perry. "From the Covenant to the Revival." In *The Shaping of American Religion*, edited by James Ward Smith and A. Leland Jamison, pp. 322–68. Princeton, 1961.

Montgomery, David. *Workers' Control in America*. Cambridge, 1979.

———. "The Working Classes of the Pre-Industrial American City, 1780–1830." *Labor History* 9 (Winter 1968):3–22.

Mott, Frank Luther. *A History of American Magazines, 1741–1850*. Cambridge, Mass., 1939.

———. *American Journalism: A History of Newspapers in the United States through 260 Years: 1690–1950*. New York, 1959.

Munsell, Joel. *A Chronology of Paper and Paper Making*. Albany, 1864.

Myers, Eloise. *A Hinterland Settlement*, n.p., n.d.

Navin, Thomas R. *The Whitin Machine Works Since 1831: A Textile Machinery Company in an Industrial Village.* Cambridge, Mass., 1950.

New England Historic Genealogical Society. *The Vital Records of Dalton, Massachusetts, to the Year 1850.* Boston, 1906. (And similar volumes for *Hinsdale*, 1902; *Lee*, 1903; *Newton*, 1905; *Otis*, 1941; and *Tyringham*, 1903.)

Niles, Grace Greylock. *The Hoosac Valley: Its Legends and Its History.* New York, 1912.

Noble, David F. *Forces of Production: A Social History of Industrial Automation.* New York, 1984.

Nobles, Gregory H. *Divisions Throughout the Whole: Politics and Society in Hampshire County, Massachusetts, 1740–1775.* Cambridge, 1983.

North, Douglass C. *The Economic Growth of the United States, 1790–1860.* Englewood Cliffs, N.J., 1961.

———. *Growth and Welfare in the American Past.* Englewood Cliffs, N.J., 1966.

150th Anniversary Committee. *The One Hundred Fiftieth Anniversary of the Town of Dalton, Massachusetts.* Pittsfield, Mass., 1934.

Paskoff, Paul F. *Industrial Evolution: Organization, Structure, and Growth of the Pennsylvania Iron Industry, 1750–1860.* Baltimore, 1983.

Pidgeon, Daniel. *Old-World Questions and New-World Answers.* London, 1884.

Pierce, Frederick Clifton. *Field Genealogy.* 2 vols. Chicago, 1901.

Pierce, Wadsworth R. *The First 175 Years of Crane Papermaking.* North Adams, Mass., 1977.

Pierson, William Harvey, Jr. "Industrial Architecture in the Berkshires." 2 vols. Ph.D. diss., Yale University, 1949.

Pollard, Sidney. *The Genesis of Modern Management: A Study of the Industrial Revolution in Great Britain.* Cambridge, Mass., 1965.

Pred, Allan R. *Urban Growth and the Circulation of Information: The United States System of Cities, 1790–1840.* Cambridge, Mass., 1973.

Prude, Jonathan. *The Coming of Industrial Order: Town and Factory Life in Rural Massachusetts, 1810–1860.* Cambridge, 1983.

Pursell, Carroll W., Jr. *Early Stationary Steam Engines in America: A Study in the Migration of a Technology.* Washington, D.C., 1969.

Ray, R. H. "Economic Geology of Northern Berkshire." M.S. thesis, Williams College, 1942.

Raynor, Ellen M. and Emma L. Petitclerc. *History of the Town of Cheshire, Berkshire County, Mass.* Holyoke, Mass., 1885.

Rodgers, Daniel T. *The Work Ethic in Industrial America, 1850–1920.* Chicago, 1978.

"The Romance of Adams Industries." Separately bound extract from the *North Adams Transcript* (1926), Adams Public Library, Adams, Mass.

Rosenberg, Nathan. *Inside the Black Box: Technology and Economics.* Cambridge, 1982.

———. *Perspectives on Technology.* Cambridge, 1976.

———. *Technology and American Economic Growth.* White Plains, N.Y., 1972.

Rothman, David J. *The Discovery of the Asylum: Social Order and Disorder in the New Republic.* Boston, 1971.

Russell, Howard S. *A Long, Deep Furrow: Three Centuries of Farming in New England.* Hanover, 1976.

Ryan, Mary P. *Cradle of the Middle Class: The Family in Oneida County, New York, 1790–1865.* Cambridge, 1981.

Scott, John A. *Tyringham Old and New.* Old Home Week Souvenir, August 7–13, 1905.

Scranton, Philip. *Proprietary Capitalism: The Textile Manufacture at Philadelphia, 1800–1885.* Cambridge, 1983.

Scull, Penrose. *Papermaking in the Berkshires: The Story of the Hurlbut Paper Company.* South Lee, Mass., 1956.

Sedgwick, Sarah Cabot, and Christina Sedgwick Marquand. *Stockbridge 1739–1939: A Chronicle.* Great Barrington, Mass., 1939.

Shlakman, Vera. *Economic History of a Factory Town: A Study of Chicopee, Massachusetts.* Northampton, Mass., 1915.

Sinclair, Bruce A. *Philadelphia's Philosopher Mechanics: A History of the Franklin Institute, 1824–1865.* Baltimore, 1977.

Siracusa, Carl. *A Mechanical People: Perceptions of the Industrial Order in Massachusetts, 1815–1880.* Middletown, Conn., 1979.

Smith, Chard Powers. *The Housatonic: Puritan River.* New York, 1946.

Smith, Cora Hitt. *A History of Dalton Methodism.* Pittsfield, Mass., 1927.

Smith, David C. *History of Papermaking in the United States (1691–1969).* New York, 1970.

Smith, Edward Church and Philip Mack Smith. *The History of the Town of Middlefield.* Menasha, Wis., 1924.

Smith, J.E.A., ed. *History of Berkshire County, Massachusetts, with Biographical Sketches of Its Prominent Men.* 2 vols. New York, 1885.

———. *The History of Pittsfield, from the Year 1800 to the Year 1876.* Springfield, Mass., 1876.

———. *Pioneer Paper-Maker in Berkshire: Life, Life-Work and Influences of Zenas Crane.* Holyoke, Mass., 1885.

Smith, Merritt Roe. *Harpers Ferry Armory and the New Technolgy: The Challenge of Change.* Ithaca, 1977.

Smith, Wellington. *Genealogical Records of Wellington Smith and Family.* Lee, Mass., 1889.

Snell, R. M. *The Story of Papermaking in the United States.* Holyoke, Mass., 1929.

Solomons, David. *Studies in Costing.* London, 1952.

Sowell, Ellis Mast. *The Evolution of the Theories and Techniques of Standard Costs.* University, Ala., 1973.

Staudenmaier, John M., S.J. *Technology's Storytellers: Reweaving the Human Fabric.* Cambridge, Mass., 1985.

"Successful Paper Makers: Representative Industrial Leaders of the Times: Hon. Byron Weston of Dalton, Mass." *Paper World* 1 (July 1880):7–8.

Sutermeister, Edwin. *The Story of Papermaking*. Boston, 1954.

Taylor, Charles J. *History of Great Barrington (Berkshire) Massachusetts, 1676–1882*. Great Barrington, Mass., 1929.

Taylor, George Rogers. *The Transportation Revolution, 1815–1860*. New York, 1951.

Taylor, Robert J. *Western Massachusetts in the Revolution*. Providence, 1954.

Teitelbaum, Michael S., ed. *Sex Differences: Social and Biological Perspectives*. Garden City, N.Y., 1976.

Temin, Peter. "Labor Scarcity and the Problem of American Industrial Efficiency in the 1850s." *Journal of Economic History* 26 (September 1966):277–98.

Tentler, Leslie Woodcock. *Wage-Earning Women: Industrial Work and Family Life in the United States, 1900–1930*. New York, 1979.

Thompson, E. P. "Time, Work-Discipline, and Industrial Capitalism." *Past and Present* 38 (December 1967):56–97.

Toynbee, Arnold. *The Industrial Revolution*. Boston, 1956.

Turner, Hadley K. *A History of New Marlborough*. Great Barrington, Mass., 1944.

Turner, Steve. "Berkshire Blacks: The Struggle for Equality Began Two Centuries Ago." *Berkshire Eagle*, August 28, 1976, p. 18.

Tyler, Alice Felt. *Freedom's Ferment*. Minneapolis, 1944.

Uselding, Paul John. *Studies in the Technological Development of the American Economy During the First Half of the Nineteenth Century*. New York, 1975.

Walkowitz, Daniel J. *Worker City, Company Town: Iron and Cotton-Worker Protest in Troy and Cohoes, New York, 1855–1884*. Urbana, 1978.

Wallace, Anthony F. C. *Rockdale: The Growth of an American Village in the Early Industrial Revolution*. New York, 1978.

Ware, Caroline. *The Early New England Cotton Manufacturers: A Study of Industrial Beginnings*. Boston, 1931.

Weeks, Lyman Horace. *History of Paper Manufacturing in the United States, 1690–1916*. New York, 1916.

Welter, Barbara. "The Cult of True Womanhood: 1820–1860." In *Dimity Convictions: The American Woman in the Nineteenth Century*, pp. 21–41. Athens, Ohio, 1976.

Weston, Byron. "History of Paper Making in Berkshire County, Massachusetts, U.S.A." In *Collections of the Berkshire Historical and Scientific Society*, pp. 3–22. Pittsfield, Mass., 1895.

Weston, Donald M. *Weston, 1065–1951*. Pittsfield, Mass., 1951.

Wilk, Joseph Addison. "A History of Adams, Massachusetts." Ph.D. diss., University of Ottawa, 1945.

Yamey, B. S. "Scientific Bookkeeping and the Rise of Capitalism." *The Economic History Review*, Second Series, 1 (1949):99–113.

Zevin, Robert Brooke. *The Growth of Manufacturing in Early Nineteenth Century New England*. New York, 1975.

INDEX

South Lee Manufacturing Company, 275, 393–94
South Windham (Conn.), 104, 164, 166
Spafford, George, 104, 106n
specialization. *See* fine paper making; news paper making
Springfield (Mass.), 16, 164, 166. *See also* Ames paper mill
stamping machines, 112, 114, 163, 341, 343, 347
standard of living, 311–15, 333, 367, 380. *See also* wages
steam, use in processing, 103, 109, 181, 223
steamboats, 61–62, 324
steam engines, 190, 215, 221, 223, 242, 253–55, 379; and workers, 43n, 276, 308, 311, 321
steam whistles, 190–91, 215, 223, 230
Steinway, Theodore, 201
Stockbridge (Mass.), 19, 25, 122–23, 291, 392. *See also* Curtisville
straw (as paper fiber), 191, 197–98, 202–203, 205, 207
stuff chest, 43, 251
success, of mill owners, 55, 128–47, 159, 235–45
suction pumps, 99, 101, 103
sulfuric acid, 75, 207
supercalender, 110–12, 114, 163, 166, 170, 172, 180; and paper damage, 177, 252; and workers, 301, 341–42, 348, 352
superintendents, 135–36, 234, 243, 259n, 286–87, 303–304, 308, 314, 326–27; owners as, 50–51, 143, 244–45
Swain turbine, 217–18

Taconic Mountains, 18, 20
Tanner, Edward P., 167–69, 392, 400
"Tartarus of Maids, The," 3–4, 7, 9, 335–36, 338, 341, 344
technical information, 126, 379; personal sources of, 134, 136–39, 141–43, 146–47; published sources of, 119, 125–28, 248
technological determinism, 3–6, 93, 158, 227, 347, 381
technological unemployment, 285–86, 304, 308, 351, 355

telegraph, 121, 248n
temperance: and mill owners, 152, 256–66, 270, 272, 275, 277–79; and mill workers, 282–83, 292–93, 318–21, 334; and religion, 81, 87, 259, 261–62, 293, 320. *See also* alcohol
temperance organizations, 265–66, 293, 319–20
Tennout, Charles, 74
textile mills, 9, 149, 228; in Berkshire County, 37, 51–52, 69–70, 75, 88–89, 168, 170, 203, 378; owners of, 141–42, 153n, 167, 219, 243–44; workers in, 281, 285–86, 293, 335n, 354, 357, 361, 367–68, 370
Thatcher, Stephen: early career of, 21–22, 32, 34, 36; as mill owners, 73–74, 76, 135, 141, 399–400
time book, 52, 151, 156
Towgood and Smith, 105
Toynbee, Arnold, 5, 7
tramping, 47, 53, 330, 331n
transmission (power), 41, 48, 224, 228; and work, 298, 311–12, 344, 377
transportation: in 1801, 20–22; in the 1820s, 61–62; and mechanization, 119–21, 128, 248, 278
trimming press, 46, 76, 78, 108–110; in Berkshire mills, 163, 167, 172, 180, 184, 252; and workers, 249, 302, 311
turbine, hydraulic, 215, 217–18, 379
turnover, labor: among female workers, 338, 345, 352–53, 356–57, 368–69, 371; in hand mills, 52–53; among male workers, 316, 317n, 327–33
Tyringham (Mass.), 19, 25–26, 122, 274; paper mills in, 120–21, 309, 375, 393

unemployment: and female workers, 359–61, 362n, 372; and male workers, 274n, 296–97, 305, 308–309, 315. *See also* employment security
Union Mill, 375, 386–87
unskilled labor, 51, 75–76; men's, 286–88, 293, 300, 302, 304, 306, 311, 314; women's, 347, 353, 355, 373, 381

Van Bergan, Ira, 136, 398
Van Bergan, William, 73, 135–36, 399

LIBRARY OF CONGRESS CATALOGING-IN-PUBLICATION DATA

McGaw, Judith A., 1946–
Most wonderful machine.

Bibliography: p.
Includes index.
1. Papermaking—Massachusetts—Berkshire County—
History.   2. Berkshire County (Mass.)—History.
I. Title.   II. Series.
TS1095.U6M38   1987   303.5'83   86–42851
ISBN 0–691–04740–5
ISBN 0–691–00625–3 (pbk.)

JUDITH A. McGAW is Associate Professor of
History of Technology at the University of Pennsylvania.
This is her first book.